California

A Multicultural
Documentary History

California
A Multicultural Documentary History

Lauren Coodley
History Department
Napa College

PEARSON

Prentice
Hall

Upper Saddle River, New Jersey 07458

Library of Congress Cataloging-in-Publication Data

Coodley, Lauren
  California : a multicultural documentary history / by Lauren Coodley.
    p. cm.
  Includes bibliographical references and index.
  ISBN-13: 978-0-13-188410-6 (alk. paper)
  ISBN-10: 0-13-188410-7 (alk. paper)
  1. Pluralism (Social sciences)—California—History—Sources—Juvenile
literature. 2. California—History—Sources—Juvenile literature. 3.
California—Social conditions—Sources—Juvenile literature. 4.
California—Ethnic relations—History—Sources—Juvenile literature. I.
Title.

F870.A1C66 2009
979.4'004—dc22

                                        2007047250

Publisher: *Charlyce Jones Owen*
Senior Editorial Assistant: *Maureen Diana*
Senior Marketing Manager: *Kate Mitchell*
Marketing Assistant: *Jennifer Lang*
Managing Editor (Production): *Mary Carnis*
Production Liaison: *Marianne Peters-Riordan*
Operations Specialist: *Maura Zaldivar*
Art Director: *Jayne Conte*
Cover Design: *Bruce Kenselaar*

Cover Photo: *Chris Stowers/Dorling Kindersley*
Director, Image Resource Center: *Melinda Patelli*
Manager, Rights and Permissions: *Zina Arabia*
Manager, Visual Research: *Beth Brenzel*
Manager, Cover Visual Research & Permissions: *Karen Sanatar*
Image Permission Coordinator: *Ang'John Ferreri*
Composition/Full-Service Project Management:
  Pine Tree Composition
Printer/Binder: *R.R. Donnelley & Sons*

Credits and acknowledgments borrowed from other sources and reproduced, with permission, in this textbook appear on appropriate page within text.

Pearson Education LTD.
Pearson Education Australia PTY, Limited
Pearson Education Singapore, Pte. Ltd.
Pearson Education North Asia Ltd
Pearson Education, Canada Ltd

Pearson Educación de Mexico, S.A. de
Pearson Education-Japan
Pearson Education Malaysia, Pte. Ltd
Pearson Education, USR, NJ

10 9 8 7 6 5 4 3 2 1
ISBN-13: 978-0-13-188410-6
ISBN-10: 0-13-188410-7

For my parents, my sister and brother, my daughter and son,
and my students, with gratitude.

*The lovers of romance can go elsewhere for satisfaction but where
can the lovers of truth turn if not to history?*
—Katherine Anthony, 1950

Contents

6   "A Thousand Plows": Farming and Citizenship, 1870–1900   85

7   Nature and Labor: Progressives and Empire, 1900–1914   111

8   "Feathery Almond Trees Against a Lavender Horizon": The Great War and Its
        Aftermath, 1915–1929   132

9   "I Produce, I Defend": Depression and the New Deal, 1929–1940   170

Preface for Students

Why is it that students often find the study of the past boring, when we all love movies set in another time, when we dream of time-traveling, our dreams themselves an invented history? Imagine then that you are stepping into a dream, or a time-traveling capsule, going back to the beginnings of California, a time when there was no concrete, no cars, no cities, no smog.

If we want to know why Californians have fought "growth" or "development," we must look at the paintings made by the first Spaniards to travel here, at the earliest photographs of indigenous dwellers' tools and baskets. If we could time travel to 1700, we'd see the skies turned black with flocks of migratory waterfowl, hear the splash of canoe oars through the bays and rivers and creeks, smell the air scented with herbs and grasses—and untouched by petroleum fumes.

I have assembled tools in this book to enable you, the student, along with your teacher, to put together the many puzzles of the past. After decades of teaching history using standard textbooks, I am turning more and more to "the real stuff," the stories everyday people tell and the images they record. These stories, these pictures, help us construct an understanding of what happened, just as looking at your parents' yearbooks would help you understand what their high school experiences were like. Of course, a yearbook is an "official" record, while private diaries and letters or emails to friends might tell a very different tale. And were you to interview your parents' parents, or their teachers, the point of view would be different, and you would see your parents as others saw them.

The documents and photos I have chosen for you are both private and public. What has been recorded in any form is only a moment out of a year, a day out of a life. This collection will help to fill in the blanks that your other textbooks may not have time to explore; equally, it could introduce your family and friends to a social and multicultural history of our "Golden State," now the seventh largest economy on this planet Earth.

As you examine the documents, I'll be asking you some questions, so I will introduce myself here. I was born and raised in Culver City and in Bakersfield, went to college and graduate school in Northern California, and have been a teacher to California college students from Napa, Vallejo, and Fairfield for the past three decades. I developed both multicultural, women's studies, and California history classes, and taught critical thinking for many years; you will find my background reflected in the questions I pose. I hope that these documents will illuminate some of the dilemmas within our own lives and those of our beautiful, complex, and struggling state of California. Let's journey into the past.

Acknowledgments

I wish to thank the archivists and historical societies who have preserved these stories in drawers and cupboards and files, and thus allowed us to listen to voices from the past. Thanks especially to my local friends at the Napa County Historical Society, the San Francisco State Labor Archives and Research Center, and the Vallejo Naval and Historical Museum. Thanks to the California State Library for their beautiful images of the past and to the photographers who have shared contemporary images with me. Thanks to Dana Gioia, Terry Beers, and Malcolm Margolin for editing and publishing through Heyday Books the luminescent collections of poetry and essays that inspired some of my selections.

To the many publishers and individuals granting generous permissions for reprints, I thank you. Deirdre Lashgari, Harvey Schwartz, Valerie Mathes, Richard Bermack, and Gray Brechin were particularly helpful. The work of scholars like these has allowed me to include new thinking about our state. Mel Orpilla and Vangie Buell kindly allowed me to access images and stories that have been largely untold until now. Lionel Rolfe and Valerie Matsumoto documented the history of two utopian communities and shared their images. I wish to thank all of the poets and photographers who shared their work and all the Napa College students who allowed me to introduce you to family history as California history.

Mesa Refuge and the Common Counsel Foundation invited me to a writer's residency to complete this work; Jason Pollack and Charlyce Jones Owen encouraged me to undertake it. I wish to thank colleagues Danielle Alexander and Benita Briones for your contributions. To my research assistants, Patty Alexander and Lisa Prince—my appreciation for your thoughtful input.

This book would not be possible without the tireless energy and imagination of Tammy Rogers nor without the brilliant and impassioned editing and epigram discoveries of Paula Amen-Judah Schmitt. I hope that the book's truths honor the memories of their beloveds, Tammy's brother and Paula's daughter. It is my deepest hope that it will do this for them and for all our dear departed.

Foreword

California history continues to evolve in new directions. Carol Kammen has noted that "the times influence what we are interested in and they influence the questions we ask about the past." [i] Jim Rawls reviewed a number of these themes in his collection of essays about California history. [ii] The idea of a "Pacific period," as explicated by archaeologists Joseph and Kerry Chartkoff, [iii] is one of these new frameworks. The Chartkoffs' research points to the beginning of this period about 4,000 years ago, when California indigenous cultures achieved cultural complexity without the development of agriculture. [iv] These researchers believe that similar developments were happening along the Pacific coast. The permanent disruption of this way of life began with the arrival of Spanish missionaries in 1769.

Currently, no racial or ethnic majority group exists within California's population, though the state contains the largest immigrant communities from many nations around the world. Our multicultural present demands a more complete understanding of our multicultural origins. A detailed understanding of Spanish settlement, for example, is now made possible by the publication of Rose Beebe and Robert Senkewicz's scholarly work. Beebe and Senkewicz not only translated a wealth of primary documents, they also opened up our visual imaginations by finding paintings of California in Spanish museums, some of which are included in this book. [v]

James Rawls tells us that "among the many new areas of inquiry in California history perhaps none is as rich in potential as the history of women and the family." [vi] In the 1920s, French historians, led by Marc Bloch and Lucien Febre, "stressed the need to see *histoire totale*, or a history explored by using a variety of sources and historical techniques." [vii] American scholars adopted these methods after World War II, creating the name "social history" to describe the study of how ordinary people lived.

History is usually told from the viewpoint of the victors; through social history we revise that story. As scholar Michael Parenti notes, "Revisionism opens up new areas of inquiry." [viii] The questions he suggests we ask include:

> Why were human beings held in slavery through a good part of U.S. history? Why were Native Americans systematically massacred time and again? Why in past generations did people work twelve hours a day or longer six and seven days a week? Where did the weekend and the eight hour

[i] Carol Kammen, *On Doing Local History* (Walnut Creek, California: Altamira Press), 2003, 2nd edition, 52.
[ii] James Rawls, *New Directions in California History* (New York: McGraw-Hill), 1988.
[iii] Joseph and Kerry Chartkoff, *The Archaeology of California*, 1984.
[iv] Rawls, 2.
[v] Rose Marie Beebe and Robert Senkewicz, *Lands of Promise and Despair: Chronicles of Early California* 1535–1846 (Berkeley: Heyday Books), 2001. See also Linda Heidenreich's research on changing notions of identity as the land transitioned from Mexican to American ownership, PhD Diss., "Family, Race and Culture in Napa County, California," Barksdale Essays in History, 2000.
[vi] Rawls, xii.
[vii] See Kammen, 163.
[viii] Michael Parenti, *History as Mystery* (San Francisco: City Lights Bookstore), 1999, 10.

day come from? Who were the Wobblies? How did poor children get to go to public schools? How did communities get public libraries? How did we get laws on behalf of occupational safety, minimum wage, environmental protection, and retirement and disability benefits?[ix]

Some of the selections in this book address these cogent and relevant questions. In his Introduction to a book about Carey McWilliams, Gray Brechin describes a panel painted for San Francisco's 1915 Panama Pacific Exhibition:

> Youthful pioneers enter the Golden State as a joyous chorus of native sons welcome them to a promised land replete with oranges, grapes, and gold. Playing the losers in this pageant, natty Spanish explorers and a pious padre bring up the rear. California Indians and Asians have fallen out of the picture frame altogether.[x]

Brechin describes this as an "ascensional view of history," free of conflict. He contrasts this idealized fantasy with the truth-telling of authors that include Charlotte Perkins, Upton Sinclair, and Lucy Thompson, all of whom are heard from in this collection. Such people, Michael Harrington believed, "constitute the secret history of the United States," according to Brechin.[xi]

Although early California historian Hubert Bancroft made strenuous efforts to construct a trustworthy narrative of the state, like most regional histories, an emphasis on "progress" became an almost inevitable characteristic of early California texts. As the authors of a more recent textbook, *Elusive Eden*, point out, "Most Californians see the state's history as a romantic, anecdotal story featuring famous people and heroic events" in a narrative that focuses on politicians and business leaders. Others, they note, are "barely visible in the typical publication, museum, or historical park."[xii] Carol Kammen has noted that "most of the records that were sought and collected . . . stem from and document a community's elite."[xiii]

How does this happen? These historians point to the traditional textbook's emphasis on themes of growth, progress, success, and social equality, while state buildings "concern themselves primarily with the documents, buildings and artifacts of the wealthy, powerful and famous individuals who constituted a small minority of all past generations."[xiv] They remind us that historical restoration has "recreated mines without miners, lung disease or strikes; farms without crop pickers. . .entire worlds with few or no women."[xv] While children continue to build sugar cube models of the missions, very few mission sites contain an acknowledgment of the cost in indigenous deaths (although the Santa Cruz mission is a notable exception).

Historians of California have in recent decades turned to other disciplines, other kinds of evidence, and other voices; stressing the diversity of our state, the authors of *Elusive Eden* conclude that "California today stands as a testament to the power of cooperation and collective action."[xvi] This cooperation found expression in movements ranging from Upton Sinclair's End Poverty in California

---

[ix]Parenti, 11.

[x]Gray Brechin, Introduction, *Fool's Paradise: A Carey McWilliams Reader* (Berkeley: Heyday Books), 2001, xix.

[xi]Brechin, xxi.

[xii]Richard Rice, William Bullough, and Richard Orsi, *The Elusive Eden* (New York: McGraw-Hill), 2002, 3.

[xiii]Carol Kammen, 43.

[xiv]Rice, et al., 5.

[xv]Rice, et al., 5.

[xvi]Rice et al., 7.

campaign to the United Farm Workers. If we want to broaden our understanding of California history, we might start with EPIC and UFW, two of its most significant and inspiring stories.

However, it is important not to revert to a view of history that negates the oppression and discrimination that characterized the past and persists into the present. Clark Davis and David Igler raise an important question: "To what extent did the heated immigration debates of the 1990's echo similar debates in the late 1870's?", noting that these debates "pose basic questions about community itself: who is inside and who is outside the community, who is welcome and who is not."[xvii]

African Americans have been almost invisible in California history texts, along with Filipino-Americans and other minorities. Susheel Bibb has done outstanding work in bringing back into awareness the forgotten history of the African American community in the Bay Area through her research and impersonation of Mary Ellen Pleasant.[xviii] Her scholarship reminds us that history can be an intensely personal journey, yet one that changes all of us. Equally, the East Bay Filipino American Historical Society has inspired many fine writers, a number of whom have contributed memoirs and photographs to this volume.

Carol Kammen writes:

> The historian, in an effort to understand the past, shapes the history of the subject in his or her hand. History is an art form and it is important to remember that if history is in the mind of the historian, then it is subject to the interests, intelligence, and even the preoccupations and era of each individual historian.[xix]

The documents in this book spoke to me. Each reader, each student will create her or his own narrative of the past based on the interpretations and experiences of her or his own era. For any given chapter, we could find an additional fifty documents that would contribute to our knowledge. This book offers a multicolored quilt of primary documents framed with critical thinking questions, aiming to turn the study of the past into a conversation, which is, after all, where story began.

[xvii]Clark Davis and David Igler, eds., *The Human Tradition in California* (Wilmington, Delaware: Scholarly Resources Inc.), 2002, xiii.

[xviii]See www.mepleasant.com and www.orpilla.com for more.

[xix]Kammen, 45.

1

"The Song She Got from the Hawk": Indigenous Life

O Beautiful Earth! Alive, aglow,
With your million things that grow
I would lay my head on your ample knee

—*Harriett L. Childe-Pemberton, "Songs of the Earth"*

Malcolm Margolin, in his pioneering collection of stories, tells us:

> "People started appearing in California more than twelve thousand years ago. Perhaps they were placed here by the Creator, as many traditional people still insist . . . or perhaps, as archaeologists tell the story, they were bands of bold explorers or maybe desperate refugees . . . who came into California over the course of many thousands of years."[i]

More than five hundred indigenous tribes have lived in California, tribes as distinct from each other in beliefs and physical characteristics as they were from faraway Midwest or Eastern tribes. Scholars estimate that about 300,000 people were here when the Spanish arrived.[ii] The one hundred different languages spoken by indigenous Californians are related to those of eastern North America, Canada, and the Southwest.

1-1 SEASONAL ROUND

Like most indigenous cultures around the world, Native Californians viewed their lives as circular—as happening in a wheel of time. The seasonal round reflects the indigenous conception of circular reality. Within its wheel the seasonal changes bear a continuing relationship to a changeless center, maintaining the harmonious balance of the universe. Margolin explains:

> Within the ritual calendar was encoded the cycle of dances and ceremonies, the timing of the salmon runs, the ripening of the acorns, and the migrating water fowl . . . timing was essential. Without it people would not know when to prepare fishnets and head to the coast, when to travel to the upland meadows to gather seeds, when to store the nuts, burn the meadows, or gather tule to make their boats.[iii]

---

[i]Malcolm Margolin, *The Way We Lived* (Berkeley: Heyday Books), 1981, 1–2.

[ii]Margolin, 4.

[iii]Malcolm Margolin, *Monterey in 1786: Life in a California Mission, the Journals of Jean Francois de la Perouse* (Berkeley: Heyday Books), 1989, 24.

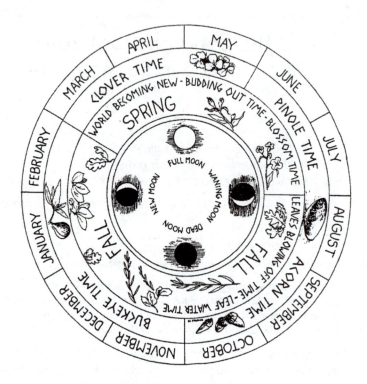

QUESTION: The past repeats itself, stretches into and connects with our present and future lives. Our modern calendar displays the months facing us, flat and separately. How does this way of tracking time compare with the round pictured here? How might our standard calendar or a calendar kept electronically through a computer affect our sense of time? Of reality?

1-2   BASKETS

Clifford Trafzer, Director of Native American Studies at the University of California in Riverside, describes baskets as "alive with spirit, beauty and motion . . . at once the past and the present, woven into the fabric of California Indian being."[iv]

Baskets represent survival for Native Americans, the center of their practical, social, and spiritual lives. Native Californians who live close to Mount Shasta believe that at the beginning of time, a huge basket filled with goodness was placed in the heart of the mountain. Indigenous people designed and crafted baskets in an extraordinary array of sizes and shapes

---

[iv]Clifford Trafzer, review, *California History*, 1996, *The Fine Art of California Indian Basketry* by Brian Bibby, and *Remember Your Relations: The Elsie Allen Baskets, Family and Friends* by Suzanne Abel-Vidor, Dot Brovarney, and Susan Billy.

to fit both daily needs and ceremonial occasions. Baskets not only stored food and water, they traced history, commemorated alliances, and held the medicines of shamans.

Pomo basket weaver Susan Billy speaks of the spirituality of baskets:

> People frequently ask me what these ceremonial baskets hold. They did not have to hold anything because the basket itself was all that was needed. The basket contained the prayers and the wonderful good energy that made it a ceremonial basket.[v]

1-3   CALIFORNIA WOMAN MAKING BASKETS

Women like the one in this picture peeled and split the stems and twigs of Redbud to form watertight baskets, interweaving them with lighter-colored stems to create patterns. She would have adorned her baskets with feathers, clamshells, and beads. She might have given her baskets as gifts at a potlatch, and cooked and stored food in them. Later, she would have used a basket for carrying her infant and perhaps worn a basket in religious ceremonies. See www.cabrillo.edu/~crsmith/calindwwwresources.html for a fascinating showcase of California Indian basketry.

---

[v]Susan Billy cited in *American Passages A Literary Survey, Native Voices* http://www.learner.org/amerpass/unit01/context_activ-4.htm/

As we look at this photograph, we can imagine her shyness or awkwardness at being asked to demonstrate her basketry skills for the photographer. We can observe her head-gear and vest, her hairstyle and her features, as if looking down a long telescope of time.

Unlike most Californians in the 21st century, indigenous people described their lives without the specifics of birth, marriage, or occupation, instead recounting dreams and contacts with the spirit world in careful detail. Imagine a culture in which your dreams would be shared with the people in your household, in your neighborhood, seen as important messages from another world. Margolin describes the setting in which these stories had been told for centuries:

> Since everyone knew the plot, the storyteller was free to concentrate on voice and performance. Imagine a rainy winter night. A fire is lit—it crackles and smokes from the moisture in the wood—and the storyteller launches forth, voice rising and falling, now talking, now singing; adopting the tone of one character, then another; shouting, whispering, grunting, laughing."[vi]

QUESTION: Women like this one have often been referred to as "squaws" (and indigenous men as "bucks"); see www.bluecorncomics.com/squaw.htm for an explanation and discussion of why these terms are so offensive to Native Americans.

[vi]Margolin, 8.

1-4 CHARLEY BROWN, POMO, *THE GIRL WHO MARRIED RATTLESNAKE*

I chose the rattlesnake tale because it is remarkably distinct from the basic values conveyed by the European representation of animals as "beasts," which are ugly and have to be transformed into human princes to be valued. In this, however, indigenous people clearly saw animals as their equals.

At a place called Cobowin there is a large rock with a hole in it and there were many rattlesnakes in this hole. At Kalesima nearby there was a village with four large houses. In one of these large houses which had a center pole there lived a girl. This was in the spring of the year when the clover was just right to eat. This girl went out to gather clover and one of the rattlesnakes watched her. When she had a sufficient amount of this food she took it home and gave it to her mother.

Rattlesnake went to the village and when he had approached very near to the house he transformed himself into a young man with a head-net on his head and fine beads around his neck. He made himself look as handsome as possible. Then he climbed up onto the top of the house and came down the center pole. He went to this girl and told her that he wanted to marry her and he remained there with the family. The following morning he went home again. This he did for four days. On the fifth evening he came back but this time he did not change his form. He simply went into the house and talked just as he had before. The girl's mother said that there was someone over there talking all the time. She made a light and looked over in the place where she heard the sound, and there was Rattlesnake. He shook his head and frightened her terribly. She dropped the light and ran.

On the following morning Rattlesnake took the girl home with him and she remained there. Finally this girl had four children and as they grew up, whenever they saw any of the people from the village, they would say to their mother, "We are going to bite those people." But she would say, "No, you must not do that. Those are your relatives." And the children would do as she told them.

Now these four rattlesnake boys were out playing around one day as they grew a little older. Finally they became curious. They came in and asked their mother, "Why do you not talk the way we do? Why are you so different?"

"I am not a rattlesnake," she replied. "I am a human being. I am different from you and your father."

"Are you not afraid of our father?" asked the boys. "No," she answered.

Then the oldest of the rattlesnake boys said that he had heard the other rattlesnakes talking and that they too thought it strange that she was so different from them and that they were going to investigate and see just why it was that she was so different. They were going to crawl over her body and find out why she was so different from themselves. She was not at all afraid; when the rattlesnakes all came they crawled over her and she was not alarmed in any way.

Then she said to her oldest boy, "It is impossible for you to become a human being and I am not really a human being any longer, so I am going back to my parents and tell them what has happened." She did go home and she said to her parents, "This is the last time that I shall be able to talk to you and the last time that you will be able to talk with me." Her father and mother felt very sad about this, but they said nothing. Then the daughter started to leave, but her mother ran after her and caught her right by the door, brought her back into the house and wept over her because she was so changed. Then the girl shook her body and suddenly she was gone. No one knew how or where she went, but she really went back to Rattlesnake's house where she has lived ever since.

1-5 CHIEF YANAPAYAK, MIWOK, SUMMONS TO A MOURNING CEREMONY

This "call" is part of a ritual used by the Miwok peoples of Marin County to signal the beginning of a yearlong mourning ceremony in which the community shared the survivors' grief.

> Get up! Get up! Get up! Get up! Get up!
> Wake up! Wake up! Wake up!
> People get up on the south side,
> East side, east side, east side, east side,
> North side, north side, north side,
> Lower side, lower side, lower side!
> You folks come here!
> Visitors are coming, visitors are coming.
> Strike out together!
> Hunt deer, squirrels!
> And you women, strike out, gather wild onions, wild potatoes!
> Gather all you can! Gather all you can!
> Pound acorns, pound acorns, pound acorns!
> Cook, cook!
> Make some bread, make some bread!
> So we can eat, so we can eat, so we can eat.
> Put it up, and put it up, and put it up!
> Make acorn soup so that the people will eat it!
> There are many coming.
> Come here, come here, come here, come here!
> You have to be dry and hungry.
> Be for a while.
> Got nothing here.
> People get up, people around get up!
> Wake up!
> Wake up so you can cook!
> Visitors are here now and all hungry.
> Get ready so we can feed them!
> Gather up, gather up, and bring it all in, so we can give it to them!
> Go ahead and eat!
> That's all we have.

Don't talk about starvation, because we never have much!
Eat acorns!
There is nothing to it.
Eat and eat!
Eat! Eat! Eat! Eat!
So that we can get ready to cry.
Everybody get up! Everybody get up!
All here, very sad occasion.
All cry! All cry!
Last time for you to be sad.

QUESTION: Try reading this piece aloud. Can you capture the rhythm, the music, the repetition, and hypnotic effect? Would you respond to such a summons?

1-6 INDIGENOUS TRIO CROSSING SAN FRANCISCO BAY

Here we see indigenous peoples, who may have been Miwok, since the Miwok lived just north of San Francisco Bay. Imagine that these people are answering the call to a mourning ceremony. Though we are seeing them through the eyes of the unknown Spaniard who took pen in hand to record his observations, we can study the drawing for clues about their boat and how they oared it through the water. Notice the baskets in the back of the boat.

1-7   TOOLS

As you look at this photograph, keep in mind that these tools trace the indigenous relationship with nature.[vii]

Indigenous peoples took only as many plants as needed, and after gathering seeds for making pinole, they would cast a few handfuls back to the ground to assure a yield the following season. When gathering bulbs and tubers, they aerated the soil with their digging sticks, assuring a large yield of bulbs the next year.[viii]

Tribes used the plants they gathered in an impressive variety of ways. They cracked the ghost pine for nuts, roasted California bay nuts in their shells, and ground the nuts into flour, forming it into cakes. They dug up the roots of the ghost pine with sticks and used them to weave large twine baskets. They fueled their fires with pine cones and chewed pitch as gum, treated rheumatism with boiled bay leaves, and rubbed branches of leaves over the body as a germicidal, placing them above doorways to keep sickness away. Indigenous peoples used poison oak leaves in cooking to spice up dishes and fed their children bits of these leaves to immunize them; they applied fresh leaves to rattlesnake bites.

[vii]See essay by L. Mark Raab in Deverell and Hise, *Land of Sunshine: An Environmental History of Metropolitan Los Angeles*, for another view on ecological and environmental sensitivity of Native Californians.
[viii]See *Tending the Wild*, M. Kat Anderson. Berkeley: University of California, 2005.

QUESTION: Today, psychologists like Howard Gardner suggest there are many kinds of intelligence.[ix] Rather than limiting the definition of intelligence to the ability to solve verbal or mathematical problems, Gardner proposes that we recognize intelligence as being evident in many kinds of thinking, including the ability to use tools and to solve practical problems in the real world. Using Gardner's definition, discuss other examples of the intelligence of the indigenous Californians.

1-8 ROBERT SPOTT, YUROK, *A DOCTOR ACQUIRES POWER*

This is how Fanny Flounder of Espeu became a doctor. She told me the story herself, at various times. For several summers she danced at Wogelotek, on a peak perhaps three miles from Espeu north of the creek. It looks out over the ocean. Then at last while she was sleeping here she dreamed she saw the sky rising and blood dripping off its edge. She heard the drops go "ts, ts" as they struck the ocean. She thought it must be *Wesona olego*, where the sky moves up and down, and the blood was hanging from it like icicles. Then she saw a woman standing in a doctor's maple-bark dress with her hair tied like a doctor. Fanny did not know her nor whether she was alive or dead, but thought she must be a doctor. The woman reached up as the edge of the sky went higher and picked off one of the icicles of blood. "Here, take it," she said, and put it into Fanny's mouth. It was icy cold.

Then Fanny knew nothing more. When she came to her senses she found she was in the wash of the breakers on the beach at Espeu with several men holding her. They took her back to the sweat-house to dance. But she could not: her feet turned under her as if there were no bones in them. Then the men took turns carrying her on their backs and dancing with her. Word was sent to her father and mother, who were spearing salmon on Prairie Creek. But her mother would not come. "She will not be a doctor," she said. Most of Fanny's sisters had become doctors before this. Her mother was a doctor, and her mother's mother also, but her mother had lost faith in her getting the power.

Now, after five days of dancing in the sweat-house, she was resting in the house. Then she felt a craving for crabmeat; so an old kinswoman, also a doctor, went along the beach until she found a washed-up claw. She brought this back, roasted it in the ashes, and offered it to Fanny. At the first morsel Fanny was nauseated. The old woman said, "Let it come out," and held a basket under her mouth. As soon as she saw the vomit she cried, "Eya," because she saw the *telogel* in it. Then everyone in Espeu heard the cry and came running and sang in the sweat-house, and Fanny danced there. She danced with strength as soon as the *telogel* was out of her body. And her mother and father were notified and came as fast as they could. Then her mother said, "Stretch out your hands [as if to reach for the pain] and suck in your saliva like this: hlrr." Fanny did this and at last the pain flew into her again.

This pain was of blood. When she held it in her hands in the spittle in which it was enveloped you could see the blood dripping between her fingers. When I saw it in later years it was a black *telogel* tipped red at the larger end. This, her first, is also her strongest pair of pains. About it other doctors might say, "*Skui ketsemin kel*" (Your pain is good).

[ix]See www.pz.harvard.edu/Pls.HG.htm

They say that sort of thing to each other when one doctor has seen a pain in a patient but has been unable to remove it and the next doctor succeeds in sucking it out. The words of Fanny's song when she sucks out blood with her strongest power are: "*Kitelkel wesona-olego kithonoksem*" (Where the sky moves up and down you are traveling in the air).

Now after a time an old kinsman at Espeu was sick in his knee. The other doctors there, who were also his kin, said, "Let the new doctor treat him." Her mother wanted her to undertake it but warned her not to try to sing in curing until she told her to. So she treated the old man without singing; and then she took on other light cases. Altogether she doctored seven times before she sang. Then her mother told her to try to sing, and the song came to her of itself.

QUESTION: Describe healers you may know or have heard of who have not had formal training.

2

"The Region of the Earthly Paradise": Spanish Conquest, 1690–1821

Our sense of the past is created for us largely by history's winners. The voices of the losers, when heard at all, are transmitted through a carefully tuned network of filters.

—John Gager

The name California was inspired by Garcia de Montalvo's sixteenth-century Spanish novel, *Las Sergas de Esplandian.* Its hero visits "California," an island full of powerful women, whose Queen, Califia, "excited the imagination of many a Spanish soldier who read it," according to historian Andrew Rolle.[i] Island myths originated in the thirteenth century from European mariners.

Historian Ken Dvorak notes that "these dream stock tales provided early explorers with an identifiable belief system that they took with them on their explorations; cartographers placed these tales on maps and globes, suggestively hinting at their location."[ii] The island image of California remained fixed in maps late into the 1700s.

---

[i]Andrew Rolle, *California: A History*, 6th edition (Wheeling, Illinois: Harlan Davidson), 2003, 20.

[ii]Ken Dvorak, review of Dora Beale Polk, *The Island of California, A History of the Myth* (University of Nebraska), 1995, review posted at H-California listserv, 1995.

2-1   GARCIA RODRIGUEZ DE MONTALVO, TITLE PAGE, *THE LABORS OF THE VERY BRAVE KNIGHT,* 1510

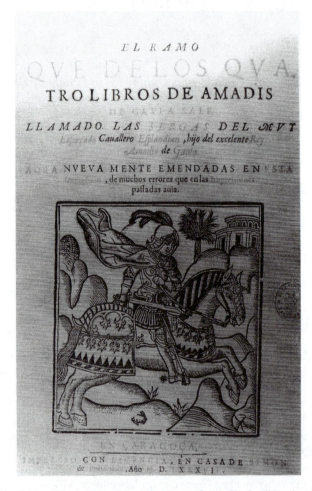

Title page of the 1588 edition of The Labors of the Very Brave Knight Esplandián, *the chivalric novel in which "California" first appeared as an island on "the right-hand side of the Indies." Courtesy of the Biblioteca Nacional, Madrid.*

2-2   GARCIA RODRIGUEZ DE MONTALVO, EXCERPT FROM *THE LABORS OF THE VERY BRAVE KNIGHT,* 1510

After his conquest of Mexico in 1520, Cortez wrote to the Spanish king about this novel. Three decades later in 1542, the Spaniards began their exploration of the land we now know as California when Juan Cabrillo's ships sailed into the harbor of San Diego.

I tell you that on the right-hand side of the Indies there was an island called California, which was very close to the region of the Earthly Paradise. This island was inhabited by black women, and there were no males among them at all, for their way of life was similar to that of the Amazons. The island was made up of the wildest cliffs and the sharpest precipices found anywhere in the world. These women had energetic bodies and courageous, ardent hearts, and they were very strong. Their armor was made entirely out of gold—which was the only metal found on the island—as were the trappings of the fierce beasts that they rode once they were tamed. They lived in very well-designed caves. They had many ships, which they used to sally forth on their raiding expeditions and in which they carried away the men they seized, whom they killed in a way that you will soon hear. On occasion, they kept the peace with their male opponents, and the females and the males mixed with each other in complete safety, and they had carnal relations, from which unions it follows that many of the women became pregnant. If they bore a female, they kept her, but if they bore a male, he was immediately killed. The reason for this, inasmuch as it is known, is that, according to their thinking, they were set on reducing the number of males to so small a group that the Amazons could easily rule over them and all their lands; therefore they kept only those few men whom they realized they needed so that their race would not die out.

On this island called California there were many griffins, because these beasts were suited to the ruggedness of the terrain, which was a perfect habitat for the infinite number of wild animals that lived there and that were not found in any other part of the world. When these griffins had offspring, the women ingeniously covered themselves in coarse hides in order to capture the young; then they took them back to their caves, where they raised them. When their plumage was even, they fed them so often and so cleverly with the captured men and the boys they bore that the griffins became well acquainted to the women and never harmed them in any way. Therefore, every man who ventured onto the island was immediately killed and devoured by the griffins; and even though they had eaten their fill, they never for that reason stopped seizing the men, carrying them aloft as they flew through the air and, when they tired of carrying them, dropping them to their certain deaths.

QUESTION: This novel gave us the name "California" for our state. Which phrases within this description of California are the most interesting?

2-3   EXCERPT, *OFFICIAL ACCOUNT OF THE CABRILLO EXPEDITION*, 1542

In Spain, the Catholic Church fought against the Moors, who were Muslims, from 711 through 1492. The Spanish considered the Jews as well as the Moors as outsiders who should be expelled from Spain.[iii] Although Pope Paul IV (1476–1559) had ruled that "Indians" were human and had rights to freedom and property, many Spanish soldiers in California prayed for divine assistance when they went into battle against the indigenous people, sometimes even calling them "Moors" "and "Jews."

[iii]In the spring of 1492, shortly after the Moors were driven out of Granada, Ferdinand and Isabella of Spain expelled all Jews from their Spain, about 50,000 families.

The following Friday they went in search of water and came upon some Indians at the watering place. The Indians, who were very quiet, showed them a pool of water and a salt marsh. Using gestures, they indicated that they did not live there, but inland, and that there were many of them. That afternoon, five Indians came to the beach and they were taken back to the ships. The Indians appeared to be intelligent. As they boarded the ship the Indians motioned to the Spaniards and began counting the number of Spaniards there. The Indians indicated with gestures that they had seen men like the Spaniards before, men who had beards. The Spaniards had brought dogs with them as well as crossbows and swords. The Indians had smeared their bodies, thighs, and arms with a white pitch which had been applied to look like slashes from a knife. They resembled half-dressed men in slashed breeches and doublets.

They motioned that there were Spaniards in the vicinity, a five-day journey away. They also indicated that there were many Indians in the area and that they had much corn and many parrots. The Indians covered their bodies with deerskins, some of which were tanned in the way Mexicans tan the hides used for their sandals. They are large and healthy people. They carry their bows and arrows like the people of New Spain do, using flint arrowheads. They had said that the Spaniards had traveled inland, so the Captain gave them a letter to take back to the Spaniards.

They left the port of La Posesión on Sunday, August 27, and sailed on course until they discovered an uninhabited island two leagues from the mainland. They named the island San Agustin. It is probably two leagues in circumference and there is a good port there. They continued sailing windward along the coast with favorable light winds. The following Wednesday, August 30, they encountered strong northwest winds, which forced them to seek shelter on the island of San Agustin. They found signs of people on this island as well as two cow horns and very large trees the sea had tossed ashore. The trees looked like cypresses and were more than sixty feet long. They were so thick that two men could not reach around one of them. Some of the trees were cedars and there was a large amount of this timber. There is nothing else of value on this island, but it is a good port. They remained on the island until the following Sunday.

They left the island of San Agustin on Sunday, September 3, and sailed on course. The following Monday they anchored at the shore, seven leagues windward along a coast running north and south. They continued on course, sailing with fair weather and light winds along a coast running north and south until Thursday, September 7, when they anchored in a small bay formed by the land. Here the coast ceases to run in a north-south direction and turns to the northwest. There is a large valley at this small bay and the land is level at the coast. Inland there are high mountains and uneven terrain that appears to be good. The entire coast is rocky. The bottom of the ocean is level and not very deep, for at half a league from shore they cast anchor at ten fathoms. There is an abundance of plant life on top of the water here.

On Friday, September 8, they sailed windward with light winds and encountered crosscurrents here. They anchored at a point that forms a cape and affords good shelter from the west-northwest winds. They named it Cabo de San Martin.[*] It forms a tip from one end and

---

[*]Now called Cape Colonet—about seventy miles south of Ensenada.

the other. Some high mountains that come from behind end here, and other, smaller mountains begin. There is one large valley, yet there appear to be many others. The land is good. The port, located at $32\frac{1}{2}$ degrees, north of the island of San Agustin, is unobstructed and shallow enough to take depth measurements.

While at Cabo de San Martin they went ashore for water. They found a small, freshwater lake and replenished their supply of water. Forty large, naked Indians came to the watering place with their bows and arrows and roasted maguey and fish to eat. They could not communicate with the Indians. They took possession of this place and remained at the cape until the following Monday.

On Monday, September 11, they left Cabo de San Martin and sailed about four leagues along the coast in a north-northeast to south-southwest direction. From there the coast turns to the northwest. The land is high and bare. The next day they sailed about six leagues along the coast in a northwest-southeast direction. The entire coast is rocky and clear. The following day, even though the weather was dreadful, they sailed about four leagues along the coast from northwest to southeast. The mountains are high and jagged. The following Thursday they sailed ahead about three leagues and cast anchor at a point that extends into the ocean and forms a cape on both sides. It is called Cabo de la Cruz and is located at 33 degrees. There is no water or wood and they did not find any sign of Indians.

They left Cabo de la Cruz, but because the weather was miserable along the coast from north-northwest to south-southeast, the following Saturday they found themselves only two leagues from the cape. Along the shore they saw Indians in very small canoes. The land is very high, bare, and dry. All the land from California to this spot is sandy ground along the shore, but another type of land begins here. The soil is reddish in color and appears to be better.

On Sunday, September 17, they continued on their voyage. About six leagues from Cabo de la Cruz they found a good, protected port. In order to reach it they passed by a small island that is near the mainland. At this port they replenished their supply of water from a small rainwater lake. There are groves of trees similar to the silk-cotton tree, except the wood is hard. They found large, thick timbers tossed ashore by the sea. This port is called San Matco and is located at $33\frac{1}{3}$ degrees. They took possession of the port and remained there until the following Saturday. The land appears to be good, the terrain is even and high. There are large savannahs and the grass is like that in Spain. They saw herds of animals similar to cattle, which wandered in droves of one hundred or more. From their appearance, gait, and long wool the animals resembled Peruvián sheep. They have small horns about the length of a *jeme* and the thickness of a thumb. Their tail is broad and round and about a palm's length.

On Saturday, September 23, they left the port of San Mateo and sailed about eighteen leagues along the coast until the following Monday. They saw very beautiful valleys, groves of trees, and terrain that was both level and uneven. They did not see any Indians, however.

The following Tuesday and Wednesday they sailed about eight leagues along the coast and passed by three uninhabited islands located at 34 degrees, three leagues from the mainland, which they named Islas Desiertas.[*] One of the islands, about two leagues in circumference, is larger than the others, and provides shelter from the west winds. On this day they saw what appeared to be smoke signals on land.[*] There are large valleys and the land appears to be good. In the interior there are high mountains.

The following Thursday they traveled about six leagues along a coast that ran in a north-northwest direction. They discovered a very good, protected port located at $34\frac{1}{3}$ degrees which they named San Miguel. After casting anchor they went ashore and encountered some Indians. Three of them waited but the others fled. They gave gifts to the three Indians, who gestured that people like the Spaniards had headed inland. The Indians appeared to be very scared. That night the Spaniards left the ships on a small rowboat and went ashore to fish. Some Indians were on shore and began to shoot arrows at them, wounding three men.

On another day, in the morning, they sailed further into the large port with the small boat. They had brought two boys with them who did not understand their attempts to communicate with gestures. They gave each boy a shirt and then sent them away.

The next morning three large Indian men came to the ship. With gestures indicated that bearded men who were clothed liked us and armed like the men on the ships were wandering about the interior. They called the Christians *"Guacamal."* They gestured that the men were carrying crossbows and swords. They ran around as if on horseback and motioned with their right arm that the men were throwing lances. They indicated that they were afraid because the Spaniards were killing many Indians in the region. These people are large and healthy and they cover themselves with animal skins. While they were at this port, a violent storm came from the west-southwest and south-southwest directions, but because this was a good port they did not suffer at all. This was the first storm they had experienced. They remained at this port until the following Tuesday.

QUESTION: If you had been a California indigenous person during Cabrillo's Landings, which of the reactions described here would you have had, and why?

2-4   GERONIMO DE MENDIETA, *FRANCISCAN MYSTIC* QUOTATION, c. 1550

The Indian with respect to the Spaniard is like a small dog in front of a mighty lion. The Spaniards have both the evil desire and the strength to destroy all the Indians in New Spain, if they were ever given the chance. The Indian is so phlegmatic and meek, that he would not harm a fly. Consequently, one must always assume in case of doubt that the Spaniard is the offender and the Indian is the victim.

QUESTION: Try putting di Mendieta's analogy in your own words. Were Spanish abusers contemptuous of those they victimized, or did they pity them and see them as in need of civilizing?

------

[*]The Coronado Islands, about ten miles off the coast just south of the present international border.

2-5 LETTER, EXPLORER VIZCAINO TO KING FELIPE III, 1602

Vizcaino was born in Spain and participated in the Spanish invasion of Portugal in 1580. Next, he traveled to the Spanish colony of Manila in the Philippines; by 1589, he was in Mexico applying for licenses for pearl fishing and mining in California.

Mexico, May 23, 1603

Among the most important ports that I discovered was one located at 37 degrees latitude, which I named Monterey. I wrote to Your Majesty from there on September 28 of this year, stating that this port is all that one could hope for. It is a convenient stopping place along the coast for ships that are coming from the Philippines. The port is sheltered from all winds, and along the shore there are many pine trees that could be used for ship masts of any size desired. There are also live oaks and white oaks, rosemary, vines, and roses of Alexandria. There are many rabbits, hares, partridges, and other genera and species found in Spain, especially in the Sierra Morena, as well as different types of birds. It is a pleasant place. The area is very populated by people whom I considered to be meek, gentle, quiet, and quite amenable to conversion to Catholicism and to becoming subjects of Your Majesty. The Indians have strong bodies and white faces. The women are somewhat smaller and have nice features.

Their clothing is made from sealskins. They tan and dress the hides better than how it is done in Castile. Seals are found in abundance. They have a large amount of flax and hemp, from which they make fishing lines and nets for catching rabbits and hares. Their boats are made of pine and are very well constructed. They go out into the ocean with fourteen oarsmen and they can sail with ease even during a strong storm.

I traveled more than eight hundred leagues along the coast and kept a record of all the people I encountered. The coast is populated by an endless number of Indians, who said there were large settlements in the interior. They invited me to go there with them. They were very friendly to us, and when I showed them the image of Our Lady they were drawn to it and wanted to join us. They were very attentive during the sacrifice of the Mass. They make use of various idols, as I already have reported to the Viceroy. They are very knowledgeable about silver and gold and said that these metals can be found in the interior.

QUESTION: Make a drawing of the land as Vizcaino describes it, inserting all the examples of plant and animal life.

2-6 FR. IGNACIO TIRSCH, HOW TWO CALIFORNIA INDIANS KILLED A DEER WITH ARROWS, HOW THEY SKINNED IT IN THE FIELD AND PREPARED IT FOR ROASTING, 1763–1768

2-7 CLOTHING WORN BY MALES IN THE MISSIONS OF CALIFORNIA, 1763–1768

Plans to establish a port in California were not realized until the 1700s when the mission system began. Fr. Ignacio Tirsch was a Jesuit priest at Mission San Diego, 1763–1768. Tirsch returned to Europe in 1778 with these paintings, which give us some of the earliest portraits of indigenous people as seen by Europeans.

When the Spanish established their mission in Monterey in 1770, stories of the changes they brought were spread to neighboring communities. Neophytes (new converts) constructed altars under the direction of the priests; those who resisted were lashed, pilloried, or chained in stocks. Within the mission, indigenous religion was replaced with Catholicism, and hunter/gatherer society replaced with agriculture.

Interestingly, visitors from the British Isles observed and documented their shock at the treatment of the indigenous. English geographer Frederick Beechey wrote that women and children were "generally the first object of capture; sometimes husbands and parents would come into captivity to be with them,"[iv] while Scotsman Hugo Reid observed that in recruiting new converts, the soldiers "tied and whipped every man, woman, and child" they found, and further humiliated male prisoners at the mission by demanding that they "throw their bows and arrows at the feet of the priest, and make due submission."[v]

Suicide due to captivity and abuse, unsanitary living conditions at the mission, and malnutrition, all contributed to the high death rate of indigenous peoples, and they fled Monterey with stories of the diseases they had contracted there. Families were at risk of disintegration: after children were baptized, women desperately submitted to baptism to stay with their children, and men followed in order to remain with their families. Malcolm Margolin writes of the mission system:

> [The] handful of soldiers and monks expected the Indians to desert everything they knew about life and to adapt overnight to a most peculiar and highly evolved European institution, the monastery—an institution under which, even at the height of its popularity, only a small number of Europeans themselves ever chose to live.[vi]

When indigenous people became part of the mission system, some tried to hold onto their religious practices, but priests insisted that they reinterpret their lives through Biblical stories and adapt their behavior accordingly. The Catholic Mass was a daily reminder of the new order: the "Indians" were called to Mass by the same bells that called them to labor. As they filed into church, soldiers stood guard to make sure no one left the building before Mass was over.

Children were taken from their parents and raised by priests. They were trained to play musical instruments to accompany the Mass and sat with the priests at Mass rather than with their families. Through Catholic religious training (Catechism), children were given gifts for reciting lessons correctly and were slowly and systematically turned away from their native religion. The mission system disrupted the custom of requiring obligations to the husband's mother that had provided older women with status and security.

[iv]Frederick Beechey, *Narrative of a Voyage to the Pacific*, 1825–28 (London: H. Colburn and R. Bentley), 1831.
[v]Hugo Reid, "Conversion," *Los Angeles County Indians; A Collection of Letters*, Bancroft Library, Scrapbook.
[vi]Malcolm Margolin, Introduction to *Monterey in 1786: Life in a California Mission, the Journals of Jean Francois de la Perouse* (Berkeley: Heyday Books), 1989, 14.

Missions were built like military fortresses with separate dormitories for single females who slept under lock and key after adolescence, to be released only for marriage. The women were taught to card, clean, and spin wool. Converted Indian women, as well as Mexican women, were the teachers and role models and guards for the imprisoned indigenous females. Indigenous women had no opportunity for privacy; while some priests allowed sweat houses for the men, no menstrual huts were permitted on mission grounds. It was common practice for Presidio soldiers and mission priests to rape indigenous women, who died in great numbers in this period, in childbirth or from venereal disease.

QUESTION: How did the European paintings of indigenous people differ from the way they really looked? Why do you think this might have been?

2-8   NARCISCO DURAN AND CHILD, FROM MISSION SAN JOSE, 1844, UNSIGNED. VIRGINIA BOUVIER USED THIS IMAGE AS THE COVER OF HER BOOK, *WOMEN AND THE CONQUEST OF CALIFORNIA 1542–1840: CODES OF SILENCE.*[vii]

It is important to know that not all Europeans agreed with or perpetrated violence upon indigenous tribes. Some were appalled by the abuse perpetrated by soldiers and clergy, and some spoke out (at great risk to their own positions, if not safety).

QUESTION: This image shows the position of women under the power system called patriarchy. Do you see evidence of this system today? What share of power do women hold in government today? In religion? Who is responsible for household labor today, the same kind of work that Indian women were taught in the missions?

[vii]Virginia Bouvier (Tucson: University of Arizona Press), 2001.

2-9   LETTER, FR. LUIS JAYME, 1772

Jayme was a priest sent to Mission San Diego three years after the establishment of the
Spanish colony. He gave this letter to Junipero Serra to deliver to Spanish officials in Mexico.

With reference to the Indians, I wish to say that great progress would be made if there were
anything to eat and the soldiers would set a good example. We cannot give them anything
to eat because what Don Pedro [Fages] has given is not enough to last half a year for the Indians from the California [Baja California] who are here. Thus little progress will be made
under present conditions. As for the example to be set by the soldiers, no doubt some of them
are good exemplars and deserve to be treated accordingly, but very many of them deserve
to be hanged on account of the continuous outrages which they are committing in seizing
and raping the women. There is not a single mission where all the gentiles have not been
scandalized, and even on the roads, so I have been told. Surely, as the gentiles themselves
state, they are committing a thousand evils, particularly those of a sexual nature. The
Fathers have petitioned Don Pedro concerning these points, but he has paid very little attention to them. He has punished some, but as soon as they promised him that they would work
at the *presidio,* he turned them loose. That is what he did last year, but now he does not
even punish them or say anything to them on this point. I suppose that some ministers will
write you, each concerning his own mission, and therefore I shall not tell you about the
cases which have occurred at other missions. I shall speak only of Mission San Diego.

At one of these Indian villages near this mission of San Diego, which said village is very
large, and which is on the road that goes to Monterey, the gentiles therein many times have
been on the point of coming here to kill us all, and the reason for this is that some soldiers
went there and raped their women, and other soldiers who were carrying the mail to Monterey turned their animals into their fields and they ate up their crops. Three other Indian villages about a league or a league and a half from here have reported the same thing to me
several times. For this reason, on several occasions when Father Francisco Dumetz or I have
gone to see these Indian villages, as soon as they saw us they fled from their villages to the
woods or other remote places, and the only ones who remained in the village were some men
and some very old women. The Christians here have told me that many of the gentiles of
the aforesaid villages leave their huts and the crops which they gather from the lands around
their villages and go to the woods and experience hunger. They do this so that the soldiers
will not rape their women, as they have already done so many times in the past.

No wonder the Indians here were bad when the mission was first founded. To begin
with, they did not know why they [the Spaniards] had come, unless they intended to take
their lands away from them. Now they all want to be Christians, because they know that
there is a God who created the heavens and earth and all things, that there is a hell, and glory,
that they have souls, etc., but when the mission was first founded they did not know all these
things; instead, they thought they were like animals, and when the vessels came at first, they
saw that most of the crews died; they were very loath to pray, and they did not want to be
Christians at all; instead, they said that it was bad to become a Christian because they
would die immediately.

No wonder they said so, when they saw how most of the sailors and California Indians died, but now, thanks be to the Lord, God has converted them from Sauls to Pauls. They all know the natural law, which, so I am informed, they have observed as well or better than many Christians elsewhere. They do not have any idols; they do not go on drinking sprees; they do not marry relatives; and they have but one wife. The married men sleep with their wives only. The bachelors sleep together, and apart from the women and married couples. If a man plays with any woman who is not his wife, he is scolded and punished by his captains. Concerning those from the Californias I have heard it said that they are given to sexual vices, but among those here I have not been able to discover a single fault of that nature. Some of the first adults we baptized, when we pointed out to them that it was wrong to have sexual intercourse with a woman to whom they were not married, told me that they already knew that, and that among them it was considered to be very bad, and so they did not do so at all. "The soldiers," they told me, "are Christians, and although they know that God will punish them in hell, they do so, having sexual intercourse with our wives." They said, "Although we did not know that God would punish us for that in hell, we considered it to be very bad, and we did not do it, and even less now that we know that God will punish us if we do so." When I heard this, I burst into tears to see how these gentiles were setting an example for us Christians. Of the many cases which have occurred in this mission, I shall tell of only two about which it is very necessary that Your Reverence should know, particularly the last one which I shall relate.

FIRST CASE

One day about the first of August of the present year of 1772, I went to the Indian village nearest the mission, which is about fifty paces from here, and the Christian Indians said to me, "Father, there is an unmarried woman here who is pregnant." "Well, how can this be?" I said to them. "Have not you told me many times that you do not have sexual intercourse with any woman except your own wife?" That is true, Father," they said to me. "We do not do so, nor have any of us done so with this woman. On the contrary, according to what the woman says, she was coming from the Rincon village (which is about a league and a half from this mission) when a soldier named Hernández and a soldier named Bravo and a soldier named Julián Murillo seized her and sinned with her, and although she was getting away, she is almost blind and could not run very fast, and so it is that she is in this condition without being married." They told me, furthermore, that she was ashamed to be in this condition without being married, and that for this reason she had made many attempts to have an abortion but could not, but that as soon as the creature was born she would kill it. I told her through the interpreter (for, although I understood her some, I used the interpreter so that she could understand better) that she should not do anything so foolish, for God would punish her in hell, that she should bear the little one and we would give her clothing for it to wear, and we would baptize it, etc. Several times I made this and other exhortations to her so that she would not carry out her evil intentions, but it was to no avail. When the time came for the child to be born, she went to the said Rincon village, where she bore the child and killed it without my being able to baptize it. The child was killed about the middle of August of this year. The Indians who saw the little boy told me that he was somewhat white and gave every indication of being a son of the soldiers.

SECOND CASE

On the eleventh day of September of the present year, there went to the Indian village called El Corral the soldiers Casteló, Juan María Ruiz, Bravo, and another who, although the Indians did not know his name, they knew his face well, and a sailor named Ignacio Marques. When they arrived at the said Indian village, they asked the Indian women for prickly-pear apples, which they graciously gave to them. They then asked them to give them some earthen pots, and when they would not do so, the soldier Casteló went forward to take them by force in front of Marques, the said sailor, and boldly seized one of the women by the hand. The said sailor left the soldiers, giving them to understand that he did not want to cooperate in such iniquity as the soldiers were going to commit, and in fact did commit, as soon as the said sailor left them.

Before the said soldiers sinned with the women, the soldier Casteló and the soldier Bravo threatened a Christian Indian named José Antonio who happened to be at the said Indian village, so that he would say nothing about what he had seen. Soldier Casteló carried a gentile woman into a corral which serves as a part of the enclosure surrounding the said Indian village, and inside the corral the said soldier had sexual intercourse with the woman and sinned with her. When he had raped her, the said soldier came out of the corral, and the soldier Juan María Ruiz entered the same corral and sinned with the said woman. After this they released the woman and went to the Indian village, and the soldier whose name is not known seized another woman violently and carried her into the same corral and sinned with her there. He came out, and the soldier Bravo entered and sinned with her. He came out and the soldier Juan María Ruiz entered and did the same. He came out and the soldier Casteló entered and did the same. They went to the Indian village and the soldier Casteló gave this last woman two tortillas and some red ribbons. The soldier Juan Maria Ruiz also gave this same woman some ribbons. The two said soldiers also gave the first woman some ribbons. In order that these outrages should not become known, soldiers Casteló and Bravo told José Antonio, the Indian (who is the one already mentioned above, he having been at the Indian village while all this was taking place) that if he told the Father they would punish him. The said José Antonio arrived here at the mission and the soldier Casteló gave him two tortillas, warning him not to tell.

On the afternoon of the same day, the two women came to tell me about what had happened. They came into the mission weeping, and were seen by many soldiers who were inside. Guessing why they had come, I sent them to the Indian village next to the mission so that the case would not become known to the public. I went to the Indian village after a little while and learned about everything that had happened from the same women with whom the said soldiers had sinned, Diego Ribera serving as my interpreter for greater clarity, he being the one whom I use to teach the Christian Doctrine.

I was informed of this case twice by the said two women, and three times by José Antonio, the said Indian, and they always agreed on everything. This evil was followed by another which, *abisus abisum invocat,* was that this same Indian who had told me about this case was placed in stocks without my being notified, and I took him out in defiance of the corporal of the guard, for I judged, and rightly so, that they were going to punish him so that he would not confess the truth concerning the said case. I am not writing you all the details. I beg Your Reverence to do everything possible (as I suppose you will) so that this conquest will not be lost or retarded because of the bad example of these soldiers, also so that it may be materially restored.

In the *memoria* I am asking for a little sundial adjustable to any latitude, one like the one which Your Reverence had made for Father Antonio Paterna when he was in the Sierra Gorda. I should appreciate it if Your Reverence would send for it or have it made. Enclosed you will find the *memoria* from the Fathers at Mission San Luis Obispo, which, since they neglected to include it among their papers, they forwarded to me so that I could submit it to Your Reverence with mine.

I remain, Your Reverence, as ever, praying that God will watch over you and preserve you for many years in His Divine Love and Grace. From this Mission of San Diego, October 17, 1772.

Kissing the hands of Your Reverence, always your most affectionate friend and faithful, humble subject,

QUESTION: Friar Jayme was what we today call a "whistle-blower." Some Americans call whistle blowing "snitching." Do you think this is right or wrong? Did Jayme owe more to the Indians or to his fellow Spaniards?

Andrew Galvan is the curator of Mission Dolores in San Francisco. He has been able to trace his ancestry all the way back to Ohlone peoples who lived in Bay Area missions in the late 1700s. He points out that everyone who came here was undocumented. Galvan believes that the result of missionaries for most American Indians was alcohol, poverty, and illiteracy. If indigenous peoples were added to the paintings of California missions, he says that it would be like seeing photographs of the liberation of concentration camps in World War II.

And yet Galvan believes in the essential moral imperative of the priests, arguing that "The friars chose to be here; today we call them social workers." Practices such as the suppression of the daily bath, which destroyed the Mission Indians' religious rituals as well as left them more vulnerable to disease, were typical of European cultural practices in that era, and were not intended to be punitive. The European/indigenous encounter was a tragic one, but not intentionally so, Galvan believes.[viii] French explorer Jean Francois de la Perouse visited the Monterey Mission in 1786, taking detailed notes on the area.

[viii]Andrew Galvan shared these perspectives in a lecture at the Napa Valley Museum in April 2006.

2-10   JEAN FRANCOIS DE LA PEROUSE, EXCERPT FROM *LIFE IN A CALIFORNIA MISSION*, 1786

The trees are inhabited by the most charming birds. Our ornithologist stuffed several varieties of sparrows, blue jays, titmice, speckled woodpeckers, and troupiales. Among the birds of prey, we observed the white-headed eagle, the large and small falcon, the goshawk, the sparrow hawk, the black vulture, the large owl, and the raven.

In the ponds and on the seacoast are found the duck, the gray and white pelican with yellow tufts, different species of gulls, cormorants, curlews, ring plovers, small water hens, and herons. Lastly, we killed and stuffed a bee-eater, which ornithologists have supposed to be peculiar to the old continent.

2-11   FR. IGNACIO TIRSCH, *CHUPA MIRTOS (FLOWER SUCKER), CARDINAL, CALIFORNIA SPARROW, BLUEBIRD*, 1763

QUESTION: The Europeans developed an elaborate classification system for birds, and also developed taxidermy, a process of preservation of bird and animal bodies. How does this practice contrast with what we read in Chapter 1 about the indigenous relationship to animals?

2-12 CALIFORNIA CENSUS, 1790

At the top of the Spanish racial system was the category, "Espanol." In Alta California (the land we now call California), all people with a quarter or less "Indian" ancestry were eventually regarded as "Espanol." One level down were the Mestizos, people of half Indian–half European descent. At the bottom were people of pure Indian ancestry, the indigenous people that the Spanish called "Indios," reflecting Columbus' misperception, in 1492, that he had arrived in India.

LOS ANGELES, 1790

María Ignacia Alvarado, española, from Loreto, 28, widow {widow of the late Juan Hismeris/Hismerto Osuna}; four children, españoles: José María Osuna, 12; Francisca Osuna, 7; Juan María Osuna, 6; Juan Nepomuceno Osuna, 3.

Juan Alvarez, cowboy, coyote, from the Yaqui River, 49; wife Bernarda Silvas, española, [from Villa Sinaloa] 17; one child from his first wife {María Lucina/Rudesinda Rodriguez}, mestiza: Gertrudis, 3; one child from his present wife, mestiza: María Rufina, two months.

Manuel Ramírez de Arellano, weaver, español, from Puebla, 46; wife María Agreda López de Haro {aka Aro}, española, [from Alamos] 30; four children, españoles: Teodoro, 7; Rosalía, 5; Martina, 3; Rafaela, seven months.

Joaquín de Armenta, farmworker, español, from Villa Sinaloa, 55; wife María Loreta de Vega, coyota, [from Culiacán] 40; one orphan child, española: María Manuela Lisalde, 12.

Domingo Aruz, farmworker, español, from Gerona [Cataluña], 43; wife Gertrudis Quintero, mulata, [from Alamos] 26; mestizo sons from his first marriage {wife was María Seraphina, a neofita from M. San Carlos}: José, 14; Domingo, 12; son from his present wife: Martín, 7.

Manuel Camero, farmworker, mestizo, from Chametla [Sinaloa], 38; wife Tomasa Garcia, mulata, [from Rosario, Sinaloa] 32.

María Ignacia Carrillo, española, from Loreto, widow, 65 {husband was Juan Diego Verdugo who died in 1780}; her adult son, Leonardo Verdugo, español, farmworker, from Loreto, 29; her grandson: José Antonio Góngora, español, 12.

Roque de Cota, farmworker, español, from El Fuerte, 66; wife Juana María Verdugo, española, [from Loreto] 47; four children, españoles: Guillermo, 22; Loreta, 18; María Ignacia, 11; Dolores, 7.

QUESTION: Had Spain continued to rule North America, its racial categorization system likely would have continued here, as it does in South America today. The American government has recently developed a new term, "biracial," for people of mixed heritage. How does this term compare to Spain's terms, or to terms that are still used today by U. S. census-takers: "white," "Black," "Hispanic," "Asian," "Other"?

3

"Hijos del Pais": Mexican Rule, 1820–1848

> *Even in a democracy, history always involves power and*
> *exclusion, for any history is always someone's history, told by that*
> *someone from a partial point of view. . . . Everyone must listen to*
> *other voices. All histories are provisional; none will have the last*
> *word.*
>
> —Joyce Appleby, et al., *Telling the Truth About History*

Mexico declared its independence from Spain in 1821. At that time, California was populated by the Spanish mission priests, Spanish civil and military officials, as well as wealthy landowners, of Spanish descent, called "Californios." Pió Pico was one of these, part of a generation of young men born in California who called themselves "hijos del pais," or Californios.[i] Pico's father had served at the San Diego Presidio and Pico grew up at the mission.

3-1 DON PIÓ PICO'S EXCERPT FROM *HISTORICAL NARRATIVE*, 1877

In 1827 or 1828, I was named scribe or secretary to Captain Don Pablo de la Portilla, who was named Attorney General, to take down declarations from one Señor Bringas, a Mexican. Señor Bringas was a merchant established in Los Angeles, and it was said that the merchandise he sold belonged to Don José María Herrera, principal Subcommissioner residing in Monterey, who was accused of misappropriation of public funds and of having purchased this merchandise with government money which had been given him in Mexico to pay the troops in California.

Captain Portilla and I arrived at Los Angeles and arranged a meeting with Señor Bringas at an office that had been established by the Captain in the home of Don Antonio Rocha, situated where the city jail is now. Señor Bringas presented himself. The Captain informed him of the object of his commission, to which Bringas answered that he respected and esteemed him very much as a private individual and as a friend, but as a Captain of the Mexican Army he was nothing more to him than the sole of his shoe. This reply impressed me profoundly, because we considered a Captain a personage of high rank and distinction. Not only Captains, but all officials, and even sergeants and corporals, and even the lowest of soldiers were treated with consideration.

---

[i]See Rose Beebe and Robert Senkewicz, *Lands of Promise and Despair* (Berkeley: Heyday Books), 2001.

I was even more surprised when I heard Bringas tell Portilla that the civilians *[paisanos]* were the sacred core of the nation, and that the military were nothing more than servants of the nation, which was constituted of the people and not of the military. Bringas declared he would not give his statement except in front of a person in civil authority, even if he were an Indian *alcalde* from the mission, but not before a military man, whatever his rank. Convinced, Señor Portilla decided to send a message to the Commandant General and another to the Commandant of San Diego, Captain José María Estudillo, laying before them Bringas's reluctance.

I offered to take the communication to the Commandant of San Diego, and my offer was accepted. I arrived at San Diego and delivered the document and was told by Señor Estudillo that I should go to my home to rest until the next day, and that I should return to take the reply back to Los Angeles. By then I was beginning to feel the effects of Señor Bringas's words.

My mother and my family were all in need of my services in San Diego and made it plain to me that, for this reason, they were opposed to my return to Los Angeles. I wanted to please my mother and at the same time show my sense of independence. I now considered myself a "sacred vessel" words which sounded very good to my ears. I presented myself to Estudillo. He had the official letter ready in his hand, and he asked me if I was prepared to depart as he handed me the letter. I told him that I was not able to return to Los Angeles, as I was needed at home. Then Señor Estudillo issued orders to the sergeant that I should be taken to the jail. They imprisoned me in a cell with other prisoners, though I had the luck not to be placed in iron. I was there all that day and that night, and the next morning Estudillo ordered my release, and that I should be taken to the Commandant's office. I went there and he asked me to excuse the manner in which I had been treated—that it had been a hot-headed action, and that I should go and look after my mother. I retired to my home and stayed at my mother's side, but always it appeared to me, deep in my soul, that the citizens were the nation and that no military was superior to us.

QUESTION: Do you recognize the pride in being a "Californio" that he expresses? What might have happened here if Californios had been able to govern this state for fifty or a hundred more years?

Another Californio, Mariano Vallejo, grew up at the Monterey Presidio, where his family owned property. He began his military career at the age of sixteen, proving his loyalty to the Mexican government by attacking some indigenous tribes, while also making treaties with other tribes who would help him maintain the Mexican rule over his part of California.

Vallejo settled in the Sonoma Valley in 1835, awarding land grants to his favorite soldiers and friends. The first land grant that Vallejo bestowed was not given to a Californio, but to American George Yount, who had migrated from Missouri to California in 1833. Yount had won the favor of the Spanish priests by working as a carpenter in the missions, and by serving in the Mexican army. American pioneer John Bidwell wrote about watching men like Yount assimilate into the Californio culture.[ii]

[ii]See Michael Gillis and Michael Magliari, *John Bidwell and California: The Life and Writings of a Pioneer* (Spokane, Washington: Arthur H. Clark Co.), 2001.

3-2   MARIANO VALLEJO, c. 1820

Any time Vallejo needed help in wars against indigenous people, he summoned other Californios (including George Yount) to meet at Los Trancas, his Rancho in Napa, which was
the site of rodeos and bear fights. The Juarez family also came to California as soldiers in
the Spanish colonial army, where Sgt. Cayetano Juarez helped Vallejo found the Sonoma Presidio. But, in 1837, when Mexico did not pay its soldiers, Sergeant Juarez organized a mass
desertion of soldiers who planned to ride from Sonoma to Monterey to demand payment.
Juarez swam across the Carquinez Straits with his horse. Just short of Monterey, he was
captured and sentenced to be shot. Vallejo intervened and ordered Juarez to marry instead
and gave him a grant in Napa to help him "civilize" the region. In return, Juarez allowed
Vallejo to direct his personal life.[iii]

[iii]See Linda Heidenreich, "Family Race and Culture in Napa County, California," Barksdale Essays in History,
v 15, 2000.

3-3 CAYETANO JUAREZ AND SON, c. 1830

QUESTION: Remember, California was part of Mexico only 160 years ago. Why then do many Americans see Mexican people as aliens today?

3-4   CALIFORNIOS CAPTURING BEAR, ARTIST UNKNOWN

3-5   CALIFORNIOS AND BULL, ARTIST UNKNOWN

Under Mexican rule, cattle ranching in California began, offering economic opportunities to Californios and Californianas, while placing those without land in a permanent position of servitude on the ranchos.

Men often left the ranchos and spent extended amounts of time socializing at the forts, or Presidios. These Mexican soldiers "civilized" Northern California, "subdued" indigenous uprisings, and were rewarded by the Mexican government for that service with vast quantities of land and indigenous servants.

3-6   LUIS MARIA PERALTA, CATTLE BRANDS, 1819

While their husbands were gone, wives managed the estates. These women, Californianas, were trained in horseback riding and the use of small arms; they did not go out without their weapons, fearing "Indian" attacks. While running the ranchos, these women were pregnant during most of their reproductive lives. Maria Juarez had eleven children at Rancho Tulocay; Mariano Vallejo's wife had sixteen children. The mandate on Californianas to reproduce was so strong that when one of Juarez's daughters, Agnes, entered the Dominican convent, her father was angry enough to threaten her with violence.

3-7   JOSÉ DEL CARMEN LUGO, EXCERPT FROM *LIFE ON A CALIFORNIA RANCHO,* 1840

José del Carmen Lugo, the author of this reminiscence, was born in Los Angeles in 1813 and grew up on San Antonio Rancho. He was granted Rancho San Bernardino in 1842.

FROM "THE LIFE OF A RANCHER"

The Californian way of life in my early years was as follows: at eight o'clock in the evening, the entire family was occupied in its prayers. In commending themselves to God, they recited the rosary and other special prayers which each one addressed to the saint of his or her name or devotion. Husband and wife slept in the same room, and nearly always in the same bed. If there were any children, and the dwelling had conveniences and separate apartments, the boys slept in the galleries outside in the open air, and the girls in an enclosed quarter to which the parents kept the key, if there was a key, a thing that was not very common.

At three o'clock in the morning, the entire family was summoned to their prayers. After this, the women betook themselves to the kitchen and other domestic tasks such as sweeping, cleaning, dusting, and so on. The men went to their labor in the field, some to herd cattle, others to look after the horses. The milking of the cows was done by the men or the Indian servants. Ordinarily some woman had charge of the milking, to see that the milk was clean and strained. The women and the Indian servants under them made the small, hard, flat cheeses, the cheese proper, butter, curds, and a mixture made to use with beans.

The women's labors lasted till seven or eight in the morning. After that they were busy cooking, sewing, or washing. The men passed the day in labor in the fields, according to the location—some preparing the ground for sowing seed, bringing in wood, sowing the seed, and so on. Some planted cotton, some hemp, some planted both. This was done by those who had facilities for it; they planted and harvested the things they needed most for the benefit of their families, such as rice, corn, beans, barley and other grains, squash, watermelons, and cantaloupes.

The lands in the immediate vicinity of Los Angeles were set to fruit trees such as grapes, pears, apples, pomegranates, here and there an olive, cactus fruit in some places, peaches, nectarines, and other minor fruits. The owners of fields could not obtain seeds of oranges, lemon, cider-producing fruits, or others that were found at the missions, because the padres selfishly refused to allow them to grow elsewhere than at their missions.

Fruit trees were not cultivated on the *ranchos*, because very few persons were able to own ranches until very recently; that is, 1836 or 1837 and on.

During the time Spain was in power here, a few *ranchos* were granted, those of the Nietos, Verdugos, Domínguez and Bartolo Tapia. I am not positive, but I have heard it said that the *Rancho de la Bayona* was also granted in the time of the King, to the family of Zúñiga. These are the only *ranchos* that I know as having been granted during the Spanish regime.

Many people occupied *ranchos* provisionally with their stock, and this was allowed because there was not room enough for them in the town or the community corral. In 1822, an order came from the *Alcalde* that the Judge should destroy corrals on the *ranchos*, and the owners of stock should place them in community corrals. At this time my father was in Monterey, and he secured permission to maintain a corral on the little ranch where he lived, the one that the river destroyed in 1825. . . .

Returning to the way of living of the Californians: the type of ordinary life that I have described was more or less followed by people living on *ranchos* as well as by those residing in the towns.

The house on a little ranch was of rough timber roofed with tules. It rarely had more than two rooms. One served as the entry and living room, the other as a sleeping room. If the family was large, the two rooms were divided. Many of these houses had a door faced with sheepskin, cowhide, or horsehide. No door had a lock or key, nor was it necessary to close it on the outside when the whole family left, because there was no one who would enter to steal, and nothing which would be worth taking. If the family was to be absent for several days, they would take with them their one thing of value, namely, the little chest of clothes, and some bedding and a cot.

Some ranchers or other people of the town had beds of cottonwood or poplar lined with leather on which they slept. On this bed there were sheets, blankets, coverlets, pillows, and so on, according to the resources of the owner.

Some slept on great frameworks resembling a hammock with cross-bars on which was thrown a cowhide. The person who had nothing else slept on a cowhide or horsehide. I am speaking, of course, of the first years that I knew. Later some conveniences were introduced when trade with the outside began. The families who were able usually had furniture of the sort most needed, such as a table, a long bench, and a few little stools. Some had seats of whalebones, other little stools, often of reeds, narrow slats, or some other splints. These stools were the most common. Outside the house on each side of the door there were benches of adobe on which people could sit; they were less than a *vara* in height. Some were plastered and whitewashed like the wall of the house. Others, like some of the houses, were not whitewashed, because lime was scarce and hard to obtain without bringing it from a distance.

The kitchen in some places was supplied with a small adobe arrangement on which were placed the cooking pots. In other places there were only stones upon which the pots were placed, the fire being underneath them. The hour for breakfast was very early for the men who had to go to their labors. Others breakfasted later. For this breakfast the wealthy had good Spanish chocolate made with milk or water according to taste, with bread, tortillas, and wheat or corn porridge with butter, and so on. The poor people had their early meal of milk with pinole or toasted corn, or perhaps parched corn. Others breakfasted on beans, while some had a solid meal of roasted or dried meat with chili, onions, tomatoes, and beans, since there would not be another until four or five in the afternoon, according to the time of the year.

During Lent, when fasting was observed, people did not have their first meal until twelve o'clock noon, and the second at eight in the evening. These two meals, at midday and at night, generally consisted of fish, abalone, *colachi* (which was merely squash chopped fine and boiled), and *quelites* (which were native herbs well boiled) mixed with beans half and half. There was no coffee or tea.

Another dish was *lechetole*, which was wheat cooked in milk with plenty of *panocha* (a sort of candy made of brown sugar), or squash cooked with milk and *panocha*, curds, cheese, cottage cheese, and clabber. The supper during Lent was of *colachi, quelite,* and beans, with cornmeal tortillas.

There was another tortilla which the old women made of corn. It was coarse, and the last that was made, and they called it *niscayote*. They added butter, and to sweeten it sugar, *panocha*, or honey was used. The only difference between the Lenten season and the rest of the year was that in Lent no meat was eaten except by the individual who had permission from the Church because of sickness or other exemption.

Those who had plates, who were few in number, ate on them. Those who did not have them used at clay bowls which had the same shape as the ordinary plates. Knives, forks, and spoons such as those used today on the table were possessed by only a few people. With the poorer class, which was the greater part of the population, the general thing was to use forks and spoons of horn. Those who did not have even this made a spoon for every mouthful by loading the meat or beans or whatever they had on a piece of tortilla, and all went together to the stomach. They used their knives for all work.

The food was generally eaten in the kitchen beside the fire. Those who had the conveniences, of course, with tables, ate as is done today, with tablecloths and so on. But the number of these was very limited.

3-8   CHRISTINA DELGADO LAND GRANT, 1834

3-9 DELGADO PROPERTY, 1834

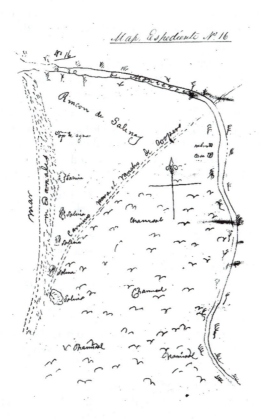

3-10 ANDREW GARRIGA, EXCERPT FROM *HERBS AND REMEDIES USED BY INDIANS AND CALIFORNIOS*, c. 1890

Many Californianas worked alongside with their indigenous servants, learning from them how to use local herbs for healing, cooking, and cleaning. These remedies were among the first written records of indigenous healing, which were adapted by the Californios.

FROM A COMPILATION OF HERBS AND REMEDIES USED BY THE INDIANS AND SPANISH CALIFORNIANS, BY ANDREW GARRIGA

Blindness: They say that the juice of *Jamatai* (soaproot) put on it with a small feather will dissolve them (cataracts).

Colds: Drink tea of *Palo Santo (lignum vitae)* and *Miel de Abejas* (bees' honey), or tea of mountain pine leaves, or tea of *Yerba de la Hiedra* (poison oak), or tea of blossoms of *Sauco* (elderberry tree), or of the root of wild *Peonia* (peony), or of *Marrubio* (white horehound), or of *Borraja* (borage), or drink powders of the root of wild *Peonia* with some water.

Earache: Put in the ear oil of Laurel (bay tree).

Deafness: Crush eggs of ants and mix with the juice of raw *Cebolla* (onion) and pour into the ear.

Eyes: Apply a poultice of *Yerba del Ojo.* Steam the leaves a little so as to make them softer, and keep the poultice on the sore eye during the night. Or wash them, from time to time, with balm of *Romero* (rosemary), or with the tea of *Rosa de Castilla* (rose of Castile), or with tea of *Yerba de la Golondrina* (swallow seed).

Hemorrhage: Drink tea of *Culantrillo* (maidenhair) and eat *Arroz* (rice), cooked plain, with plenty of salt, or do either of the two, or take a spoonful of the juice of apples every five minutes, till relieved. If it repeats, do it again. If it comes from a wound:

1. Put *Hollin* (soot from chimney) with white of eggs;
2. Or catch frogs, roast in a well-covered vessel and, when dry, reduce them to powder and put it on the wound;
3. Or fill the wound with clean cobwebs dipped in wheat flour.

Insanity: When insanity is not from a hopeless cause, this may be tried. It has brought several back to their senses. Anyway, it can do no harm. A poultice of Laurel (bay tree) leaves, some nutmeg, cinnamon, and olive oil cooked together and put on the head. It starts an abundant perspiration. Change poultice when it begins to get cold. Soon the patient will come to, as if he awoke from a sleep.

Rheumatism: Inflammatory. It swells the joints. Drink the pure juice of a lemon every morning half an hour before breakfast, or drink tea of *Yarcas* (tarweed), or take powders of sulfur, niter, *Mostaza* (mustard), *Rubardo* (rhubarb), one ounce each, and of gum of *Guaicaca* (guaicum), one-half ounce. Mix powders well. Take two teaspoons of it with some water the first night and then only one teaspoon every other night. This prescription is very old and famous. It has cured many hard cases. Do not mind the trouble the first dose will give you. . . .

Sciatica: This is rheumatism of the nerves. It does not swell the joints.

1. Make tea of the leaves of Eucalyptus (gum tree).* Drink some of it and put a plaster of the leaves (steamed) on the pain every night.
2. Change of climate and giving the mind a rest may relieve or even cure it permanently. The same is good for all neuralgias.

Teeth: For numb or too-sensitive teeth: boil *Romero* (rosemary) in vinegar and wash your mouth with it, or boil roots of *Lanten* (plantain) instead of *Romero* in the same way.

For toothache: Chew green *Yerba de la Muela,* or make tea of it and wash your mouth to and fro with it, and spit it out.

QUESTION: How do people today use herbs in healing?

What happened to the missions? Secularization was a plan to transfer ownership of the missions from the church to indigenous people, but this plan was rarely honored. Corrupt commissioners routinely sold off the mission land for profit before indigenous people could receive it. Therefore, most former mission Indians ended up as laborers on the ranchos or in the pueblos.

Mexican soldiers and peasants formed the labor force that performed the hard work on ranchos for the wealthy Mexican landholding families. The former mission Indians intermarried with these landless Mexicanos to produce a mixed-race labor force.

3-11, 3-12, 3-13   WORKERS ON RANCHOS

Field hands identified as Californios on the porch of the former San Fernando Mission probably in the 1880's.

Left: A vaquero at San Jan, near Los Angeles. *Right:* A Neophyte Indian serving as a zanjero (keeper of the irrigation ditch).

QUESTION: How did the lives of the workers contrast with those of the owners of the Mexican ranchos, based on what you've read and seen in these documents?

Juana Machado was the daughter of a Mexican soldier. The land described in her story was 22 miles southeast of Mission San Diego and had been claimed by the Pico family since 1829.

3-14   JUANA MACHADO, EXCERPT FROM *TIMES GONE BY IN ALTA CALIFORNIA* 1837

Early one afternoon, an Indian woman named Cesárea came to where Doña Eustaquia was sitting at the door looking toward the street and, in a loud voice, asked her for salt. The mistress ordered that salt be brought her, but the Indian woman, by sign, gave her to understand that she wished her to give it to her, herself. The mistress got up and the Indian woman followed her. Arriving at a secluded spot, the Indian woman, in a tongue which Doña Eustaquia understood well, told her that the Indians were going to rise, kill the men, and make captives of the women.

Doña Eustaquia, with much prudence, went to the room where her daughters were sewing; she told them to leave their work, take their *rebozos* (all of the women wore *rebozos* at that time), and go for a walk along the edge of the cornfield, saying that she would soon follow them.

With much secrecy she called the majordomo, a relative of hers named Juan Leiva, and told him what Cesárea had revealed to her, saying besides that she herself had for some days noticed things among the Indians which had made her suspicious, although these had not been great.

The majordomo assured her that there was no danger whatever, advising her to calm herself, as he had men and twelve firearms well loaded. Doña Eustaquia again urged him to place her and her family in safety. He, confident of his strength, refused to do what she advised. Then Doña Eustaquia told him to send a *carreta* with oxen along the road to the cornfield. She started on the road to meet her daughters. The *carreta* came along to them, with only one hide in it; in this *carreta* they arrived at Jamacha ranch (belonging to the already mentioned Doña Apolinaria, who had a majordomo in charge there) in the middle of the night; thence after telling the majordomo and his family what was going on, they continued the journey to San Diego and reported to the *Alcalde*, Don José Antonio Estudillo, who at once sent people to protect those at the ranch, but they arrived late.

The Indians did not attack the same night but the following; all of a sudden they fell upon servants at the ranch, who were the majordomo, Juan Leiva, his son José Antonio, a youth name Molina, and another from Lower California named Comancho. They killed all at the cornfield except Juan Leiva, who broke away toward the house to defend his family.

When he went toward the gun room, an Indian cleaning woman of the house who had locked that room and put the key in her pocket mockingly showed him the key, saying that there were no hopes in that direction.

Leiva ran to the kitchen and defended himself with coals of fire for a while; but at the end they killed him and threw his body into the hall of the house. Afterward they overcame his wife, Doña María, a little son named Claro, and his two daughters, Tomasa and Ramona (fifteen and twelve years old, respectively).

The Indians were going to kill Doña María and the boy, when the supplications of Doña Tomasa made them desist. They took off all the woman's clothes and those of the boy, and in spite of the screams and moans of all the family, they carried off the two girls toward the Colorado River. Before starting they removed everything from the ranch, taking with them horses, cattle, and all other things of value, and burned the houses.

Poor Doña María covered her nakedness with grasses and thus reached Mission San Diego, where Fathers Vicente Pasqual Olivas and Fernando Martín were in charge.

All the efforts that were made to recover the lost property and much great effort to ransom the kidnapped girls were useless. To this day, what was the fate of those unhappy creatures is unknown. Sergeant Macedonio Gonzales, celebrated Indian fighter, told us that once he went from Mission San Miguel in Lower California to Jacumba Mountain with a considerable force to see about rescuing these girls, who were his nieces. On reaching the foot of the mountain he saw many men and women Indians above, eating meat of the cattle which they had stolen. When they saw him they began to shout and threaten him, saying that they also had courage, and if he wanted to come up where they were, Tomasa and Ramona were there.

He said that he actually saw these two girls, apparently with white bodies painted and with hair cut in Indian fashion. He saw their bodies because in that time the Indians did not wear clothes, except a covering of rabbit skins, which they called *pajales*, over their privates; he did not dare to fire, fearing that they really were his nieces and the shots might kill them.

Afterwards the Indians left the rock to which they had ascended and disappeared. It was not possible for him to climb with his horses to that height. He spoke kindly to the Indians and made them very generous offers of cattle, horses, etc. as ransom for the girls, but the Indians accepted nothing.

Some years afterwards, when these same Indians were at peace, he again offered them ransom, but all his efforts were in vain.

QUESTION: Like slaves in the Southern states, indigenous people in California put up more resistance to domination than has usually been credited to them. What evidence of their strategies and planning do you find in this account?

Great waves of epidemics of European diseases rolled into the former "Indian country" in the early 1830s. A group of trappers came from the Pacific Northwest to trade, unknowingly bringing smallpox that killed seventy-five percent of the indigenous Californians. In May 1838, Mariano Vallejo announced that a second epidemic had killed an additional 70,000 indigenous people. Cayetano Juarez's great-niece Juarez Vivian Metcalf writes: "The death toll was so great because the Indians used sweat boxes and then plunged into the water of the river," bringing on pneumonia.[iv]

[iv]Juarez-Rose, Vivian. *The Past is Father of the Present: Spanish California History and Family Legend*s, *San Francisco and Napa County* (Vallejo: Wheeler Publishing), 1974.

4

"The Road to California Will Be Open to Us": American Settlement, 1840–1849

Every new generation must rewrite history in its own way; every new historian, not content with giving new answers to old questions, must revise the questions themselves—since historical thought is a river into which none can step twice.

–R.G. Collingwood, The Idea of History

As we examine the effect of the migration of people from the Eastern and Midwestern states to California, it helps to listen to multiple voices that are now speaking through the careful research of scholars and translators. In this chapter you will read Mariano Vallejo's description of the arrival of the American wagon trains alongside the Proclamation by the Commander in Chief of the U.S. Naval Forces. Fellow Californio Antonio Osio responds to the arrival of the Americans, while Americans John Bidwell and George Yount weigh in with their own eyewitness accounts of what happened.

Finally, the Treaty of Guadalupe Hidalgo, which concluded the U.S. war with Mexico, along with a page from the first California Constitution, supply us with an understanding of what was promised to the Mexican peoples who saw California as their rightful home. Remember, California belonged to Mexico until 1848, 72 years after the American Revolution; it did not become part of the United States until 1850.[i]

4-1 MARIANO GUADALUPE VALLEJO, EXCERPT FROM LETTER, 1841

Most Excellent Sir: On the return of Captain Don José Castro to this Department, I had a number of conferences with him; and I had decided that he should return to that capital in company with Captain of Militia and Secretary of the Commandancy General Don Victor Prudón, to place in Your Excellency's hands an exact report of the state in which this country finds itself, a country that is so promising but which can accomplish nothing; for its happiness is conditional, and its misery positive. Its geographic location, the mildness of its climate, the fertility of its soil, the amenity of its fields, the safety of its ports, among which

---

[i]See http://encarta.msn.com/media_461546354//Mexican_War.html for map of borders in 1845. See http://www.pbs.org/kpbs/theborder/history/morphingmap.html for progression of borders.

that of San Francisco deserves to rank among the principal ones of the world, its navigable rivers and inlets, etc. guarantee it a state of prosperity which it is not permitted to attain, due to its lack of population. From that lack of population results its lack of defense, and from this, its insecurity. Thus it is that daily, throughout the whole extent of the Department with the exception of this frontier, where I maintain a military force of forty men at my own expense, there are Indian raids which ravish the fields with impunity and destroy the only effective wealth of the country, the cattle and horses. The otter and beaver which abounded in California have been exterminated, the first by the Russians and the latter by the Columbians [trappers from the Columbia River], who still continue to trap them to the point of extinguishing the species, as the Russians have done with the otter. And we have to endure all those ills because we cannot prevent them, since we have not troops. All that we have suffered and shall endure, if we do not avert the tempest which is presaged for us by the thick clouds that darken our political horizon, is derived from one and the same source; it comes from one single cause: all of it we should attribute to the lack of troops.

This has been, Your Excellency, the motive which inspired me with the idea of addressing to you, by the aforementioned Commissioners, the various notes which they shall have the honor to place in Your Excellency's hands, all of them relative to the exigencies of the country, with the hope that Your Excellency's zeal and acknowledged patriotism will be exerted to contribute toward the salvation of this valuable portion of Mexican Territory. The Commissioners will be able to satisfy Your Excellency about all of which you may judge opportune to inform yourself.

On the ninth of November, last, while at Mission San José, during a conference with Don José Castro, I received word of the arrival at the town of San José of a party of thirty-three foreigners from Missouri. I had them appear before me to demand their passports, and I was told that they had none, because they did not deem them necessary, since they did not use them in their country. I took a list of their names and the object of their journey. I asked them to return to their country and to get the required documents, and I gave them provisional papers so that they might travel in safety to Monterey to see the Governor and get the necessary permission from him to travel in the country. I gave the Governor an account of everything but do not know the results. I took what seemed to me the only way to reconcile justice with the present circumstances, since we find ourselves forced to accept them, as we cannot prevent them from entering, and all because we lack troops. This party numbers thirty-three, but it is said that a larger one is on the way.

The total population of California does not exceed six thousand souls, and of these two-thirds must be counted as women and children, leaving scarcely two thousand men. But we cannot count on the fifteen thousand Indians in the towns and missions, because they inspire more fear than confidence. Thus we have this lamentable situation in a country worthy of a better fate. And if the invasion which is taking place from all sides is carried out, all I can guarantee is that the Californians will die; I cannot dare to assure you that California will be saved. This people, loyal to their flag, will follow the same course and fate. They will be replaced by or dominated by another race at least. Those others will probably conserve their great past, raising their flag to wave in the breeze. Thus also the noble people of California will preserve their noble attitude of free men while a drop of blood remains in their veins, and will bite the dust before kissing the enemy's hand.

Have the kindness to excuse this burst of feeling in a soldier who laments not having arms when he sees the treasure being stolen. I regret to bother Your Excellency's patriotic zeal, but I must be a truthful steward when speaking of the national interests. The danger seems closer than the help, and it is urgent, and it is with the hope of getting it that I have the honor of addressing Your Excellency.

4-2   EMIGRANTS OVERLAND TRIP

4-3   THOMAS JONES, COMMANDER IN CHIEF OF THE U.S. NAVAL FORCES, PROCLAMATION TO THE PEOPLE OF THE CALIFORNIAS, 1842

To the inhabitants of the two Californias:

Although I come in arms, as the representative of a powerful nation upon whom the central government of Mexico has waged war, I come not to spread desolation among California's peaceful inhabitants.

It is against the armed enemies of my country, banded and swayed under the flag of Mexico, that war and its dread consequences will be enforced.

Inhabitants of California! You have only to remain at your homes in pursuit of peaceful vocation to ensure security of life, persons, and property from the consequences of an unjust war into which Mexico has suddenly and rashly plunged you.

Those Stars and Stripes, infallible emblems of civil Liberty–of Liberty of speech, freedom of the press, and above all, the freedom of conscience, with constitutional rights and lawful security, to worship the Great Deity in the way most congenial to each one's sense of duty to his Creator, now float triumphantly before you and henceforth and forever will give protection and security to you, to your children, and to unborn countless thousands.

All the rights and privileges which you now enjoy, together with the privilege of choosing your own magistrates and other officers for the administration of justice among yourselves, will be secured to all who remain peaceably at their homes and offer no resistance to the forces of the United States.

Each of the inhabitants of California, whether natives or foreigners, as may not be disposed to accept the high privilege of citizenship and to live peaceably under the Free Government of the United States will be allowed time to dispose of their property and to remove out of the country without any other restriction, while they remain in it, than the observance of strict neutrality, total abstinence from taking part directly or indirectly in the war against the United States or holding any intercourse whatever with any civil or military officer, agent, or other person employed by the Mexican Government.

All provisions and supplies of every kind furnished by the inhabitants of California for the use of the United States, their ships, and their soldiers will be paid for at fair rates.

No private property will be taken for public use without just compensation.

Thomas ap C. Jones

Commander in Chief of the United States Naval Forces on the
Pacific Station and of the Naval and Military Expedition for the
occupation of Old and New California.

Flag ship United States. Monterey Bay, October 19, 1842

QUESTION: "Whether native or a foreigner . . . " Who is the native and who is the foreigner in Jones's proclamation? If Mexican Californians didn't want to accept American rule, what choices did they face? Why was Vallejo so sure that the American settlers would be able to "take" California from its Mexican governors?

4-4   ANTONIO MARIA OSIO, CHIEF CUSTOMS ADMINISTRATOR OF MONTEREY, RESPONSE TO JONES'S PROCLAMATION, 1842

. . . A few days later, the frigate *United States* and the sloop *Cyane,* commanded by Commodore Jones, anchored in Monterey. Jones then sent a message to Señor Alvarado informing him that he would take possession of Monterey, since war had been declared between Mexico and the United States. He advised Alvarado not to expose his people to the horrors of war, because he did not have sufficient soldiers to oppose Jones's troops. He also stated that he expected Alvarado to comply with his demands by eleven o'clock the following day. The message was delivered by the Commodore's secretary and Don Juan Armstrong, the commander of the frigate. Señor Alvarado was in shock as he read the note, which was written in Spanish. After a period of silence, his face suddenly became pale and then immediately turned red, as if blood were about to burst from his eyes. In a voice choked with emotion, he told the Commodore's secretary, who was a Spaniard, that if he had only half the number of men in the Commodore's force he would consider their forces equal. Then he would not have needed to try to frighten him with threats. It would bring him pleasure as well as honor to fight him in defense of his country. However, since he could not do this, he would comply.

It was almost sunset when the Commodore's representatives left Señor Alvarado's house. That night Alvarado sent a communiqué posthaste to General Micheltorena informing him of the unexpected arrival of the American warships under the command of Commodore Jones. Alvarado attached a copy of Jones's demand, and the reply he would give the Commodore the following day. It stated that he was compelled to surrender, because his force was not large enough to oppose Jones, and because he and his men wanted to protect his people from bombardment. Jones could accordingly take possession of Monterey at the appointed hour or before. Alvarado also informed Jones that he had sent an urgent communiqué, dated that day, to the Commander General of the Territory to advise him of the situation.

Flying flags of truce, yet with their guns aimed at the town, the ships maintained their positions as they waited for the appointed hour to arrive. At ten o'clock on that ill-fated day, all the small boats were lowered into the water to transport the soldiers, who were commanded by Captain Armstrong. Once ashore, Armstrong headed for the Governor's home. There, the true *Californios,* people who loved their country and were proud of their nationality, were forced to witness a painful ceremony for the very first time. The national flag of the three guarantees was lowered from its native flagpole so that it could be replaced by the stars and stripes. This flag was alleged to be the symbol of liberty, but that was actually a lie. It belonged to an oppressor who displayed arrogance against the weak. As he was inspecting the papers in the government archives, the Commodore found some recent newspapers that completely convinced him that Mexico and the United States were not at war. Therefore, since he had acted wrongly, he promised that he would evacuate the town at four in the afternoon, and as soon as the Mexican flag had been raised, he would honor it by firing his cannons in salute.

4-5   ANTONIO MARIA OSIO

1842: REHEARSAL FOR INVASION

QUESTION: Osio writes, "The symbol of liberty was actually a lie." Why would he think so? Does a symbol have a universal meaning, or does it depend on what side you're on?

4-6   GEORGE C. YOUNT, EXCERPT FROM *GEORGE C. YOUNT AND HIS CHRONICLES OF THE WEST: COMPRISING EXTRACTS FROM THE MEMOIRS AND FROM THE ORANGE CLARK NARRATIVE*

George Yount was impressed by the religious devotion of California's indigenous people. He watched them passing mounds that marked spirit places, carefully placing a bead or a pin, a seed or a stone out of respect for each monument. He described the trances he witnessed, during which "they communicated with the gods who were ghosts and after which they would tell what they had learned."[ii] Richard Dillon says that Yount "saw their prophecies as Delphic [comparable to Greek mythology]; their frenzies as akin to the religious possession of the most religious Christians."[iii]

[ii]George Yount, *George C. Yount and His Chronicles of the West: Comprising Extracts from the Memoirs and from the Orange Clark Narrative* (Denver, Colorado: Old West Publishing), 1966.

[iii]Richard Dillon, *Napa Valley's Natives,* Napa County Historical Society, 2001, 19.

As described in Chapter 3, Yount was immersed in the Californio culture. He helped Vallejo subdue indigenous people, yet he strongly objected to their subjugation by Americans. George Yount's account was dictated to an interviewer because Yount could neither read nor write.

They roamed from Rancho to Rancho, from Rancheria to Rancheria, and left behind only traces of tears and blood—they would shoot down the Indian and even the Spaniard for more sport, or as some have confessed upon the gallows, "only to see them jump and struggle, and to hear them yell and groan."—They stole cattle by the hundreds from the Ranchos and drove them to market in the cities—they often entered houses on remote farms, and robbed in open daylight, prepared for murder indiscriminately if resisted, or in any danger of being exposed—sometimes they have been known, in organized bands, of from 20–50, to embark in an indiscriminate slaughter of all the Indians they could find . . . . On one occasion they even skinned their wretched victim alive from the sole of the foot to the crown of the head—and exultingly to mock and exult over his expiring agonies.

QUESTION: What is the importance of the eyewitness testimony Yount offers?

4-7 WARM SPRINGS WOMAN

QUESTION: How might the American settlers or the indigenous woman pictured here tell the story differently?

4-8 JOHN BIDWELL, LIFE IN CALIFORNIA BEFORE THE GOLD DISCOVERY, *CENTURY MAGAZINE*, DECEMBER 1890

Bidwell led one of the first emigrant parties across the Sierras, and eventually founded the town of Chico. He ran for president as Prohibition Party candidate in 1882, and may have been the first person to import "Bermuda grass," which became an efficient way to keep levees from eroding in the Central Valley.[iv]

The party at Sonoma now received some accessions from Americans and other foreigners living on the north side of the bay. Rumors began to reach them of an uprising on the part of the native Californians, which indeed began under Joaquin de la Torre. Henry L. Ford and other Americans to the number of thirty met De la Torre—whose force was said to number from forty to eighty—near the Petaluma Ranch, and four or five of the Californians were said to have been killed or wounded. The repulse of the Californians seems to have been complete, though reports continued alarming, and a man sent from Sonoma to Russian River for powder was killed. A messenger was sent in haste to Sacramento for Frémont, who hurried to Sonoma with nearly all his exploring party and scoured the country far and near, but found no enemy.

I tried to make the prisoners at Sacramento as comfortable as possible, assisting to see that their meals were regularly and properly brought, and sometimes I would sit by while they were eating. One day E. M. Kern, artist to Frémont's exploring expedition, called me out and said it was Frémont's orders that no one was to go in or speak to the prisoners. I told him they were in my charge, and that he had nothing to say about them. He asserted that they were in his charge, and finally convinced me that he had been made an equal, if not the principal, custodian. I then told him that, as both of us were not needed, I would go over and join Frémont at Sonoma. Just at this time Lieutenant Washington A. Bartlett of the United States Navy arrived from the bay, inquiring for Frémont. The taking of the horses from Arce, the capture of the prisoners, and the occupation of Sonoma, had been heard of, and he was sent to learn what it meant. So he went over to Sonoma with me.

On our arrival Frémont was still absent trying to find the enemy, but that evening he returned. The Bear Flag was still flying, and had been for a week or more. The American flag was nowhere displayed. There was much doubt about the situation. Frémont gave us to understand that we must organize. Lieutenant Gillespie seemed to be his confidential adviser and spokesman, and said that a meeting would be held the next day at which Frémont would make an address. He also said that it would be necessary to have some plan of organization ready to report to the meeting; and that P. B. Reading, W. B. Ide. and myself were requested to act as a committee to report such a plan. We could learn nothing from Frémont or Gillespie to the effect that the United States had anything to do with Frémont's present movements.

[iv]See Michael Gillis and Michael Magliari, *John Bidwell and California: The Life and Writings of a Pioneer* (Spokane, Washington: Arthur H. Clark Co.), 2001.

In past years rumors of threats against Americans in California had been rather frequent, several times causing them and other foreigners to hasten in the night from all places within one or two hundred miles to Sutter's Fort, sometimes remaining a week or two, drilling and preparing to resist attack. The first scare of this kind occurred in 1841, when Sutter became somewhat alarmed: the last, in 1845. But in every case such rumors had proved to be groundless, so that Americans had ceased to have apprehensions, especially in the presence of such an accessible refuge as Sutter's Fort. And now, in 1846, after so many accessions by immigration, we felt entirely secure, even without the presence of a United States officer and his exploring force of sixty men, until we found ourselves suddenly plunged into a war. But hostilities having been begun, bringing danger where none before existed, it now became imperative to organize. It was in everyone's mouth (and I think must have come from Frémont) that the war was begun in defense of American settlers! This was simply a pretense to justify the premature beginning of the war, which henceforth was to be carried on in the name of the United States.

So much has been said and written about the "Bear Flag" that some may conclude it was something of importance. It was not so regarded at the time: it was never adopted at any meeting or by any agreement; it was, I think, never even noticed, perhaps never seen, by Frémont when it was flying. The naked old Mexican flagstaff at Sonoma suggested that something should be put on it. Todd had painted it, and others had helped to put it up, for mere pastime. It had no importance to begin with, none whatever when the Stars and Stripes went up, and never would have been thought of again had not an officer of the navy seen it in Sonoma and written a letter about it.

QUESTION: Compare Bidwell's account to what you find from an Internet search on "The Bear Flag Revolt." Can the story of any war ever be told without taking sides?

The U.S. war against Mexico was vigorously debated in Congress. Notable Americans like abolitionist Frederick Douglass opposed the war and called it "the present disgraceful, cruel, and iniquitous war with our sister republic."[v] In the eastern U.S. colonies, Irish workers in New York and Massachusetts demonstrated against the war; some enlisted in the Mexican Army and formed the Saint Patrick's Battalion. Desertion of American troops from this war grew to over 9,000 men.

Opposition to the war was the inspiration for the essay "Civil Disobedience," which Henry David Thoreau wrote to explain why he chose jail rather than pay what he called "war taxes." One hundred and fifty years later, most Americans don't know the story of the U.S. Mexican War. A recent PBS film attempted to give multiple perspectives on what one of its writers, Rob Tranchin, calls "the birth event for the Mexican-American people," but both Mexican historians and American viewers were critical of the finished product.[vi]

---

[v]Frederick Douglas, cited in John Schroeder, *Mr. Polk's War: American Opposition and Dissent 1846–1848* (Madison: University of Wisconsin), 1973.
[vi]See www.current.org/hi/hi815m.html.

4-9   TREATY OF GUADALUPE HIDALGO, 1848

Mexico surrendered to the United States in February 1848. Under the Treaty of Guadalupe Hidalgo, the U.S. was given possession of half of Mexico, which included much of the Southwest as well as California. The guarantees to Californios of property and equality were not honored.

TREATY OF PEACE, FRIENDSHIP, LIMITS, AND SETTLEMENT BETWEEN THE UNITED STATES OF AMERICA AND THE UNITED MEXICAN STATES CONCLUDED AT GUADALUPE HIDALGO, FEBRUARY 2, 1848; RATIFICATION ADVISED BY SENATE, WITH AMENDMENTS, MARCH 10, 1848; RATIFIED BY PRESIDENT, MARCH 16, 1848; RATIFICATIONS EXCHANGED AT QUERE-TARO, MAY 30, 1848; PROCLAIMED, JULY 4, 1848.

IN THE NAME OF ALMIGHTY GOD

The United States of America and the United Mexican States animated by a sincere desire to put an end to the calamities of the war which unhappily exists between the two Republics and to establish Upon a solid basis relations of peace and friendship, which shall confer reciprocal benefits upon the citizens of both, and assure the concord, harmony, and mutual confidence wherein the two people should live, as good neighbors have for that purpose appointed their respective plenipotentiaries, that is to say: The President of the United States has appointed Nicholas P. Trist, a citizen of the United States, and the President of the Mexican Republic has appointed Don Luis Gonzaga Cuevas, Don Bernardo Couto, and Don Miguel Atristain, citizens of the said Republic; Who, after a reciprocal communication of their respective full powers, have, under the protection of Almighty God, the author of peace, arranged, agreed upon, and signed the following: Treaty of Peace, Friendship, Limits, and Settlement between the United.

ARTICLE I

There shall be firm and universal peace between the United States of America and the Mexican Republic, and between their respective countries, territories, cities, towns, and people, without exception of places or persons.

ARTICLE VIII

Mexicans now established in territories previously belonging to Mexico, and which remain for the future within the limits of the United States, as defined by the present treaty, shall be free to continue where they now reside, or to remove at any time to the Mexican Republic, retaining the property which they possess in the said territories, or disposing thereof, and removing the proceeds wherever they please, without their being subjected, on this account, to any contribution, tax, or charge whatever.

Those who shall prefer to remain in the said territories may either retain the title and rights of Mexican citizens, or acquire those of citizens of the United States. But they shall be under the obligation to make their election within one year from the date of the exchange of ratifications of this treaty; and those who shall remain in the said territories after the expiration of that year, without having declared their intention to retain the character of Mexicans, shall be considered to have elected to become citizens of the United States.

In the said territories, property of every kind, now belonging to Mexicans not established there, shall be inviolably respected. The present owners, the heirs of these, and all Mexicans who may hereafter acquire said property by contract, shall enjoy with respect to it guarantees equally ample as if the same belonged to citizens of the United States.

ARTICLE IX

The Mexicans who, in the territories aforesaid, shall not preserve the character of citizens of the Mexican Republic, conformably with what is stipulated in the preceding article, shall be incorporated into the Union of the United States, and be admitted at the proper time (to be judged of by the Congress of the United States) to the enjoyment of all the rights of citizens of the United States, according to the principles of the Constitution; and in the mean time, shall be maintained and protected in the free enjoyment of their liberty and property, and secured in the free exercise of their religion without; restriction.

ARTICLE X

[Stricken out]

ARTICLE XI

Considering that a great part of the territories, which, by the present treaty, are to be comprehended for the future within the limits of the United States, is now occupied by savage tribes, who will hereafter be under the exclusive control of the Government of the United States, and whose incursions within the territory of Mexico would be prejudicial in the extreme, it is solemnly agreed that all such incursions shall be forcibly restrained by the Government of the United States whensoever this may be necessary; and that when they cannot be prevented, they shall be punished by the said Government, and satisfaction for the same shall be exacted all in the same way, and with equal diligence and energy, as if the same incursions were meditated or committed within its own territory, against its own citizens.

It shall not be lawful, under any pretext whatever, for any inhabitant of the United States to purchase or acquire any Mexican, or any foreigner residing in Mexico, who may have been captured by Indians inhabiting the territory of either of the two republics; nor to purchase or acquire horses, mules, cattle, or property of any kind, stolen within Mexican territory by such Indians.

And in the event of any person or persons, captured within Mexican territory by Indians, being carried into the territory of the United States, the Government of the latter engages and binds itself, in the most solemn manner, so soon as it shall know of such captives being within its territory, and shall be able so to do, through the faithful exercise of its influence and power, to rescue them and return them to their country, or deliver them to the agent or representative of the Mexican Government. The Mexican authorities will, as far as practicable, give to the Government of the United States notice of such captures; and its agents shall pay the expenses incurred in the maintenance and transmission of the rescued captives; who, in the mean time, shall be treated with the utmost hospitality by the American authorities at the place where they may be. But if the Government of the United States, before receiving such notice from Mexico, should obtain intelligence, through any other channel, of the existence of Mexican captives within its territory, it will proceed forthwith to effect their release and delivery to the Mexican agent, as above stipulated.

For the purpose of giving to these stipulations the fullest possible efficacy, thereby affording the security and redress demanded by their true spirit and intent, the Government of the United States will now and hereafter pass, without unnecessary delay, and always vigilantly enforce, such laws as the nature of the subject may require. And, finally, the sacredness of this obligation shall never be lost sight of by the said Government, when providing for the removal of the Indians from any portion of the said territories, or for its being settled by citizens of the United States; but, on the contrary, special care shall then be taken not to place its Indian occupants under the necessity of seeking new homes, by committing those invasions which the United States have solemnly obliged themselves to restrain.

ARTICLE XII

In consideration of the extension acquired by the boundaries of the United States, as defined in the fifth article of the present treaty, the Government of the United States engages to pay to that of the Mexican Republic the sum of fifteen millions of dollars.

Immediately after the treaty shall have been duly ratified by the Government of the Mexican Republic, the sum of three millions of dollars shall be paid to the said Government by that of the United States, at the city of Mexico, in the gold or silver coin of Mexico The remaining twelve millions of dollars shall be paid at the same place, and in the same coin, in annual installments of three millions of dollars each, together with interest on the same at the rate of six per centum per annum. This interest shall begin to run upon the whole sum of twelve millions from the day of the ratification of the present treaty by—the Mexican Government, and the first of the installments shall be paid—at the expiration of one year from the same day. Together with each annual installment, as it falls due, the whole interest accruing on such installment from the beginning shall also be paid.

QUESTION: If you were a Californio, what sentence from the treaty would you cite in order to defend your right to your property?

4-10   CONSTITUTION OF THE STATE OF CALIFORNIA, 1849

PROCLAMATION TO THE PEOPLE OF CALIFORNIA

The delegates of the people assembled in Convention have formed a Constitution, which is now presented for your ratification. The time and manner of voting on this Constitution, and of holding the first general election, are clearly set forth in the Schedule; the whole subject is therefore left for your unbiassed and deliberate consideration.

The Prefect (or person exercising the function of that office) of each District will designate the places for opening the polls, and give due notice of the election, in accordance with the provisions of the Constitution and Schedule.

The people are now called upon to form a government for themselves, and to designate such officers as they desire to make and execute the laws. That their choice may be wisely made, and that the government so organized may secure the permanent welfare and happiness of the people of the new State, is the sincere and earnest wish of the present Executive, who, if the Constitution be ratified, will, with pleasure, surrender his powers to whomsoever the people may designate as his successor.

Given at Monterey, California, this 12th day of October, A.D. 1849.

B. RILEY,

Bvt. Brig. Gen'l U.S.A., and Governor of California.

Official: II. W. HALLECK,

Brev. Capt. and Secretary of State.

WE, the People of California, grateful to Almighty God for our freedom, in order to secure its blessings, do establish this Constitution.

ARTICLE I

Declaration of Rights

Sec. 1.   All men are by nature free and independent, and have certain inalienable rights, among which are those of enjoying and defending life and liberty; acquiring, possessing, and protecting property; and pursuing and obtaining safety and happiness.

Sec. 2.   All political power is inherent in the people. Government is instituted for the protection, security, and benefit of the people; and they have the right to alter or reform the same, whenever the public good may require it.

Sec. 3.   The right of trial by jury shall be accured to all, and remain inviolate for ever; but a jury trial may be waived by the parties, in all civil cases, in the manner to be prescribed by law.

Sec. 4.   The free exercise and enjoyment of religious profession and worship, without discrimination or preference, shall for ever be allowed in this State; and no person shall be rendered incompetent to be a witness on account of his opinions on matters of religious belief; but the liberty of conscience, hereby accured, shall not be so construed as to excuse acts of licentiousness, or justify practices inconsistent with the peace or safety of this State.

Sec. 5.   The privilege of the writ of *habeas corpus* shall not be suspended, unless when, in cases of rebellion or invasion, the public safety may require its suspension.

Sec. 6.   Excessive bail shall not be required, nor excessive fines imposed, nor shall cruel or unusual punishments be inflicted, nor shall witnesses be unreasonably detained.

Sec. 7.   All persons shall be bailable by sufficient sureties; unless for capital offences, when the proof is evident or the presumption great.

Sec. 8.   No person shall be held to answer for a capital or otherwise infamous crime (except in cases of impeachment, and in cases of militia when in actual service, and the land and naval forces in time of war, or which this State may keep with the consent of Congress in time of peace, and in cases of petit larceny under the regulation of the Legislature), unless on presentment or indictment of a grand jury; and in any trial in any court whatever, the party accused shall be allowed to appear and defend in person and with counsel, as in civil actions. No person shall be subject to be twice put in jeopardy for the same offence; nor shall he be compelled, in any criminal case, to be a witness against himself, nor be deprived of life, liberty, or property, without due process of law; not shall private property be taken for public use without just compensation.

Sec. 9.   Every citizen may freely speak, write, and publish his sentiments on all subjects, being responsible for the abuse of that right; and no law shall be passed to restrain or abridge the liberty of speech or of the press. In all criminal prosecutions on indictments for libels, the truth may be given in evidence to the jury; and if it shall appear to the jury that the matter charged as libellous is true, and was published with good inotives and for justifiable ends, the party shall be acquitted; and the jury shall have the right to determine the law and the fact.

Sec. 10.   The people shall have the right freely to assemble together, to consult for the common good, to instruct their representatives, and to petition the Legislature for redress of grievances.

Sec. 11.   All laws of a general nature shall have a uniform operation.

Sec. 12.   The military shall be subordinate to the civil power. No standing army shall be kept up by this State in time of peace; and in time of war no appropriation for a standing army shall be for a longer time than two years.

Sec. 13.   No soldier shall, in time of peace, be quartered in any house, without the consent of the owner; nor in time of war, except in the manner to be prescribed by law.

Sec. 14.   Representation shall be apportioned according to population.

Sec. 15.   No person shall be imprisoned for debt, in any civil action on *means* or final process, unless in cases of fraud; and no person shall be imprisoned for a militia fine in time of peace.

Sec. 16.   No bill of attainder; *ex post facto* law, or law impairing the obligation of contracts, shall ever be passed.

Sec. 17. Foreigners who are, or may hereafter become *bona fide* residents of this State, shall enjoy the same rights in respect to the possession, enjoyment, and inheritance of property, as native born citizens.

Sec. 18. Neither slavery, nor involuntary servitude, unless for the punishment of crimes, shall ever be tolerated in this State.

Sec. 19. The right of the people to be secure in their persons, houses, papers, and effects, against unreasonable seizures and searches, shall not be violated; and no warrant shall issue but on probable cause, supported by oath or affirmation, particularly describing the place to be searched, and the persons and things to be seized.

Sec. 20. Treason against the State shall consist only in levying war against it, adhering to its enemies, or giving them aid and comfort. No person shall be convicted of treason, unless on the evidence of two witnesses to the same overt act, or confession in open court.

Sec. 21. This enumeration of rights shall not be construed to impair or deny others retained by the people.

ARTICLE II

Right of Suffrage

Sec. 1. Every white male citizen of the United States, and every "white" male citizen of Mexico, who shall have elected to become a citizen of the United States, under the treaty of peace exchanged and ratified at Queretaro, on the 30th day of May, 1848, of the age of twenty-one years, who shall have been a resident of the State six months next preceding the election, and the county or district in which he claims his vote thirty days, shall be entitled to vote at all elections which are now or hereafter may be authorized by law: Provided, that nothing herein contained shall be construed to prevent the Legislature, by a two thirds concurrent vote, from admitting to the right of suffrage, Indians or the descendants of Indians, in such special cases as such a proportion of the legislative body may deem just and proper.

Sec. 2. Electors shall, in all cases except treason, felony, or breach of the peace, be privileged from arrest on the days of the election, during their attendance at such election, going to and returning therefrom.

Sec. 3. No elector shall be obliged to perform militia duty on the day of election, except in time of war or public danger.

Sec. 4. For the purpose of voting, no person shall be deemed to have gained or lost a residence by reason of his presence or absence while employed in the service of the United States; nor while engaged in the navigation of the waters of this State, or of the United States, or of the high seas; nor while a student of any seminary of learning; nor while kept at any almshouse, or other asylum, at public expense; nor while confined in any public prison.

Sec. 5. No idiot or insane person, or person convicted of any infamous crime, shall be entitled to the privileges of an elector.

Sec. 6. All elections by the people shall be by ballot.

ARTICLE III

Distribution of Powers

The powers of the Government of the State of California shall be divided into three separate departments: the Legislative, the Executive, and Judicial; and no person charged with the exercise of powers properly belonging to one of these departments, shall exercise any functions appertaining to either of the others, except in the cases hereinafter expressly directed or permitted.

ARTICLE IV

Legislative Department

Sec. 1.   The Legislative power of this State shall be vested in a Senate and Assembly, which shall be designated the Legislature of the State of California; and the enacting clause of every law shall be as follows: "The people of the State of California, represented in Senate and Assembly, do enact as follows."

Sec. 2.   The sessions of the Legislature shall be annual, and shall commence on the first Monday of January, next ensuring the election of its members, unless the Governor of the State shall, in the interim, convene the Legislature by proclamation.

Sec. 3.   The members of the Assembly shall be chosen annually, by the qualified electors of their respective districts, on the Tuesday next after the first Monday in November, unless otherwise ordered by the Legislature, and their term of office shall be one year.

Sec. 4.   Senators and Members of Assembly shall be duly qualified electors in the respective counties and districts which they represent.

Sec. 5.   Senators shall be chosen for the term of two years, at the same time and places as Members of Assembly; and no person shall be a member of the Senate or Assembly, who has not been a citizen and inhabitant of the State one year, and of the county or district for which he shall be chosen six months next before his election.

Sec. 6.   The number of Senators shall not be less than one third, nor more than one half, of that of the Members of Assembly; and at the first session of the Legislature after this Constitution takes effect, the Senators shall be divided by lot as equally as may be, into two classes; the seats of the Senators of the first class shall be vacated at the expiration of the first year, so that one half shall be chosen annually.

QUESTION: The Constitution was written in both Spanish and English; what does that suggest about the vision of the new American government?

5

"Cooking Eggs at Three Dollars a Dozen": Gold Rush and Immigration, 1849–1869

History is two things: it is the past, and it is what happens in the minds of historians who bring to the documents their own interests and concerns, as well as the interests, concerns, and historical understandings of their eras.

—Carol Kammen, *On Doing Local History*

5-1   SAM PITT, "SPIRIT GUIDE" TO JAMES MARSHALL

John Marshall's assistant, Sam Pitt, served as his "spirit guide" to discover gold.

5-2　STEAMER TRIP AROUND CAPE HORN

5-3　"CROSSING THE PANAMA ISTHMUS"

After James Marshall discovered gold, tens of thousands of people came to the Mexican territory of California. The cost of getting to California was the equivalent of more than a year's worth of wages for the average American in 1849. Although most were white, married, and middle-class Americans, thousands of others came from Mexico, Hawaii, China, Chile, and England, France, and Spain. Half of the Americans came from the Eastern states by sailing ship around Cape Horn or by steamship to Panama, crossing the Isthmus on foot. The Americans from the Midwestern states took the Overland Route over the Sierra Nevada Mountains. At least ten percent of these overlanding "Forty-niners" were female and some were freed slaves. Within one year of the beginning of the Gold Rush, California entered the union as the fiftieth state.

5-4   GOLDFIELDS, 1852

5-5 EXCERPT FROM *DAILY ALTA CALIFORNIA,* 1849

There are only eight historic landmarks in California honoring women's lives. One of them is in Downieville and is "in memory of Juanita." Juanita, whose given name was Josefa, was sentenced to hang for stabbing a man to death who had broken into her house in the middle of the night and attempted a sexual assault. Josefa said at trial that she would defend herself exactly the same way if it happened again.

SACRAMENTO INTELLIGENCE.

Gregory was first to furnish us with the Times and the Union of yesterday from Sacramento. We have also the Marysville Herald of the 8th.

In the Herald we find an account of a murder and the hanging of the perpetrator, who was a woman! We can hardly credit the report, but we transmit the statement entire, as it is made through the columns of the Herald:

A WOMAN HUNG AT DOWNIEVILLE.—We are informed by Deputy Sheriff Gray, that on Saturday afternoon a Spanish woman was hung for stabbing to the heart a man by the name of Cannan, killing him instantly. Mr. Gray informs us that the deceased, in company with some others, had the night previously entered the house of the woman and created a riot and disturbance, which so outraged her, that when he presented himself the next morning to apologize for his behavior, he was met at the door by the female, who had in her hand a large bowie knife, which she instantly drove into his heart.

She was immediately arrested, tried, sentenced, and hung at 4 o'clock in the afternoon of the same day. She did not exhibit the least fear, walking up a small ladder to the scaffold, and placing the rope round her neck with her own hands, first gracefully removing two plaits of raven black hair from her shoulders to make room for the fatal cord. Some five or six hundred witnessed the execation. On being asked if she had any thing to say, she replied, "Nothing; but I would do the same again if I was so provoked"—and that she wished her remains to be decently taken care of.

On Saturday evening a man was shot in Marysville, while handling a pistol carelessly. He was an English sailor. Under the treatment of the physician he is expected to recover from the wound.

The Sacramento Union learns from Major Henry P. Sweetser, that gold has been recently discovered upon one of the highest summits of the Nevada range. (Under the eternal snows of thirty feet depth, we suppose.) The story goes that the ledge is 200 yards from a point 9000 feet above the level of the valley, and is near the Truckey trail, within 25 miles of Grass Valley. The yield of the ore is said to be 14 cts. to the lb.

The first overland companies of immigrants are reported by a correspondent of the Union to be at Carson Valley. At Sty Park, June 28th, six wagons with three families were met coming in from the Salt Lake.

A New Yorker, named Eustace, was killed on the night of July 3d, at Smith's Bar, North Fork of the American. The Times says he was shot by a man named Page, who afterwards escaped. Both are said to have been intoxicated.

QUESTION: What happens to women today who are victims of sexual assault? What happens to women today who kill their attackers? How has it changed from 150 years ago?

5-6   MINERS AT THE HEAD OF AUBURN RAVINE, 1852

Captioned "Head of Auburn Ravine, 1852," this daguerreotype shows white and Chinese miners sluicing near Auburn's town plaza.

5-7   FOREIGN MINER'S TAX, 1852

Kevin Starr comments that California during the Gold Rush "is not a pretty story; but it is a true story and it must be faced."[i] Many American miners imagined that they would find an ideal community where everyone would be rich, and no one would have to compete. Instead, they found gold mining to be unprofitable, dangerous, and exhausting. Most of these men had never worked with their hands, and the majority lost everything. Sometimes they turned their hostility onto each other but also against Mexican, Chinese, and African-American miners, ousting them from the most promising of the gold fields, sometimes beating or outright murdering them. American miners resented the competition of "foreign" miners and pressured the state to exclude them. To that end, the Legislature passed the Foreign Miner's License Tax.

---

[i]Kevin Starr, *Rooted in Barbarous Soil: An Introduction to Gold Rush Society and Culture* (Berkeley: University of California), 1998.

Chapter XXXVII
An Act

To provide for the protection of Foreigners, and to define their liabilities and privileges: Whereas, great prejudices exist in the Mixing districts in relation to the propriety of Foreigners being permitted to work Placer and Quarts diggings, inasmuch as they are not liable to the same duties as American citizens, whilst they enjoy the same privileges; and whereas these contests produce great expenditure by the State in the maintenance of order, and whereas, in consideration of the protection and privileges extended, and secured to them by the Constitution and laws of our country, therefore,

The People of the State of California, represented in Senate and Assembly, do enact as follows:

To present license.

Sec. 1. That from and after the first day of June next, and until the Congress of the United States shall by law assume control of the mining lands of California, no person not being a citizen of the United States, (California Indians excepted,) shall be allowed to take gold from any of the mines of this State, unless he shall have a license therefor as hereinafter provided.

Duty of the State Comptrollers.

Sec. 2. It shall be the duty of the Comptroller of State to procure a sufficient number of blank licenses, which shall be substantially in the following form, and numbered consecutively, and a record thereof be filed in his office. He shall deliver the said licenses to the Treasurer of State, and take his receipt for the same, upon the books of his office.

FORM OF LICENSE.

Form

| To be renewed upon expiration of term. | *No.*

County (date)

185

has paid three dollars mining license, which entitles him to labor in the mines one month. | No._____   County, (date,)
   This certifies that ....
has this day paid the Sheriff of ....
................County, three dollars which entitles
him to labor in any mines within this State for
one month from date. | To be renewed upon explnation of term. |

Comptroller of State.

By .... *Sheriff.*

Sheriff to act as collector.

QUESTION: Was it reasonable for native-born and naturalized citizens to make it very difficult for men from other countries to make a profit in the gold mines? Why or why not?

5-8   THE OLD STONE HOUSE, HOME OF MANUEL VIERRA, GEORGIA STREET, VALLEJO

This was the home of Californio Manuel Vierra, who shot a squatter who illegally settled on his land. He was confined to a Vallejo boardinghouse while officials debated whether to charge him. On May 6, 1863, a group of vigilantes (those who take or advocate the taking of law enforcement into their own hands) rode into town, dragged Vierra into the street, and murdered him. The killers were never prosecuted.

QUESTION: What is the value of buildings like this in teaching us about the past?

5-9   TRAVEL SUGGESTIONS FOR STAGECOACH PASSENGERS, *OMAHA HERALD*, 1864

The best seat inside a stage is the one next to the driver. Even if you have a tendency to sea-sickness when riding backwards, you'll get over it and will get less jolts and jostling. Don't let any sly elphtrade you his midseat.

In cold weather don't ride with tight fitting boots, shoes or gloves. When the driver asks you to get off and walk, do so without grumbling. He won't request it unless absolutely necessary. If the team runs away—sit still and take your chances. If you jump; nine out of ten times you will get hurt.

In very cold weather abstain entirely from liquor when on the road; because you will freeze twice as quickly when under the influence.

Don't growl at the food received at the station; stage companies generally provide the best they can get. Don't keep the stage waiting. Don't smoke a strong pipe inside the coach—spit on the leeward side. If you have anything to drink in a bottle pass it around. Procure your stimulants before starting as "ranch" (stage depot) whiskey is not "nectar."

Don't swear or lop over neighbors when sleeping. Take small change to pay expenses. Never shoot on the road as the noise might frighten the horses. Don't discuss politics or religion. Don't point out where murders have been committed if there are women passengers.

Don't lag at the wash basin. Don't grease your hair because travel is dusty. Don't imagine for a moment that you are going on a picnic. Expect annoyances, discomfort and some hardship.

5-10   TERMINUS RAILROAD, 1867

The first passengers to travel by train in California traveled between Sacramento and Roseville in April 1864, at 22 miles per hour. When the company tried to expand into the Sierras, it could find few laborers willing to work in the snow for $35 a month. Charles Crocker ordered that Chinese be hired but for considerably less pay than white workers. Thousands of Chinese labored on the railroad, with more imported from China. By the spring of 1867, conditions were so unbearable that the Chinese struck for more pay and shorter hours.[ii] But Crocker cut off supplies and starved them back to work. In 1869, the Central Pacific met the Union Pacific in Utah in a triumphant celebration. Then the Chinese were fired. Joseph Amato writes:

> The train ended one kind of local history and began another. The steam engine, off its mooring, put on wheels, and turned loose in the countryside, trumpeted the triumph of the Industrial Revolution . . . . It accounted for the dust and din of constructing hundreds of thousands of miles of beds, trestles, and bridges, the leveling of hills, the tunneling of mountains, and the filling of valleys. The train marked the beginning of the machine's acoustic tyranny over the landscape.[iii]

[ii]See Richard Rice, William Bullough, and Richard Orsi, *The Elusive Eden: A New History of California* (New York: McGraw-Hill), 2002, for an outstanding bibliography on this issue.

[iii]Joseph Amato, *Rethinking Home* (Berkeley: University of California), 2002, 67.

QUESTION: What is your favorite piece of advice from the stagecoach pamphlet? How does it help you imagine what the ride was like? How might the completion of the transcontinental railroad in 1869 have expanded the kinds of people who could travel to California?

5-11   CARRIE WILLIAMS, EXCERPTS FROM DIARY, 1858–1864

"I thought I would feel better if I work right hard."

by Carrie Williams

January the 1st 1859 Saturday: I begin this year with the determination to read every day not less than 3 chapters in my Bible and with the help of God to try and profit thereby. Today I cleaned the dining room, kitchen, also some little starching and ironing. Adelia came down in the afternoon, & her and Mary went to town. She took the velvet braid and went to Coen's, where she found a beautiful sheniel [chenille] braid for me. In the evening Teresa & Tom came down on his way to the Division. Thomp and Adelia eat supper with us. Then the girls after supper sent Thompson up after his flute, and they all three came into my room. A & M got their Carmina sacra. Thompson accompanied their singing with his flute, and so they had quite a singing school for about an hour. When Wallace, his father and

Tom came home we had a down right candy pulling. Then after that was over Wallace got his fiddle and Thomp with his flute played for us and we danced till 15 minutes after 11. Thompson danced with me, the first time he ever tried to. We had considerable fun over the old fashioned french four that Wallace's father would persist in dancing, none of us having ever danced it. Well, the amount of it was there was a terrible dust kicked up. Then all hands took their candy & went home. Little Walla did act so cunning that I cannot refrain from speaking about it. When they commenced playing he kept his body going to and fro, till he would get tired. Then he would keep his hands going up and down, keeping perfect time with the music. It was quite amusing to see him perform. He looked just as serious all the time. He did not go to sleep till $\frac{1}{2}$ after ten. I did not get to bed till one. So passed off New Year's day 1859 in this house, district of Gold Flat. County of Nevada.

Sunday 2nd: I got up this morning about 9 and tried to get ready for church, but did not succeed. Well, after breakfast which I got, and burnt up the bread, the dancing room of the preceeding evening was so impure that although twas Sunday I could not refrain from mopping it out. Lockwood came over after $\frac{1}{2}$ after ten to practice with Wallace. He staid to lunch. Teres and Tom came back from church and Mrs. W & I persuaded Teresa to sit down and take a snack with us. Adelia and Mary went off to Sunday school, flaunting, in the blue merino dresses. Wallace staid with me with evening, and read to him a very interesting Sunday school book, with which he was very much pleased. The title of the book is *Ten Mile Stones the Life of Jesse Palmer.*

Monday 3rd: I have felt quite unwell today, but I thought I would feel better if I wold turn in and work right hard. Therefore no Monday's washing is done, all but the rencing of the white clothes. They are now on boiling as I write. Wallace's mother has been quite miserable all day. She took ten drops of Electric Oil last night and this morn. It is her intention to take it regular, while I rub shoulder, to see if it will relieve the rheumatic pains with which she is affected. Adelia & Mary went to town today. A got a bra for my green plaid. Neither W nor his father was to supper tonight. Walla's grandma washed and put him to sleep at 6 oclock this evening. Wallace wanted me to go to a slight of hand show in theatre, but not fancying that kind of performance in the least I declined. He went, and he practices with the band also.

Tuesday 4th: Today has been bright and pleasant as a May day. Only think of it, in the depth of winter too. I rensed my clothes this morning & mopped the dining, kitchen and porch before 12. Walla's grandma took the entire charge of him while I was doing it, and the little toad went [to] sleep on the lounge, the first time he ever done such a thing. About two oclock I got redy and went up to see Teresa. I hauled Walla and also tipped the little chap over by Wentworth's Mill. He was very much afraid of "palling" after that, as he calls it. When his grandma fixed him to go he kissed her and said "By by Granma." He speaks a number of words quite plain. Wallace and his father went to town this morning and have not yet returned.

Wednesday 5th: What beautiful weather we have, almost as warm as summer, and quite as bright and plesant. I cut out 6 night caps today and made one after Mary's pattern. It runs up into a point, sugar loaf fashion, before it is bottoned down, and Wallace thinks it an odious fashion. Mrs. Wentworth came down this afternoon to invite Mrs. W to go up and take tea with her this evening, her and the squire. Well the sq came home about dark, all mud as usual, and M[rs.] W could not prevail on him to change a thing he had on. They went and said they spent a very pleasant evening. Wallace brought me an apple.

Thursday 6th: Lovely day this. My geranium looks superb, and the new shoot that my flower[ing] pea made two or three days ago looks fine also. Wallace and I, Mary and Adelia talks some this morning of attending a little dance in Temperance Hall Friday evening. Mary is as usual in a peck of trouble about what she will wear. I put a braid on my cashmere today and starched 4 shirts for Wallace, ironed 2 and the rest of my week's washing too.

Friday 7th: Pleasant as yesterday. Mrs. Williams expected Mr. & Mrs. Turner over to spend the day with her. She sent word she would be here at 11, but the children came home at noon and she had not yet made her appearance, so Mrs. W was all expectation yet. She had got Walla washed and his hair curled, herself all ready too, so as to receive them, but little W could not stay awake. I in the meantime was busy scrubbing. I mopped the dining, kitchen, hall and my room before she got here, which event happened about 1 oclock, she having taken the wrong trail over the hill. Mr. T did not come with her but came in the evening in time for supper. I staid in the parlor this afternoon, a great wonder for me. Mrs. Turner is a very amiable lady, I think. Wallace, Mary, Adelia and I went to the dance this evening before mentioned. We all had a good time generally, danced till 1 oclock.

Saturday 8th: Nice day, but I felt very much like someone that had been to a ball. Wallace is having trouble with the water works. He went to town this morning but came immediately back to turn on more water. The folks in town, he said, had no water at all, for some cause or other. The water works, I think, are a great trouble and so trying to the temper, Wallace says. Walla's grandma mopped the dining room today. Adelia wore her blue merino double skirt and Mary her maroom with velvet down the sides last night. Wallace brought me a pair of congress gaiters to dance in, black, $3.00. Adelia was down today. I gave her some oiled silk to put in hers and Teresa's bonnet[s].

Sunday 9th: Another lovely day. I was very good today, did not say one cross, ill natured word, and so I coaxed him to go to church with me, which he done without a single word of impatience, and the consequence was we have both been happier today than any Sunday before in a long time. Our intention was to go to hear Mr. McCollum, but we saw Lockwood standing at the church door, and he said there would be no service there this afternoon. The court house bell was ringing for Episcopal service, so [we] went there and listened to a very good sermon. The text was: be not afraid, only believe. Walla's grandma staid at home and took care of him. I wore my cashmere dress and white bonnet. Walla has come running in and reached up to the table, got a pin and commenced picking his teeth, so I'll have to stop and tend to him. Last night some one asked him what his name [is] and he said John, just as big as though he was 6 years old instead of a little tyke 22 months old. He sticks to it that his name is John. No one has ever trained him about it either.

Monday 10th Tuesday morning 11th: Really I was so tired last night, and it was so cold to go off in my room to write that I did not do it. Therefore the task this morning, and I am stealing time to do it too. My washing was done yesterday. Walla's grandma tried to commence the making of a winter bonnet for herself but did not get much done at it for running after him. Wallace worked hard all day making a reservoir up at the head of the spring that supplies us with water. He had an Irishman helping him, one that I think from Wallace's account ought to carry cloves with him and use the same freely. Wallace's father had his troubles yesterday too. To quote his own language, it was a blue Monday with him. In the evening Wallace talked of going to town to practice with the band, and then he talked of going to the theatre, but by dint of some coaxing from me and being tired as he was, he finally decided to stay at home, so he went and got his horn and rendered night hideous about here with the thing. Today I cleaned the dining, kitchen, and commenced making a pair of linen pillow cases. Walla's grandma worked hard today trying to make a pair of drawers, linen, edged with embroidery, for him. Wallace finished his reservoir about noon. When he came home I was busy mopping, and his mother turned in and got dinner for him. She made soup. Then about 2 oclock his father came home, and she had to set dinner for him. He was going to Wentworth's for lumber to fix some boxes about the flume. He seemed very much care worn and troubled about those diggings. I hope the constant care he experiences on account of them will not have a bad effect. They work all night tonight. He was not to supper. W was. I was thinking some today of going up to call on Mrs. Wentworth tomorrow. I don't know whether my courage will hold out or not. Wallace and little Toad.I.buss are to accompany me.

Wednesday 12 Thursday 13th: Half past 8 oclock. I sit down to record the ups and downs of the last two days. I did not write last night for this reason. I got interested in a story that I accidentaly came across, and I was bound to finish it, to the exclusion of Roman history, my writing, Bible reading & c. I read aloud to the family. The story was the Glorious Forth in Boston. During the reading we all laughed not a little at the misfortunes of Mr. & Mrs. Ben on that memorable day. Mrs. Furston called yesterday after noon with her young son all dressed in an officer's uniform, cap and all. He did look so comical when I opened the door to let then in (for I did do it) that I was tempted to laugh. Wallace, Walla and I have made the long talked on call on Mrs. Wentworth. That lad received us very placidly and invited us into the dining room to sit down, there not being any fire in the parlor she said. She made great parade over Walla and his curls, and he in return was as saucy to her as though it had been Mary or George, as he call[s] them. He told her his name was John, and finally when we came away he went up to her and kissed her, said by by, and shook hands. Mr. Furston came in while we were there. Tuesday I plaited a green satin ribbon into Adelia's bonnet braid, took out the black velvet in it. I today have been heron bone stiching on my linen pillow cases, done my week's ironing this evening. Wallace's father still in a great deal of trouble about the diggings, working hard all day came home wet this evening. Wallace came home about 4 oclock all wet, had to change. He was completely out of patience with the flume. Him and his father were both to supper. Wallace is practicing tonight. Yesterday he got some new music from below. Two or three days ago he received a long drawn out letter from a man in Tuolome county wanting him to send him a description of the improvement on quartz mills that Wallace got a patent for last winter. He said he had saw something of it in the Scientific American.

Friday 14th: I mopped the dining room this morning, cleaned up my little Walla. He then went to sleep, and I made out to finish my linen pillow cases, all but the lace. That I do not intend to put on till have used them some. Adelia came down with her bonnet, and I put in the braid, before mentioned, made of green and pink satin. The bonnet now becomes her very much. Walla's grandma baked pies and cakes this afternoon, and Walla troubled her not a little, running around teasing for a good sing. She made him a little turnover that is to be all his own. Bless his baby heart, when he beed so dear. Wallace's father went to the diggings this morning and has not yet returned. Tis ten now. Wallace had some trouble today with some person or persons that will persist in cutting wood off his land whether he will or not. Now I must go and rub Wallace's mother's back with Electric Oil. Then I must try and get to bed some time before midnight, for twas about that time before I did last night.

Saturday 15th Sunday 16th Evening about 9 oclock: Yesterday I was very busy all day, mopped the dining room, hall, kitchen and my room, then cut out a night shirt for Wallace. Teresa and Tom were down in the evening, and her and I had so much running to do after little Kate and Walla that neither of us accomplished much but a little neighborhood gossip. Then twas so late when they went away that I did [not] write any, read some in the *Book of Life*, tended to a few little chores about and went to that receptable for the weary and sleepy of earth, that matter of fact concern, a bed. Wallace practiced after Division. Wallace brought Walla a little whip with a whistle in the end, 25cts, and himself a small lamp for which he paid 2.50. This morning we were up later than usual, and the consequence was Mr. Lockwood, one of Wallace's fellows in the horn operation, catched us at breakfast. He sat down and took a cup of coffee. Walla[ce] and him then adjourned to the barn to tute (as little Walla styles playing the cornet). I went up to mother's this evening and staid till Wallace came after me, which he did about 7. I eat supper with them. Mother and I had such a good time talking over about the shadows and sunshine of the past, the trials that mother and you children, as she is wont to style her great grown up daughters and son, have borne unknown to any but ourselves. Wallace's mother this evening received a letter from her friend Mrs. Kelso in the States. Now I will just stop writing and go into the dining room and read awhile. Wallace is now down to the chicken pen making night hideous with that odious horn.

Monday 17th Tuesday 18th: My washing was done yesterday. During the day little Walla gave Wallace and I quite a fright. The little toad was missed, and I looked out of the back door and saw Mr. Wentworth looking very hard from the road down in the direction of the bridge. I turned my eyes in that direction, and there stood Walla on the extreme end of the bridge, where there is a plank, one end on the bridge and the other resting on the bank, which had partly caved away. His hat was thrown down at his feet. Wallace run down after him, when baby commenced climbing up the railing, to look down at the river. Wallace told him to come and get a pretty sing, when he let go and came running as fast as [his] little feet could carry him, so he was captured. Yesterday was the first day this winter that the ground was dry enough to let him out to play. Therefore his adventure. Wallace and his father both went to the theatre last night. Wallace played for the establishment, or rather the Union Brass Band of which he is a member are engaged to play this week (outside). They get free tickets and 50 dollars in money for the week's playing.

Tuesday: How busy I have been this day. Mopped dining, kitchen and part of [the] porch, starched 7 shirts for Wallace, ironed one, mended considerable on two of them before starching. Also cleaned, or tried to, a very dirty, muddy pair of pants, broiled steak for Wallace's dinner and boiled a mess of bacon and cabbage to end with. The reason why I did not write any in my diary last night was that I wrote a long letter to Amanda, which was sent off this morning. I forgot to mention in my writing last Sunday that Saturday Walla got hold of a match and eat the sulphur end off. We felt some what uneasy and went immediately and gave him a good dose of sweet oil and in the course of 15 minutes after gave about a half pint of warm milk. Wallace to day received a letter from H. Merrow, also one from Old Man Fool, and O what hyeroglypicks.

Wednesday 19th Thursday 20: About 2 oclock in the afternoon that I am now writing. Walla is asleep, and I must improve the moments as they fly, for baby is very cross and will not let me do much of anything. Yesterday I felt very unwell, indeed the most part of the day. My head felt heavy and miserable, though along towards night I began to feel better, so that when Wallace's father came home and asked me to go to the theater why I went. Wallace had to be there in the evening to play with the band. That is the reason why I could not go with him. It was to see the celebrated Mrs. Wood that I wished to go, and she certainly is a very beautiful woman. The plays were both comedy, the first *Sketches in India*: I forget the name of the other. We were there early. The band had not been playing long when we got there. Walla's grandma took good care of him. Thursday. This morning Wallace whipped Walla for laying down and screaming when some books were taken away from him. I felt so bad about it that I cried too, but he deserved it, I suppose. I know though that Wallace will feel bad all day when he thinks about it. His grandma finished the waist for his linen drawers that she made. I feel very stupid and miserable all day today. I can hardly hold up my head it feels so oppressed somehow. I commenced supper 5 oclock so as Wallace could eat with us before he went to town. I went to bed at 9 oclock tonight.

Friday 21st: Today has been so pleasant that it has been hard for me to stay within doors, and particularly so for to keep Wallace. I commenced supper a few minutes past five, and so we had Wallace to eat with us again but not his father. The band went out on a playing excursion this afternoon, for tonight is Mrs. Wood's benefit. How I do wish Wallace did not belong to the concern. Him and his father have attended evry night this week. Adeli went to town today, and when she came back she teased me to let Walla go home with her, and so I did. Bless his sweet soul, he always talking about some "poory chicky dead" whenever he sees a feather or dusting wing. I commenced making me a merino skirt today, sewed up the breadths and based the hem, hemmed half breadth. Now I must go and pick over a mess of beans to soak tonight.

Saturday 22nd Sunday 23rd: In the morning after sweeping and putting to rights, George being out hauling Walla in his little waggon, so I may write a little now without being disturbed. Wallace and Lockwood are down in the barn practicing on the machines infernal! Yesterday was a very busy day for me. I hemmed $2\frac{1}{2}$ breadths on my merino skirt, cooked a capital kettle of beans, washed out my room, the dining and kitchen and then ironed eleven oclock. Walla's grandma worked at her bonnet all day did not get it quite done. She is some in the bonnet making line, and not a proffessional hand either. George took almost the entire charge of Walla yesterday. His grandma washed and put him to sleep after supper. Sunday Well I guess none of us will go to church this day, but I know what I will do. I'll go and clean Walla and myself and then perhaps he will go to sleep and then I can study or read just as I please in the afternoon. Wallace went to town and brought me two magazines, 75cts for the two, *Harpers* and *Graham's* that used to be but is now changed its name to the *Ladies Magazine*.

Monday 24th Tuesday 25th: About $1/2$ after 12. I have just laid Walla in his cradle. The sun shines pleasantly, but there has been quite a high wind and cold today. Yesterday done my week's washing. Walla's grandma finished her bonnet, and I think she has made quite a bonnet. Wallace was summoned on the jury Saturday, but he did [not] understand and so did not attend. He was again summoned yesterday to appear this afternoon. He dressed and went to town for that purpose, but having some work to do on the flume, he came home for a saw and walked it from town here in 8 minutes! Almost locomotive speed! A man named Hanson and a Miss Mead were married last night at the brick church. He had his wedding advertised in the *Journal*, and the public were invited to attend. None of the Williams however made their appearances. Mary staid all night with Adelia. She says A is $1/2$ an inch taller than her. Today I mopped the dining room, kitchen and porch thoroughly. Wallace's father eat supper home last night for a wonder, after the rest were done however.

Wednesday 26th Thursday 27th: 8 oclock, raining and snowing all day. Yesterday nice and pleasant. Teresa called on Mrs. McCutcheon yesterday afternoon. She has a feminine baby born last Tuesday 25th. Walla's grandma commenced to write a letter to Mrs. Kelso last night. She intends to finish it this evening, but she took little Walla to bathe his feet in mustard water, for he is quite unwell this evening. I think he felt feverish and bad about 4 oclock this morning when he first awaked. He has considerable fever tonight. I think this spell has been brought on by his running out on the damp ground the last day or two. I allowed him to stay out too late yesterday evening. I was so busy trying to finish a merino skirt I was making. This was wrong, and if heaven spares him this time I will try to be very careful in future as to how I let the little darling be exposed. I have just rocked him to sleep. Mary received a letter from Jany Keloff this evening, and her mother one from Louisa in which she says Frank has another boy, born the last day of the last month of 1858. Wallace has worked all day in the diggings. He got off the jury for that purpose. He practiced last night and was to again tonight, but being tired and raining so he did not go. I ironed from 6 yesterday evening to 11 last night, about the time Wallace came home. All I have done today besides taking care of Walla has been to mend a pair of pants for Wallace and put feet in a pair of stockings for myself.

QUESTION: In colonial America, women were valued for hard work and contributions to their households. By the nineteenth century, the "cult of true womanhood" had limited what a typical European American female was allowed to do or be.[iv] The California Gold Rush provided an opportunity for some women to experience adventure, camaraderie, and a sense of being valued. What examples from Williams's diary illustrate this statement?

[iv]See Michael Goldberg, *Breaking New Ground: American Women, 1800–1848* (New York: Oxford University Press), 1997.

5-12   GOLD RUSH RECIPES, *THE CALIFORNIANS*, 1942

SOURDOUGH BREAD

Not too long ago bread was baked as needed and often was a daily chore.

starter sponge	1 teaspoon salt
4 cups flour	2 tablespoons lard, melted
2 tablespoons sugar	

To starter add equal quantities of flour and lukewarm water to make about 3 cups of sponge. Let stand 6 to 8 hours or overnight in a warm location. It should bubble and emit a yeasty odor. Take out 2 cups of this sponge, leaving remainder for next starter. To these two cups of sponge add flour, sugar, salt and lard, and mix until a soft dough is formed. If dough is stiff, add a little milk; if too soft, add more flour. Knead for 3 or 4 minutes on a clean floured surface. Shape into two loaves and place in well greased loaf pans. Cover and set in a warm place until loaves have swelled to double size. Bake 50 to 60 minutes in a preheated moderate oven (350°). Bread is done when loaves are golden brown and shrink away from sides of pan. Turn out on rack and rub top surface with butter or lard.

BEAR PAWS BOILED

A favorite of the mountain men.

¼ pound salt pork	salt and pepper
2 pounds skinned front bear paws	

Clean paws well and marinate in vinegar if available, as it is a good tenderizer. Place in a deep pot, cover with water, add salt and pepper, and simmer for about 8 hours. Add more water if needed during cooking. Slice and serve.

AMERICAN BAKED HAM

Hams available in the mining camps were not the pink, oozy, anemic-looking ones sold in today's supermarkets. In those days hams were rubbed well with salt and hung in the meat-house, to be cured by hanging over a slow-burning apple-wood fire or hung in the chimney for a month or so. The texture was fine, the meat a rich, dark red, the taste substantial. It might have been a bit salty if the meat had not been properly treated before cooking.

Pour boiling water over ham and let it stand until cool. Scrape clean with a coarse hairbrush used for this purpose. Place in a clean boiler with cold water enough to cover; bring to the boiling point and then place on back part of stove to simmer steadily for six or seven hours, or till tender when pierced with a fork. Be careful to keep water at boiling point and not to allow it to go much above it. Turn ham once or twice while cooking. When done, take up and put into baking-pan. When cool enough to handle, remove skin by dipping hands in cold water, taking the skin between your fingers and peeling as you would an orange. Set in a moderate oven, placing the lean side of the ham downward, and if you like, sift over pounded or rolled crackers. Baking brings out a great quantity of fat, leaving the skin much more delicate. If desired, the ham may be glazed with strong meat jelly or any savory jelly at hand, boiled down rapidly until it is like glue. Brush this jelly over the ham when cool and it makes an elegant dish. The nicest portion of a baked ham may be served in slices, and the ragged parts and odds and ends chopped fine for sandwiches, or by adding three eggs to one pint of chopped ham a delicious omelet may be made. If the ham is very salty, it should lie in water overnight.

GOLD NUGGET PORK AND BEANS

Miners who did not have ovens could still bake a pot of beans by placing the pot in a hole beneath the camp fire, though it may have required a little time and patience to keep the fire going. This recipe for a dark golden brown pot of beans approximates one in the collection of old family recipes compiled by the Ladies of Columbia Church of the '49ers. It came from New England.

1 quart white navy beans	molasses (about 1 cup)
½ teaspoon soda	salt and pepper
½ pound salt side pork	

Boil beans with soda for 30 minutes. Drain. Wash pork and place in earthen bean pot. Add beans, salt, pepper and molasses. Cover with boiling water, set lid on pot and bake in moderate oven (350°) for six hours or until done. If necessary, add a little more water. Remove lid about 45 minutes to an hour before serving time and add more seasonings if desired.

CARAMEL PUDDING

The basic ingredient of this interesting pudding is bread, and the cooking procedure demonstrates how cooks managed to get by without fancy kitchen equipment, and maybe even ovens.

4 slices bread (lightly buttered)	2 cups milk
2/3 cup brown sugar	$1/2$ teaspoon salt
(firmly packed)	$1/2$ teaspoon vanilla
2 eggs, beaten with a fork	$1/4$ cup raisins

Cut bread into small cubes and place in heavy saucepan. Sprinkle sugar and raisins over the top. Mix eggs and milk with salt and vanilla and pour over bread mixture. Do not stir. Cover and cook very slowly for an hour.

CRYSTALLIZED CHINESE ORANGES

The Chinese do not top off their meals with cakes, pies, ices or other desserts as we do in the Western world. Candied fruit is served throughout the year, most particularly at New Year's. Crystallized orange is taken to Chinese temples as food offerings. The plethora of California citrus fruit is a boon to the cook who wishes to try this recipe.

Take oranges not quite ripe, cut off the colored part of the rind carefully with a sharp knife, cut a hole where the stem has been, sufficiently large to take out all the inside. Be careful not to change the form of the orange. When the oranges are clean inside and outside, cover them with water and salt for 24 hours. Change the water, but this time omit the salt. Do this for 5 or 6 days, or until all the bitterness has disappeared. Drain, place oranges in boiling water and boil for 20 minutes. Remove from pan and drop into cold water immediately, allowing them to drain while preparing the syrup. The syrup is made by putting equal quantities by weight of sugar and fruit in enough water to give the consistency of ordinary syrup. Boil the fruit in the syrup over a slow fire until the syrup attains the consistency of honey. Take the fruit out and let it dry in a convenient place.

NOTE: Small lemons or limes are crystallized by the same process, except that they are simply cut in two before being placed in the brine.

5-13   MARY ELLEN PLEASANT, 1902

MARY ELLEN ("MAMMY") PLEASANT AT 87 YEARS OF AGE
The first and only photograph taken since she was 13 years old

5-14   MARY ELLEN PLEASANT COURT CASE, 1868

Born a slave in Georgia around 1815, Mary had no surname of her own. After she was bought out of slavery, she adopted the last name of Ellen Williams, her first employer and member of a Quaker family who were, themselves, abolitionists. She stole onto plantations in disguise to plan slave escapes. Her motto was "I'd rather be a corpse than a coward."

When California wanted to join the Union as an antislavery state, Senator Henry Clay proposed a compromise that included a Fugitive Slave Law. This law impelled Mary Ellen Pleasant to relocate West. She arrived in San Francisco on a steamer in 1852, where she found six men to every woman and a million gallons of liquor per year flowing through the city. Mary fashioned herself into what her biographer Susheel Bibb calls a "capitalist by trade," earning millions of dollars in a number of San Francisco businesses.[v] At one point, her fortune was $30 million.

---

[v]Susheel Bibb, *Mary Ellen Pleasant: Mother of Human Rights in California* (San Francisco: MEP Publication), 1996. *Heritage of Power* (San Francisco: Voodoo Authentica), 2000.

Mary Ellen Pleasant worked to repeal legislation in California known as "black laws," passed to prevent people of color from voting, serving in the militia, or testifying against white people in court. She employed hundreds of ex-slaves in her own businesses, which included dairy farms, livery stables, and laundries. Mary sent more than $30,000 to abolitionist John Brown's efforts to end slavery with the slave revolt in 1859 at Harper's Ferry in Virginia. After the Emancipation Proclamation, Mary became the leader of the Franchise League in testing civil rights legislation in court. Her case set precedent in the Supreme Court, by suing to desegregate the trolleys in San Francisco. Historian Sue Thurman calls her the "Mother of Civil Rights" in California."[vi]

12   Action, by William W. Crane, Jr., its attorney, and for answer to the complaint of John J. Pleasants, and Mary E., his wife, the plaintiffs therein, Denies each and every, all and singular, the allegations in said complaint contained. Wherefore, defendant prays to be hence dismissed, with its costs in this behalf incurred.

W. W. CRANE, Jr.,
Attorney for Defendant.

13   [Indorsed:] "Service of a copy admitted November 23d, 1866.

G. W. Tyler.

"Filed November 23d, A. D 1866."

_____

[Title of the Cause.]

JUDGMENT

This cause came on regularly for trial, Mr. G. W. Tyler appearing as counsel for the plaintiffs, and Mr. W. W. Crane, Jr., for the defendant. A jury of twelve persons was regularly
14   impanneled and sworn to try said cause. Witnesses on the part of plaintiffs and defendant were sworn and examined. After hearing the evidence, the arguments of counsel, and instructions of the Court, the jury retired to deliberate upon their verdict, and subsequently returned into Court, and being called answered to their names, and said: "We, "the jury, find for the plaintiffs, and assess their "damages at the sum of five hundred dollars."

15   Wherefore, by virtue of the law, and by reason of the premises aforesaid, it is ordered, adjudged and decreed that John J. Pleasants and Mary E. his wife, plaintiffs, do have and recover from the North Beach and Mission Railroad Company, defendant, the sum of five hundred dollars ($500), with interest thereon at the rate of ten per cent per annum from the date hereof till paid, together with said plaintiffs' costs and disbursements incurred in this action, amounting to the sum of one hundred and 75–100 dollars ($100.75).

16   Judgment recorded February 20th, A.D. 1867.

_____

Title of the Cause.]

_____

[vi]Sue Bailey Thurman, *Pioneers of Negro Origin in California* (San Francisco: Acme Publishing Co.), 1949. Pleasant is buried in Tulocay Cemetery in Napa (former rancho of Cayetano Juarez from Chapter 4) and asked that her tombstone read "She was a Friend of John Brown."

NOTICE OF MOTION FOR A NEW TRIAL

You will please take notice that the defendant in the above entitled action intends to move for a new trial of said action, upon the following grounds:

17   1st. Irregularity in the proceedings of the Court, jury, and adverse party, and orders of the Court, and abuse of discretion, by which the defendant was prevented from having a fair trial.

2d. Misconduct of the jury.

3d. Accident and surprise, which ordinary prudence could not have guarded against.

4th. Newly discovered evidence, material for the party making the application, which it could not with reasonable diligence have discovered and produced at the trial.

QUESTION: Why is it important to know that civil rights struggles in California began in the 1860s rather than the 1960s, as people often assume?

5-15   JOAQUIN MILLER ON ENVIRONMENTAL DETERIORATION IN THE GOLD COUNTRY, 1890

As lone as God, and white as a winter moon, Mount Shasta starts up sudden and solitary from the heart of the great black forests of Northern California. You would hardly call Mount Shasta a part of the Sierras: you would say rather that it is the great white tower of some ancient and eternal wall, with nearly all the white walls overthrown. . . .

Ascend this mountain, stand against the snow above the upper belt of pines, and take a glance below. Toward the sea nothing but the black and unbroken forest. Mountains, it is true, dip and divide and break the monotony as the waves break up the sea: yet it is still the sea, still the unbroken forest, black and magnificent. To the south the landscape sinks and declines gradually, but still maintains its column of dark-plumed grenadiers, till the Sacramento Valley is reached, nearly a hundred miles away. Silver rivers run here, the sweetest in the world. They wind and wind among the rocks and mossy roots, with California lilies, and the yew with scarlet berries dipping in the water, and trout idling in the eddies and cool places by the basketful. On the east, the forest still keeps up unbroken rank till the Pitt River Valley is reached; and even there it surrounds the valley, and locks it up tight in its black embrace. To the north, it is true, Shasta Valley makes quite a dimple in the sable sea, and men plow there, and Mexicans drive mules or herd their mustang ponies on the open plain. But the valley is limited, surrounded by the forest, confined and imprisoned.

Look intently down among the black and rolling hills, forty miles away to the west, and here and there you will see a haze of cloud or smoke hung up above the trees; or, driven by the wind that is coming from the sea, it may drag and creep along as if tangled in the tops.

These are mining camps. Men are there, down in these dreadful cañons, out of sight of the sun, swallowed up, buried in the impenetrable gloom of the forest, toiling for gold. Each one of these camps is a world of itself. History, romance, tragedy, poetry, in every one of them. They are connected together, and reach the outer world only by a narrow little pack

---

From Joaquin Miller, *My Life amongst the Indians* (Chicago: Morril, Higgins & Co., 1892 [1890]), pp. 18–22, 54–55.

trail, stretching through the timber, stringing round the mountains, barely wide enough to admit of footmen and little Mexican mules, with their apparajos, to pass in single file.

But now the natives of these forests. I lived with them for years. You do not see the smoke of their wigwams through the trees. They do not smite the mountain rocks for gold, nor fell the pines, nor roil up the waters and ruin them for the fishermen. All this magnificent forest is their estate. The Great Spirit made this mountain first of all, and gave it to them, they say, and they have possessed it ever since. They preserve the forest, keep out the fires, for it is the park for their deer.

This narrative, while the thread of it is necessarily spun around a few years of my early life, is not of myself, but of this race of people that has lived centuries of history and never yet had a historian; that has suffered nearly four hundred years of wrong, and never yet had an advocate.

Yet I must write of myself, because I was among these people of whom I write, though often in the background, giving place to the inner and actual lives of a silent and mysterious people, a race of prophets, poets without the gift of expression—a race that has been often, almost always, mistreated, and never understood—a race that is moving noiselessly from the face of the earth; dreamers that sometimes waken from their mysteriousness and simplicity, and then, blood, brutality, and all the ferocity that marks a man of maddened passions, women without mercy, men without reason, brand them with the appropriate name of savages.

I have a word to say for the Indian. I saw him as he was, not as he is. In one little spot of our land, I saw him as he was centuries ago in every part of it perhaps, a Druid and a dreamer—the mildest and tamest of beings. I saw him as no man can see him now. I saw him as no man ever saw him who had the desire and patience to observe, the sympathy to understand, and the intelligence to communicate his observations to those who would really like to understand him. He is truly "the gentle savage"; the worst and the best of men, the tamest and the fiercest of beings. . . .

A singular combination of circumstances laid his life bare to me. I was a child, and he was a child. He permitted me to enter his heart. . . .

All this city [Sacramento] had been built, all this country opened up, in less than two years. Twenty months before, only the Indian inhabited here; he was lord absolute of the land. But gold had been found on this spot by a party of roving mountaineers; the news had gone abroad, and people poured in and had taken possession in a day, without question and without ceremony.

And the Indians? They were pushed aside. At first they were glad to make the strangers welcome; but, when they saw where it would all lead, they grew sullen and concerned. . . .

I hurried on a mile or so to the foot-hills, and stood in the heart of the placer mines. Now the smoke from the low chimneys of the log cabins began to rise and curl through the cool, clear air on every hand, and the miners to come out at the low doors; great hairy, bearded, six-foot giants, hatless, and half-dressed.

They stretched themselves in the sweet, frosty air, shouted to each other in a sort of savage banter, washed their hands and faces in the gold-pans that stood by the door, and then entered their cabins again, to partake of the eternal beans and bacon and coffee, and coffee and bacon and beans.

The whole face of the earth was perforated with holes; shafts sunk and being sunk by these men in search of gold, down to the bed-rock. Windlasses stretched across these shafts, where great buckets swung, in which men hoisted the earth to the light of the sun by sheer force of muscle.

The sun came softly down, and shone brightly on the hillside where I stood. I lifted my hands to Shasta, above the butte and town, for he looked like an old acquaintance, and again was glad.

QUESTION: How does Miller describe the changes in "the Indian" he observes and why do you think Miller's perspective is so little known or told?

5-16   BOGUS CHARLEY, THE FUTURE LEADER OF THE MODOC TRIBE

Historian Brian Roberts notes that few Forty-Niners "would have arrived in California as one-dimensional racists."[vii] Although many indigenous Californians were killed by American miners, other American observers recorded these atrocities, "not," says Roberts, "because they were proud of these acts, but to criticize their fellows."[viii] Joaquin Miller was one of these; he took the name of one of the West's legendary outlaws, Joaquin Murieta, a Mexican "Robin Hood." His autobiography, *Life Among the Modocs*, was a pioneering work of social protest.

[vii]Brian Roberts, "Diversity and the Anglo Forty Niner," in *The Human Tradition in California* (Wilmington, Delaware: Scholarly Resources, Inc.), 2002, 55.

[viii]Roberts, 60.

In 1850, California had passed "An Act for the Government and Protection of Indians," making it legal for Americans to indenture (bind as a servant for a set amount of time) indigenous children. Boys could be kept until the age of eighteen and girls until the age of fifteen. In 1860, the indenture laws changed to keep boys and men until the age of twenty-five and girls and women until the age of twenty-one.

When we see a picture of an indigenous Californian labeled "Bogus Charley," there is much to wonder about him. He stares out at us from his life, leaving a haunting mystery of what we will never know about him. Who named him Charley? Who decided he was "Bogus"? This Modoc Indian left no oral or written history of his own, but we will learn something about him in the next chapter.

6

"A Thousand Plows": Farming and Citizenship, 1870–1900

The landscape that took shape reflected the goals of the people who settled there. Advantages exist only in the imagination: they are the riches that people read into soil and climates and water.

—Steven Stoll, The Fruits of Natural Advantage

In California, as in America as a whole, the last three decades of the nineteenth century was an era of cultivation and of "the closing of the West." The final defeat of the California indigenous peoples occurred in Modoc County in 1873. The animosity toward indigenous people quickly extended to the Chinese immigrants who had come to mine gold. As this resentment escalated, the Chinese were forced out of mining and into railroad work, and then into agriculture. Ultimately, the Chinese were expelled from California, and the Chinese Exclusion Act of 1880 banned further Chinese immigration for 10 years. By the next century, the definition of the "other" would expand again, this time to include residents of the Philippines.

However, many Americans actively opposed these attitudes, as Frederick Douglas denounced the war against Mexico, and reformers like Helen Hunt Jackson worked unrelentlessly on behalf of the rights of indigenous peoples. Mark Twain, who we will hear from later about the Filipino-American War, visited California in the 1870s. His description of Mono Lake epitomizes the way that Americans saw California as a site of adventure and self-exploration. Sarah Bixby's story of life for wealthy children in Los Angeles offers us an unusual description of that city when it was still a frontier village.

The explosion of agriculture in California was made possible by the ingenuity and hard work of Chinese immigrants and is documented in the letters of a Vacaville woman and the World's Fair Report. Meanwhile, women of all races, like the ones pictured in this chapter, were still without legal rights, and so the chapter concludes with a discussion of the nineteenth century struggle for "votes for women" in California.

6-1 WILLIAM HENRY BOYLE, EXCERPT FROM *PERSONAL OBSERVATIONS ON CONDUCT OF MODOC WAR*, 1873

Historian Lee Davis writes that between 1850 and 1865, "Bounties for Indian scalps were advertised in local papers. The money was paid by local citizen groups that presented their bills to the Legislature for reimbursement, which in turn billed Congress for its Indian Wars."[i]

---

[i]Lee Davis, davislee@sfsu.edu, posting to H-California@h-net.msu.edu, February 14, 2003. She cites Paula Giese, *California History: The Hidden Genocide* (www.kstrom.net/isk/stories/normtrea.html), 1997.

The state paid from fifty cents to five dollars per scalp and paid out over a million dollars for scalps before these wars ended.[ii]

. . . Everything was soon in readiness and the day had been determined on—April 15th, 1873—to make the attack on "Captain Jack's Stronghold."[1] A consultation was held at the HdQrs and General Gillem had decided to make the attack at seven o'clock. But Colonel Mason, who had been with Wheaton in the previous fight, asked to be allowed to take his command, consisting of three companies of the 21st Infantry, two companies of the 1st Cavalry, and the Warm Springs Indians,[2] who had arrived the same day and were commanded by Captain Donald McKay, a halfbreed Indian, that very evening, so he could take up a position without loss of any of his men. He was allowed to do so and the command left camp at midnight, succeeded in getting into position and would have almost advanced to the stronghold had it not been for some of the Indians being fishing on the Lake that night.

They went into position in the following order—the Battalion, 21st Infantry, on the right, resting on the Lake; the two companies of Cavalry (dismounted) on the left of them; and the Indians on the extreme left; and a Battery of two howitzers in charge of Lieutenant Chapin, 4th Artillery, with their left in the air.

General Gillem, who remained in camp although in command, sent the troops on his side in charge of Major Green, at 8 o'clock, to take up their positions and they were met by the Indians some distance from the Lava Beds and they held the troops in check.

This shows they should have taken their position at night and not waited until daylight to make the advance. Green's command consisted of Batteries E, B and M, 4th Artillery, and E and G, 12th Infantry, (Thomas's Battalion, 4th Artillery, remaining in camp with the mortars ready mounted for use), Captain Perry, 1st Cavalry, with Company F, 1st Cavalry, having taken up a position during the night without the loss of any men.

At about 9 o'clock, A.M., the battle became general along the whole line. Mason's command, being under cover, suffered no loss with the exception of one Warm Springs Indian, wounded. On Major Green's side of the Lava Beds, the loss was one officer, Lieutenant Eagan, wounded in the leg, three enlisted men killed and nine wounded. Major Green made one or two unsuccessful attempts to carry the enemy's position but did not succeed, and as the darkness came on, the troops remained in the position they had taken that day, General Gillem and staff in their camp, the remainder of the officers remaining at their post with the troops. Cooked rations and hot coffee were furnished the troops and they passed the night building breastworks to cover them and taking up a more advanced position. Occasional firing occurred along the line all night but no general engagement occurred.

April 16, 1873, the day broke fair and, as soon as it was light, the [Modoc] Indians discovered that the troops had advanced during the night. They commenced firing on the pickets but without doing any damage. At about 10 o'clock, a general advance was made but with

---

[ii]See "California and the Indian Wars, The Modoc War, 1872–1873" by Warren A. Beck and Ynez D. Hasse at www.militarymuseum.org/Modoc1html

[1] Captain Jack (or Chief Kientepoos) had camped with about 200 Modoc Indians, including 150 women and children, in the Modoc Lava Beds near the Oregon border in northern California.

[2] These were 72 Indian allies brought in to supplement the army troops.

little success and with a loss on our side of two killed and four wounded, these being in Colonel Green's command.

A general fusillade was kept up all day and, at evening, the firing ceased on both sides. Our troops were rationed during the night, which they passed much in the same manner as the last. The soldiers were instructed to build stone breast-works sufficient to hold five or six men and at no time to allow themselves to be surprised. So they managed to allow two or three to sleep while the others watched and you could see all the soldiers sleeping as soundly, with their heads pillowed on a rock, as if they had been in their camp.

Lieutenant Chapin took advantage of the darkness to advance his howitzers during the night on a small hill that overlooked the stronghold of Jack, and in the morning he was prepared to throw his shells into the very mouth of the cave and Captain Thomas succeeded in getting his mortars in a good position to land his shells on the heads of the Modocs. Everything was in splendid condition to do execution in the morning.

The troops were in fine condition to fight and in good spirits, and as the Modocs had been cut off from water the previous evening, they thought they had them sure. But, while the preparation was going on outside the caves, Jack and his warriors were also at work, removing all of their property, women and children from the caves about two miles to a safe retreat. When the army rested the previous evening, there was a gap left open between the left of Miller's command and the right of the Warm Springs Indians, through which the Modocs carried their property, women and children, and old men.

The Warm Springs Indians reported hearing children crying during the night but did not report the fact to the Commanding Officer, so the Modocs were permitted to escape and take with them all their property, leaving sufficient men to make an appearance of their being still in position.

APRIL 17TH, 1873

This day was as fine as could be expected and as soon as it was light, the firing began on our side, seemingly with little attention from the Modocs until about 11 o'clock, when a few that were left in the caves were reinforced by a few more of the party that had assisted the women and children to escape. Then a regular engagement ensued and all the troops were brought into the field and advanced over the Lava Beds. But the Modocs had made good their escape and were again perched on top of the rocks about two miles distant. How they escaped was a miracle to the soldiers. But, when they came to examine the cave, they found a fissure in the rocks leading to the distant hills, thrown up by nature, making an avenue protected on both sides by rocks.

This pass the Modocs had carefully guarded and marked by sticks and stones piled on top of one another so that they could pass out as well by night as day. The troops marched over the dreaded caves, searching for the Modocs. In one fissure they found two squaws, more dead than alive, and, soon after, an old man who had been left behind.

The dead bodies of three Indians were also found and some of the rags of plunder of the Indians, too worthless to carry so [they] were left behind. Thus ended the three day's fight under General Gillem and with the only success of having driven the Indians from their caves and to a better position in the rocky hills. . . .

6-2 CAPTAIN DONALD MCCAY, COMMANDER OF WARM SPRINGS INDIANS, C. 1870

The worst atrocities took place in northern California and culminated in the Modoc War, which occurred as a consequence of government policy that repeatedly uprooted the Modoc Indians from their homeland. In 1864 the Modoc had been forced to move to a reservation in Oregon. Modoc Chief Kientepoos (known as "Captain Jack") protested the order, imploring: " You . . . have driven us from mountain to mountain, from valley to valley, like we do the wounded deer."[iii] Upon reaching their destination in Oregon, the Modocs found themselves having to trespass on the fishing and hunting land of the Klamath Indians. Hostilities

---

[iii]www.cheewa.com/modoc.html.

between the Klamaths and the Modocs escalated, but the Modoc chief's pleas to the government for protection were ignored. Outnumbered and at the brink of war with the Klamaths, Captain Jack and 300 Modocs again left the Klamath Reservation to return to their homeland on the Lost River in northern California.

Historian Andrew Rolle describes how "disturbed settlers, in an atmosphere of confusion, spoke of organizing a force to protect themselves."[iv] Despite Captain Jack's assurances to the Army that his group would not attack settlers, the military decided to force the tribe back onto the Klamath reservation in Oregon. In November 1872, troops were dispatched to bring the Modocs out of their homeland peacefully if possible, forcefully if necessary.

A young Modoc woman named Wi-ne-ma rode 75 miles on a bay mare from Yreka to warn her people and urge them not to resist the army, becoming a hero to her tribe.[v] However, Captain Jack refused to surrender, beginning the final chapter of the Modoc War.[vi] He led his people into the lava beds a few miles south of the Oregon border where the tribe survived in caves by eating field mice and bats and successfully defending multiple attacks by the army.

The next phase of the war was an attempted peace counsel, set up by Wi-ne-ma. Wi-ne-ma set up a peace meeting of the two sides, but at Modoc's council of war preceding the meeting however, Captain Jack's call for peace was overruled, and the council voted to assassinate the army peace commissioners. When they met the Modocs opened fire on the army peace commissioners and fled. In the final battle, the Army prevailed. In October 1873, Captain Jack and three of his braves were tried and hung at Fort Klamath, specifically for killing a general. Two other captured warriors were spared and sentenced to life imprisonment at Alcatraz.

A few days after Captain Jack's hanging, the remaining Modoc Indians—39 men, 54 women, and 60 children—began the long boxcar trip to exile in Oklahoma. Many of the tribe died there, including Bogus Charley (he had sided with the U.S. Army rather than with his chief), who died in 1881 at age 32. Clyde James, a descendant of a Modoc warrior, has posted a moving account of the war:

> The year they were exiled, few Modocs spoke English; by the turn of the century, few Modocs spoke Modoc. . . . The war resulted in great devastation to the Modoc people—as well as tremendous suffering of military soldiers, the settlers in the land originally inhabited by early Modocs, and the families involved. . . . In war it is very simplistic to label opposing sides as "good" or "bad," "right" or "wrong." . . . War itself is the true evil.[vii]

[iv]Andrew Rolle, 202.

[v]For more on Wi-ne-ma (aka Toby Riddle), see *The Indian History of the Modoc War*, by her son Jeff Riddle (Urion Press), 1914.

[vi]www.cheewa.com/modoc.html.

[vii]www.cheewa.com/modoc.html.

6-3 TWO SCOUTS FROM WARM SPRINGS WITH *SAN FRANCISCO BULLENTIN* REPORTER, CALIFORNIA LAVA BEDS, 1872

McKay, the *San Francisco Bulletin* correspondent taking notes on the California lava beds. At left are two Warm Springs scouts on the lookout for Modocs, 1872. *Courtesy of the National Archives (NWDNS-111-SC-82307).*

QUESTION: Donald McKay was considered a "half-breed." What does this term convey? Half of what? To which half of his heritage should he have been loyal? Go to www.cheewa .com/modoc/html, and read about his choice to betray the Modoc Indians to the U.S. Army. Was that the right choice? Write him a letter telling him why he made the right or wrong choice.

6-4 C.W. MENEFEE, EXCERPT FROM *HISTORICAL AND DESCRIPTIVE SKETCHBOOK NAPA, SONOMA, LAKE AND MENDOCINO, 1873*

These people were a different race, lower in intelligence than any other upon the continent of America: It is simply impossible for any man to civilize a Digger Indian . . . at the first impulse, he returns to his vagabond life of idleness, his grasshopper diet and his wretched wigwam of bows. . . . [He believed that they] did not make the slightest advance in moral or religious culture in spite of the most zealous efforts of the Fathers . . . the whole subject of religion was beyond the reach of their untutored intellects.

6-5   CHILDREN DRESSED UP AS "INDIANS," 1895

QUESTION: The imagination of white Americans was haunted by the Indian presence, or absence. Note the children "dressing up" to "play Indian."[viii] What part of the Indian "wildness" fascinated Americans?

6-6   LETTER, HELEN HUNT JACKSON TO JOSEPH BENSON GILDER, MARCH 12, 1883

Los Angeles
March 12 — 1883

Dear Mr. Gilder,

I have the general feeling that it is not worth while to correct any misstatements in newspapers; but I really feel as if your wording of your paragraph about my errand to So.

[viii]See *Playing Indian* by Phillip Deloria (New Haven, Connecticut: Yale University Press, 1999), which is an "exploration of the ways non-Indian Americans have acted out their fantasies about Indians in order to experience national, modern and personal identities," according to www.powells.com.

California conveyed so false an impression, that it should be followed by some sort of *re*-statement.—

You say that I have gone out, "empowered to act in behalf of certain ill treated Indians in the southern part of etc.—"—

Now all that I am commissioned to do, is to make a *Special Report* to the Interior Dept. on the general subject of the Mission Indians — their present condition, and the best way of providing them with lands in such a way that they can never be dispossessed. — This is of course in one sense, "acting for" them — ie. — in their behalf. — But I think your paragraph conveys the idea of something far more than acting *on paper* — simply by a report to the Int. Dept. —

What I hope is, that I shall be able to make so strong a report, that if the Secretary submits it to Congress, in connection with a Bill, based upon it, & asking for an appropriation for buying lands for these Indians, the Bill will pass. — In no other way can anything be effected. —

Mr. Abbot Kinney of San Gabriel, a young friend of ours, is associated with me in the Commission. Except for his assistance I should never have dared to undertake it. —

The third paper of my Century Series will be on the Present Condition of the Mission Indians.

Perhaps you will think this is all hypercritical. — If so, never mind. But as these little personal paragraphs always go journeying about from paper to paper for months, it seemed to me better for many reasons to have it set right.

The Secretary of the Interior might very well be annoyed at being suffered to have sent out a woman to do the impossible! — He himself cannot do anything to help these Indians except on an appropriation from Congress. —

A whole village — 150 or 200 — all just about to be "ejected" — from a tract they have cultivated for nearly 100 years — It is a horrible outrage — Yet I myself, cannot see what the Int. Dept. can do to help it. — The Indians had no title — never have had, in any sense which our Land Laws recognize. — The whole valley in which their village[1] lies has been *patented* to a Colony. — The 700 acres on which this little handful of Indians live, are worth $50 an acre! — What can you do? — It is heartrending: — but I see no help. — Yours ever truly

Helen Jackson

6-7   HELEN HUNT JACKSON, AUTHOR AND HUMAN RIGHTS ACTIVIST

Jackson was orphaned at sixteen, and by the time she was thirty-four had lost both her husband and two children. She spent years of her life visiting Indian villages, both as a magazine writer and later as a federal agent. She wrote privately to a friend: "My opinion of human nature has gone down 100% in the last 30 days. Such heart-sickening fraud, violence, cruelty as we have unearthed here—I did not believe could exist in civilized communities."[ix]

[ix]Kate Phillips, book review, *San Francisco Chronicle*, Valerie Mathes, editor, *The Indian Reform Letters of Helen Hunt Jackson 1879–1885* (Norman: University of Oklahoma Press), 1998, December 20, 1998.

Jackson's novel *Ramona,* published in 1884, was the first American novel ever published about life in Southern California. The book was misunderstood and seen as a romantic depiction of life on a California ranch rather than as the protest novel it was. Jackson wrote hundreds of letters on behalf of Native Americans. Historian Valerie Mathes has edited them for publication, wanting us to know Jackson and to remember that she was "one of 19th century America's most outspoken and formidable reformers."[x]

QUESTION: Why is it important to know about the roles of *both* Helen Hunt Jackson and C.W. Menefee in California history?

---

[x]Phillips, December 20, 1998.

6-8 RUTH BERG LONGHURST, HOMESTEADER AND JOURNALIST, OAKLAND, C. 1895

Maggie Cole describes her grandmother, seen in this photo taken in Oakland around 1895 as "the daughter of German Jewish parents, who came to the U.S. in the 1870s. As a single independent woman, my grandmother homesteaded near Susanville, wrote a column of her adventures for the Oakland paper, and became friends with Mark Twain."[xi]

[xi]Maggie Cole, Faces of America contest, Napa College, 2000.

6-9   MARK TWAIN, EXCERPT FROM *ROUGHING IT,* 1872

The lake [Mono] is two hundred feet deep, and its sluggish waters are so strong with alkali that if you only dip the most hopelessly soiled garment into them once or twice and wring it out, it will be found as clean as if it had been through the ablest of washerwomen's hands. While we camped there our laundry work was easy. We tied the week's washing astern of our boat, and sailed a quarter of a mile, and the job was complete, all to the wringing out. If we threw the water on our heads and gave them a rub or so, the white lather would pile up three inches high. This water is not good for bruised places and abrasions of the skin. We had a valuable dog. He had raw places on him. He had more raw places on him than sound ones. He was the rawest dog I almost ever saw. He jumped overboard one day to get away from the flies. But it was bad judgment. In his condition, it would have been just as comfortable to jump into the fire. The alkali water nipped him in all the raw places simultaneously, and he struck out for the shore with considerable interest. He yelped and barked and howled as he went—and by the time he got to the shore there was no bark to him—for he had barked the bark all out of his inside, and the alkali water had cleaned the bark all off his outside, and he probably wished he had never embarked in any such enterprise. He ran round and round in a circle, and pawed the earth and clawed the air, and threw double somersets, sometimes backwards and sometimes forwards, in the most extraordinary manner. He was not a demonstrative dog, as a general thing, but rather of a grave and serious turn of mind, and I never saw him take so much interest in anything before. He finally struck out over the mountains, at a gait which we estimated at about 250 miles an hour, and he is going yet. This was about nine years ago. We look for what is left of him along here every day.

—Mark Twain, from *Roughing It* (1872)

6-10   SARAH BIXBY SMITH, EXCERPT FROM *ADOBE DAYS,* 1925

Los Angeles was about ninety years old and I about one when we first met, neither of us, I am afraid, taking much notice of the other. For over twenty years San Francisco had been a city, a most interesting and alive city, making so much stir in the world that people forgot that Los Angeles was the older; that her birth has been ordained by the governor and attended with formal rites of the church and salutes from the military way back in 1781, when the famous revolution on the East Coast was just drawing to a successful close. Until the stirring days of '49, San Francisco was insignificance on sand hills. Then her rise was sudden and glorious and the Queen of the Angels was humble. But she was angelic only in name. She was a typical frontier town with primitive, flat-roofed dwellings of sun-dried bricks, much like those built in ancient Assyria or Palestine. Saloons and gambling houses were out of proportion in number, and there were murders every day. The present crime wave is nothing in comparison.

My father first saw Los Angeles in January 1854, when he was camped with his sheep on the Rancho San Pasqual; his arrival was a few months later than that of Mr. Harris Newmark, who, in his book *Sixty Years in Southern California*, so vividly describes the village as he found it.

By the time I knew it there had been a great change. There were some sidewalks, water was piped to the houses, gas had been introduced; several public school buildings had been built; there were three newspapers, the *Star*, the *Express*, and the *Herald*. The public library had been founded—it occupied rooms in the Downey Block where the Federal Building now stands. Compared with what it had been twenty years before, Los Angeles was a modern, civilized city; compared with what it is now, it was a little frontier town. At school I once learned its population to be 11,311.

We lived first on Temple Street, near Charity. Once Los Angeles boasted Faith and Hope streets as well, but only Hope remains, for Faith has turned to Flower, and Charity masquerades as Grand.

Next door to us lived a Jewish family whose girls sat on the front porch and amazed me by crocheting on Sunday. I had not known that any Jews existed outside the Bible. Perhaps this family was the nucleus for the present large colony of Hebrews that now fills the neighborhood.

Temple Street was new and open for only a few blocks. Bunker Hill Avenue was the end of the settlement, a roof of scattered houses along the ridge fringing the sky. Beyond that we looked over empty, grassy hills to the mountains. Going down the first hillside and over towards Beaudry's reservoir for a picnic, I once found maidenhair ferns under some brush, and was frightened by what sounded like a rattlesnake—probably only a cicada. Court Street disappeared in a hollow at Hope, where a pond was made interesting by a large flock of white ducks.

Across the street from us on top of a hill that is now gone, at the head of a long flight of wide steps, stood "The Horticultural Pavilion," destroyed a few years later by fire. It was replaced by Hazard's Pavilion, an equally barn-like, wooden building on the site of the present Philharmonic Auditorium. The first Pavilion held county fairs, conventions, and operas. It was in this place that I once had a great disappointment, for when I was hearing *Pinafore* a child ahead of me suddenly coughed and whooped, and I was removed with haste just at the most entrancing moment. The opera had been put on in London first in the spring of '78. It had reached Los Angeles by '79, and we reveled in its wit and melody with the rest of the world.

Here, I once saw a strange instrument, a box into which one could speak and be heard half a mile away at a similar contraption—a very meek and lowly promise of our present telephone system.

At this fair, where there were exhibited fruits, jellies and cakes, quilts and long strings of buttons, when the mania for collecting them was at its height, I remember that some ladies, interested in the new Orphans' Home, served New England dinners—coffee, doughnuts, and beans. Among them were my mother and Mrs. Dan Stevens, two slender, dark-haired young women, wearing colonial costume and high combs—my mother, who so soon after left this world, and Mrs. Stevens, still among us, loved and honored for her many good works.

It may have been at this same time that all Los Angeles turned out to welcome President and Mrs. Hayes and the party of senators and cabinet officials who accompanied them. Earlier in the day there had been speaking at the grandstand built in front of the Baker Block, and a reception had been given to Mrs. Hayes and the ladies accompanying her in the parlors of the fashionable St. Elmo Hotel, still standing, but no longer fashionable. However, the great event for us in this connection was in the Pavilion where a little boy who had brought a bouquet for Mrs. Hayes suffered from stage fright, and my small sister, standing near the platform, was substituted. She marched serenely across the stage, delivered the flowers, was kissed by the president and returned safely—I am sure it was the most lime-lighty occasion of Nan's modest life. And, showing how bitter the political feeling of the day was, our little neighbor who was similarly gowned in pale blue silk and black velvet, resented very much being mistaken for the "little girl whom the president kissed." Her family, Southern Democrats, had come to look at "the man who held Tilden's rightful place," but refused to shake his hand as they passed by.

Speaking of politics recalls the wonderful torchlight processions of a later period when I, with my cousins, shouting little Republicans, perched on the fence at their residence on the corner of Second and Broadway and delightedly recognized our fathers under the swinging, smoky lights.

I happened to be in Maine during the Blaine-Cleveland campaign and once rode upon a train to which Mr. Blaine's special car was attached. It interested me to see that when he got out at one station for a hasty cup of coffee at a lunch counter, he poured the hot liquid into his saucer to drink. Was that doing politics, being one of the people, or was it simply that the mouth of a presidential candidate is as susceptible to heat as that of an ordinary mortal? I was much edified, as I was not accustomed to saucer-drinking. When the train reached Boston towards midnight, it was met by a most gorgeous torchlight parade and a blare of music.

When Garfield died, Los Angeles had a memorial service and a long daylight procession headed by a "Catafalque," (a large float, gruesomely black), on which one of my schoolmates, Laura Chauvin, rode to represent, I suppose, a mourning angel. Later its black broadcloth draperies were used to make souvenirs and sold for some deserving cause. We purchased a pin-ball the size of a dollar, decorated with a green and white embroidered thistle—a curious memento of a murdered president.

But I have been lured by memories of processions, as is a small boy by martial music, away from my ordered account of where I have lived in Los Angeles. The second year we moved to the Shepherd house (so-called because of its owner), where presently my brother, Llewellyn Bixby, Junior, in direct answer to my prayers, came through the ceiling of the front bedroom straight into the apron of Mrs. Maitland—a two-day-late birthday present for me. So I was told. My skeptical faculty was dormant.

This house still stands at the top of the precipice made by the cutting of First Street between Hill and Olive streets.

The lot in front was very steep, with zig-zag paths and terraces, in one of which was a grove of banana trees, where fruit formed, but, owing to insufficient heat, never ripened well. Do you know the cool freshness of the furled, new, pale green leaves? Or how delightful it is to help the wind shred the old ones into fringe? One by one the red and gray covers for the circled blossoms drop, and make fetching little leather caps for playing children.

In those days the hill had not been hacked away to make streets, and where now is a great gash to let First Street through there was then a breezy, open hilltop, whereon grew brush and wildflowers. The poppies in those days were eschscholtzias (the learning to spell the name was a feat of my eighth year) and were not subjected to the ignominy of being painted with poinsettias on fringed-leather souvenirs for tourists. The yellow violets were gallitas, little roosters, perhaps because in the hands of children they fought to the death, their necks hooked together until one or the other was decapitated. The brodiaeas, or wild hyacinths, sometimes now called "rubber-necks," were then known to us all by the name cocomitas. I have been unable to find the derivation of this word, or even find it in print, but I spell it as it used to sound, and I like to think that it meant little coconuts, a diminutive from coco, but the etymologically wise cannot, because of the *m* in the middle of the word. But nature favors me, for the bulbs look like tiny hairy coconuts, and are good eating, with an odd sweetish taste. They were a much valued article of Indian food.

Between the weeds and bushes there were bare spots of ground where, by careful searching, one might find faint circles about the size of a "two-bit" piece. Wise ones knew that these marked the trapdoors of tarantula nests. It was sport to try to pry one open, with mother spider holding it closed. We young vandals would dig out the nests, interested for a moment in the silky lining and the tiny babies and then would throw away the wrecked home of the gorgeous black velvet creatures that did no harm on the open hillside.

At this house Harry and I conducted an extensive "essence factory," collecting old bottles far and near, and filling them with varicolored liquids, obtained by soaking or steeping different flowers and leaves. We used to drink the brew made from eucalyptus leaves. The pepper infusion was pale, like tea; that made from old geraniums was of a horrible odor—hence we liked to inveigle innocent grown folks into smelling it. The cactus solution was thick, like castor oil, and we considered it our most valuable product, having arrived thus early at the notion that difficulty of preparation adds to the cost of a manufactured article.

North of us were several houses containing children—and here I found my first girl playmates—Grace and Susie, Bertha and Eileen. The level street at Court and Hill—protected on three sides by grades too steep for horses, was our safe neighborhood playground. I never go through the tunnel that now has pierced the hill without hearing, above the roar of the Hollywood car, the patter of flying feet, the rhythms of the witch dances, the thud-thud of hop-scotch, the shouting boys and girls defending goals in Prisoner's Base, the old, old song of London Bridge, or the "Intry mintry cutry corn" that determined who was "it" for the twilight game of Hide-and-Seek—and then the varied toned bells in the hands of mothers who called the children home.

QUESTION: Interview your own grandparents or great grandparents to add to the histories of California that we have. Ask your informants to describe one particular event in their lives, like a trip to a lake (Twain) or a description of their neighborhoods in childhood (Bixby Smith). You might share these accounts and photographs with them to stimulate the conversation. Tape your interview, listen to it, and then go back with questions a second time. For more on doing family histories, see www.myhistory.org.

6-11   WHEAT THRESHING, GEORGE ROUND RANCH, AMERICAN CANYON

WHEAT THRESHING. A crew harvests wheat at George Rounds's ranch in American Canyon. Rounds later went into the lumber business in Vallejo and in the 1890s served as a member of the city's board of trustees. During Vallejo's pioneer era, the surrounding hills and countryside supported wheat farming, dairy ranches, and other agricultural production.

6-12   HIGH-SPEED FREIGHT TRAIN, 1869

By 1889, California was the second largest producer of wheat in America, generating field hands who followed the harvest; these men were called "bindle stiffs" because they carried their sleeping rolls over their shoulders. Historian Cletus Daniels writes that "family farming gave life to humane and enduring society, while large scale farming created only personal fortunes."[xii] Eventually, the owners of large farms in California would become known as "growers," and most family farms would not survive. By 1900, single-crop wheat farming had depleted the soil, and overproduction of wheat pushed prices down. Steven Stoll, who has recently written a history of California orchards, writes: "With no more cheap land to bust, farmers abandoned their dismal acres, leaving behind a desolation that was the agricultural equivalent of ripped out gold hills."[xiii]

[xii]Cletus Daniel, *Bitter Harvest: A History of California Farmworkers 1870–1941* (Berkeley: University of California), 1982.

[xiii]Steven Stoll, *The Fruits of Natural Advantage: Making the Industrial Countryside in California* (Berkeley: University of California), 1998, 29.

However, horticulturalist Luther Burbank's experiments in Santa Rosa had produced a vast array of new species of fruits and vegetables. The development of high-speed freight service, the population boom in California who wanted fruit, and finally the glamour that out-of-state consumers attached to fruit from California, all combined to produce a completely new kind of rural landscape. California's two major fruits, prunes and oranges, quickly transformed American breakfast tables.[xiv] Dried fruits began to appear in American grocery stores, and, writes Sunsweet historian Robert Couchman: "Boarding houses everywhere in the country made dried prunes a standard dessert a good part of the year."[xv]

The demand for California fruit increased the need for hands to pick it. Stoll explains that cheap labor emerged from the nature of the crops themselves: pruning, watering, picking, and packing could not be mechanized. Thus, even family-owned farms were forced to exploit labor.[xvi] California orchard owners intended to hire Americans to pick their trees, but it was difficult to recruit them away from higher paying jobs in other states. The owners advertised in national newspapers and hired speakers to show illustrated lectures about the California orchard—but young people would not cross the continent for "the shallow promise of two dollars a day in a vineyard," says Stoll.[xvii] Therefore, the only willing and available workers were the bindle stiffs, Indians, and former Chinese miners who combined to form a new agricultural workforce.

QUESTION: Is there a family farm in your history? Where was it, and what is on the land now? For information on how you can help family farms survive, see www.caff.org.

[xiv]See *Orange Empire: California and the Fruits of Eden* by Douglas Cazaux Sackman (Berkeley: University of California Press), 2005, for more about the California citrus industry.

[xv]Robert Couchman, *The Sunsweet Story* (San Jose: Sunsweet Growers Inc.), 1967, 20.

[xvi]See David Vaught's *Cultivating California: Specialty Crops and Labor, 1875–1920* (Baltimore: Johns Hopkins University Press), 1999.

[xvii]Stoll, 136.

6-13 CHINESE FAMILY, LATE 1800'S

Chinese men originally came to California to mine gold, but soon became truck gardeners and farmers, shipping dried food to mining camps, and by the 1860s, had established gardens in every mining town. When the Gold Rush ended, Chinese settlers began to lease and buy land. They built levees and grew asparagus, potatoes, and rice, which transformed the San Joaquin delta into an agricultural region. After helping to build railroads, Chinese laborers took jobs in factories and became servants to wealthy Californians like Mariano Vallejo, who built a kitchen and bunkhouse for his Chinese servants on the Sonoma property where he lived after California became a state.

Chinese families built rows of wooden buildings in small California towns along the rivers, down below the mines. They opened laundries, general stores, and barbershops and built religious temples that served as social and spiritual centers. These temples, called Joss Houses, smelled of sandalwood incense and were illuminated by peanut oil–fueled glass lanterns. Many communities had red-uniformed musical bands that performed at funerals and New Year's festivals.

Although Chinese children were forbidden from attending school, in some towns this law was not strictly enforced; however, the Chinese were always buried separately, segregated from white residents in the town cemetery. Chinese history in these towns has almost disappeared. Our memories of the Chinese presence are found primarily in photographs, like this one of Fire Chief Otterson, with "Gow Ling," his callman, or assistant.

6-14   FIRE CAPTAIN AND "CALL BOY"

6-15   MAJOR LOCATIONS OF ANTI-CHINESE VIOLENCE

An article from the 1872 *San Francisco Post* states:

> These Mongols pay a ridiculously small amount of revenue to the government in the
> shape of property taxes. They live mainly on rice, dried meats (which are imported) and
> vegetables, which they raise themselves. They patronize the white merchants but little.
> Now bring in the same number of Caucasians who would come to make homes . . . live
> in respectable houses, patronize the carpenters, masons, furniture dealers, grocers,
> butchers . . . this would prove vastly more efficient to us than the present incubus of hea-
> thens who only weigh us down.[xviii]

[xviii]*San Francisco Post*, 1872.

QUESTION: Notice the use of language in the newspaper article. How do words like "Mongol," "incubus," and "heathen" attempt to direct the reader's ideas? Do you remember children in your school who were looked down upon for how they dressed or talked?

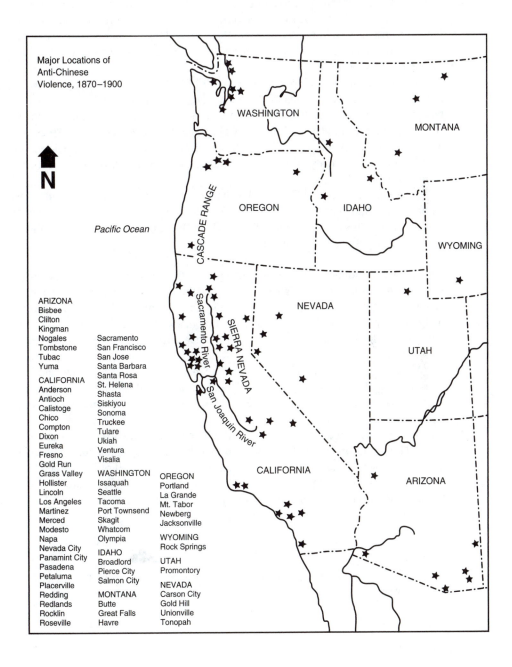

6-16   ELISE BUCKINGHAM DIARY, VACAVILLE

In the nineteenth century women were pregnant from menstruation to menopause and routinely died in childbirth. As a result of high maternal death rates, most men married several times during their lifetimes. Elise Pierson was the twelfth of thirteen children born to her family in upstate New York. She married Thomas Buckingham after his first wife, her older sister Harriet, died. Elise eventually moved with her husband to San Francisco where he manufactured shoes.

We know from the *San Francisco Chronicle* of 1880 that Elise Buckingham was granted a divorce that year on grounds of "adultery." Hoping to provide a living for her son, she bought 400 acres in Vacaville in 1884, and by 1888, Buckingham was running the farm herself without a ranch manager. Edward Wickson described her ranch in 1889 as "the most notable example of woman's work in California fruit growing," and he also noted Buckingham's efforts for women's suffrage, commenting that "women grow restless in the bonds of conventionality."[xix]

Wickson suggested that Elise Buckingham wanted women to "recognize their own ability and strength, to lead them to action rather than restlessness or repining, to demonstrate that a woman can succeed in horticulture." Elise Buckingham spoke publicly in Vacaville in 1911 on behalf of votes for women.[xx]

I would go out and look at the great field where nothing was to be seen on the brown earth but some short sticks not as high as my knee; without a single leaf, then go home and toss and turn hour after hour at night, possessed by the thought that I had done a most unwise thing. If I slept I dreamed of endless rows of tiny black twigs standing year after year, silent witnesses to the folly of a woman who had wandered from her sphere and was being justly punished for it.

My courage was gone. Afraid to undertake the cultivation of the ground and care of the trees, I engaged an overseer. He was six feet eight inches tall, and I think I must have taken him in the hope that he would save me in stepladders when I might need them for picking fruit.

My little trees were planted in a field where wheat and barley had grown for thirty years. The sun was warm and the volunteer wheat and barley sprang up and grew tall and strong, completely hiding the little trees. I could see one head of barley nod to another a rod away, and hear them say 'We'll show them what will grow here.' All about the borders and through the fields the yellow poppies and purple lupin bloomed. Clumps of

---

[xix]Edward Wickson, *California Illustrated #1, 1888.*

[xx]Information on Elise Buckingham from Sabine Goerke-Shrode, "Making History as Female Fruit Rancher," *Solano Reporter*, January 14, 2001.

sweet elder sprang up as if by magic, making a beautiful picture set in a framework of soft green hills, which comforted me when I tired of figuring what my loss would be on this enterprise.

Sometimes in driving about I met a neighbor who would inquire how my trees were getting on, or compliment me on my fine crop of volunteer barley. Another would ask if I intended to plow this year. One said, 'I suppose you know the barley would grow without the trees?' Then I overheard a man saying 'Look at that now—where are the trees? Pretty expensive crop of barley, I think.' To which another replied, 'What can you expect of a woman, and a city woman at that?'

All these things made me begin to doubt the ability of my tall overseer, who seemed in no hurry to commence plowing, and during a sleepless night I decided I must get a new man. I told him so the next morning. It was while I was hunting for another overseer that my courage came back, and I proved to myself that I could get along perfectly well without one.

I could not do all the work myself, but the man at the head of a big business does not sweep his office, keep his books, write his letters, buy and sell all his goods himself. I could not plow, but I could take the plow points to town for sharpening, and thus save the time of a man and two horses. I found many things I could do to further the work and I hesitated at nothing within my power. Once when all the men were busy pruning, planting, and rolling a field of barley that was growing rank and tall, a horse became sick, and the man who was driving the roller had to go to the hills for another. I knew the horse he went for and knew it would take time to catch her. The roller was a borrowed one. I had promised to return it that night. If the work stopped I must break my word or let the barley go unrolled. I looked at my clean white dress, hesitated a moment, then mounted the roller. I confess that as I came each time to the county road that bordered one side of the field, I scanned it closely to see if anyone was coming. But the roller went home that night, and the barley was rolled.

6-17 VALLEJO STEAM LAUNDRY

Laundry workers like the women in the picture were often at the mercy of their husband or father's alcoholism. Most towns in California had organizations that worked for passage of laws prohibiting sale and use of alcohol and for women's suffrage (the right to vote). Groups like the Women's Christian Temperance Union advocated for both, believing that alcohol destroyed family life by the violent behavior it caused and the paychecks it consumed. Women knew that the only way to eliminate this problem was to get the vote and pressure Congress to pass prohibition legislation. The campaign for women's suffrage traveled to California in 1896, where Susan B. Anthony, at the age of seventy-six, spoke to enthusiastic crowds.

VALLEJO STEAM LAUNDRY. Workers at the Vallejo Steam Laundry take a break from their jobs to pose for a photograph. The laundry was established in 1893 at the southeast corner of Marin and Pennsylvania Streets. Although the work was often hard and tedious, one writer for the Vallejo *Times Herald* said that "to make wheels, gears, tubs, ironers, pressers, whirling dryers and quantities of soap and water all mesh together might better be called an art."

6-18 CHERRY PICKING IN NAPA

Picking Cherries, Napa, Cal.

QUESTION: Women have struggled for independence in America since the Declaration of Independence. One of the goals of the women's rights movements of the 1840s was to allow women to leave abusive marriages by making divorce legal. There are so many women whose lives have never been recorded. You can pursue this kind of project as you continue your education. If you could record a woman's life story, do you know whom you would interview?

6-19 SUFFRAGE LEADERS, 1896

San Francisco was the seat of the California Women's Movement. Delegates to women's Suffrage meetings wore campaign badges of silky yellow, the official color of the suffrage movement. The Equal Suffrage ballot measure of 1896 failed by a large margin due to lobbying by alcoholic beverage associations. Historian Mae Silver concludes, "Considering the city's powerful saloon and liquor interests . . . it was no wonder that the 1896 Suffrage Amendment failed."[xxi]

Suffrage leaders, 1896. Lucy Anthony, Dr Anna Shaw, Susan B. Anthony, Ellen Sargent, Mary Hayes (first row); Ida Husted Harper, Selina Solomons, Carrie Chapman Catt, Ann Bidwell (second row).

[xxi]Mae Silver, *The Sixth Star* (San Francisco: Ord Street Press), 2000, 9.

QUESTION: Does voting really make a difference? Do your friends see voting as part of being a citizen? If they don't, what might change their attitudes?

6-20   DRYING RAISINS

5320.   Picking and Drying Raisins California.

6-21   CALIFORNIA EXHIBITS AT CHICAGO COLUMBIAN EXPOSITION, 1894

As in the Horticultural, Mining, and other departments, nearly duplicate exhibits of California's agricultural products were made in the California and in the Agricultural Buildings. In the former, the State agricultural exhibit occupied a space about 100 feet long and 18 feet wide on the west side of the lower floor, the Butte County exhibit being to the north, and that of horticulture and viticulture to the south. On a portion of the space large glass inclosures were built, reaching to the gallery. Within these were placed pyramidic forms, entirely covered with green felt cloth and with neat white shelves arranged thereon at convenient distances. Over fifteen hundred pear-shaped inverted globes and bottles of different sizes, filled with cereals and soils of various kinds, were artistically set upon the shelves, the whole presenting an attractive appearance. Running along the wall beneath the windows was a wide table stacked with sheaves of wheat, oats, rye, and barley, and with vegetables of different sizes and varieties.

The San Francisco Produce Exchange was the largest contributor to this department. Two beautiful cases, well filled with products, were furnished. One case was of polished redwood, with a base about 4 feet high, upon which rested a pyramid holding nearly every variety of cereals and fibers grown in California. This splendid collection comprised four varieties of oats, fifteen of barley, seventeen of wheat, two of buckwheat, eight of corn, ten of peas, and thirty of beans, beside Egyptian corn, broomcorn, maize, sorghum, farina, cracked wheat, rolled oats and barley, semola, graham flour, oat groats, oatmeal, hominy, split peas; canary, flax, rape, alfalfa, mustard, millet, coriander, and hemp seed; hops, ramie, silk cocoons and raw silk, grades of cotton and wool; also, a fine display of wheat, oats, and barley in sheaf from the crop of 1893. The other case was a cabinet of black walnut, within which were placed on shelves inverted globes filled with various kinds of wheat; set off by a delicate green background.

Besides this exhibit the Produce Exchange furnished seven silk banners, prettily lettered in gilt upon a dark garnet ground and bordered with long golden fringe. The largest banner was about 15 feet long, and bore this inscription: "San Francisco Produce Exchange—Products of California." The other six were smaller, but of uniform size, and contained a clear statement in brief of the agricultural products of the State. Comparative figures were given for the years 1879 and 1892, the former year being chosen, as it marked the beginning of a new era in agriculture and horticulture. The lettering upon the banners gave the following valuable information:

Wheat—Crop 1879, 33,500,000 bushels; crop 1892, 40,000,000 bushels. Export 1879—Wheat 16,660,000 bushels; flour, 527,440 barrels. Export 1892—Wheat, 21,400,000 bushels; flour, 1,056,000 barrels.

Wines—Vintage 1879, 7,000,000 gallons; 1891, 20,000,000 gallons. Brandies—Product 1879, 158,393 gallons; 1892, 1,475,525 gallons.

Barley—Largest production of any State in the Union. Crop 1879, 11,000,000 bushels; 1892, 15,000,000 bushels.

Hops—Crop 1879, 1,335,700 pounds; 1892, 7,500,000 pounds.

Wool—Production 1879, 46,903,360 pounds; 1891, 33,200,000 pounds.

Raisins—Pack 1879, 65,000 boxes; 1891, 2,150,000 boxes.

Dried fruit—Product 1884, 5,285,000 pounds; 1891, 63,710,000 pounds.

Green fruit—Shipments overland, 1879, 3,126,140 pounds; 1891, 98,680,000 pounds.

Canned fruit—Pack 1879, 298,356 cases; 1891, 1,460,000 cases.

In addition to generous contributions to this department of wheat, rye, oats, and barley from the manager of the Butte County exhibit, General John Bidwell, of Chico, furnished some very fine samples of cereals, embracing sixty-five varieties of wheat, twelve of barley, five of oats, and four of rye.

San Luis Obispo County sent a greater diversity of products than any other county, the exhibit consisting of beans, peas, corn, wheat, rye, barley, oats, onions, buckwheat flour, corn meal, cracked wheat, shorts, middlings, rolled oats and wheat, breakfast food, semola, rice, alfalfa seed, walnuts, flax, ramie, jute, yxtle, soils, and a variety of small seeds. This collection was prepared and forwarded by J. V. N. Young, of Arroyo Grande.

Los Angeles County made a fine showing of wheat, barley, corn, oats, rye, beans, walnuts, onions, squashes, potatoes, beets, etc.

Ventura County forwarded twenty-five varieties of beans, also several kinds of wheat, corn, oats, barley, nuts, and potato starch.

A very creditable exhibit was received from Merced County, including wheat, barley, rye, oats, beans, corn, cotton, tobacco, walnuts, peanuts, almonds, Egyptian corn, alfalfa, and various grasses.

Other counties contributed as follows: Sacramento—six varieties of wheat, four of barley, two of rye, and three of oats; Santa Clara—collection of two hundred varieties of seeds; Alameda—three varieties of choice barley, and the same of wheat; Sutter—choice selection of wheat, oats, and barley; El Dorado—samples of very fine rye; Orange County—walnuts and peanuts; San Diego—samples of wheat, barley, and oats; Kern—miscellaneous cereals.

The University of California, through Prof. E. W. Hilgard, loaned three hundred varieties of grains—wheat, barley, rye, oats, flax, alfalfa, clover, and numerous fine grasses. These samples were all of the best quality, and the tastily disposed sheaves of cereals and forage-plants, with a neat array of phials, to show the results of the threshing, constituted one of the finest displays in the State exhibit.

Taken as a whole, the State agricultural exhibit was a comprehensive one, and fairly represented the agricultural products of California. . . .

QUESTION: Notice that General John Bidwell is mentioned in this report. Where have we met him earlier in California history? What was produced from Sarah Bixby's home? From the county where you live? If your county isn't mentioned, how would you find out what was produced there in 1894?

7

Nature and Labor: Progressives and Empire, 1900–1914

It was on the day that the Weaver Maiden met the Cowherd
That I took passage on the President Lincoln.
I ate wind and tasted waves for more than twenty days.
How was I to know I would become a prisoner
Suffering in the wooden building?

—Poem carved into the wall at Angel Island internment center

The first fifteen years of the twentieth century have been known as the Progressive Era. Opinions of this era, like those about the 1960s, have everything to do with what people define as the problem and with whom they identify. The reformers of this time attempted to partially remedy what historian Steve Fraser describes as:

> A convulsive economy marked by deadly competition, wild booms and panics, chronic deflation, deep depression—in a word, chaos. A later more complacent time would characterize all this as the "takeoff" stage of American industrial development. Back then, however, what people lived through was more raw and ugly. One process involved the near extinction of the family farm . . . the second upheaval transformed millions of one-time European peasants and skilled artisans into proletarians, native-born and immigrant, who together found themselves descending into a world of brutal exploitation and abject powerlessness.[i]

If you ask people, perhaps your own parents, to summarize an era they lived through—say, the 1980s—their answers will also reflect their own sense of personal and political priorities.

This period was an agonizing transition for Filipino people who were transported here like slaves after the defeat of their rebellion against the American invasion of their country. Some were exhibited at the St. Louis World's Fair in breechcloth and bolo, and billed as the new "Wild Indians." Meanwhile, those Chinese who had not been expelled under the Exclusion Act continued their efforts to gain full citizenship, as did women, whose final push for suffrage has been often untold in histories of California. The elected representatives of those who were allowed to vote debated (and eventually passed) the initiative, the referendum, and the recall—measures that would change the nature of decision making in California.

This was also a time when idealistic Angelinos founded a society in the San Bernardino desert, while hops pickers in Wheatland battled police, in a "riot" that was one of the first

---

[i]Steve Fraser, "Crowds and Power," in *The Nation*, April 3, 2006, 34–36.

battles of agricultural laborers for basic human rights. Republican President Theodore Roosevelt supported some of the Progressive reforms; while camping with the president in Yosemite, John Muir persuaded Roosevelt to preserve some of California from development. As a result, Yosemite National Park was created in 1890.

The Spanish American War was made possible because powerful American business and political leaders wanted it. Theodore Roosevelt, who was the Secretary of the Navy before becoming President, was enthusiastic about America expanding its spheres of influence. As his ally Senator Albert Beveridge proclaimed: "American factories are making more than the American people can use; American soil is producing more than they can consume. Fate has written our policy for us; the trade of the world must and shall be ours."[ii]

The Americans participated in the "Spanish American War" against Spain, with the expressed purpose of helping Cuba achieve its independence. However, after the victory over Spain in Cuba in 1898, American businesses seized most of Cuba's assets, then debated whether to take another part of the Spanish empire, the Philippine Islands. President McKinley told a group of visitors to the White House: "There was nothing left for us to do but to take them all and to educate the Filipinos, and uplift and civilize and Christianize them."[iii] But Filipinos resisted in a war that is often ignored in American history textbooks. The Filipino-American War lasted from 1899 to 1902. Thousands of Filipinos died, and many more Americans died there than in Cuba.

7-1   EDITORIAL CARTOON, *NEW YORK EVENING JOURNAL,* MAY 5, 1902

Historian Victor Nebrida has written, "They [American soldiers] were very young men, poorly educated and conditioned by the racism and provincialism of their upbringing. They were determined to prove their manhood by shooting "niggers."[iv] All Filipinos who resisted the occupation were regarded as enemies. The last war that American soldiers had experienced was the Civil War when an army faced an army. Because these soldiers were familiar only with hand-to-hand fighting, the guerilla warfare practiced by the Filipino population frustrated and angered them.

In a shocking move, General Jake Smith instructed Major Littleton Waller to "clean up" the Philippine island of Samar, and his orders are illustrated in the cartoon. Eventually, both men were court-martialed by the Secretary of War; Waller was acquitted for having followed orders and Smith was convicted, admonished, and then retired. Nebrida notes that these two men had spent their earlier careers "chasing Apaches, Comanches, Kiowas and Sioux. It was easy for these commanders to order similar tactics in the Philippines, because that warfare was waged against an enemy [also] belonging to an inferior race."[v]

[ii]Beveridge, in Philip Foner, *The Spanish-Cuban-American War and the Birth of American Imperialism* (New York: Monthly Review Press), 1972.

[iii]McKinley, in Robert Beisner, *Twelve Against Empire: The Anti-Imperialists 1898–1902* (New York: McGraw-Hill), 1968.

[iv]Victor Nebrida, "The Balangiga Massacre: Getting Even" in Hector Santos, ed., *Philippine Centennial Series,* at http://www. bibingka. com/ phg/ balangiga, June 1997.

[v]Nebrida, see also Stuart Miller, *Benevolent Assimilation: The American Conquest of the Philippines,* 1899–1903 (New Haven, Connecticut: Yale University Press), 1982.

"KILL EVERY ONE OVER TEN."
Criminals because they were born ten years before we took the Philippines.
— *The New York Evening Journal.*

Former slaves who had become Indian fighters known as "Buffalo soldiers" were sent to help subdue the Filipino population. Once they were there, they encountered the reality of a dual racism: one toward the Filipino people, another toward themselves. Some Buffalo soldiers fell in love with Filipinas, left the Army, and eventually moved their new families to California.[vi]

QUESTION: The Filipino people fought for independence first against the Spanish and then against the Americans. What emotions would the U.S. soldiers have experienced when the people they came to "liberate" tried to throw them out?

A group of American businessmen and politicians formed the Anti-Imperialist League to oppose the Filipino-American War. They published the letters of soldiers, who saw the Filipino people as being treated as if they were the Indians or black slaves in America. Eventually more than a million pieces of literature opposing this war were circulated, and a large part of the League's half million members were working-class people.[vii] Mark Twain joined the Anti-Imperialist movement and wrote angrily:

[vi]See Willard Gatewood, *"Smoked Yankees" and the Struggle for Empire: Letters from Negro Soldiers 1898–1902* (Urbana: University of Illinois), 1971.

[vii]Rebecca Dowell and Kendra Kuhl have created a webpage about this war, which they describe as "one of the bloodiest conflicts in American history, the first Vietnam." www.geocities.com/Athens/Crete/9782/main.htm?200518.

We have pacified some thousands of the [Philippine] islanders and buried them; destroyed their fields; burned their villages, and turned their widows and orphans out of doors . . . and so, by these Providences of God—the phrase is the government's, not mine—we are a World Power.[viii]

7-2   DAVID STARR JORDAN, EXCERPT FROM "COLONIAL EXPANSION" OCTOBER 1898, SPEECH TO THE CONGRESS OF RELIGIONS, OMAHA, NEBRASKA

Last May I spoke before my people at home on the subject of Imperialism. I took my title, as I take now my text, from Kipling's "   ," the noblest hymn of our century: "Lest we forget." For it seemed to me then, just after the battle of Manila, that we might forget who we are and for what we stand. In the sudden intoxication of far-off victory, with the consciousness of power and courage, with the feeling that all the world is talking of us, our great stern mother patting us on the back, and all the lesser peoples looking on in fear or envy, we might lose our heads. But greater glory than this has been ours before. For more than a century our nation has stood for something higher and nobler than success in war, something not enhanced by a victory at sea, or a wild bold charge over a hill lined with masked batteries. We have stood for civic ideals, and the greatest of these, that government should make men by giving them freedom to make themselves. The glory of the American Republic is that it is the embodiment of American manhood. It was the dream of the fathers that this should always be so, —that American government and republican manhood should be co-extensive, that the nation shall not go where freedom cannot go.

This is the meaning of that America should grow strong within herself, should keep out of all fights and friendships that are not her own, should secure no territory in which a free man cannot live, and should own no possessions that may not in time be numbered among the United States. In other words, America should not be a power among the nations, but a nation among the powers. This view of the function our country rests on is no mere accident of revolution or isolation. It has its base in sound political commonsense, and in the rush of new claims and new possibilities we should not forget this old wisdom.

This year 1898 makes one of the three world-crises in our history. Twice before have we stood at the parting of the ways. Twice before have wise counsels controlled our decision. The first crisis followed the war of the Revolution. Its question was this, What relation shall the weak, scattered colonies of varying tempers and various ambitions bear to one another? The answer was, the American Constitution, the federation of self-governing United States.

The second crisis came through the growth of slavery. The union of the States, we found, could not "permanently endure half slave, half free." These were the words of Lincoln at Springfield in 1858, — the words that made Douglass Senator from Illinois, that made Lincoln the first President of the re-united States. These are the words which, fifty years

---

[viii]Quoted in Daniel Boone Schirmer, *Republic or Empire: American Resistance to the Philippine War* (Cambridge, Massachusetts: Schenkman), 1972.

ago, drove the timid away in fear, that rallied the strong to brave deeds in face of a great crisis. And this was our decision: Slavery must die that the Union shall live.

The third crisis is on us today. It is not the conquest of Spain, not the disposition of the spoils of victory which first concerns us. It is the spirit that lies behind it. Shall our armies go where our institutions cannot? Shall territorial expansion take the place of Democratic freedom? Shall our invasion of the Orient be merely an incident, an accident of a war of knight-errantry, temporary and exceptional? Or is it to mark a new policy, the reversion from America to Europe, from Democracy to Imperialism?

It is my own belief that the crisis is already passing. Our choice for the future is made. We have already lost our stomach for Imperialism, as we come to see what it means. A century of republicanism has given the common man common sense, and the tawdry glories of foreign dominion already cease to dazzle and deceive. But the responsibilities of our acts are upon us.

QUESTION: David Starr Jordan, who was one of California's anti-imperialists, would go on to found Stanford University, help John Muir found the Sierra Club, and work for women's suffrage. Does Jordan make a convincing argument? Why or why not?

7-3 JOHN MUIR AND WILLIAM KENT, MUIR WOODS, 1908

John Muir first saw the Sierra Nevada in 1868 and called it "Range of Light." He studied the trees, the plants, and the rocks, proposing a theory of glacial formation of Yosemite that later proved to be correct. In 1892, he co-founded the Sierra Club, named for his favorite location. The club supported legislation that added Yosemite Valley to Yosemite National Park. Muir believed that "nature existed for its own mysterious purposes, all beings were interrelated, and the long-term welfare of humanity depended on the preservation of nature's fullness."[ix] Inspired by Muir, William Kent donated the redwood grove now known as Muir Woods to posterity.[x] Yone Noguchi, born as Noguchi Yonejiro in 1875 in Japan, traveled to San Francisco in 1893, where he worked first as a servant and later as a journalist. A visit to Joaquin Miller in Oakland convinced him to become a poet; he became part of the Imagist poetry circle in San Francisco.[xi]

7-4   YONE NOGUCHI, "I HEAR YOU CALL, PINE TREE", 1904

I hear you call, pine tree, I hear you upon the hill, by the silent pond where the lotus flowers bloom, I hear you call, pine tree.

What is it you call, pine tree, when the rains fall, when the winds blow, and when the stars appear, what is it you call, pine tree?

I hear you call, pine tree, but I am blind, and do not know how to reach you, pine tree. Who will take me to you, pine tree?

QUESTION: Muir implored Californians to: "Climb into the mountains. Nature's peace will flow into you as the sunshine into trees."[xii] Noguchi wrote: "Who will take me to you, pine tree?" Discuss experiences you have had in nature. Perhaps you have visited the Sierras or a national park or a forest in California or have fished or climbed trees as a child. Have you felt the peace of nature? Do visitors to parks and forests realize what a battle it was to save these sites from development? See www.npca.org for information on how you can help our national parks survive.

At any given moment, people in small towns were having very different experiences: in Vallejo, a Filipino woman and a former Buffalo soldier were raising a child together, Portuguese immigrants (many of whom were dairy farmers on the former ranchos of the Californios) were holding their annual picnic at Blue Rock Springs park, a traveling circus with elephants and Lotta the Fire Dancer was marching through downtown, and young Black women were going to a school modeled on Booker T. Washington's Tuskegee Institute.[xiii]

[ix]Rice, Bullough, Orsi, *Elusive Eden*, 291.

[x]Kent was later elected to Congress from the 2nd District; his grandson Clarence teaches college history with me.

[xi]See www.noguchi.org/yone_noguchi.html

[xii]Sally Miller, ed., *John Muir: Life and Work* (1993), cited in *Elusive Eden*, 291.

[xiii]See www.nps.gov/bowa/tuskin.html

7-5 MARIA MARTINEZ, c. 1915, WHO MARRIED BUFFALO SOLDIER GEORGE WASHINGTON CARTER IN THE PHILLIPINES AND MOVED TO VALLEJO IN 1912

(Courtesy of Alice Realiza.)

7-6   PORTUGUESE PICNIC, BLUE ROCK SPRINGS PARK, VALLEJO, c. 1900

PORTUGUESE PICNIC AT BLUE ROCK SPRINGS. Members of Vallejo's Portuguese community gathered for a portrait on the steps of the Blue Rock Springs hotel around 1900. Portuguese
immigration to Vallejo dates well back into the 19th century when many Portuguese fishermen settled in South Vallejo. Later, Portuguese families became active in dairy ranching in the area.
Among the many Portuguese social organizations active in Vallejo is the *Sociedade Da Coroa Do
Divino Espirito Santo*.

7-7   DOWNTOWN STREET FAIR, VALLEJO, c. 1900

LOTTA THE FIRE DANCER. From its earliest days, downtown Vallejo has been the scene of parades, carnivals, festivals, and open-air markets. This *c.* 1900 downtown street fair was sponsored by the Fraternal Order of Eagles and featured the exotic Lotta the Fire Dancer. The Streichan House (background, at left) was built in 1899. The Times Building (at right) housed Vallejo's public library from 1891 to 1904.

7-8   VALLEJO INDUSTRIAL AND NORMAL INSTITUTE, MARIN ST., VALLEJO

VALLEJO INDUSTRIAL AND NORMAL INSTITUTE. Charles H. Toney came to Vallejo from his home state of Texas in 1907. In 1911 he established the Vallejo Industrial and Normal Institute at 2100 Marin Street. The school stressed classroom education and job training for African-American students and was patterned after Booker T. Washington's famous Tuskegee Institute. Toney's institute provided classes and training for students in first through twelfth grades, and was the first school of its type in California. Ironically, the school was ordered closed in 1934 after Toney faced criticism for operating a segregated facility.

QUESTION: If you could visit any of these four scenes and interview the participants, whom would you choose and what would you ask them?

7-9   MAUD YOUNGER, "TAKING ORDERS: A DAY AS A WAITRESS IN A SAN FRANCISCO RESTAURANT," *SUNSET*, OCTOBER 1908

"What's your first name?" asked Kittie, coming toward me.

"Mary," said I. (Mary is my professional name; its meekness just expresses my professional feelings.)

"Well, Mary, fill the sugars," said she. I did my best. I wanted to please, for Kittie was both captain of three rows of tables and, president of the Waitresses' Union. The sugars were soon filled, and I looked about for new and just as easy worlds to conquer.

With a mental vista of tables I'd washed down the aisles of my waitress career, I went over to Kittie and said politely: "Shall I wash the tables or floors or anything?"

She laughed. "Women don't wash floors in San Francisco."

I stared. I tried to realize it. I thought of the New York scrubwomen who had so wrung my heart, and a load was lifted from my soul. It was as though a ton of canned tomatoes had been crushing me down and each little tin had suddenly taken wings and departed. Kittie smiled as though she saw them go and, pressing her fingertips firmly together, she said: "Waitresses don't do any heavy work since the Union. It's all done by the men who wash dishes—the cook's helpers."

Kittie told me to give a glass of water to each customer, as a signal to the other girls that the order was taken, just as in New York. "Be sure it's boiled," she laughed over her shoulder, as she went to seat a woman in mourning. This was the only woman who came in that day, which was very pleasant. Waitresses dread women. "They're so fussy," said one, "specially if they're ladies. They want everything just so. Now, men mostly take what you give them."

I think this is because men are too busy to fuss. I don't think it is consideration. The same men would probably let an old woman stand in a streetcar. Whatever the cause, men certainly are the clams in a waitress's chowder. I never enter a restaurant without wishing to apologize for being a woman.

In New York we said "Union" under our breath, and exchanged names under the table, like conspirators of the Middle Ages. Here, though one heard such hatred of unions, they spoke freely and fearlessly. I soon asked, "What has the Union accomplished?"

"Everything," said Cora, forsaking a tart halfway to her mouth to turn upon me. "We girls have got everything ourselves, inch by inch, and we'll fight to the finish to keep it," and rising, tart in hand, she strode off, flashing a scornful glance at me over her shoulder.

"You mustn't mind Cora," said Louise. "She's fiery and suspicious of anyone not in the working class. We've been fooled so often."

"None of you seem exactly—er— crushed," I suggested, choosing my words with temperance.

"Sure not," said Annie, who had waited all over the country, "we know our strength."

When I had got into my street clothes, I went back to Kittie who was looking over my tables to see if I had cleared up properly. "Was I all right?" I asked, a little anxiously.

"Sure," she smiled, patting my shoulder. "I'll give you a job any time."

I tried to slip past the door, but the proprietor called me over.

"Here's your pay, Miss," he said, and put down 85 cents. Eighty-five whole cents, and for three hours only I had never been so valuable in my life! The most I had earned was 67 cents for five hours work. San Francisco seemed a good place to live, or, as Kittie would say, "The Union's a good thing to work under."

7-10 MAUD YOUNGER, LABOR AND SUFFRAGE ORGANIZER, C. 1900

Maud Younger was a wealthy young woman from San Francisco when she dropped in at a New York settlement house on her way to Paris in 1900. Settlement houses were homes where activist women lived with, learned from, and taught immigrant women and their children. Historian Mae Silver notes, "That 'tour of the slums' took five years. Maud Younger emerged as a radical, an organizer, and a champion for working women."[xiv]

Having worked as a waitress in New York, "Younger could hardly contain her delight and approval"[xv] when returning to San Francisco in 1906 and observing working conditions in San Francisco's unionized restaurants. By 1908 she had been elected President of Waitresses Union Local 48.[xvi]

Maud Younger gave her first suffrage speech at the Santa Clara Equal Suffrage convention in 1907. By 1908, she traveled to Sacramento with Waitress Union Vice President Louise LaRue and Lillian Harris Coffin of the San Francisco Equal Suffrage League to ask the California Federation of Labor to support the amendment to the state Constitution giving women the ballot. They were joined by members of the United Garment Workers, Local 131, and Steam Laundry Workers, Local 26, and the resolution passed. Lillian Coffin reported in 1909 "all labor leaders supported woman suffrage."[xvii]

By the end of August 1911, Younger and other women unionists, including Lizzie Williams of the Steam Laundry Workers and Daisy Mank of the Cracker Baker's Auxiliary Union, had visited seventy-eight unions, the majority of which endorsed suffrage unanimously. They had even achieved the endorsement of the Brewery Workers Union, despite its opposition to temperance. Historian Sue Englander notes that "involvement in the Wage Earners Suffrage League meant sacrificing their evenings after spending their days at work, putting in a 'double shift' to work for woman suffrage."[xviii]

On September 4, the League and the Waitresses Union created a float for the Labor Day Parade, which marched from the Mission District to the Embarcadero. Younger held the horses' reins, while behind her, women dressed in the uniforms of their trades performed their duties on a flatbed cart, costumed as cannery workers, nurses, or shop girls. Shields on the side of the float proclaimed "Justice for Women." The College Equal Suffrage League wrote: "The sincerity of the appeal, the plain, tired faces of some of the women reached men who know what it is to work for wages, and know what it is to ask for a withheld right."[xix] When the votes were counted, according to Sue Englander's analysis:

> Those areas with predominately working-class residents cast a higher percentage of affirmation votes than any other neighborhood. Over forty percent of male residents of South of Market and the Mission districts voted for suffrage, in contrast to only a little more than one man in three in the more professional and middle class districts of the Western Addition and Richmond areas.[xx]

[xiv]Mae Silver, *The Sixth Star* (San Francisco: Ord Street Press), 2000, 76.

[xv]Sue Englander, *Class Conflict and Class Coalition in the California Woman Suffrage Movement 1907–1912* (San Francisco: Mellen Research University Press, 1992), 113.

[xvi]Maude Younger wrote, "I do not think in looking back that any honor in all my life has meant so much or been more appreciated," *Labor Clarion*, January 1, 1909, "Along the Way—President of the Waitresses Union."

[xvii]Lillian Coffin, cited in Mary McHenry Keith, "California 1901–1920," McHenry Papers, Bancroft Library, Suffrage collection.

[xviii]Englander, 131.

[xix]College Equal Suffrage League, *Winning Equal Suffrage in California* (San Francisco: James H. Barry Co., 1913), 97–98.

[xx]Englander, 137.

Contrasting this with the 1896 election, Englander notes that only a quarter of the residents of working-class San Francisco supported suffrage at that time, and credits this dramatic change to the activism of the trade union suffragists.

QUESTION: What do you identify with in Younger's account from your own experiences waiting on people? Why would a wealthy woman want to join forces with poor women to improve their lives?

Working with Maud Younger and other union members, members of the College Equal Suffrage League drew attention to their cause by campaigning in a special car named the Blue Liner. Mae Silver says, "Trimmed like a pet horse, the car sported yellow streamers and was especially appealing to men."[xxi] Mrs. B. Grant Taylor (this is how married women were identified at that time) spoke to the Berkeley Equal Suffrage League during this campaign:

> It has always been conceded that "the hand that rocks the cradle rules the world." That would all be very well if we women could keep the occupant IN the cradle and spent our time rocking it. But how soon is it out, into the kindergarten, on the public streets, in the public schools and out of our hands entirely unless we have some say in the management of these."[xxii]

After the October 10 election, both leading San Francisco papers, *The Examiner* and *The Chronicle*, declared the women's cause had been defeated, but suffrage won when 3,587

[xxi]Mae Silver, 77.
[xxii]From the Bancroft Library archives, courtesy of Danielle Alexander's research.

rural votes came in. In gratitude to their male supporters, the League wrote an "Ode to the Farmers Who Voted a Majority for Us":

> But from the strength of the hills
> Men's voices hailed us;
> God bless our farmer-folk,
> Scarce a man failed us![xxiii]

7-11   FIRST WOMEN VOTERS IN CALIFORNIA, 1912

After the California suffrage victory, Maud Younger moved to Washington, D.C., to work toward a constitutional amendment so that all women would achieve the right to vote. She toured the country with Alice Paul's National Women's Party.[xxiv]

[xxiii]"Out of the Dust," poem from College Equal Suffrage League, files in Bancroft Library, Berkeley, California.
[xxiv]For a dramatic recreation of this crusade, see *Iron Jawed Angels* (HBO), 2003.

7-12 CAMPAIGNER FOR WILLIAM HENRY TAFT, PRESIDENTIAL CANDIDATE, 1909

The man in the photo appears to be campaigning for William Howard Taft, candidate for President in 1909. It would be thirty years more, however, before Chinese immigrants were granted the right to vote.[xxv]

QUESTION: Often, recent immigrants are anxious to participate in citizenship and show their patriotism to their new country. Do you know anyone who worked on a political campaign? Do you think political participation of citizens is important to living in and maintaining a democracy?

[xxv]See http://www.jimcrowhistory.org/scripts/jimcrow/lawsoutside.cgi?state=California for more.

7-13   EDWARD FRANCIS ADAMS, SPEECH AGAINST RECALL LEGISLATION, TRANSACTIONS OF THE COMMONWEALTH CLUB OF CALIFORNIA VI, SEPTEMBER 1911

If the referendum be bad the initiative is worse. It is the uncorking of all the bottles of crankiness, and it is one of the strongest arguments of the proponents of the initiative that the people will probably vote down most of the laws that are proposed. But why subject ourselves to the torment and expense? Any law that ought to be passed, and any law that the people really demand, whether it ought to be passed or not, will be passed by a Legislature; but in the process of legislation it will be licked into some kind of reasonable shape, and can be amended if not right, or repealed when we are tired of it. The more direct legislation you have, the greater and the more costly will be our litigation, and the greater the body of our judge-made law.

The recall is an abomination. It is evidence of almost inconceivable hysteria in the American people that they cannot wait to get rid of an official, whom in the fulness of their wisdom they have just elected, until the expiration of his brief term of office. What we seem to need is a dose of soothing syrup. The recall of judges would be an atrocity. The talk about the people being as competent to recall as to elect is nonsensical. Personally I do not believe the people more competent to elect judges than to elect railroad commissioners, and I heartily favor that change in the glorious constitution of 1879, which takes from us that power which we have shown our incompetence to use wisely, and place it in the hands of our good Governor and his successors forever. But when we do elect judges we elect them on their general reputation at the bar or on the bench, and if we ever recall them we shall do it not because of their general conduct on the bench, but because we are mad about some particular decision—which the recall will not change—just as some of the people in one of the judicial districts of Oregon are now trying to recall a judge whose charge to the jury on the Oregon law of self defense is assumed to have set free a murderer whom the recallers think should be hanged. What is wanted of the recall is that judges may be terrorized into deciding law points to produce the result which popular clamor demands, regardless of what the judge thinks the law really is. It would never be invoked in a single instance except as the result of popular clamor against some special decision, in which the judge is far more likely to be right than the people. It is as wicked to terrorize a judge as to bribe him, and far more dangerous to society. . . .

QUESTION: Progressive legislators introduced a number of measures to increase the involvement of California citizens (as long as they were not Asian!) in their government. Here you have one of the arguments posed AGAINST the idea of recall elections. What would be the argument FOR recall elections?

Progress is rarely linear; often there are setbacks as well as steps forward. For example, the recall and the initiative were passed in order to increase citizen involvement in politics, and in 1918 the first African American was elected to the California Legislature.

Frederick Roberts championed desegregating public facilities, like restrooms and restaurants.[xxvi]

Yet at the same time, the 41,000 Japanese in California were facing worse discrimination than did Mexican immigrants. For example, in 1903, in Oxnard, 200 Mexican farm workers joined with 1000 Japanese farm workers to form the Japanese-Mexican Labor Association. The American Federation of Labor, under the leadership of Samuel Gompers, agreed to accept only the Mexican workers into a recognized union, but these workers refused to join without their Japanese coworkers.[xxvii]

In a "Gentleman's Agreement" Japan consented in 1907 to limit migration to America. Yet, Japanese who were already here were able to buy land, and they successfully introduced rice and potatoes to California agriculture. Legislators introduced bills to restrict Japanese land ownership and to permit segregation in schools and neighborhoods. In 1913, these legislators succeeded in passing the Alien Land Law, which blocked "aliens" from purchasing land, or from leasing it for more than three years.

7-14   LOS ANGELES RESIDENTS MOVING TO LLANO DEL RIO, 1914

Throughout American history, and beginning with the Pilgrims, Americans have established "colonies" or "communes," intentional communities with shared values and economies. Most of us have heard about the ones that have survived, like the Amish, but not the ones that didn't. Llano del Rio was founded in the San Bernardino desert in 1912 by idealistic workers from Los Angeles. Families who wanted to join donated $500 cash and $2,000 in personal property, which went into a "common storehouse" to be used for everyone.

By 1915, one thousand people were living in Llano, successfully growing potatoes, alfalfa, and corn. The community published a monthly magazine and opened its own school system. Like many residents of American communes, they were misunderstood and resented by neighbors, which caused internal problems. By 1917, they had deserted their land. You can visit the ruins of Llano del Rio twenty miles east of Palmdale on State Highway 138.

[xxvi]See www.sacobserver.com/government/blacks_in_state_government.shtml for more.

[xxvii]See John Murray, "A Foretaste of the Orient," *International Socialist Review*, 4 (August 1903): 72–79, available online as http://historymatters.gmu.edu/d/5564.

7-15   BLACKSMITH SHOP, LLANO DEL RIO

7-16   LLANO COLONY BASEBALL TEAM

QUESTION: Communes offered an opportunity for people to live among others of like mind and to share the work and the wealth. Research the history of other such "colonies." See http://www.slis.indiana.edu/CSI/WP/wp96-02B.html and list one that you find most appealing or practical.

7-17   MORTIMER DOWNING, "REPORT ON WHEATLAND RIOT," *SOLIDARITY*, JANUARY 3, 1914

The Industrial Workers of the World (IWW) had been organizing men and women workers since 1905. Dockworkers, loggers, and factory workers were considered unskilled, so they were excluded from the American Federation of Labor. They turned to the IWW, which accepted members of both sexes and all races, as their only hope.

Members of the IWW believed in the concept of "one big union." Although there were no more than 100,000 members over the course of its existence, Howard Zinn writes, "their energy, their persistence, their inspiration to others, made them an influence on the country far beyond their numbers. They traveled everywhere; they organized, wrote, spoke, sang, spread their message and their spirit."[xxviii]

Journalist Dick Meister has written about the story of Wheatland, an IWW battle that he believes is "long forgotten but still one of the most dramatic and significant in American history."[xxix] He notes:

[xxviii]Zinn, 242.

[xxix]Dick Meister, "The Legacy of Wheatland," *San Francisco Bay Guardian*, August 21, 1996, 19.

For the first time the severe plight of farm workers was exposed to general view through newspaper reports and government probes that led to passage of more than three dozen safety laws to improve workplace conditions on farms. A commission was created to investigate farms and to enforce regulations on sanitation and living arrangements. . . . Anything that will be done by and for those vital workers who harvest our food must draw inspiration from the foundation laid down in Wheatland on that hot, dusty, terror-filled afternoon of August 3, 1913."[xxx]

Bloody Wheatland is glorious in this, that it united the American Federation of Labor, the Socialist Party and the I.W.W. in one solid army of workers to fight for the right to strike.

Against the workers are lined up the attorney general of the state of California, the Burns Agency, the Hop Growers' Association, the ranch-owners of California, big and little business and the district attorney of Yuba County, Edward B. Stanwood. For the army of Burns men, engaged in this effort to hang some of the workers, somebody must have paid as much as $100,000. The workers have not yet gathered $2,000 to defend their right to strike.

Follow this little story and reason for yourself, workers, if your very right to strike is not here involved.

By widespread lying advertisements Durst Brothers assembled twenty-three hundred men, women and children to pick their hops last summer. A picnic was promised the workers.

They got:

Hovels worse than pig sties to sleep in for which they were charged seventy-five cents per week, or between $2,700 and $3,000 for the season.

Eight toilets were all that was provided in the way of sanitary arrangements.

Water was prohibited in the hop fields, where the thermometer was taken by the State Health Inspector and found to be more than 120 degrees. Water was not allowed because Durst Brothers had farmed out the lemonade privilege to their cousin, Jim Durst, who offered the thirsting pickers acetic acid and water at five cents a glass.

Durst Brothers had a store on the camp, and would not permit other dealers to bring anything into the camp.

Wages averaged scarcely over $1 per day.

Rebellion occurred against these conditions. Men have been tortured, women harassed, imprisoned and threats of death have been the portion of those who protested.

When the protest was brewing, mark this: Ralph Durst asked the workers to assemble and form their demands. He appointed a meeting place with the workers. They took him at his word. Peaceably and orderly they decided upon their demands. Durst filled their camp with spies. Durst went through the town of Wheatland and the surrounding country gathering every rifle, shot gun and pistol. Was he conspiring against the workers? The attorney general and the other law officers say he was only taking natural precautions.

When the committee which Ralph Durst had personally invited to come to him with the demands of the workers arrived, Durst struck the chairman, Dick Ford, in the face. He then ordered Dick Ford off his ground. Dick Ford had already paid $2.75 as rental for his shack. Durst claims this discharge of Ford broke the strike.

[xxx]Meister, 20.

This was on Bloody Sunday, August 3, 1913, about two o'clock in the afternoon.

Ford begged his fellow committeemen to say nothing about Durst's striking him.

At 5:30 that Sunday afternoon the workers were assembled in meeting on ground rented from Durst. Dick Ford, speaking as the chairman of the meeting reached down and took from a mother an infant, saying, "It is not so much for ourselves we are fighting as that this little baby may never see the conditions which now exist on this ranch." He put the baby back into its mother's arms as he saw eleven armed men, in two automobiles, tearing down toward the meeting place. The workers then began a song. Into this meeting, where the grandsire, the husband, the youth and the babies were gathered in an effort to gain something like living conditions these armed men charged. Sheriff George Voss has sworn, "When I arrived that meeting was orderly and peaceful." The crowd opened to let him and his followers enter. Then one of his deputies, Lee Anderson, struck Dick Ford with a club, knocking him from his stand. Anderson also fired a shot. Another deputy, Henry Dakin, fired a shot gun. Remember, this crowd was a dense mass of men, women and children, some of them babies at the breast. Panic struck the mass. Dakin began to volley with his automatic shot gun. There was a surge around the speaker's stand. Voss went down. From his tent charged an unidentified Puerto Rican. He thrust himself into the mass, clubbed some of the officers, got a gun, cleared a space for himself and fell dead before a load of buckshot from Henry Dakin's gun.

Thirty seconds or so the firing lasted. When the smoke cleared, Dakin and Durst and others of these bullies had fled like jack rabbits. Four men lay dead upon the ground. Among them, District Attorney Edward T. Manwell, a deputy named Eugene Reardon, the Puerto Rican and an unidentified English lad. About a score were wounded, among them women.

Charges of murder, indiscriminative, have been placed for the killing of Manwell and Reardon. This Puerto Rican and the English by sleep in their bloody graves and the law takes no account—they were only workers.

Such are the facts of Wheatland's bloody Sunday. Now comes the district attorney of Yuba County, the attorney general of the state of California and all the legal machinery and cry that these workers, assembled in meeting with their women and children, had entered into a conspiracy to murder Manwell and Reardon. They say had no strike occurred there would have been no killing. They say had Dick Ford, when assaulted and discharged by Durst, "quietly left the ranch, the strike would have been broken." What matters to these the horrors of thirst, the indecent and immodest conditions? The workers are guilty. They struck and it became necessary to disperse them. Therefore, although they, the workers were unarmed and hampered with their women and children, because a set of drunken deputies, who even had whiskey in their pockets on the field, fired upon them, the workers must pay a dole to the gallows. . . .

QUESTION: The editor of the Industrial Workers of the World newspaper wrote the report on the Wheatland Riot near Yuba City. Can you imagine an account written by the owner of the Durst ranch? Which one would be biased? Can journalism be unbiased, or does it always have a point of view?

8

"Feathery Almond Trees against a Lavender Horizon": The Great War and Its Aftermath, 1915–1929

Dying

I will go down in peace,
But when I sink,
I will take something with me

—Pomo tribal chant

Usually when we hear about World War I, we picture battles in Europe, and when we think about the 1920s, we picture jazz bands and flappers. However, for most Americans, that time was one of struggle and trauma. Prosperity was concentrated at the top while each year, 25,000 workers were killed on the job, and 100,000 were permanently disabled.[i] Labor, immigrant rights, and civil liberties were all under siege. The Klan, which had formed in the South in 1866, was re-founded in 1915, with the addition of anti-Catholic, anti-Semitic (Jewish), and anti-immigrant sentiments to the original anti-Black philosophy. By 1924, the KKK had 4.5 million members.

The selections in this chapter introduce you to some well-known and some forgotten Californians who describe life in this era, beginning with utopian writer C.P. Gilman and ending with Hisaye Yamamoto DeSoto, who remembers growing up amidst oil wells just as the stock market crashed. You'll examine photos of Californians from the Pan-Pacific Expo in San Francisco and read a memoir by an indigenous woman healer.

You'll look at photos of men leaving and returning from the "Great War." Susan Minor shares one story of the joys of fellowship in the "Women's Land Army," while the a photo of a Mexican immigrant working in the fields and Ernesto Galarzo's memoir offer a different picture.

You will read Upton Sinclair's response to a dockworkers' protest in San Pedro. You'll look at family photos from Filipino, Italian, and Chinese immigrants for clues to what life was like in this era before chain stores, when every business was family owned—a time before radio, when sports-hungry men would gather in the street below newspaper offices, as the newspaper employees received the play-by-play of a ballgame via telegraph and then relayed it to the fans by diagramming the position of each runner on a large board.

---

[i]See Irving Bernstein, *The Lean Years: A History of the American Worker 1920–1933* (Boston: Houghton Mifflin),1960.

8-1   CHARLOTTE PERKINS GILMAN, *CALIFORNIA COLORS*, 1915

Charlotte Perkins Gilman was widely recognized during her lifetime as an important intellectual of the early twentieth century. Her most famous book was *Women and Economics*, but she wrote hundreds of stories for magazines from her humanist/socialist perspective. In her fiction and science fiction, she promoted economic independence for all adults, and advocated her view that household chores should be done only by those who chose it, like shoemaking or carpentry.

Charlotte Perkins was born in Connecticut. After her father's desertion, she grew up in poverty. After marriage and the birth of her daughter in 1875, she suffered from depression. Her husband sent her to a famous physician, who prescribed a "rest cure" for women that required total inactivity and isolation. Under this regimen, Charlotte almost went mad. Her description of this experience, "The Yellow Wallpaper," was widely published as a horror story.[ii]

Gilman gathered the courage to leave her marriage and relocated to Pasadena where she supported her mother, daughter, and herself by running a boardinghouse. In 1894 she became coeditor of *The Impress, a Journal of the Pacific Coast Women's Association*, and began to earn a living speaking about her ideas. Writer Upton Sinclair was so impressed that in 1907 he founded a utopian colony, Helicon Hall, based on her ideas, the only time that a woman's theories were used by a male reformer.[iii]

> A Song
> I came from Santa Barbara,
> I went to San Jose,
> Blue sky above—blue sea beside,
> Wild gold along the way—
> The lovely lavish blossom gold
> Ran wild along the way.
>
> The purple mountains loomed beyond,
> The soft hills rolled between,
> From crest to crest, like smoke at rest,
> The eucalyptus screen
> Its careless foliage drifting by
> Against that all-enfolding sky
> In dusky glimmering green;
> With live-oak masses drowsing dark
> On the slopes of April green;
> More joy than any eye can hold,
> Not only blue, not only gold,
> But bronze and olive green.

[ii]Her memoir about this experience, "The Yellow Wallpaper," was anthologized originally as a ghost story. See www.scribblingwomen.org/cgwallpaper.htm for more.

[iii]For more on Gilman, see Carl Degler, *Introduction to Women and Economics* (New York: Harper Torchbooks), 1966. Recently, Peggy Ann Brown writes that "Helicon Hall may be unique in its attempts to structure a year round colony based on the writings of Charlotte Perkins Gilman [with] its emphasis on equality between husbands and wives and communal childcare." Peggy Ann Brown, "Not Your Usual Boardinghouse Types: Upton Sinclair's Helicon Home Colony 1906–1907." Diss., American University, 1993.

8-2   JOSEPH DE SERPA AND FAMILY, PAN-PACIFIC EXPOSITION, SAN FRANCISCO, 1915

On the right in the photo is Joseph Alexander, an electrician whose parents immigrated to Monterey when it was still a site for whaling. Joseph moved to San Francisco from Monterey to help rebuild the city after the 1906 earthquake. Joseph's sister Mary is in the middle, her husband John de Serpa on the left. His grandson writes that a few years after this photo was taken, "Joseph moved his family to a southern San Joaquin Valley ranch where one of his sons, his grandsons, and his great-grandsons continue in the electrical business."[iv]

[iv]Joseph Alexander, Faces of America contest, Napa College, 2000.

8-3 JAMES EARLE FRASIER "THE END OF THE TRAIL," PAN-PACIFIC EXPOSITION

At the same exposition, you might have turned the corner and seen this statue by James Earle Fraser, "The End of the Trail," commemorating the final defeat of California Indians. The indigenous models for the sculpture stand in front of it. Robert Levine tells us that when photography was developed after 1850, men and women believed photographic images "to be 'scientific' and therefore 'objective' but today we understand that all photographic images are subjective . . . most photographs are as composed as a piece of writing." He believes that we bring ourselves and our own imaginations and histories to every photograph.

QUESTION: Notice the difference in dress, and in expression, of the Alexander family and the unnamed Indian models. See the difference in dress between the men and the women. Notice the expressions on the faces of the Alexander family measured against the facial expressions of the Indians. How do you interpret them? Write down a sentence or two that someone in each photograph might be thinking while posing for these photographs.

8-4   LUCY THOMPSON (CHE-NA-WAH WEITCH-AH-WAH), EXCERPT FROM *TO THE AMERICAN INDIAN: REMINISCENCES OF A YUROK WOMAN,* 1916

Under the 1887 Dawes General Allotment Act, reservation tribal lands were divided into small parcels that were given out only if a head of household would agree to build a house, engage in farming, send his children to government schools, and renounce his tribal allegiance. The program was opposed by traditional peoples and it was finally repealed in 1934. By 1900, the indigenous population in California, which had been 300,000 at the time of the Spanish conquest, had declined to 15,000. In 1916, Yurok elder Lucy Thompson was interviewed about the traditional practices of her people.

As there has been so much said and written about the American Indians, with my tribe, the Klamath Indians, included, by the white people, which is guessed at and not facts, I deem it necessary to first tell you who I am, for which please do not criticize me as egotistical.

I am a pure, full-blooded Klamath River woman. In our tongue we call this great river by the name of Health-kick-wer-roy, and I wear the tattoos on my chin that has been the custom for our women for many generations. I was born at Pec-wan village, and of highest birth or what we term under the highest laws of marriage. I am known by my people as a Talth. My maiden name was Che-na-wah Weitch-ah-wah, Che-nawah being my given name.

My father, being also a Talth, took me at a very early age and began training me in all of the mysteries and laws of my people. It took me years to learn, and the ordeal was a hard one. I was made a Talth and given the true name of God, the Creator of all things, and taught the meaning of every article that is used in our festivals, together with all the laws governing our people. I understand every word, every nod and gesture made in our language. Therefore, I feel that I am in a better position than any other person to tell the true facts of the religion and the meaning of the many things that we used to commemorate the events of the past.

In the high marriage of the Talth the woman is most beautifully dressed on her wedding day in a buckskin dress all strung with beads and shells that clink and rattle with her every graceful step. Her hair is parted in the middle, brought down on each side and rolled with the skin of the otter. This skin is nicely dressed or tanned and then cut into about one-inch strips, thus holding the hair so it hangs down to their hips or lower, according to its length. Around her neck are strings of most beautifully arranged beads of high value; they hang down to her waist, almost completely covering her chest. A buckskin, dressed and made as white as it can be made, goes over the shoulders and fastens around the neck and hangs down the back. This makes her very beautiful. She is so quick in movement that one has to keep their eyes on her closely to see all of her actions, while she speaks low and softly. These high marriages are very few, and this beautiful sight of the bride is seldom seen. The girls born of these marriages were always looked up to by the Indians. When these girls came along or were met by any children of other births, the latter would always get out of the trail and let them pass.

The Klamath Indians never had a chief like the other large tribes but were ruled by these men and women of such births that became members of the order [Talth].

Another system is the "half-married" one, the woman taking her husband to her house to live with her. By this marriage she is the absolute boss of the man and has complete control of all the children. She has the power to correct her husband in all his actions and can send him out to hunt, fish or work just as she deems proper, he being a slave to her, as they usually both belong to the class that are slaves. It amuses one to hear them use the term against white men that marry white women, the man having no home of his own, and the woman taking him to her home. They say that white man is half-married just the same as our people are-half-married, and that the white man cannot walk out at any time as he is not boss, for the women owns everything.

They have a third form of marriage that belongs to the middle class. These marriages are considered by the whole tribe as good marriages, and the children born by these marriages have a good standing in all walks of life. The marriage is performed by a part barter and trade, such as giving in exchange a boat or fishing place or any other property of a personal nature. This ceremony is more common than the imposing way. Since the coming of the white man, he has brought this marriage around to a simple form of buying outright by giving a price as one would for a horse, cow or any other purchase. The old Indian law was an exchange of valuable articles, and often the woman did not go to the man she married and live with him in his own home until they had been married one, two or three years.

Indian enslaving Indian. The Klamath Indians were, at the coming of the white man, a very large tribe, there being several thousand of them. It taxed every resource of the country in which they lived for all of them to obtain a subsistence; therefore everything was owned in the same way that it is now owned by the white man. The land was divided up by the boundaries of the creeks, ridges and the river: all open prairies for gathering grass seeds, such as Indian wheat, which looks similar to rye, besides other kinds of seed; the oak timber for gathering acorns, the sugarpine for gathering pine nuts, the hazel flats for gathering hazelnuts and the fishing places for catching salmon.

The most frugal and saving of the families had become the owners of these places and their ownership undisputed, and these ownerships were handed down from one generation to another by will. In time this left a great many Indians owning no property by which they could make a living, and many of their own people became slaves to the wealthy class. They made the slaves work and kept them from starving, and by this there came about the "half-married" system. [There are some of these Indians that are always ready to tell the white man all of the Indian legends in a way to fit their own cases.] They cannot tell the true legends at all, as they are ignorant of such facts. The wealthy ones would see that the [slave] men got wives and that the girls got husbands, built them houses; and some families were very kind to their slaves. When they were sick they saw that they had doctors and the proper care. Some families were mean and overbearing to their slaves; giving no care to the sick, letting them die, and going so far as to throw them into a hole, leaving them there to suffer and starve until they died. This sort of treatment was looked down upon by the ones that had better humane feelings, and they sometimes prevented such inhuman actions.

Most of the doctors are women, and they exercised great power (especially those who had a high standing as to family) and the art of curing most all diseases or cases of sickness. A few of the doctors were men, and they used roots and herbs of different kinds, and they are hard to beat as doctors in a great many kinds of sickness. They can cure the bite of a rattlesnake, not one of them ever dying from the bite. I knew many of the people that were bitten by the rattlesnake at different times, and they were cured and lived to be very old. For this cure they use saltwater out of the ocean and the root of the onion of what you call kelp and which is taken out of the ocean. They pound the onion of the kelp and make a poultice out of it, place it over the wound and keep it wet with the saltwater, at the same time letting the patient drink all he can of the saltwater. The patient is kept perfectly still and not allowed to move about more than is necessary. They bind the limb or place where the part is bitten to prevent the free circulation of the blood through these parts.

In other things they are equally as good. In childbirth they prepare a woman for giving birth to her child, and at the birth of the child they have an old woman to take care of the mother and child. After the birth of the child the cord is cut and tied; then they take the black part of a large snail, which has an oily substance, and place it over the navel. They put a bandage around the child which is kept there for some time. I have never known an Indian of the old tribe to be ruptured, and yet they do not know anything about surgery. If anything of a serious nature happens to a woman during childbirth they are at a loss to know what to do to save her.

If the woman gives birth to twins and they are a boy and girl, they try to raise them both; but if it be two boys or girls they pick one of them and raise it while the other one is neglected and starved to death; and when it died they went through all the forms of sorrow by crying and mourning over the loss of the child just the same as if they tried to raise it. . . .

Two meals a day. My people were in the habit of eating but two meals a day, the first meal or breakfast came about 11 o'clock, and in the evening, after dark, the women prepare the supper, the menu differing according to the season of the year.

As soon as it begins to get cold, the men would go out and get large loads of small limbs and brush, tie it up in a bundle which they placed on their backs and held with both hands; and as they came in, they sang a song for luck in whatever they might wish for, such as making money, good health and many other things. With this wood they make a fire in the sweathouse and the smoke coming out of the crevices would make it look as if the house was afire for a short time, when the wood would burn down to a bed of coals and the smoke all disappeared. And then the men and boys would strip and creep into them, one at a time, and in about 30 or 40 minutes would all come crawling out of the small round door, steaming and covered with perspiration, weak and limp, appearing as if they could hardly stand up. After crawling out they lay flat on the stone platform that is fixed for the purpose and sing the same songs, only at this time in a more doleful way.

They lay in this way for 30 or 40 minutes, then get up and, still looking weak, start off down to the bank of the water, one at a time, and plunge into the cold water and swim and splash for a time. Then all go back to the dwelling-house and go in where the women folks are preparing the evening meal; take their seats around the basement floor, out of the way of the women while they are cooking; and all will join in laughing and talking until the evening meal is over. Then the men and boys go back to the sweathouse for the night and prepare for a big smoke, all laughing and talking about different topics and telling amusing tales. Some of the older ones would discuss points on Indian law; others tell how things are changing, how this and that used to be and is different now, how they fought the other tribes, when they were victorious and when they were defeated; praising one that was the leader or condemning another, one that was a good general; and many other things. And some were very interesting talkers. They talked until they were ready to go to sleep for the night, and then they would place the wooden pillows under their heads. Some of them would not use any kind of covering and would be almost naked, as the sweathouses would keep very warm for at least 12 hours after a big fire had been built in them.

Early in the morning they would come out and each take his own way for the day, such as hunting, trapping, fishing or getting something that might be needed for the family. The old men dressed deerskins, many of which the hair was left on, and these were for the women to use as blankets and for shawl-like coats which they wear; for moccasins (noch-i), they take a dressed deerskin and smoke it and then make it up into moccasins. They make dresses and many other things out of skins. Others would dress furs which they use in many ways. They use the fisher skin for quivers to carry arrows in; also the young panther skin. The freshwater otter they dress very nicely for the women to tie their hair with. Some would make awls and wedges for future use, and others were making bows and arrows, while a few would give directions to the others. The women went about their work, such as pounding acorns, soaking the flour and preparing it to make bread or mush, some cutting fresh salmon and preparing it for cooking; others go out after wood for their parts of the living and cooking quarters, and others make baskets for cooking purposes. Some make hats and baskets they used for storing away food, while others make the fine dresses for wearing and anything that was to be done, but few of them being idle, unless it was some of the old women that were very wealthy. . . .

QUESTION: Is there any way that California Indians could have continued their traditional lifestyles and practiced their own religion under U.S. settlement and statehood? What if several counties had been set aside for them to continue their traditional lifestyle—could this have worked?

8-5 POSTER OF MONTICELLO STEAMSHIP STRIKE, 1916

In 1916, steamboat workers employed by the Monticello Steamship Company went on strike. The company operated the steamers between San Francisco and Vallejo. The issues for the workers were a request for a pay raise from $50 to $55 a month, and a reduction in the work day from $17^1/_2$ to $13^1/_2$ hours.

Once the strike began, non-union crews (ex-convicts and men from the Thiele Detective Agency) were hired to keep the boats running. Stevedores and longshoremen joined the strike, closing down the entire San Francisco waterfront, while the San Francisco Chamber of Commerce organized a committee to condemn the strikers.

Unfair Monticello Steamship Co.

June 14, 1916.

To the Traveling Public:

Please be advised that there is a boycott on all vessels of the Monticello Steamship Company. This company operates the Steamers "Schome," "General Frisbie" and "Napa Valley," doing a general passenger business between San Francisco and Vallejo.

Our grievance against this company dates from June 1st, 1916, when we requested the company to reduce the working day from seventeen (17) hours per day to eleven (11) hours per day. On the refusal of the company to comply with this modest request, our men quit the boats and ex-convicts and men from the Thiele Detective Agency were hired in their places, and are paid three and four dollars per day and are willing to work the full seventeen hours—the former class of men, ex-convicts and employment office men, are paid three dollars and the men from the detective agency are paid four dollars per day.

All that we are asking of the Monticello Company is an eleven-hour-day with no increase in pay (our men received $60.00 per month), and you, the traveling public, can force this company to terms by STAYING OFF THEIR BOATS. Please do so and have your friends do likewise.

The people of Vallejo have built up this company with their liberal patronage and doubtless expect them to work their employees reasonable hours, as the majority of the workers in Vallejo work only eight hours per day.

Remember that we are not asking for more pay, only that the 17-hour-day be reduced in order that we can live like other men and have our share of relaxation lengthened.

The railroad fare between San Francisco and Vallejo is the same for the round trip as the boat fare.

Trains leave Vallejo for San Francisco:	Trains Leave San Francisco for Vallejo:
7:10 A. M.	6:20 A. M.
8:05 A. M.	8:00 A. M.
9:45 A. M.	9:00 A. M.
11:15 A. M.	10:40 A. M.
12:25 P. M.	1:40 P. M.
2:25 P. M.	4:00 P. M.
4:12 P. M.	5:00 P. M.
5:43 P. M.	6:00 P. M. Sunday only.
6:40 P. M.	
7:50 P. M. Sunday only.	

Assist us by not patronizing the Monticello Steamship Company. Don't litter the street with this circular—give it to your friend.

BAY AND RIVER STEAMBOATMEN
10 EAST STREET, SAN FRANCISCO, CAL.

Affiliated with International Seamen's Union of America, San Francisco Labor Council, Waterfront Workers' Federation, and California State Federation of Labor.

The year that Lucy Thompson wrote her memoir was also the year that Tom Mooney was arrested, a year that saw many strikes, such as that by the steamboat-men in San Francisco. Within a year America had entered into what was then called the Great War in Europe.

Tom Mooney had been a union leader in San Francisco, involved in a strike of street-car workers in 1916. That year, a "preparedness march" to promote American involvement in World War I was organized by business interests in San Francisco. At the march, a bomb went off, killing ten people. Mooney was arrested despite the fact that no witnesses placed him at the scene, and even though the police ignored other exculpatory evidence.

Mooney was tried, sentenced to death, and sent to Folsom Prison. Many citizens believed he had been framed and worked for his release, which became a statewide and then a national cause. At the request of President Woodrow Wilson, Governor Stephens commuted Mooney's sentence to life imprisonment. By 1921, several men testified that they had helped to frame Tom Mooney.

In 1917, America entered World War I. That year, Congress passed the Espionage Act, which imprisoned people who spoke or wrote against the war for up to twenty years. Teachers who opposed the war were fired from colleges and the first woman in Congress, Jeanette Rankin, lost her seat for her anti-war position. Nationally, nine hundred people went to jail under the Espionage Act. In Los Angeles, a film called *The Spirit of 76* was produced, showing British atrocities during the American Revolution. The filmmaker was prosecuted under the Espionage Act, *U.S. v. Spirit of 76*, because his movie criticized a U.S. ally. He was sentenced to ten years in prison.[v]

In my own town of Napa, I discovered that George Peterson, a member of the International Workers of the World, was arrested in 1918. The *Napa Daily Journal* reported that the Farm Labor Committee of the state recommended to Governor Stephens that if the law failed to protect people from the IWW, "citizens should take them by the neck and drown them in the river."[vi] Perry Schriver, a German who was staying at the Connor Hotel at the corner of Third and Main, was jailed for what the *Napa Daily Journal* called "treasonable utterances" while Harry Sawyer of Martinez was featured on the front page of that paper for stating that "America has no business in this war."[vii] He was escorted by guards to Angel Island.

Meanwhile, a marching band escorted draftees to the Southern Pacific Depot. At a war rally, Napa's Judge Henry Gesford said that "seditious [anti-war] people should be shot."[viii]

---

[v]See Zechariah Chafee, *Free Speech in the United States* (New York: Atheneum), 1969.

[vi]*Napa Daily Journal*, 17 March 1918.

[vii]*Napa Daily Journal*, 14 April 1918.

[viii]*Napa Daily Journal*, 27 April 1918.

8-6 WORLD WAR I DRAFTEES ON COURTHOUSE STEPS, NAPA, OCTOBER 8, 1917

QUESTION: When people disagree with their government about sending soldiers to war, should public protest be allowed or banned? Why or why not?

8-7   ARMISTICE DAY PARADE, NAPA, 1918.

The men are wearing masks because they are in the midst of the influenza epidemic that year.

8-8   SUSAN MINOR, "SISTERS ALL", *OVERLAND MONTHLY, 73* (MAY 1919)

Beginning with the Great War, American women took "men's jobs" in factories and fields. For college girls, working communally on a fruit farm was a great experience: the beauty of the landscape thrilled them and camaraderie nourished them.

Two hand-cars dashed furiously and somewhat jerkily down the railroad track, each manned by a desperate looking crew of five or six. These hardened individuals were similarly attired in curiously cut trousers and coats of dark blue cotton stuff, faded, muddy, and torn, their heads bound about in red or blue bandanas. They carried themselves with gay abandon and though they pulled at the levers of the hand-cars with tense fury they laughed joyously.

The second car seemed to be in pursuit of the first for ever anon one or another of the leading crew glanced behind and then urged the rest to yet wilder pulling on the propelling handle.

Were they a bandit gang of the woolly days of California?

Were they staging a moving picture?

Look carefully around the edges of the bandanas. Look carefully at the hands gripping the metal bar. Long hair is tidily tucked away under the coarse, gay head wrappings. The hands are brown and hard but too small for men's hands.

The desperate bandits are really farm laborers out for a holiday, those weary women workers of the Woman's Land Army.

Weary in body we might be at times. I know because I was one a them, that we did get backaches and leg-aches from stooping to the ground for peaches and prunes, from reaching above out heads for peaches and prunes, from bending over grapevines. But weary in spirit—never.

The first California Land Army Camp where I labored was situated about fifteen miles south of Chico in the broad, level, hot and fertile. Sacramento Valley, between the distant, dim Sierras and the equally dim Coast Range.

Here, close by hundreds of acres of peaches, prunes, figs, olives and nuts, forty-five of us lived in eight little screened and electric lighted bungalows built for us on what had been, in the season, a wheat field and was now, except that part occupied by our camp, the drying field for fruit. . . .

We rattled away to the orchards every day except Sunday at 7 A.M. weak and emaciated condition. There you might possibly be permitted to blanket on one of the popular dormitories, two hay stacks, for which a number of girls nightly deserted their cots until a three days' rain soaked the stacks.

This easy good-fellowship that was regardless of age, education, and previous condition of servitude arose from a combination of causes. The cotton uniform, soon muddy and fruit stained, in which some girls looked picturesque, but no one overwhelmingly beautiful leveled all distinction except those of personality, manners and speech. As in the old Western frontier days our past had no direct bearing on our life in camp. The camp life was an isolated experience and we were taken for what we were worth at the moment. After a while we began to inquire into each other's previous occupation and habits, but from curiosity only and from no desire to establish any social standards.

The nature of the work also was a democratizer, work requiring speed in judging the color of fruit, speed of motion, and grit to maintain that speed. The possession of these qualities made two or three girls accustomed to piece-work in factories, two or three college students, a waitress, and an office clerk, the fastest workers. And when day after day in the orchard you have sprawled together for fifteen heavenly minutes of relaxation, morning and afternoon, on the ground beside the common water can, when any two of you have raced any other couple to see which could fill more boxes with the big, golden peaches, when the telephone girl beside you at the table offers you her tomatoes, and asks for nothing in return, when a college student loans you her cherished washboard to facilitate the laundering of your nightgown, a fellow-feeling grows. . . .

And we worked, oh, how hard we worked! We wanted to be really good laborers, not just good "for women." In spite of the fact that we were paid by the hour, and not by the amount accomplished, the rivalry for speed was keen. It was a matter of honor and pride to pick rapidly and yet pick only the best fruit, and the fastest workers were greatly revered by the slow ones.

The result has proved highly satisfactory to our employers, and almost every rancher and fruit company that employed women last year wants them back this year. We are said to have a better eye than men, for judging fruit in the right stage for picking and to be quicker of hand. We are slow in moving ladders and boxes of fruit, but this slowness is compensated for, in the opinion of our employers, by greater industry, intelligence, and reliability. . . .

The organization that makes possible this general introduction of women into agriculture is the Woman's Land Army of America. It came on the floor of the motor truck with our tin fruit-picking pails, singing, swaying our relaxed bodies with the motion of the machine, swinging our legs over the edge. And here we rattled back in the late afternoon after eight, nine or ten hours of work, dusty, perspiring, limp, contented, still singing.

After work, by way of recreation, we went swimming in the neighboring irrigation canal that cleared today of past fatigue and future fears or cantered about the plain on a horse that the lender soon had to remove from us, as we were riding him to his grave. Then came a show-bath, a change into some costume other than uniform, and, lo, Richard was herself again. In some paradoxical way these exertions had rested us.

Once a week those of us who cared to do so, struggled with our back-to-nature hair, girt a corset about our back-to-nature figures, powdered our sunburned noses, donned the best apparel at our command, and were motored to a dance in the nearest town, so getting a taste of the outside world that gave us food for thought and conversation for many a day as we climbed ladders and filled fruit boxes. . . .

These women who lived together in such easy good-fellowship, who rose while it was yet dark, and with many semi-humorous protests stumbled out in bath-robes, sweaters, kimonos, or unaugmented pajamas to go through setting-up exercises beneath moon and stars, who got sweaty and grimy and stuck up with rotten fruit, who combed their hair by hand-mirrors, and used shelves for dressing tables, and who not only tolerated such an existence as a patriotic need, but reveled keenly in the gay freedom of it, who paused a moment in their work to glory in the long rows of green peach trees against the cloudless sky, in a bunch of red grapes glittering with the clinging dew, in a line of feathery almond trees against a lavender horizon; these women varied in private life from factory girl to college student; ranged from eighteen to forty-five years, or thereabout, and were, almost without exception, from cities.

There you would see, sitting side by side on benches at the long, white-oilcloth covered tables, and eating with avidity from enamel plates, a waitress who used with freedom "ain't" and "his'en" and double negatives in good-natured argument, with a charming Swiss lady who read, or at least, had with her to read, Darwin and Nietzsche. There you might listen when in the evening or while at work, the Hawaiian girl, a Mills College student, sang the "Gypsie Trail," or one of her native songs, when the beautiful shadowy-eyed French girl sang "The Bluebird," or "The Marseillaise," or the Swiss woman yodle songs of the Alps. There you might stroke the amiable, homely kitten named "Measley," which had been adopted and fondly nourished by us when it strayed to us into existence in February, 1918, after the successful experiment of the preceding summer in placing women on the fields in New York State. It is managed by a national board of directors having headquarters at 19 West 44 street, New York City. This board is made up of women from various parts of the country and operates through state boards having offices in each of the forty states in which the Land Army has to this time been organized. In the fall of 1918 the Land Army was affiliated with the United States Department of Labor at the request of the Secretary of Labor in recognition of its excellent work.

QUESTION: How does Minor's experience remind you of your own bonding with coworkers at a jobsite, even if the work was routine or exhausting? Have you ever worked on a farm or garden where food was grown? What was your experience of this kind of work?

8-9   ERNESTO GALARZA, EXCERPT FROM *ON THE EDGE OF THE BARRIO*, 1971

Between 1910 and 1930, over a million Mexicans migrated to the United States, historian Debra Weber tells us, forming a new base of manual labor for California's emerging agribusiness. A new system of landholding in Mexico, the hacienda system, had been swallowing up village communal lands and turning agriculturalists into wage-earners for decades. Weber explains: "By 1910 over nine and a half million people, 96 percent of Mexican families, were landless."[ix]

Dr. Vicky Ruiz is one of the first Latina historians, earning a Ph.D. at Stanford University in 1982. On her website, http://www.hnet.uci.edu/history/faculty/ruiz/, she writes:

> For me, history remains a grand adventure, one, which began at the kitchen table listening to the stories of my mother and grandmother and then took flight aboard the local bookmobile. As a historian, I have had the privilege of interviewing people whose quiet courage made a difference in their lives and in their communities.

Ruiz interviewed women like Jesusita Torres, who described how her mother fled an abusive marriage in Mexico, sneaking out the house with the nine-year old Jesusita in 1923. They

---

[ix]Devra Weber, *Dark Sweat, White Gold: California Farmworkers, Cotton, and the New Deal* (Berkeley, University of California), 1994.

traveled by train to El Monte, where Torres and her mother worked in the berry fields from February till June, when they moved to the San Joaquin Valley to pick grapes and then cotton.[x]

Ernesto Galarza was born in Jalcocotán, Nayarit, Mexico, on August 15, 1905, and came to the United States when he was 8 years old. As a youth, Galarza worked as a farm laborer in Sacramento—and he dedicated his life to the struggle for justice for farm workers and the urban working-class Latinos, and to changing curricula in the schools. During the 1950's, Dr. Galarza helped build the first multiracial farm worker union, which set the foundation for the emergence of the United Farm Workers Union. His civil rights legacy also includes the founding of the Mexican American Legal Defense Fund (MALDEF) and the National Council of La Raza (NCLR). In 1979, Dr. Galarza was the first U.S. Latino to be nominated for the Nobel Prize in Literature.

I had been reading stories in the *Sacramento Bee* of the Spanish influenza. At first it was far off, like the war, in places such as New York and Texas. Then the stories told of people dying in California towns we knew, and finally the *Bee* began reporting the spread of the flu in our city.

One Sunday morning we saw Uncle Gustavo coming down the street with a suitcase in his hand, walking slowly. I ran out to meet him. By the front gate he dropped the suitcase, leaned on the fence, and fainted. He had been working as a sandhog on the American River, and had come home weak from fever.

Gustavo was put to bed in one of the front rooms. Uncle José set out to look for a doctor, who came the next day, weary and nearly sick himself. He ordered Gustavo to the hospital. Three days later I answered the telephone call from the hospital telling us he was dead. Only José went to Gustavo's funeral. The rest of us, except my step-father, were sick in bed with the fever.

In the dining room, near the windows where the sunlight would warm her, my mother lay on a cot, a kerosene stove at her feet. The day Gustavo died she was delirious. José bicycled all over the city, looking for oranges, which the doctor said were the best medicine we could give her. I sweated out the fever, nursed by José, who brought me glasses of steaming lemonade and told me my mother was getting better. The children were quarantined in another room, lightly touched by the fever, more restless than sick.

Late one afternoon José came into my room, wrapped me in blankets, pulled a cap over my ears, and carried me to my mother's bedside. My stepfather was holding a hand mirror to her lips. It didn't fog. She had stopped breathing. In the next room my sister was singing to the other children, "A birdie with a yellow bill/hopped upon my windowsill,/cocked a shiny eye, and said,/'Shame on you, you sleepyhead.'"

The day we buried my mother, Mrs. Dodson took the oldest sister home with her. The younger children were sent to a neighbor. That night José went to the barrio, got drunk, borrowed a pistol, and was arrested for shooting up Second Street.

A month later I made a bundle of the family keep-sakes my stepfather allowed me to have, including the butterfly sarape, my books, and some family pictures. With the bundle

---

[x]Torres, cited in Ruiz, 15. Torres was interviewed on January 8, 1993.

tied to the bars of my bicycle, I pedaled to the basement room José had rented for the two of us on O Street near the corner of Fifth, on the edge of the barrio.

José was now working the riverboats and, in the slack season, following the round of odd jobs about the city. In our basement room, with a kitchen closet, bathroom, and laundry tub on the back porch and a woodshed for storage, I kept house. We bought two cots, one for me and the other for José when he was home.

Our landlords lived upstairs, a middle-aged brother and sister who worked and rented rooms. They were friends of doña Tránsito, the grandmother of a Mexican family that lived in a weather-beaten cottage on the corner. Doña Tránsito was in her sixties, round as a barrel, and she wore her gray hair in braids and smoked handrolled cigarettes on her rickety front porch. Living only three houses from doña Tránsito, saying my saludos to her every time I passed the corner, I lived inside a circle of security when José was away.

José had chosen our new home because it was close to the Hearkness Junior High School, to which I transferred from Bret Harte. As the jefe de familia[1] he explained that I could help earn our living but that I was to study for a high school diploma. That being settled, my routine was clearly divided into school time and work time, the second depending on when I was free from the first.

Few Mexicans of my age from the barrio were enrolled at the junior high school when I went there. At least, there were no other Mexican boys or girls in Mr. Everett's class in civics, or Miss Crowley's English composition, or Mrs. Stevenson's Spanish course. Mrs. Stevenson assigned me to read to the class and to recite poems by Amado Nervo, because the poet was from Tepic and I was, too. Miss Crowley accepted my compositions about Jalcocotán and the buried treasure of Acaponeta while the others in the class were writing about Sir Patrick Spence and the Beautiful Lady Without Mercy, whom they had never met. For Mr. Everett's class, the last of the day, I clipped pieces from the *Sacramento Bee* about important events in Sacramento. From him I learned to use the ring binder in which I kept clippings to prepare oral reports. Occasionally he kept me after school to talk. He sat on his desk, one leg dangling over a corner, behind him the frame of a large window and the arching elms of the school yard, telling me he thought I could easily make the debating team at the high school next year, that Stanford University might be the place to go after graduation, and making other by-the-way comments that began to shape themselves into my future.

Afternoons, Saturdays, and summers allowed me many hours of work time I did not need for study. José explained how things now stood. There were two funerals to pay for. He would pay the rent and buy the food. My clothes, books, and school expenses would be up to me.

On my vacations and when he was not on the riverboats, he found me a job as water boy on a track gang. We chopped wood together near Woodland and stacked empty lug boxes in a cannery yard. Cleaning vacant houses and chopping weeds were jobs we could do as a team when better ones were not to be had. As the apprentice, I learned from him how to brace myself for a heavy lift, to lock my knee under a loaded hand-truck, to dance rather than lift a ladder, and to find the weakest grain in a log. Like him I spit into my palms to get

_____
[1]*jefe de familia* head of the household (literally, "head of the family")

the feel of the ax handle and grunted as the blade bit into the wood. Imitating him, I circled a tree several times, sizing it up, *tanteando*, as he said, before pruning or felling it.

Part of one summer my uncle worked on the river while I hired out as a farmhand on a small ranch south of Sacramento. My senior on the place was Roy, a husky Oklahoman who was a part-time taxi driver and a full-time drinker of hard whiskey. He was heavy-chested, heavy-lipped, and jowly, a grumbler rather than a talker and a man of great ingenuity with tools and automobile engines. Under him I learned to drive the Fordson tractor on the place, man the gasoline pump, feed the calves, check an irrigation ditch, make lug boxes for grapes, and many other tasks on a small farm.

Roy and I sat under the willow tree in front of the ranch house after work, I on the grass, he on a creaky wicker chair, a hulking, sour man glad for the company of a boy. He counseled me on how to avoid the indulgences he was so fond of, beginning his sentences with a phrase he repeated over and over, "as the feller says." "Don't aim to tell you your business," he explained, "but as the feller says, get yourself a good woman, don't be no farmhand for a livin', be a lawyer or a doctor, and don't get to drinkin' nohow. And there's another thing, Ernie. If nobody won't listen to you, go on and talk to yourself and hear what a smart man has to say."

And Roy knew how to handle boys, which he showed in an episode that could have cost me my life or my self-confidence. He had taught me to drive the tractor, walking alongside during the lessons as I maneuvered it, shifting gears, stopping and starting, turning and backing, raising a cloud of dust wherever we went. Between drives Roy told me about the different working parts of the machine, giving me instructions on oiling and greasing and filling the radiator. "She needs to be took care of, Ernie," he admonished me, "like a horse. And another thing, she's like to buck. She can turn clear over on you if you let'er. If she starts to lift from the front even a mite, you turn her off. You hear?"

"Yes, sir," I said, meaning to keep his confidence in me as a good tractor man.

It was a few days after my first solo drive that it happened. I was rounding a telephone pole on the slightly sloping bank of the irrigation ditch. I swung around too fast for one of the rear tracks to keep its footing. It spun and the front began to lift. Forgetting Roy's emphatic instructions, I gunned the engine, trying to right us to the level ground above the ditch. The tractor's nose kept climbing in front of me. We slipped against the pole, the tractor bucking, as Roy said it would.

Roy's warning broke through to me in my panic, and I reached up to turn off the ignition. My bronco's engine sputtered out and it settled on the ground with a thump.

I sat for a moment in my sweat. Roy was coming down the ditch in a hurry. He walked up to me and with a quick look saw that neither I nor the tractor was damaged.

"Git off," he said.

I did, feeling that I was about to be demoted, stripped of my rank, bawled out, and fired.

Roy mounted the machine, started it, and worked it off the slope to flat ground. Leaving the engine running, he said: "Git on."

I did.

"Now finish the disking," he said. Above the clatter of the machine he said: "Like I said, she can buck. If she does, cut'er. You hear?" And he waved me off to my work.

Except for food and a place to live, with which José provided me, I was on my own. Between farm jobs I worked in town, adding to my experience as well as to my income. As a clerk in a drugstore on Second and J, in the heart of the lower part of town, I waited on Chicanos who spoke no English and who came in search of remedies with no prescription other than a recital of their pains. I dispensed capsules, pills, liniments, and emulsions as instructed by the pharmacist, who glanced at our customers from the back of the shop and diagnosed their ills as I translated them. When I went on my shift, I placed a card in the window that said "Se habla español." So far as my Chicano patients were concerned, it might as well have said "Dr. Ernesto Galarza."

From drugs I moved to office supplies and stationery sundries, working as delivery boy for Wahl's, several blocks uptown from skid row. Between deliveries I had no time to idle. I helped the stock clerk, took inventory, polished desks, and hopped when a clerk bawled an order down the basement steps. Mr. Wahl, our boss, a stocky man with a slight paunch, strutted a little as he constantly checked on the smallest details of his establishment, including myself. He was always pleasant and courteous, a man in whose footsteps I might possibly walk into the business world of Sacramento.

But like my uncles, I was looking for a better chanza, which I thought I found with Western Union, as a messenger, where I could earn tips as well as wages. Since I knew the lower part of town thoroughly, whenever the telegrams were addressed to that quarter the dispatcher gave them to me. Deliveries to the suites on the second floor of saloons paid especially well, with tips of a quarter from the ladies who worked there. My most generous customer was tall and beautiful Miss Irene, who always asked how I was doing in school. It was she who gave me an English dictionary, the first I ever possessed, a black bound volume with remarkable little scallops on the pages that made it easy to find words. Half smiling, half commanding, Miss Irene said to me more than once: "Don't you stop school without letting me know." I meant to take her advice as earnestly as I took her twenty-five-cent tip.

It was in the lower town also that I nearly became a performing artist. My instructor on the violin had stopped giving me lessons after we moved to Oak Park. When we were back on O Street he sent word through José that I could work as second fiddler on Saturday nights in the dance hall where he played with a mariachi. Besides, I could resume my lessons with him. A dollar a night for two hours as a substitute was the best wages I had ever made. Coached by my teacher, I second-fiddled for sporting Chicanos who swung their ladies on the dance floor and sang to our music. Unfortunately I mentioned my new calling to Miss Crowley when I proposed it to her as a subject for a composition. She kept me after school and persuaded me to give it up, on the ground that I could earn more decorating Christmas cards during the vacation than at the dance hall. She gave me the first order for fifty cards and got subscriptions for me from the other teachers. I spent my Christmas vacation as an illustrator, with enough money saved to quit playing in the saloon.

It was during the summer vacation that school did not interfere with making a living—the time of the year when I went with other barrio people to the ranches to look for work. Still too young to shape up with the day-haul gangs, I loitered on skid row, picking up conversation and reading the chalk signs about work that was being offered. For a few days of picking fruit or pulling hops I bicycled to Folsom, Lodi, Woodland, Freeport, Walnut Grove,

Marysville, Slough House, Florin, and places that had no name. Looking for work, I pedaled through a countryside blocked off, mile after mile, into orchards, vineyards, and vegetable farms. Along the ditch banks, where the grass, the morning glory, and the wild oats made a soft mattress, I unrolled my bindle and slept.

In the labor camps I shared the summertime of the lives of the barrio people. They gathered from barrios of faraway places like Imperial Valley, Los Angeles, Phoenix, and San Antonio. Each family traveling on its own, they came in trucks piled with household goods or packed in their secondhand fotingos[2] and chevees. The trucks and cars were ancient models, fresh out of a used-car lot, with license tags of many states. It was into these jalopies that much of the care and a good part of the family's earnings went. In camp they were constantly being fixed, so close to scrap that when we needed a part for repairs, we first went to the nearest junkyard.

It was a world different in so many ways from the lower part of Sacramento and the residences surrounded by trim lawns and cool canopies of elms to which I had delivered packages for Wahl's. Our main street was usually an irrigation ditch, the water supply for cooking, drinking, laundering, and bathing. In the better camps there was a faucet or a hydrant, from which water was carried in buckets, pails, and washtubs. If the camp belonged to a contractor and it was used from year to year, there were permanent buildings—a shack for his office, the privies, weatherworn and sagging, and a few cabins made of secondhand lumber, patched and unpainted.

If the farmer provided housing himself, it was in tents pitched on the bare baked earth or on the rough ground of newly plowed land on the edge of a field. Those who arrived late for the work season camped under trees or raised lean-tos along a creek, roofing their trucks with canvas to make bedrooms. Such camps were always well away from the house of the ranchero, screened from the main road by an orchard or a grove of eucalyptus. I helped to pitch and take down such camps, on some spot that seemed lonely when we arrived, desolate when we left.

If they could help it, the workers with families avoided the more permanent camps, where the seasonal hired hands from skid row were more likely to be found. I lived a few days in such a camp and found out why families avoided them. On Saturday nights when the crews had a week's wages in their pockets, strangers appeared, men and women, carrying suitcases with liquor and other contraband. The police were called by the contractor only when the carousing threatened to break into fighting. Otherwise, the weekly bouts were a part of the regular business of the camp.

Like all the others, I often went to work without knowing how much I was going to be paid. I was never hired by a rancher, but by a contractor or a straw boss who picked up crews in town and handled the payroll. The important questions that were in my mind—the wages per hour or per lug box, whether the beds would have mattresses and blankets, the price of meals, how often we would be paid—were never discussed, much less answered, beforehand. Once we were in camp, owing the employer for the ride to the job, having no means to get back to town except by walking and no money for the next meal, arguments over working conditions were settled in favor of the boss. I learned firsthand the chiseling

---

[2]*fotingos* old cars (often travel-worn Fords)

techniques of the contractors and their pushers—how they knocked off two or three lugs of grapes from the daily record for each member of the crew, or the way they had of turning the face of the scales away from you when you weighed your work in.

There was never any doubt about the contractor and his power over us. He could fire a man and his family on the spot and make them wait days for their wages. A man could be forced to quit by assigning him regularly to the thinnest pickings in the field. The worst thing one could do was to ask for fresh water on the job, regardless of the heat of the day; instead of iced water, given freely, the crews were expected to buy sodas at twice the price in town, sold by the contractor himself. He usually had a pistol—to protect the payroll, so it was said. Through the ranchers for whom he worked, we were certain that he had connections with the Autoridades, for they never showed up in camp to settle wage disputes or listen to our complaints or to go for a doctor when one was needed. Lord of a ragtag labor camp of Mexicans, the contractor, a Mexican himself, knew that few men would let their anger blow, even when he stung them with curses.

As a single worker, I usually ate with some household, paying for my board. I did more work than a child but less than a man—neither the head nor the tail of a family. Unless the camp was a large one, I became acquainted with most of the families. Those who could not write asked me to chalk their payroll numbers on the boxes they picked. I counted matches for a man who transferred them from the right pocket of his pants to the left as he tallied the lugs he filled throughout the day. It was his only check on the record the contractor kept of his work. As we worked the rows or the tree blocks during the day, or talked in the evenings where the men gathered in small groups to smoke and rest, I heard about barrios I had never seen but that must have been much like ours in Sacramento.

The only way to complain or protest was to leave, but now and then a camp would stand instead of run, and for a few hours or a few days work would slow down or stop. I saw it happen in a pear orchard in Yolo when pay rates were cut without notice to the crew. The contractor said the market for pears had dropped and the rancher could not afford to pay more. The fruit stayed on the trees while we, a committee drafted by the camp, argued with the contractor first and then with the rancher. The talks gave them time to round up other pickers. A carload of police in plain clothes drove into the camp. We were lined up for our pay, taking whatever the contractor said was on his books. That afternoon we were ordered off the ranch.

In a camp near Folsom, during hop picking, it was not wages but death that pulled the people together. Several children in the camp were sick with diarrhea; one had been taken to the hospital in town and the word came back that he had died. It was the women who guessed that the cause of the epidemic was the water. For cooking and drinking and washing it came from a ditch that went by the ranch stables upstream.

I was appointed by a camp committee to go to Sacramento to find some Autoridad who would send an inspector. Pedaling my bicycle, mulling over where to go and what to say, I remembered some clippings from the *Sacramento Bee* that Mr. Everett had discussed in class, and I decided the man to look for was Mr. Simon Lubin, who was in some way a state Autoridad.

He received me in his office at Weinstock and Lubin's. He sat, square-shouldered and natty, behind a desk with a glass top. He was half-bald, with a strong nose and a dimple in the center of his chin. To his right was a box with small levers into which Mr. Lubin talked and out of which came voices.

He heard me out, asked me questions, and made notes on a pad. He promised that an inspector would come to the camp. I thanked him and thought the business of my visit was over; but Mr. Lubin did not break the handshake until he had said to tell the people in the camp to organize. "Only by organizing," he told me, "will they ever have decent places to live."

I reported the interview with Mr. Lubin to the camp. The part about the inspector they understood and it was voted not to go back to work until he came. The part about organizing was received in silence, and I made my first organizing speech.

The inspector came and a water tank pulled by mules was parked by the irrigation ditch. At the same time the contractor began to fire some of the pickers. I was one of them. I finished that summer nailing boxes on a grape ranch near Florin.

When my job ended, I pedaled back to Sacramento, detouring over country lanes I knew well. Here and there I walked the bicycle over dirt roads rutted by wagons. The pastures were sunburned and the grain fields had been cut to stubble. Riding by a thicket of reeds where an irrigation ditch swamped, I stopped and looked at the red-winged blackbirds riding gracefully on the tips of the canes. Now and then they streaked out of the green clump, spraying the pale sky with crimson dots in all directions.

Crossing the Y Street levee by Southside Park, I rode through the barrio to doña Tránsito's, leaving my bike hooked on the picket fence by the handlebar.

I knocked on the screen door that always hung tired, like the sagging porch coming unnailed. No one was at home.

It was two hours before time to cook supper. From the stoop I looked up and down the cross streets. The barrio seemed empty.

I unhooked the bicycle, mounted it, and headed for the main high school, twenty blocks away, where I would be going in a week. Pumping slowly, I wondered about the debating team and the other things Mr. Everett had mentioned.

QUESTION: In thinking about Ernesto Galarzo and Jesusita Torres' experiences, how would you describe their lives in the fields compared to those of Susan Minor? What do you think made the difference?

While agricultural workers struggled under brutal conditions in the valleys, industrial workers in cities fought their bosses and the police to build unions. Most of these battles are still left out of history books, but because Upton Sinclair involved himself in one of them, at least one story has been recorded. When the San Pedro dock strike occurred in 1923, Sinclair was living a few miles away in Long Beach.

The "Pedro" strike was one of the last actions of the IWW before the organization was effectively crushed. Some of the IWW songs, written by their most famous poet Joe Hill, captured the imagination of a whole generation of workers. Fifty IWW members in California were tried in Sacramento, after being locked up for five months in a disease-ridden jail where five of them died. Twenty-four of them were given ten years in prison. But they left court, heads held high, singing "Solidarity Forever," a song written by IWW member Ralph Chaplin in 1915:

> When the union's inspiration and the workers blood shall run
> There can be no power greater anywhere beneath the sun
> For what force on earth is greater than the feeble strength of one?
> It's the union makes us strong.

Sinclair was not an IWW member; but as historian Martin Zanger notes,

> The 44 year old novelist found it difficult to concentrate on his writing while a short distance away, men were being herded into lice-infested tanks. . . . A woman visited their home describing how a hired mob raided an IWW meeting, beating workers and throwing a little girl into a great receptacle of boiling coffee scalding her almost to death.[xi]

Sinclair's belief that the next move of the police would be to take over the hillside where the dockworkers regularly met, called Liberty Hill, proved to be correct. Labor journalist Art Shields describes what happened:

> The strikers continued to sing as each was arrested. From jail, the message came to carry our message from door to door. And the biggest and longest parade in San Pedro's history began. 5000 men, women and children wound through the streets singing our songs, with jailed workers singing to them from inside the jailhouse. . . . I felt better after calling Upton Sinclair again. "I'm coming tomorrow with three friends to speak on Liberty Hill," he said and told reporters: "We're testing the right of police to suppress free speech and assemblage."

The minute Upton Sinclair stepped up onto the speaker's box, the police captain threatened to arrest him. Defiantly, Sinclair recited the First Amendment, and "The captain grabbed the people's novelist by the collar and turned him over to a cop."[xii] Sinclair was held incommunicado and denied access to a lawyer for several days. After his release, his wife wrote that she had expected him to be killed by the police, with either the Klan or the IWW framed for the murder.[xiii]

8-10   UPTON SINCLAIR, LETTER TO THE CHIEF OF POLICE OF LOS ANGELES, 1923

Having escaped from your clutches yesterday afternoon, owing to the fact that one of your men betrayed your plot to my wife, I am now in position to answer your formal statement to the public, that I am "more dangerous than 4,000 IWW." I thank you for this compliment,

---

[xi]Martin Zanger, "The Politics of Confrontation: Upton Sinclair and the Launching of the ACLU in Southern California," *Pacific Historical Review* XXXVIII:4 (November 1969), 386. Retired longshoreman Art Almeida has obtained oral and written corroboration of these events.

[xii]Shields.

[xiii]Mary Craig Sinclair, letter to John Hamilton, May 31, 1923, quoted in Zanger, 394. The Klan revived in the 1920s and had 4.5 million members by 1924.

for to be dangerous to lawbreakers in office such as yourself is the highest duty that a citizen of this community can perform.

In the presence of seven witnesses I obtained from Mayor Cryer on Tuesday afternoon the promise that the police would respect my constitutional rights at San Pedro, and that I would not be molested unless I incited to violence. But when I came to you, I learned that you had taken over the mayor's office at the Harbor. Now, from your signed statement to the press, I learn that you have taken over the district attorney's office also; for you tell the public: "I will prosecute Sinclair with all the vigor at my command, and upon his conviction I will demand a jail sentence with hard labor." And you then sent your men to swear to a complaint charging me with "discussing, arguing, orating, and debating certain thoughts and theories, which thoughts and theories were contemptuous of the constitution of the State of California, calculated to cause hatred and contempt of the government of the United States of America, and which thoughts and theories were detrimental and in opposition to the orderly conduct of affairs of business, affecting the rights of private property and personal liberty, and which thoughts and theories were calculated to cause any citizen then and there present and hearing the same to quarrel and fight and use force and violence." And this although I told you at least a dozen times in your office that my only purpose was to stand on private property with the written permission of the owner, and there to read the Constitution of the United States; and you perfectly well know that I did this, and only this, and that three sentences from the Bill of Rights of the Constitution was every word that I was permitted to utter—the words being those which guarantee "freedom of speech and of the press, and the right of the people peaceably to assemble, and to petition the government for the redress of grievances."

But you told me that "this Constitution stuff" does not go at the Harbor. You have established martial law, and you told me that if I tried to read the Constitution, even on private property, I would be thrown into jail, and there would be no bail for me—and this even though I read you the provision of the State constitution guaranteeing me the right to bail. . . .

I charge, and I intend to prove in court, that you are carrying out the conspiracy of the Merchants' and Manufacturers' Association to smash the harbor strike by brutal defiance of law. . . . It is you who are doing the job for [I. H.] Rice [president of the association], and the cruelties you are perpetrating would shock this community if they were known, and they will be punished if there is a God in Heaven to protect the poor and friendless. You did all you could to keep me from contact with the strikers in jail; nevertheless I learned of one horror that was perpetrated only yesterday—fifty men crowded into one small space, and because they committed some slight breach of regulations, singing their songs, they were shut in this hole for two hours without a breath of air, and almost suffocated. Also I saw the food that these men are getting twice a day, and you would not feed it to your dog. And now the city council has voted for money to build a "bull-pen" for strikers, and day by day the public is told that the strike is broken, and the men, denied every civil right, have no place to meet to discuss their policies, and no one to protect them or to protest for them. That is what you want—those are the orders you have got from the Merchants' and Manufacturers' Association; the men are to go back as slaves, and the Constitution of the United States is to cease to exist so far as concerns workingmen.

All I can say, sir, is that I intend to do what little one man can do to awaken the public conscience, and that meantime I am not frightened by your menaces. I am not a giant physically; I shrink from pain and filth and vermin and foul air, like any other man of refinement; also, I freely admit that when I see a line of a hundred policemen with drawn revolvers flung across a street to keep anyone from coming onto private property to hear my feeble voice, I am somewhat disturbed in my nerves. But I have a conscience and a religious faith, and I know that our liberties were not won without suffering, and may be lost again through our cowardice. I intend to do my duty to my country. I have received a telegram from the American Civil Liberties Union in New York, asking me if I will speak at a mass meeting of protest in Los Angeles, and I have answered that I will do so. That meeting will be called at once, and you may come there and hear what the citizens of this community think of your efforts to introduce the legal proceedings of Czarist Russia into our free Republic.

8-11   ACTORS IN UPTON SINCLAIR'S PLAY, *SINGING JAILBIRDS*, 1924

After the letter to the police chief was published, Sinclair wrote the play *Singing Jailbirds*, in order to arouse the indignation of the public about conditions for political prisoners. It was performed in New York City and later as far away as India.

8-12   POSTER FOR PERFORMANCE OF *SINGING JAILBIRDS* IN INDIA, 1934

QUESTION: Why would the police chief call Sinclair "more dangerous than 4,000 IWW"? Should celebrities carry the same obligation as ordinary citizens to involve themselves in fighting for justice, or should they confine themselves to their own careers?

Sinclair's wife, Mary Craig, owned property in Signal Hill (near Long Beach), site of a Shell Oil 'wildcat' well that had spouted a 114-foot black geyser, proclaiming the birth of one of the world's greatest oil fields. His wife recalled:

> "Are you going to write about it?" I asked. "Gosh!" came the response. "Don't you see what we've got here? Human nature lay bare! Competition in *excelsis*. The whole industry—free, gratis, for nothing! How could I pass it up!"[xiv]

By 1927 Sinclair had published the novel (as well as a play) that he first titled *Black Gold*, and then *Oil!*[xv] When Julian Petroleum Corporation collapsed after an overissue of $5 million in stocks, tens of thousands of Californians lost everything, while a handful of stockbrokers made large profits. The scandal boosted the sales of *Oil!*

[xiv]Mary Craig Sinclair, *Southern Belle* (New York: Crown Publishers, 1957), 280.

[xv]In 2001, Word for Word Theater Company presented *Chapter One* for rapt audiences in San Francisco. The company commissioned a sculptor to create a giant musical car; in the driver's seat sat Dad, often cited as one of the most sympathetic portrayals of a businessman in American literature. *There Will Be Blood* (2008) is based on *Oil!*

8-13   HISAYE YAMAMOTO DESOTO, "LIFE AMONG THE OILFIELDS", 1979

There has been some apprehension this year about the possibility of another depression such as overtook this country in the autumn of 1929. I was eight years old at the time and was unaware that there were people then who were leaping out of windows to their deaths. But our family was never distant from poverty, so we probably did not have that far to fall.

Over the years, however, I have managed to piece together this or that homely event with the corresponding dates—the Flaming Twenties, the Volstead Act, Al Capone, Black Thursday—and realize that there were signs of the great debacle around us all along.

My mother has given me four pennies to take to school. Two cents are for me to spend, but the other two cents are for candy for my little brother Johnny at home. At noon, a little Japanese girlfriend and I cross over to the little grocery near the school so that I can make my purchases. After due deliberation over the penny Abba-Zabbas, which are supposed to resemble the bones worn through their noses by the black figures on the checkered wrapper, the long white strips of paper pebbled with pastel buttons of graduated hue, the large white peppermint pills, the huge jaw-breakers with the strange acrid seed in the middle, the chicken bones covered with golden shredded coconut, the bland imitation bananas, the black licorice whips, I settle for two white wax animals filled with colored syrup, one for me and one for Johnny, and, always one for a bargain, eight little wrapped caramel and chocolate taffy squares, which come four for a penny. The man behind the counter, white-haired and kindly, gives me one wax candy and four chews, then hands the same to my little friend.

Before I can protest, my friend dashes off with the candy clutched tightly in her fist, the candy which I am supposed to take home to my brother. I sputter my inadequate English at the storekeeper and give furious chase to my friend, who knows what the deal is. But, running like the wind, she has already escaped. The rest of the school day I spend seething about this introduction to incredible treachery and worrying about what to tell my mother.

It does not occur to me to forego eating my share of the candy, to take it home to my brother.

It was at the same school, Central School in Redondo Beach, that I once watched in wonderment as two thin tow-headed children, a boy and a girl, delved into one of the trash baskets filled with lunchtime litter. They came up with a banana skin which they gravely shared, taking turns scraping the white insides of the yellow peeling with their lower teeth.

But I don't know why I was attending Central School, when I had begun kindergarten at South School, since we were still living at the same house with the enormous piano and orchard. I do know that I went back to South School subsequently, where, at the beginning of the second grade, I encountered obstacles in being admitted to the proper classroom. On the first day of that school year, I was among the milling children lining up to march into the building. When I tried to line up with the second-grade children, a teacher steered me over to the first-grade column. I did not command enough English or nerve to argue, but meekly joined the first-graders and prepared to go through the first grade all over again.

After some weeks, though, I must have made enough noise about it at home, because my mother was upset. Since the same bus serviced both Central and South Schools, unloading first at Central School, she counseled me to get off at Central School, there to see if the second grade wouldn't accept me. In trepidation I obeyed, but there, too, I was consigned to the first grade. I sat woefully at the rear of the room that day, like one suspended in limbo, while Central School tried to figure out how to handle this deluded Oriental shrimp with second-grade pretensions. As it turned out, probably because of my grass-roots revolt, South School found out that I did indeed belong in the second grade. The bus driver came after me in his own car later that day and transported me to South School, where I was finally delivered to the second grade. I was secretly so delighted to be in my proper niche at last that I took steps to make myself known to the teacher. Taking my reader up to her, I asked how to read the word "squirrel" which I knew very well. I guess this was like pinching myself to make sure there was order in the world again, the seconds of his personal attention constituting the confirmation.

When I was still in second grade, we moved to our last location in Redondo Beach, going a little distance south to a farm among the oilfields. We were not the only oilfield residents. There was a brown clapboard house diagonally across the road, first occupied by an Italian family whose home garden included Thompson seedless grapes, then by a Mexican family. At the far end of the next oil tract to the west, next to a derrick, lived an older gentleman in what I recall as more of a tent than a house. Once, a few years later, after we had moved inland, we stopped by to visit with him and found him tending a baby in a canvas swing set up outside his canvas-and-wood abobe. It seemed to be a grandchild left in his care. He showed us the special canned milk he fed the baby. Each can came completely wrapped in plain cream-colored paper, so it seemed a more elegant product than the condensed Carnation milk we used.

There was a white family in the corner of a diagonal tract, where we played with the children. A Japanese family with two little ones farmed in the middle of a tract to the north, and I remember one day watching the father smear a poisoned red jam on little pieces of bread in order to kill the rats in his barn. Beyond, I remember visiting a blonde schoolmate named Alice, whose older sister was named Audrey.

Our house, bathhouse, barn, stable, long bunkhouse, outhouse, water tower and kitchen garden were set down adjoining a derrick along the country road. Derricks then were not disguised by environmental designers to be the relatively unobtrusive, sometimes pastel-colored pumps that one comes across nowadays. Constructed of rough lumber, tar-smeared and weathered, they were ungainly prominences on the landscape. They reared skyward in narrow pyramids from corrugated tin huts and raised platforms whose planks accommodated large wooden horseheads nodding deliberately and incessantly to a regular rhythm. Each derrick had its rectangular sumphole, about the size of an olympic swimming pool. The reservoir of rich dark goop, kept in check by sturdy, built-up dirt walls, might be a few inches deep or nearing the top. Occasionally a derrick caught fire, but I remember only a couple of times when, off in the distance, we could see the black smoke rising in a column for days.

We must have lived day and night to the thumping pulse of black oil being sucked out from deep within the earth. Our ambiance must have been permeated with that pungency, which we must have inhaled at every breath. Yet the skies of our years there come back to me blue and limpid and filled with sunlight.

But winter there must have been, because there was the benison of hot *mochi* toasted on an asbestos pad atop the wood-burning tin stove, the hard white cake softening, bursting, oozing out dark globs of sweet Indian bean filling. Or Mama would take out from the water in the huge clay vat a few pieces of plain *mochi* which she would boil. The steaming, molten mass, dusted with sugared, golden bean flour, would stretch from plate to mouth, and the connection would have to be gently broken with chopsticks.

It must have been a chilly January, too, when my father, with horse and plow, dug up the ground. After the earth was raked and leveled, he would pull after him the gigantic pegged ruler which marked off the ground for planting, first one way and then across, so that seen from the sky, the fields would have been etched with a giant graph.

Some of the preparation was done in the empty bunkhouse at night, the bulging, thin-slatted crates of strawberry plants arriving from somewhere to be opened up, each damp plant to be trimmed of old leaves and its clump of earthy roots to be neatly evened off with a knife.

Each plant was inserted into the soil where the lines on the ground intersected—first a scoop of dirt out, the plant in, followed by a slurp of water, the dirt and quick tamping. Once in a while, before the strawberry runners started to grow, we could find tiny red berries to pop into our mouths.

Then, with the horse again, my father would make long furrows between the plants. Others, including my mother, would go crawling down the rows with wooden paddles with which to mound the dirt up around the strawberry plants; then they would plug in the roots of the runners at suitable intervals. Regular irrigation would smooth the channels between the rows and, voila, there would be the strawberry fields, row upon row thick with green leaves and white blossoms and, by early summer, gleaming red berries.

Our fields stretched to the east end of that particular tract, to another road whose yonder side was a windbreak of fir trees, but there was an interruption in the center, a long corrugated tin building with a neat sand-and-gravel yard. Also sand and gravel was the compacted narrow road which sliced the tract in half lengthwise and which must have been for the convenience of the oil company. (We used our end of it as a driveway.) The building was visited from time to time by inspectors of some kind but was usually kept locked. I remember entering that building once, but its contents were mysterious and mechanical.

I do not know how reliable my memory is in conjuring up a giant hangarful of gas pump-size gauges that stood at attention like robot troops.

My mother learned how to drive among the oilfields. The whole family, which by then would have included three brothers and me, went along in the open car while my father instructed her in the fine points of chauffeuring. Chugging around with her at the steering wheel was for me a harrowing experience, and I insisted on being let off when we arrived at an intersection near the house. I walked home by myself, relieved to be on terra firma. In later years, my mother even drove trucks, but she never seemed to have learned how to get across an intersection after a stop without the vehicle undergoing a series of violent jerks and spasms that were terribly disconcerting. Besides, as one endured the eternity it took to traverse the intersection, one knew the whole world was laughing at the spectacle.

It was among the oilfields that we first subscribed to an English-language newspaper. I remember the thud of the newspaper arriving on Sunday morning. First out to the porch, I would open up the funny papers and spread them out right there, to be regaled by nouveau-riche Maggie and Jiggs arguing over his fondness for corned beef and cabbage; Barney Google and the dismal, blanketed excuse for a horse named Spark Plug; Tillie the Toiler at the office with her short boyfriend Mac whose hair grew in front like a whiskbroom; the stylized sophisticates of Jefferson Machamer. There were several assortments of little boys who were always getting into mischief. Hans and Fritz, the Katzenjammer Kids, usually got away with murder but sometimes would get caught by the Captain or Mama and soundly spanked, to wail their pain as they felt their smarting behinds. The little rich boy Perry, in his Fauntleroy suit, associated with a rag-taggle gang. There was also a chunky little guy named Elmer, with a baseball cap that he sometimes wore backwards. Was it Perry or Elmer who had a chum who was always saying, "Let's you and him fight!" who was always offering to hold coats so the fight could commence? The only comic strip I had reservations about was Little Nemo, a little kid who seemed to spend an inordinate amount of time wallowing in a welter of bedclothes, surrounded by a menagerie of ferocious animals from (I gathered) his nightmares.

We still used kerosene lamps then. One of my jobs was to remove the glass from the lamp and blow my breath into it, so that I could wipe off the soot inside with a wadded newspaper. I remember my mother saying how disillusioned she was to come to America and find such primitive conditions. In rural Japan, she said, her family had already had electricity running the rice-threshing machinery.

Our staples included 100-pound sacks of Smith rice; the large *katakana* running down the middle of the burlap sack said Su-mi-su. The sack must have cost less than five dollars because I seem to hear my mother exclaiming some years later about the price going up to five. We had five-gallon wooden tubs of Kikkoman soy sauce, wooden buckets of fermented soy bean paste, green tea in large metal boxes, lined with thick, heavy foil, with hinged lids. There were quart jars of red pickled plums and ginger root, Japanese cans of dark chopped pickles. The house was redolent with the fragrance of some vegetable or other—cabbage, Chinese cabbage, white Japanese radish—salted in a crock and weighed down with a heavy rock.

But we also bought bread from the Perfection Bakery truck that came house-to-house, fish and tofu and meat from the Italian fishman, who would break off wieners from a long chain of them and give them to us as treats. In summer, the iceman brought fifty-pound chucks of ice which he hefted to his leather-clad shoulder with huge tongs, and we always rummaged around the back of the dripping truck to find a nice piece to chomp on.

We used butter but also white one-pound blocks of oleo margarine which we made butter-colored with a small packet of red powder, mixing and mixing so as not to leave orange streaks hiding inside. Coffee came in a red can dominated by a white-bearded gentleman in a white turban, long yellow gown sprinkled with flowers, tiny black slippers that curled up at the toe. Salt was always in a blue carton with the girl under the umbrella happily strewing her salt into the rain. The yellow container of scouring cleanser pictured a lady in a white poke bonnet chasing dirt with a stick.

Medicines were bought from a tall Korean gentleman who spoke fluent Japanese. He brought us ginseng in pale, carroty roots and silvery pills. There was the dark dried gall of a bear for stomachaches; fever called for the tiniest pills of all: infinitesimal black shot that came in a wee black wooden urn in a teeny brocaded box.

The financial world might have been on the verge of collapse, but I was wealthy, well on my way to becoming a miser. In my little coin purse of Japanese brocade, I managed to save four shiny dimes which had been given to me over a period of time by friends of the family, particularly by one childless man who once even brought me a pair of shiny roller skates.

The day that cured me of money was a horrible one, on which I came home from school with one of my splitting headaches. Neither my parents nor I connected my increasing headaches with the fact that, as I learned to read English, I used to read all the way home on the schoolbus (especially *The Blue Fairy Book, The Red Fairy Book, Tanglewood Tales*). It was not until much later, after Redondo Beach, that I was discovered to be seriously myopic and the miracle of glasses banished my headaches forever. But, in the meanwhile, the headaches grew worse and more frequent, so that I often, close to nausea, had to take to bed as soon as the bus dropped me off.

I tried to crawl into my crib (I was such a midget that I slept in a baby bed even when I was in the second grade), but my mother stopped me. "Where did you get all that money?" she demanded. I had left my little purse under the pillow and she had found it in making my bed. Perhaps my illness did not make me a convincing defendant. Mama, alas, did not believe me and confiscated my life savings. I guess it *was* a suspicious hoard for a mere child when a grown man might make ten cents an hour at a regular job. I think I learned then and there the folly of saving and have managed to keep insolvent ever since.

I can evoke the strains of only two songs of that era. Radio must have been coming into its own but my only brush with it was once when we visited our cousins among the vast strawberry fields of Carson. My cousin Kaz had wired his crystal set to the socket of the light bulb that hung from the ceiling and he let me use the earphones to hear a little bit of Amos and Andy.

Another time when we were visiting with my aunt and uncle there in Carson, one of the boys came rushing in to get some pennies for bread. In great excitement, he announced that there was a bread war on, that sliced bread—a relatively new development—was selling for a cent a loaf.

Either my cousin Isamu or Nor would come to help us during the summer, and it was Nor who was not shy about using his nice baritone. I remember him crooning one of the songs.

> Skeeters am a hummin'
> 'round the honeysuckle vine,
> Sweet Kentucky babe . . .

The other song was sung by my best friend Isoko, whose family had moved to a tract on the other side of the highway to the south. That area there seemed to have several Japanese families living the length of a dirt road with tall eucalyptus trees fending off the wind from the west. Isoko, an only child, and I became inseparable at South School, Japanese school, prefectural and village picnics, and home, except when she would go off to the city to stay with her older cousin Asako, whose mother operated a bathhouse. When she came back, she would be insufferable for a time, talking about buying dresses at Mode O'Day (much as someone today might drop the name of Givenchy) and singing,

> There's a rainbow
> 'round my shoulder . . .

which her cousin had taught her.

As I have said, I cannot recall that the great depression immediately plummeted us into a grimmer existence. It was only years later that I remembered overhearing adult talk of a man who was a pillar of the Japanese community, who farmed a stretch beyond Isoko's house. For some reason I see him as forbidding, as a disciplinarian with his children. Probably the most prosperous Japanese farmer around, he one day went to bed with his shotgun and blasted his head open by pulling the trigger with his toe.

Likewise, living alongside derricks and sumpholes did not interfere with our daily routine. If we could not ignore their considerable presence, we accepted them, worked and played around them, and made respectful allowances for the peril connected with them. We might venture onto the derrick platforms, but investigations were conducted gingerly to avoid contact with the pounding pistons and greasy pulleys, except that we sometimes tried to ride the long steel bars that moved back and forth.

Once a pigeon or two entrapped by the thick oil of the reservoir was served up at dinner. Was it my cousin Isamu who, appalled, objected as my father crouched to pluck the feathers of the bird? A coyote that wandered in too close was kept caged under a cabbage crate for a while, but I don't know what eventually became of it. We made kites from Japanese newspapers and sticks, using boiled rice as glue, and flying them in between the derricks, a-flutter with rag strips tied together for tails.

Only once did we come face-to-face with oilfield danger, when my folks were working in the far fields to the east, near the road with the windbreak of fir trees. Little Jemo, probably three or four at the time, was playing on the earthen embankment of the sumphole nearest there when he fell in. His frantic yelling must have brought Mama and Papa running. They told us later (Johnny and I must have been at school) that they had siphoned gasoline from the car to clean the tar baby off.

Indeed, Jemo seems to have had the most traumatic of childhoods during our stay among the oil wells.

One evening my two brothers and I race home from the neighbors. We have about reached the far end of our stable when we hear a car coming up the road. We separate to opposite sides of the road and continue running, my brothers on the side nearest our property and I on the other. The car speeds by and all of a sudden, there is Jemo lying over there on the shoulder of the road.

He does not move. His eyes are closed. His still face is abraded by dirt and gravel. I run the fifty or so steps past the stable and tall barn. The house is set back from the road, from where I, terror-stricken, scream my anguished message, *"Jemo shinda, Jemo shinda!"*

My mother must be putting supper on the table, my father perhaps reading the Japanese paper while he waits. My unearthly shrieks summon the father of the friends we have been visiting. He comes running up the slope to the scene and is carrying Jemo's body towards our house when Mama and Papa finally dash out to the road in response to my cries.

As it turned out, no limbs were broken. He was only stunned, probably flipped aside by the car's front fender. But his concussions and contusions had to be attended to at the hospital in Torrance. When he came home, he was clothed in bandages, including one like a turban around his head and face. When we took him back for a checkup and Papa afterwards bought us a treat of vanilla ice cream and orange sherbet in paper cups, I had to spoon-feed him with the little balsa spoon as we rode home.

My folks thought the hit-and-run driver of the car ought to pay something towards the hospital costs. The *hakujin* neighbor who had come running up the hill was acquainted with the couple in the car, who lived way down the road in a two-story house. He must have seen the car go zooming by, as it frequently did, before the accident and had some kind of foreboding. Else how had he, farther away, reached the scene before my parents even?

My father and the neighbor conferred, and the neighbor offered to try and negotiate a settlement of some kind for us. He came back shaking his head; the couple had refused to accept any responsibility for Jemo's injuries. They said it was all Jemo's fault.

Mama and Papa were indignant. Mostly, it was because such coldness of heart was not to be believed. The couple had not even had the decency to come and inquire after Jemo's condition. Were we Japanese in a category with animals then, to be run over and left beside the road to die? My father contacted a Japanese lawyer in the city, who one day came out to talk first with us and then with the couple. He, too, returned with bad news: the couple absolutely denied any guilt.

But the scenario was not played out as simply as I have written it. This is more of a collage patched together from the fragments of overheard conversations, glimpses of the earnest expressions on the faces of my father, our neighbor, the young lawyer in the dark suit, their comings and goings, my own bewildered feelings.

So that must have been the end of the matter. I have no recollection of the roadster whizzing by our place after that. The couple must have chosen an alternate route out from the oilfields to the highway.

When I look back on that episode, the helpless anger of my father and my mother is my inheritance. But my anger is more intricate than theirs, warped by all that has transpired in between. For instance, I sometimes see the arrogant couple from down the road as young and beautiful, their speeding open roadster as definitely and stunningly red. They roar by; their tinkling laughter, like a long silken scarf, is borne back by the wind. I gaze after them from the side of the road, where I have darted to dodge the swirling dust and spitting gravel. And I know that their names are Scott and Zelda.

8-14　MAIN ST., LOCKE, c. 1920

One man remembered: "In the past, the whites would attack you with stones when you walked through some of these towns. We never dared to walk on the streets alone then—except in Locke. This was our place."[xvi]

[xvi]Big Fai Chow, quoted in by Sucheng Chang in Introduction to Gillenkirk and Motlow, *Bitter Melon: An Oral History of the Last Chinese Town in California* (Seattle: University of Washington), 1987.

8-15   BERNARDO BALAO BACOL WITH SOME OF HIS BACHELOR FRIENDS, MARE ISLAND NAVAL SHIPYARD, c. 1920.

Filipino men like Bernando Bacol were allowed into California only if they came unmarried and formed "bachelor societies" to support each other. Mare Island Naval Shipyard was a major source of employment for Filipino and European immigrants, and eventually African Americans as well. Basalt Rock Corporation sent supplies and workers to Mare Island on river barges. Basalt workers helped build the San Francisco Bay Bridge.

8-16 SISTERS ROSIE MARTINI AND THERESA TAMBORELLI, NAPA, c. 1920

People rode the ferry from San Francisco to Vallejo, where they could take the electric train straight up to Lake County. Next to the train stop in Napa was a restaurant called The Depot, founded by sisters Rosie and Theresa Tamborelli. Across the street was the unionized clothing factory Rough Rider and next to the station was the Brooklyn Hotel, where Italian railroad workers played bocce ball.

8-17   BASEBALL BROADCAST, VALLEJO, 1920

Men gathered below the office of the *Vallejo Evening News* to follow the baseball game. Newspaper employees would receive the play-by-play via telegraph or radio and describe the game to the crowd, illustrating the position of each runner on a large board, as shown here.

8-18   GROUNDBREAKING CEREMONY FOR THE CARQUINEZ BRIDGE, MARTINEZ, 1923 (DR. PLATON VALLEJO, CENTER, WAS THE SON OF MARIANO VALLEJO)

The construction of the Bay and Golden Gate Bridges during the 1930s—what railroad historian Ira Swett called "the hangman's scaffold"[xvii]—destroyed the financial success of ferries and electric trains because people no longer needed them to reach Vallejo or Lake County from the East Bay or San Francisco.

Once the bridges across San Francisco Bay were built in 1930, people could drive or take buses over the water. Greyhound Bus Lines worked to establish a monopoly in bus service in California. By 1938, buses had completely replaced the ferries and the electric train.

QUESTION: What could we gain if we brought back electric trains and ferries? What would be the benefits to society of not having to rely on private cars? How might it help you or your community?

[xvii]Ira Swett and Harry Aitken, *The Napa Valley Route* (Ira Swett), 1975.

9

"I Produce, I Defend": Depression and the New Deal, 1929–1940

> *People of every place in time deserve a history. . . . What they thought; how they felt; what they got angry, fought, and cursed about; what they prayed for; what drove them insane; and finally, how they died and were buried.*
>
> Joseph Amato, *Rethinking Home*

This chapter documents both personal and public responses to the economic crisis of the 1930s. As California's agricultural revenues plunged $400 million between 1929 and 1932, its rural areas became poverty stricken. Two of the state's chief sources of revenue—tourism and specialty crops—made California particularly vulnerable. Meanwhile, businesses crumbled, "revealing a sad picture of fraud, embezzlement, and other forms of financial chicanery that spelled ruin for thousands,"[i] according to the authors of *Elusive Eden*, a recent history of California.

Yet Californians survived and some even thrived during this difficult period. Christina Granero is proud of her grandmother's hunting skills in Oroville, while Catherine Mulholland celebrates her childhood in the San Fernando Valley, living in what was still the countryside. Valerie Matsumoto's recent research has recovered for us the forgotten history of a Japanese farm colony in Merced County, while Carlos Bulosan has written powerfully about a latter-day "Robin Hood" in the Filipino community of Salinas.

Photographs from the Santa Barbara relief camps for the unemployed and songs sung by Dust Bowl migrants introduce us to the images and voices of those who flooded California in search of land and work. In San Francisco, a strike of longshoremen cost the lives of two workers, yet ended in a powerful victory. Upton Sinclair ran for Governor and swept the state with his plan to "End Poverty in California" (EPIC). Despite the Hollywood-backed campaign against Sinclair, many of his ideas were quickly enacted through Franklin Roosevelt's New Deal projects. Californians sought recreation as well: some people stood in line to enter the glamorous new movie palaces, while others, like widows of the Buffalo soldiers, gathered for high-stakes poker in places like West Oakland. This, then, is California in the 1930s, where life expectancy was age 58 for men and age 62 for women, the average salary was $1,368 per year, unemployment was 25 percent, milk cost 14 cents a quart and bread, 9 cents a loaf.

---

[i]*The Elusive Eden*, by Rice, Bullough, and Orsi (New York: McGraw-Hill, 2002), 424.

9-1 EDITH CECILIA GARRIGAN GENTRY, HUNTER, PACIFIC GAS AND ELECTRIC CAMP, OROVILLE, 1933

Christina Granero describes her grandmother as holding the day's bounty:

> This was taken in a Pacific Gas and Electric camp, where my grandparents and family lived during the Depression and my grandfather worked as an electrician on the Oroville Dam. My grandmother had two small children and a husband to feed, note the hunting license stuck in her hat.[ii]

[ii]Christina Granero, Faces of America Photo Contest, Napa College, 2000.

9-2 CATHERINE MULHOLLAND, *RECOLLECTIONS OF A VALLEY PAST,* 1985

Five generations of my family have lived in the San Fernando Valley. My mother's people arrived as homesteaders in Calabasas during the 1880s and never left the Valley. My father's story is more complex. Although he lived his adult life in the Valley, he was born in Los Angeles, the oldest son of William Mulholland, the noted and controversial builder of the Owens River Aqueduct, and for many years, Chief Engineer of the Los Angeles Department of Water and Power (DWP). Although the older Mulholland never lived in the Valley—his home was in town—he bought the land which my father ranched and on which I grew up.

Born in 1923, I was taken as a newborn to the family's 640-acre ranch in the northwest valley, an area between two almost nonexistent hamlets known, respectively, as Chatsworth and Zelzah (now Northridge). Although I do not claim, as Mark Twain once did, that I increased the population of either village by one percent, I did augment my immediate family by one-third and became the first of a fourth generation to grow up in the San Fernando Valley. In later years, my mother was to say that she thought I had seen more change in the Valley in my lifetime than she and her mother had seen in theirs combined. She meant, I think, that while she and my grandmother passed most of their lives in an area that remained essentially rural, I was to be more deeply altered by the urbanization of the Valley. They remained at heart country ladies, while I did not.

But I did grow up on a ranch—on land which between 1912 and 1919, my grandfather Mulholland had bought for between 50 and 150 dollars an acre, the price determined by how much hay the land would grow, dry farming being all that was feasible before the arrival of water from the Owens River. There, in 1914, Mulholland sent his son, my father, Perry Mulholland, to grow hay and beans, which he did until the end of World War I, at which time he set out orchards of citrus and walnuts. When he died in 1962, my father's forty years of work on the ranch had spanned the era of large-scale irrigated agriculture in the San Fernando Valley—finally forced out by the press of population and commercial development after World War II. When Perry Mulholland first came to the Valley, he could stand on his ranch land and see the dust from a wagon or car leaving Van Nuys, twelve and fifteen miles away. By the time he died, so many roads were paved and so many cars ran on them that he could scarcely find a spot to maneuver a tractor from one grove to another.

William Mulholland did not purchase Valley land for speculation, but with a landless Irish immigrant's dream of permanency, had hoped that each of his five children would establish homes where he, the patriarch, would end his days, blessed amidst his groves and heirs. Nor was he alone among those who desired land for their children. During this period a number of Los Angeles business and professional men bought ranching land in the Valley and sent their sons out to work it. But because both before and during the building of the Aqueduct, a powerful group of capitalists had acquired vast tracts of Valley land, leading to outcries and accusations of land grabbing and collusion with the city, my grandfather and many of his associates assiduously avoided buying land from or near those under attack. Thus, the location of my childhood home was determined in part by the land and water politics of southern California; for my grandfather cast a long shadow, not only over the city, but also over his family.

He loomed over us all and I do not remember that ever a week went by that he did not arrive at the ranch, chauffeured by either his second son, Thomas, or by his driver from the DWP (he himself never learned to drive). Often he was accompanied by his companions from the department, especially Harvey Van Norman, his closest colleague, who also owned ranch land nearby. As his arrival required that we all snap to attention, his frequent appearances must have sometimes seemed intrusive to my busy young parents, and as I grew older, I sometimes resented the call of "Come inside. Grandpa's here, and he wants to see you," which meant a reluctant breaking off of play, as my brother and I went in to greet him and answer his queries about our progress in school, which formed the chief staple of our conversation with him. In his dark suit, stiff-collared shirt, and cravat, wreathed in the smoke of his ever-present cigar, he was a given in my life, and I loved him as one loves a grandparent—respectfully and unquestioningly.

He bore about him an aura of authority, even after the disastrous failure of the St. Francis Dam in 1928, which resulted in the loss of hundreds of lives and for which he took full responsibility, saying, "I envy the dead." Even then, as he seemed to draw into himself and become at family gatherings a silent specter at the feast, he remained a powerful presence. He was gruff in manner, but once, as my eighth birthday approached, he asked me what I wanted for the occasion. I told him a bicycle. Pulling out his wad, I can still see his shaky old hand peeling off a twenty-dollar bill and handing it to me. In 1931, twenty dollars bought a very handsome bicycle! He was an intimate and unquestioned part of childhood on our ranch, while the family dinners at his home in town, with its polished mahogany staircase and wood-paneled dining room with leaded casements and painted panels of sylvan scenes, afforded glimpses of life in a metropolitan style, and opened to me, at least, vistas of a world with less isolation and, therefore, larger possibilities.

For although there were friends, relatives and workers on the ranch who provided sociability, when I think of growing up in the Valley during the 1930s, I remember solitude: the lorn sound of a train whistle disrupting the country stillness, the howl of a coyote, the solitary jackrabbit darting across my path and loping ahead as I biked to school over bumpy dirt roads. Our closest neighbors were almost a mile away and were rarely visited. School provided the mental stimulation and social life I hungered for, while my mother and other ranchers' wives arranged outings for us—picnics in Brown's Canyon, day-long treks to the beach, and most wonderful of all, swimming lessons when a municipal plunge finally opened in Reseda in the 1930s.

Occasionally, excitement interrupted the country quiet, as on an afternoon at Winnetka Avenue Grammar School when our principal, Mrs. Ethel B. Newman, visited each classroom to announce that a wild boar had been sighted in Mr. Reichart's walnut orchard and that we children were to exercise extreme caution going home. She advised that if we were to come face-to-face with the beast, we were to remain still and make no sudden move, for then it might charge us. Armed only with this information and the will to live, I left the safety of the school grounds and friends to face the unknown. Never in my life was I less inclined to loiter along the way as I set about to establish some kind of speed record pedaling those two miles home, expecting, at each turn in the road, to meet my final doom.

The Mulholland name may have overshadowed that of my mother's family, but those old Valley pioneers from whom she came were lively and compelling presences in my young life. My maternal grandmother, Katie Ijams Haas, was, at the time of my birth, a widow living in the town of Owensmouth (now Canoga Park). She and my grandfather, John Haas, were among the original purchasers of land when the town site had opened in 1912, but they were not newcomers to the area as they and their families had homesteaded land almost thirty years earlier in nearby Calabasas, and had feuded with Miguel Leonis, the overlord of Rancho El Escorpion, who tried to drive them out, claiming the government land as his own. Forming a Settlers' League, the homesteaders took him to court and won their case. The often-told stories from those days made a deep mark on me and led me finally to write *Calabasas Girls* (1976), an account of three homesteading families coping with life in that tough little frontier settlement.

Always, I was touched by the stories of the grandfather I never knew, John Haas. Of German immigrant parents who arrived in northern California in the 1850s, and who himself was born in Santa Clara County in 1867 and came to Calabasas with his father in 1888, this even-tempered man of the Old West advanced from ranch hand and cowboy to rancher, deputy sheriff and then constable in Calabasas, and finally county road-master in charge of construction of the north side of Topanga Canyon Drive, the old Topanga road, and Decker Canyon Road. According to my mother, it was a political bounty job, and "the reason we were Republicans is that when the Republicans were in office, Papa had his job." Just when it seemed that he and his family could begin to enjoy a more comfortable life in the fledgling town of Owensmouth, he was struck down senselessly. Found dead in a corral, killed by the kick of a horse as he had been dragging a bale of hay into the enclosure, the finest of horsemen was undone. My mother would always remember what the men who had found him said: that there was a perfect hoofprint outlined on his temple.

I was blessed with knowing a third grandfather, who, if not the most famous nor noblest in character, remains very dear to my heart. Isaac Clay "Judge" Ijams was my great-grandfather. (The "Judge" was an honorific he picked up when he acted as Justice of the Peace in Calabasas and later in Toluca/Lankershim—now North Hollywood.) At the time of his death in 1938 at the age of ninety-seven, the local papers described him as the Valley's oldest resident. (He had lived in the Valley for fifty-four years.) When he'd first ridden through during the terrible drought of the 1860s, he said you could ride across the entire Valley on the bones of dead sheep and cattle. An authentic frontiersman and goldseeker who made three prairie crossings in the 1850s, he was a romancer with a gift of gab, and as he grew older, none of his stories shriveled. Newspaper reporters loved to hear him spin his tales of hard times on the trail, Indian skirmishes and much else about the Old West, real or imagined. He claimed once to have founded Boise City, although nobody up in Idaho ever seems to have heard about it. Whatever the truth, he was memorable, had a love of language, and should have commanded a pulpit, stage or courtroom. If ever a man missed his true calling because of poverty and lack of opportunity, it was Grandpa Ijams, for his gifts were imaginative, not practical; verbal, not commercial. He often tried to get things down in writing, and in 1912, a Lankershim editor asked him to write an account of his early days in southern California. What follows is a draft (original spelling and all) from one of his old ledger books:

"I came to Los Angeles Co in 1867 at that time she was scarsly on the map. her principal population being of the dark shade her chief amusements was cock fighting and hurdy gurdy dancing all of which the writer was convercent with . . . After riding horse back many hundred miles from the head of the Misury to LAngeles through Montana Utah and Arizona I first struck camp at ElMonte a damp spot where they raised corn and punpkins played a game of cards that my traveling companion called crack loo 30 beans for a cent it took all day to win a sufficiency to justify the venture. I spred my blankets under the open canopy of heaven and laid down for the first time feeling safe without my gun and saddle for a pillow. The next day I visited the San Gabriel Mission. There was a small groop of Indians there but no americans I engaged the proprietor of a small store in a conversation told him I just arrived from the north he manifested an interest in entertaining me. Took me to the rear of the store and entered an inclosure surrounded by an Adoby wall it was full of birds some parrots all merily singing and orange trees in full bloom the air was fragrant with the oder. This was in January and when I contrasted it with my mountain home in Montana in 5 foot of snow it made me a true convert to California."

I don't know when I first realized that my parents did not intend that I should remain forever with them in the Valley, for the process to move me away was gradual, and the weaning program largely took the form of sending me to "better schools," which were always at some distance from the local heath. The first venture, in 1930–31, was in Hollywood at the Progressive School on Highland Avenue across from the Hollywood Bowl. Each morning for a year, a neighboring rancher's son, my brother and I were driven to an early-morning bus which we rode, along with sleepy adult commuters, into town, a trip of almost twenty miles (talk about busing!). But it was worth it. The Progressive School deserves a page in the history of private schools in southern California. With its small classes, excellent teachers and imaginative learning programs, it proved to be one of the most valuable years I ever spent in school. Moreover, the physical setting was a delight—an old Hollywood estate set against the hills with a streambed running through the grounds. (In 1987, not a jot remains; it is all a blacktopped parking lot.) We learned multiplication tables while snuggled in a treehouse built in the branches of an enormous California sycamore overhanging the wash bed. Although the school was a wonder, the daily commuting from our distant location in the Valley proved too arduous and so we resumed our attendance in the local public schools. All went well until my sixth-grade class turned rowdy and unmanageable. Teachers from town came and went, driven out by our shameful country impudence and unmanageability. I began to receive failing marks in Dependability (talking, giggling and passing notes in class). Apparently behind-the-scene conferences between my parents and teachers resulted in a decision that I should go live with my grandmother and great-grandfather in Studio City where I should attend a "better school," North Hollywood Junior High. I lasted there for one fairly miserable, lonely semester, until I began to manifest unaccountable but perturbing physical symptoms, which promptly disappeared once I was returned to my disreputable and loved schoolmates at Winnetka Avenue Grammar School.

The quest for better schools continued. After a freshman year at Canoga Park High School, I was sent to Marlborough School for Girls in Los Angeles, a really better school; but after two years, I again fell sick (no one spoke of or considered psychosomatic possibilities in those days), and was allowed to return to Canoga Park. There, in a final, glorious senior year, I bounced over dirt roads to school in a 1933 Chevy coupe with a rumble seat, which was often loaded with girlfriends in the good weather as we headed for the beach through Topanga Canyon. The times we had! Beach parties, school dances in the gym, jitterbugging at the Palladium . . . I remember those times as the halcyon days, that last moment before World War II ended the innocence of our generation. On a June night in 1940, when I stood among my classmates in the lovely old Greek amphitheatre on our school grounds (also, alas! a victim of change and long gone), I knew that soon I would be leaving the Valley to attend the University of California at Berkeley, and did not know how I could endure the parting from my comrades. But I also knew that I had to go, for by now, I had become imbued with the sense that to remain in southern California, especially the San Fernando Valley, would be to remain forever culturally inferior. As it turned out, I was gone for thirty-seven years and never thought that I would live again in southern California.

I used to keep a cartoon from *The New Yorker* over my desk, in which a New Englandish matron, gazing in bafflement at an oil portrait in a gallery, remarks to her companion: "I had no idea people from California had ancestors." The assumptions implicit in the cartoon: that to sophisticated Easterners we are a land of yahoos and Johnny-come-latelies; that although San Francisco may pass muster, southern California is something of a bad joke— or worse, a large mistake; those assumptions I came to share, as I also still clung to my identity of one who had grown up on a ranch in the San Fernando Valley. Eventually, I lived for a while in the East and experienced firsthand how deep the prejudices and ignorance ran. Once, when I was in my late twenties, I was taken by friends to a cocktail party on Cape Cod, and was introduced as a native of California to the hostess, a gracious old dame of pure Massachusetts lineage. Later, she presented me to some new arrivals.

"This is Catherine," she grandly announced; and then pausing as if to remember who, indeed, I was, she continued: "Catherine is the oldest living Californian."

No. I was never going to live again in southern California. But who foresees his own end? Or controls his destiny? My grandfather Mulholland, who dreamed of spending his final days among his children, lay a long year dying in his town home, with his family scattered, all dreams of dynasty blasted. My grandfather Haas, who, at a moment when all life's obstacles seemed behind him, found his quietus in the dirt of a corral in Calabasas. And my father? After forty years of ranching—and seeing that commerce had conquered and that agriculture in the Valley was doomed—oversaw the destruction of the groves he had planted, pulled out root and branch. And then he too was gone.

So the ranch on which my parents had lived and struggled—their life's work—the ranch from which I derived so much of my identity—vanished in the face of a growth no one could prevent, or perhaps, would even have wanted to. No. I was never going to live in the San Fernando Valley again. But for my mother's eightieth birthday, I undertook to write a story of her family in Calabasas, and in the doing of it, found another way back home, for their lives so touched me that again I was drawn to those whom I had spiritually abandoned. I knew I could not reclaim the past, certainly could not reclaim the land, but I could recall them. I could tell those who would come after that once we were here, and that we did thus and thus. And so, at long last, I came home.

9-3 CORTEZ NISEI IN COSTUME FOR TURLOCK MELON CARNIVAL, MERCED COUNTY, 1931

The Cortez Nisei in costume for the Turlock Melon Carnival parade, August 1931, posing in front of the Cortez Educational Society Hall. Front row, seated left to right: Mrs. Yuge, Kiyoko Ogata, June Morimoto, Peggy Taniguchi, Masae Kubo, Miyoko Sakaguchi, Rose Narita, Buichi Kajiwara, Ernest Yoshida, Ray Yuge, Fred Miyamoto, Tsutomu Sugiura, Jim Yamaguchi, Susumu Yenokida, and Hiro Asai. Middle row, standing, left to right: Mrs. Shimizu, Sachiko Kimura, Grace Narita, Matsuye Miyamoto, Frances Yuge, Jean Morimoto, Shizuma Kubo, Dorothy Kajioka, Y. Sugiura, Naoko Kajioka, Bob Morimoto, Yeichi Sakaguchi, Eddie Nakagawa, Tom Inano, Kaoru Masuda and Henry Kajioka. Back row, left to right: Aiko Ogata, Mari Shimizu, Tomiye Baba, Edna Maeda, Yaeko Yotsuya, Clara Yamaguchi, Mr. Yotsuya, Frank Date, Key Kobayashi, Jack Nakagawa, Yoshio Asai, and Ben Yenokida. Photo courtesy of Pat Sugiura.

9-4   SAM KUWAHARA, THE FIRST FULL-TIME NISEI MANAGER OF CORTEZ GROWERS ASSOCIATION, c. 1933

Cortez was established in 1919 as a Japanese American farming colony in Merced County, the third farming settlement founded by Abiko Kyutaro. Although the Alien Land Law of 1913 had banned the sale of California land to non-citizens, by 1920 many Issei (Japanese Americans who arrived in the United States before the Immigration Act of 1924) had acquired land title in names of their American-born children. Each family was given a 20-40-acre plot, where parents and children dedicated themselves to the cultivation of rice and potatoes in what had been unusable swamps.

9-5 CORTEZ BASEBALL TEAM, MAY 1939

In May 1939 the Cortez baseball team beat Lodi, 6–0. The Cortez Wildcats were the only team in a league of six Japanese American teams to own their own ballpark. Posing after the Cortez-Lodi game are, front row, from left: George Tashiro, George (Cobby) Kajioka, Ernest Yoshida (manager), Nobuhiro (Nogi) Kajioka, Henry (Hank) Kajioka, and Yukihiro (Yuk) Yotsuya. Back row, from left: Keichi (Deacon) Yamaguchi, Yeichi Sakaguchi, Fred (Pinto) Kajioka, Shizuma (Shiz) Kubo, Kaoru Masuda, Kaname (Ben) Miyamoto, Bill Noda, and Minoru (Min) Yenokida. Photo courtesy of Yukihiro Yotsuya.

9-6 CARLOS BULOSAN, "THE THIEF" N.D., ORIGINALLY PUBLISHED IN *BULOSAN: AN INTRODUCTION WITH SELECTIONS,* EDITED BY E. SAN JUAN JR., 1983

Carlos Bulosan was born on Luzon Island in a rural farming village. His was one of the many families who suffered, according to the memorial in his honor, "because of the conditions in the Philippines created by U.S. colonization; a few ruling families were very wealthy and everyone else was very poor."[iii] In 1930, at the age of seventeen, Bulosan traveled to Seattle, hoping to support his family and get an education. He began to work in hotels and in the fields, but as the economic and racial brutality toward Filipinos persisted, his health was weakened, and he developed tuberculosis.

Bulosan underwent surgery in Los Angeles, losing several ribs and one lung; while recuperating, he began to read and write, becoming a self-educated writer, determined to record what he had witnessed. Bulosan's first collection of stories, *The Laughter of My Father,* became a surprise wartime bestseller, and he was picked by President Franklin Roosevelt to write one of the essays in "The Four Freedoms," a popular collection that appeared in the *Saturday Evening Post.*[iv]

His name was Cesar Terso. Nobody knew him twenty years ago. Some say that he borrowed his name from an unknown Philippine poet. Others say it was his real name. I saw him in Salinas in the summer of 1933. He had been in this country eight years then, and his exploits were beginning to assume the fantastic proportions that spread among our people.

It was the leanest year of my life. I had been traveling through California, sometimes on foot, sometimes in the freight trains. Once I tried to cross the country, went as far as Montana where the cold winter stopped me. I returned to California through Nevada, passing through the tunnels between that state and California. I went to Stockton and tried to find some work at the packing houses there. Then I proceeded to San Jose, and from there I went to Salinas.

The cold winter was almost over. Salinas, however, was still teeming with migratory farm workers. For days I walked on Soledad Street and sat in the Chinese gambling houses.

It was in a little Mexican restaurant where I met Cesar Terso. I remember the hour vividly because a few years afterward all of us who were there remembered him.

He was drinking in a booth with three young men. They probably belonged to the same tribe in the Philippines because there was something similar in their faces. He was the youngest in the group. Suddenly one of the fellows with him, who had been forced to stop his studies at the University of Washington due to financial reasons, said aloud: "I need a few hundreds of that filthy money in the Chinese gambling house!"

[iii]http://carlosbulosanmemorial.com.
[iv]See www.best-norman-rockwell-art.com/four-freedoms.htm for the essay itself.

Cesar said quietly, "Will you go back to the University if I give you some money?"

His companions thought he was joking. The student found some money in his drawer one morning, so he went back to the University of Washington. Upon graduation he returned to Manila and taught ichthyology at the University of the Philippines. Later he was awarded a Guggenheim Fellowship for having discovered a new way to hatch salmon eggs.

Cesar Terso's career started that night in Salinas. He traveled up and down the coast, helping destitute Filipino students. Once I heard that he robbed a gambling house in Seattle, and five Chinese were killed in the commotion. He had nothing to do with the murders. Throughout his career he never hurt anybody.

The Seattle affair spread throughout the Pacific Coast. It was at that time that Chinese and Japanese vice-lords started hiring Filipino killers to protect their business. Then a gambling house was burned in Stockton, and suddenly a destitute Mexican-Filipino family became luxurious. It was rumored that Cesar Terso had something to do with these mysterious bounties.

What fascinated me was his kindness toward poor students. I think he had sent to school more than a dozen Filipinos, and five of them made names for themselves in the Philippines.

I saw Cesar Terso again in 1948. I was then living in Los Angeles. It was sixteen years after I first saw him. He had become a different person. He had just arrived from Chicago and he did not know where to go next. One evening I invited him to my room where we sat and talked. Then we went out and walked in the streets.

It was New Year's Eve. He started to tell me about his life, and for the first time I began to understand him. I tried to piece the fragments together, and suddenly I discovered that I was also piecing the fragments of my life together. I was then beginning to write, and I felt like writing the complete story of his life.

Cesar Terso was a genius, but adverse conditions distorted his mind. What could have been a positive contribution to society became a destructive weapon.

Cesar Terso disappeared again that year. I did not hear from him again for quite some time. He wrote me from Oklahoma where, he said, he had found the girl of his dreams. I knew marriage was not in his cards. Some weeks later I received a card from him. He was in San Francisco, where he was waiting for a "big stake." The big day came, but he was caught. Poor man, poor Cesar Terso!

But another decade of Filipino life in the U.S. had been ushered in. Cesar's generation had grown old and weary. Cesar Terso was tried and deported to the Philippines. I received a letter from him a few weeks ago. He did not mention anything about his activities. But I knew that he would rob somebody to send a poor boy to school.

It is because of my association with Cesar Terso that I write this brief story about him. Yes, there is a Robin Hood for every oppressed people. Legend sometimes becomes a weapon when a people that is oppressed too long remembers heroes like Cesar Terso. I know that another such character will be born out of the chaos of Filipino life in this country. But he will be a different hero, intelligent, political, human, and charged with a wonderful dream of a better America. . . .

QUESTION: Do you know what your relatives were doing during the Great Depression? If they hadn't yet come to America, how did they survive the worldwide economic collapse in their own country? Did they have individual strategies, like Christina's grandmother or Bulosan's friend, "The Thief"? Or were they part of a mutually supportive community, like the ones in San Fernando Valley or Cortez?

9-7   A SHELTER THAT FED AND HOUSED MEN FOR ONE NIGHT, AND DISCOURAGED ALL POLITICAL AND RELIGIOUS DISCUSSIONS, SANTA BARBARA, c. 1933

9-8   UNEMPLOYED WOMEN REPAIRED CLOTHING FOR WAGES AT THE NEIGHBORHOOD HOUSE, SANTA BARBARA, c. 1933

These photos and memoirs discuss how a variety of Californians survived a period when many had no jobs, no homes, and no food, a time before unemployment insurance, Social Security, or Medicare.

9-9   WILMA ELIZABETH MCDANIEL, *FIRST SPRING IN CALIFORNIA,* 1936

Wilma McDaniel's parents were Oklahoma sharecroppers. When the land there turned to dust, they sold everything and headed West. Relatives in Merced took them in, where Wilma and her sisters worked in a fruit-packing house. Because paper was a luxury, McDaniel began to scribble poems on grocery bags, junk mail, and used envelopes and eventually was published. When Wilma McDaniel was interviewed in her small apartment in the Central Valley, she said, "What we went through is at a point of being totally forgotten and ignored. . . . What I know and what I could pass on, I must."[v]

---

[v]Mark Yi, "1930's Poet Records the Tales of her Generation," *Napa Register*, n.d.

The Okies wrapped their
cold dreams in army blankets
and patchwork quilts
and slept away the foggy
winter mights of 1935

From doorways of tents
and hasty shacks
now and then a boxcar
they watched for spring
as they would watch for
the Second Coming of Christ

And saw the Valley change
from skim milk blue
still needing sweaters
to palest green that filled
their eyes with hope

As they waited for odd jobs
the Valley burst forth
with one imperial color
poppies flung their gold
over acres of sand
like all the bankers in California
gone raving mad

Women wept in wonder
and hunted fruit jars to can
the precious flowers
in case next year
did not produce a bumper crop

QUESTION: How do these photos and McDaniel's words paint a picture for you of "what we went through"? Describe poverty you've seen in recent times. How do the two compare?

9-10   JACK BRYANT, "ARIZONA" FROM *VOICES OF THE DUSTBOWL,* 1940

We were out in Arizona
On the Painted Desert ground
We had no place to call our own home
And work could not be found.

We started to California
But our money, h it didn't last long
I want to be in Oklahoma
Be back in my old home.

A way out on the desert
Where water is hard to find
It's a hundred miles to Tempe
And the wind blows all the time.

You will burn up in the day time
Yet you're cold when the sun goes down
I wanna be in Oklahoma
Be back in my home town.

You people in Oklahoma
If you ever come west
Have your pockets full of money
And you better be well dressed.

If you wind up on the desert
You're gonna wish that you were dead
You'll be longing for Oklahoma
And your good old feather bed.

QUESTION:　What are some of the ideas conveyed in this song? What does it tell us about what migrant workers were thinking?

9-11　FRANK AND MYRA PIPKIN BEING RECORDED BY CHARLES TODD AT SHAFTER FSA CAMP, SHAFTER, 1941

Your parents or grandparents may have grown up listening to singers like Merle Haggard, who was born in Oakdale in 1937, son of Dust Bowl migrants.[vi] During the 1930's, music was performed for Dust Bowl refugees in tents like you see in this photograph.

QUESTION:　How important do you think it was to the residents of the camp for singers to visit them there? Discuss.

[vi]http://www.ucpress.edu/books/pages/8182.html. Merle Haggard's life is one of the many included in *Workin' Man Blues* by Gerald Haslam. Historian James Gregory describes the book, "With all the pathos of a Rose Maddox ballad and more edges than a Merle Haggard song, Haslam has spun together the stories of the artists who have made California part of country music and country music part of California."

9-12   OTTO HAGEL, *OUTSTRETCHED HANDS*, 1934

The strike of longshoremen in San Francisco was a defining event for all California workers. The photograph, *Outstretched Hands*, shows what art historian Mark Johnson describes as the "chaotic and desperate reach for work by longshoremen who knew full well that, for reasons both unfair and corrupt, they would likely not be hired."[vii] This was the situation prior to the strike. The art that was inspired by this struggle; the families like June Stephenson's, whose financial and emotional security was won by the union movement; the homes of strike leaders like Bill Bailey, all are mostly forgotten today.

[vii]Mark Dean Johnson (ed.), *At Work: The Art of California Labor* (California Historical Society Press and Heyday Books), 2003, 30.

9-13   JUNE STEPHENSON (BAILEY) MEMOIR, 2005

I was fourteen years old in 1934 when my father was late coming home one night from his daily commute from San Francisco to our home in Albany. It was most unusual for him not to be on the Key West Train at the time my brother and I met him every night of his work-week. We waited for the next train, and then the next. Finally we walked home with great foreboding. Where was he? And worse yet, what would we do without him if he never did come home?

We walked up the steps of one of our neighbors and announced, "Our father didn't come home." Because we were living without a mother, many neighborhood mothers acted as surrogate mothers and always made us feel welcome in their homes. We were given a dinner and then just as we were all trying to decide what to do about our sleeping for the night, the doorbell rang and my father appeared. No two children were ever happier to see their father they thought might be lost forever.

"What happened?"

"I was in the police station. I got mixed up in the waterfront strike. It was my cover-alls," he smiled, showing us his packing. Then he explained that as he was leaving Schilling Coffee Company on 2nd and Folsom Street in San Francisco, walking to the Ferry Building to take the boat that would connect him with the Key West train, he was grabbed by two policemen, shoved into truck and driven to a makeshift police tent at the waterfront.

My father wore coveralls at Schillings because he did factory work in the coffee canning department. Each Friday evening he brought his coveralls home, wrapped in newspaper, so he could wash them and have them clean for Monday. This Friday the police said they suspected that package under his arm might be a bomb. Rather silly of them now when you think about it, but fear was running high at the waterfront strike. The longshoremen who unloaded the boats in the San Francisco Bay, were striking to keep non-union men from taking jobs.

When a thousand police officers tried to clear pickets from the waterfront in order for strikebreakers to unload the cargo, there was a riot. My father, in trying to get to his ferry boat, got caught in the middle of the riot. He was released when the police saw that his "package" was nothing more than a pair of dirty coveralls. That riot, however, left two strikers dead and prompted the governor to send in the National Guard.

At the beginning of the riot, The Longshoreman's Association called for a general strike which virtually every union in San Francisco and Alameda counties joined. Eventually the federal arbitrators granted the longshoremen most of their demands.

As a fourteen-year-old I was not so interested in the details of the strike as I was in my father's safety. As long as the waterfront strike lasted, which was for most of that summer, I worried about my father's getting home safely. It was my first experience of learning about low wages, long grueling hours, the indefiniteness of being hired from day to day, the lack of concern from employers for their workers. These are not things teenagers learn from a book so much as they learn from the emotional impact of a parent's scary encounter with forces working against employees who were attempting to improve their working conditions at their own risk.

My father got through that 1934 summer but didn't carry any more packages which might invite suspicion as long as the strike lasted. He did work at Schilling's Coffee Company for the next ten years, thirty years in all, with only one day off for illness for which he was docked a day's pay. His hours were reduced to 40 hours a week when his factory workers, encouraged by the Longshoremen's strike, unionized in 1936, which was wonderful for my brother and me. Our father no longer had to work fifty or sixty hours a week and he was not so tired.

The forty-hour week was included in the National Recovery Act (NRA) which was declared unconstitutional on the basis that the executive branch was intruding on the legislative branch.

The forty-hour week work was left intact, which called for family rejoicing.

My father retired when I married in 1943. There was no pension. He had thirty-six-dollars a month Social Security which President Roosevelt had instituted, and he rented our Albany home for fifty dollars a month. He moved up to Lake County to a small cabin in the mountains on a creek, one he had bought in 1932 for four hundred dollars. Without a mortgage or children to raise he lived adequately and happily on eighty-six dollars a month.

The 1934 Longshoremen's Waterfront Strike in the midst of a depression was a grudging success. Any strike, fought brutally by employers, helped to stabilize working conditions, leading eventually to a better standard of living for working people.

9-14   BILL BAILEY, LONGSHOREMAN AND VETERAN OF 1934 GENERAL STRIKE, SAN FRANCISCO

9-15   BILL BAILEY AND HIS HOUSE, SAN FRANCISCO

Bill Bailey had been a member of the IWW before helping to organize this strike. Pictured here is his home, which was saved from demolition after his death in 1995. Note his photo and his life story posted on its door.

9-16   ELAINE BLACK YONEDA INTERVIEW, BY RICHARD BERMACK, 1980

Elaine Black Yoneda had been involved in raising bail, finding attorneys, and generating community support for the longshoremen.

Reflections on Three Days That Shook San Francisco

It was the height of the depression and the main organizing going on was of the unemployed—unemployed councils. When people were evicted we would help bring the furniture back into the house, turn back on the lights and the gas, especially if there were children so that they wouldn't freeze. And arrests resulted. . . . Social Security and Unemployment Insurance all came about from people getting their heads busted in these demonstrations.

With Roosevelt came the right to organize unions. The turning point for the San Francisco labor movement was the maritime strike, which led to the General Strike. The maritime strike started on May 9, 1934, with a great big rally at Civic Center. Somebody sabotaged the loud-speaker system, but they could hear my bellowing voice when I spoke, offering them the services of the ILD. I told them we would do everything in our power to see that their rights were preserved, and that should there be arrests, we had this little pamphlet, "What To Do If Under Arrest."

On July 3, the employers tried to run in some scabs, and a battle ensued. Everything was quiet on July 4 because of the patriotic holiday; then on July 5 the police attacked the pickets. In the ensuring battle two men were killed, and many were wounded and arrested. One of those killed was a member of the ILD, Nick Bordoise, an uptown cook. I had the very unpleasant task of having to go down to the morgue and identify the body. There was a big funeral march—over 50,000 attended. In one limousine rode [labor martyr] Tom Mooney's family, Bordoise's widow, and myself. There were innumerable speakers. I also addressed the services saying, "This must never happen again. We have to close our ranks and main-tain our rights under the Constitution and the Bill of Rights. The powers that be have no right to trample on that. That is why a good many of us and our parents came here [United States], and those rights have to be extended to all people regardless of race, color or religious beliefs."

The murders touched off a general strike, and on July 16 the entire city of San Francisco was shut down. On July 17 a reign of terror started, led by the police and the American Legion. They broke into the ILD and [Communist] Party offices, smashing all belongings and arresting the people there. I was arrested that night on $1000 Vag. [vagrancy]. They used that a lot—vagrancy was usually $10 or $20. I was arrested several times on that charge, even though I was employed by the ILD. At one point I was in the Hall of Justice with $2000 in my purse going upstairs to bail out two people, and I was stopped by the [Police] Red Squad and arrested on $1000 Vag. This was in the Hall of Justice! I defended myself in court, and we won an appeal. As a result of that case, $1000. Vag is no longer used.

The strike ended with the longshoremen winning a hiring hall and union recognition. Before they had been worse than the lowest of the low, because of the shape-up system where they were forced to pay bribes to get work. Now they won a hiring hall where a worker could apply for work with dignity. . . .

Mark Johnson writes:

> Adelyne Cross Eriksson's rendering of the funeral march [for the two workers killed on "Bloody Thursday" that Yoneda describes] captures its somber mood and the enormous crowd, which stretched the full length of Market Street. The people here look like stars in the night sky, streaming from the Ferry Terminal.[viii]

[viii]Johnson, 33.

9-17   ADELYNE CROSS ERIKSSON, *FUNERAL MARCH*, 1950

QUESTION: The San Francisco labor community has made an effort to memorialize what they struggled and died to gain. Union members today do not want people to forget their sacrifice. Go to the following websites: http://www.sfmuseum.org/hist/thursday.html or http://historymatters.gmu.edu/d/124/ Do you think the stories and information in these sites help us understand the meaning of "Bloody Thursday"?

9-18   DOROTHY DAY, REPORT ON TOM MOONEY, *THE CATHOLIC WORKER*, NOVEMBER 1937

One of Dorothy Day's earliest memories was watching her mother help quake victims during the 1906 San Francisco earthquake. As a young woman, Day traveled to join suffragists picketing the White House, the first use of mass civil disobedience in American history. The picketers were jailed and force fed through nasal tubes.[ix] Day cofounded The Catholic Worker Movement in 1933, an organization that worked for nonviolence, voluntary poverty, and hospitality for the homeless (see www.catholicworker.org). Its newspaper reached a circulation of 90,000 by 1938.

"Greater love hath no man than this, that he give up his life for his friend."

Tom Mooney is starting his twenty-second year in jail. Who has not heard of him, framed for trying to organize the street car employees of San Francisco, exercising a natural right, a right emphasized by Pope Leo XIII in 1891, and in 1931 reemphasized by Pope Pius XI, since he found it so necessary to try to make his own Catholic children understand.

Freedom is as dear to us as life and Tom Mooney has given up his. I went out to see him at San Quentin the other day, Father O'Kelly, the seamen's priest driving me. Two members of the Marine Cooks' and Stewards' Union went with us. The drive was a beautiful one, out over the Golden Gate Bridge (where 23 workers lost their lives in building it), out through the hills and around the tortuous bays where seagulls shrilly proclaimed their freedom. San Quentin is a buttressed fortress on a bay, surrounded by a village of guards' houses and by flower gardens and sunlight and fresh sea breezes that Tom Mooney seldom feels.

WORK OF MERCY

We waited a long time to see him and we wondered whether it was petty persecution on the part of the guards. But we were unjust in our suspicions because it was Mooney himself, unwilling to leave the bedside of a dying prisoner in the hospital ward where he is orderly, that caused the delay. He started telling us about it right away.

"I've been holding a funnel from the oxygen tank over his face for about three hours," he explained. "We haven't got very modern equipment here. First one arm would get paralyzed and then the other. But I had to wait until someone could spell me." He smiled as he explained the delay.

[ix]Dorothy Day report, Chapters 9–18.

He has a happy, serene face. He has the joy a man has who loves to serve his fellows, and who loves his fellows where he serves. And he seizes the opportunities afforded him by his work in jail, as he would seize any opportunity outside.

"It's the little things that make up the big things," he said, when I told him I was glad that he could throw himself into his work like that. "I've had to live from day to day. Right now I look forward to nothing. I expect nothing. Why should I hope for freedom from the Supreme Court? We'll cross that bridge when we get to it."

We asked him if he had time to read much. "My hours are from five-thirty in the morning until nine-thirty at night sometimes," he said. "And when I'm through I fall into bed and sleep like a log. If I have a chance to get off in the afternoon, I go out in the sun, but usually there's too much to do. I've got nineteen patients, and their comfort depends on me. I can't get out of it. Meals, bedpans, temperatures, charts, and like today, the oxygen tank. There's always something. Men after an operation don't have sedatives, morphine or anything like that here. After all, their aim is not to make men comfortable. So there's lots to do.

IRONY

Mooney had heard of THE CATHOLIC WORKER for a long time and occasionally he sees copies of it. "Some of your readers write to me," he said. "One of them, Miss Metcalf, in Los Angeles, sends her dividend check from the Power and Light Company, the very gang that railroaded me, to my defense committee. She must be a swell person."

We asked Mooney about his religious belief—he was born a Catholic—and he said he believed Christ to be a great Leader of the workers who set an example of laying down His life for the poor and the dispossessed of this world. "But as for organized religion, I am not for it. The great masses of workers throughout the world have protested against the injustice done me, but few churchmen. There was Father Bleakly, though," he remembered, "one of the editors of "America," who came out in my defense. And another whose name I don't remember from St. Ignatius in Chicago who spoke of my case when he was out here in California. And Archbishop Hanna signed a petition for my release. Another defender was Msgr. John A. Ryan."

Since Mooney's imprisonment, the labor movement has been winning the right to organize all over the country, but painfully, with blood and tears. Mooney's example has lent them courage, and their efforts have given him courage to face his life of imprisonment.

PRIVILEGE TO BE A MARTYR

"Someone asked me once if I had any regrets,—if I mourned the fact that I have had to spend my life imprisoned. And I said to them, and I say now, that I consider it a privilege to have been permitted to give myself in this way to the cause of the working class.

When I was a boy back in Chicago I worked hard and saved my money that I made as a moulder, and took a trip to Europe. I went around with a Baedeker, enjoying everything. Then when I got back, I wandered from one end of the country to the other, looking for work, finally landing out here. That experience made me convinced that only the organized efforts of the masses could better their conditions. I started organizing. I do not think if I had remained outside I could have done more to encourage unionization of the workers than I have done behind prison bars. It is an honor and a privilege to have been awarded this part to play."

9-19   UCAPAWA, LOCAL 3 NEGOTIATING COMMITTEE, INCLUDING LUISA MORENO, FAR LEFT, AND CARMEN ESCOBAR, THIRD FROM LEFT, 1943

One half million Mexican Americans (citizens and noncitizens) were deported during the Depression. An estimated one-third of the Mexican population in the United States was sent across the border. "La Migra" (the immigration service) went through the barrio of Los Angeles in a dogcatcher's wagon. Rather than be snatched from their families, some decided to accept the offer of free train fare to return to Mexico; others piled all their possessions into jalopies and headed south on their own: a "curious parallel to the Dust Bowl migration into California," notes historian Vicky Ruiz.[x]

Ruiz learned that those who were able to stay, like Jesusita Torres, got through the Depression by picking berries and string beans in Ontario County, and following the crops to the San Joaquin Valley. John Steinbeck describes a typical diet in good times as beans, baking powder biscuits, jam, coffee, and in bad, dandelion greens and boiled potatoes.[xi] Torres was able to raise her children and buy a house for $17.00, where she has lived for the last 50 years.

Other Mexican American women found work in canneries. In Los Angeles, the California Sanitary Canning Company (Cal San) hired Mexican and Russian Jewish women. Ruiz learned that:

> Standing in the same spots week after week, month after month, women workers often developed friendships crossing family and ethnic lines. Their day-to-day problems (slippery floors, peach fuzz, production speed-ups, arbitrary supervisors, and sexual harassment) cemented feelings of solidarity. . . . The phrase "We met in spinach, fell in love in peaches, and married in tomatoes" indicates that a couple met in March, fell in love in August, and married in October.[xii]

---

[x]Douglas Monroy, "Mexicanos in Los Angeles 1930–1941: An Ethnic Group in Relation to Class Forces" (PhD diss., University of California, 1978, and Carey McWilliams, *North from Mexico: The Spanish Speaking People of the United States* (Philadelphia: Lippincott), 1949, both cited in Ruiz, 30.

[xi]John Steinbeck, "Their Blood is Strong," Simon J. Lubin Society Pamphlet, 1938, 2.

[xii]From interviews conducted for Vicki Ruiz, *Cannery Women, Cannery Lives: Mexican Women, Unionization and the California Food Processing Industry 1930–1950* (Albuquerque: University of New Mexico Press), 1987.

In the middle of the peach season in 1939, four hundred workers walked off their jobs. The workers picketed the plant and the grocery stores that carried Cal San products, and eventually, they even took their picketing to the front lawn of the owners. Within days, a settlement was reached. Carmen Bernal Escobar joined the United Cannery Agricultural Packing Allied Workers of America Local #3 negotiating committee. When interviewed forty years later, she told Ruiz that the union was "the greatest thing that ever happened to the workers at Cal San. It changed everything and everybody."[xiii]

[xiii]Escobar was interviewed twice by Ruiz, in 1979 and in 1986.

9-20   OTTO HAGEL, SALINAS LETTUCE STRIKE, 1939

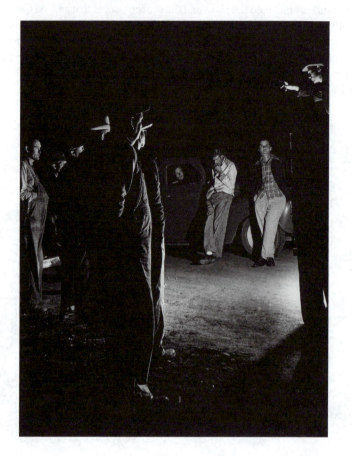

Mark Johnson writes:

> Hagel and Mieth met in Germany at the age of 15, at the beginning of their lifelong commitment to writing and photography. The rise of fascism in Germany led Hagel to immigrate to the United States in 1928; Mieth followed him to San Francisco two years later. During the Depression, the couple supported themselves as migrant workers and continued their photography.[xiv]

QUESTION: Historian John Burnett has noted: "the direct, personal records of working people have not so far been regarded as a major historical source."[xv] Who decides what is of historical importance? Would history be more interesting if it focused on more "ordinary" people like those in this book?

[xiv]Johnson, 36.

[xv]John Burnett, *Annals of Labour—Autobiographies of British Working Class People 1820–1920* (Bloomington: University of Indiana), 1974.

9-21 *END POVERTY IN CALIFORNIA* CAMPAIGN PAMPHLET COVER, 1934

In June 1934, beloved radio commentator Will Rogers told his readers that the author Upton Sinclair was running for governor—"a darn nice fellow, and just plum smart, and if he could deliver even some of the things he promises should not only be governor of one state, but president of all of 'em."[xvi] Sinclair aimed his campaign at the needs of citizens who had been disenfranchised: small property owners, the unemployed, the poor, the aged, widows, and the disabled.

His book *I, Governor of California, and How I Ended Poverty: A True Story of the Future,* became the best-selling book in the history of California.
Journalist Carey McWilliams describes the campaign as one of the most successful experiments in mass education ever performed, with Sinclair's pamphlets exhibiting "matchless skill, lucidity and brilliance."[xvii]

[xvi]Will Rogers, *Weekly Articles*, VI. Oklahoma State University Press, 1982.
[xvii]Carey McWilliams, "The Politics of Utopia" in *Fools Paradise* (Berkeley: Heyday Books, 2001) 66.

9-22   *EPIC* POSTER; THE BEE WAS THE SYMBOL OF THE EPIC MOVEMENT; THESE WERE ITS BASIC PRINCIPLES, 1934

What is especially notable about the EPIC campaign was that Sinclair used popular culture to reach the public. Imagine a candidate presiding over a "grand rodeo" complete with "rough riders," foot races, "*aeroplanes* releasing parachutes," and cowboy bands! EPIC clubs in communities across California sponsored barbeques, picnics, sewing bees, dances, and athletic competitions.

One example of how EPIC inspired "ordinary" Californians is that of Lorna Smith who titled her only work, *My Life Was Changed by Upton Sinclair*. Her father told her, "When you go into a meat market and see the government seal on a quarter of beef, you will know it's there because of Upton Sinclair." She went to the library, got the book, and "His quotation, 'I aimed at their hearts and hit their stomachs' did not apply to me. He hit my heart."[xviii] Smith began to write to Sinclair, and he responded. She established an EPIC Club in her Glendale home and even left her church when it would not defend Upton Sinclair. The depth of the support for Sinclair was such that he received more votes in the primary than his six opponents put together.[xix]

9-23 SINCLAIR DOLLAR. HUNDREDS OF THOUSANDS OF THESE WERE CIRCULATED IN CALIFORNIA, 1934

In June 1934, William Randolph Hearst was in Germany visiting with Mussolini and Hitler when he learned that Sinclair had swept the Democratic primary. As journalist Greg Mitchell describes it in his book:

> Up and down the state, terrified Republicans and outraged Democrats faced a nightmare of their own making. Earl Warren in Oakland, A.P. Giannini in San Francisco, Herbert

---

[xviii]Lorna Smith, "My Life was Changed by Upton Sinclair," *Upton Sinclair Centenary Journal*, 1:1, September 1978, 1.

[xix]Upton Sinclair Marshall was born the day of the primary, named by Los Angeles parents who were thrilled by the hope of EPIC movement.

Hoover in Palo Alto, Harry Chandler in Los Angeles, Irving Thalberg in Hollywood—they all knew they could no longer sit back and let California be captured by the muckraking author, militant vegetarian, erstwhile Socialist, scourge of the ruling class, and now Democratic nominee for governor, Upton Sinclair.[xx]

Although other major newspapers first ignored Sinclair's campaign, *The Los Angeles Times* denounced his candidacy and characterized his supporters as a "maggot-like horde." To answer this attack, supporter Aileen Barnsdall paid Sinclair's radio time over national hook-ups, until his followers were able to publish and distribute *The EPIC News*; the paper sold for 5 cents a copy and achieved a weekly distribution of over one million copies.

Times publisher Otis Chandler and the Chamber of Commerce joined forces to hire the advertising firm of Lord and Thomas, the first time an ad agency was used in an electoral campaign. In addition, *The Los Angeles Times* teamed up with *The Oakland Tribune* and *The San Francisco Chronicle* to discredit EPIC in every way possible. Metro-Goldwyn-Mayer (MGM) Studios created fake newsreels portraying homeless people flocking to California in anticipation of Sinclair's election. When theater owners were forced to show them, Sinclair's supporters fought back by standing up in theatres and denouncing the broadcasts.

Although he was defeated by the Republican incumbent, who received one million votes to Sinclair's 900,000, Sinclair had received twice the number of votes of any previous Democratic candidate in California.[xxi] Despite Sinclair's defeat, fifty other EPIC-backed candidates won races for the state legislature, and EPIC established the Democratic Party as a progressive force in California.[xxii] And four years after the campaign, Culbert Olsen, the first Democratic governor elected in forty-four years, ordered Tom Mooney released from San Quentin Prison. Many years later, McWilliams was to see the slogans of the campaign still present, "painted on rocks in the desert, carved in trees in the forest, and scrawled on the walls of labor camps in the San Joaquin Valley."[xxiii]

QUESTION: Negative advertising during newsreels emerged as a new campaign technique during the Sinclair campaign, and it worked. Many American politicians have since "gone negative" to win. What could change this problem? Do you think Californians would be more connected or less connected to politics if negative campaigns were eliminated? See www.publicampaign.org for more information.

[xx]Greg Mitchell, *The Campaign of the Century* (New York: Random House 1992), 3, 4.

[xxi]Greg Mitchell explains that a few days after the election, Will Rogers observed that if Sinclair had only a few more dollars, he would have won. In August 15, 1935, Rogers died in the crash of small plane. When rescue workers discovered Rogers's typewriter, the sheet of paper carried his final message: "Now I must get back to my Democrats." The nation mourned him with the largest display of affection for a public figure since the death of Abraham Lincoln (Mitchell, 565).

[xxii]Upton Sinclair oral history with Ron Gottesman, "When I talked to Franklin Roosevelt I told him my immediate demands in the EPIC movement . . . he checked them off on his fingers and said 'Right, right, right,' and so on. He brought about a great many of those changes," 61.

[xxiii]McWilliams, 66.

9-24   HELEN K. FORBES, MURAL, SUSANVILLE POST OFFICE

Gray Brechin has been collecting images created by FDR's New Deal programs in California. See www.livingnewdealberkeley.edu for details.

New Deal projects, championed by Franklin Delano Roosevelt, were based on a bold new idea that government could create meaningful jobs (and lives) for American citizens. After a decade as a Broadway star, Helen Gahagan Douglas and her husband, actor Melvyn Douglas, moved to California in the 1930s. She worked with the Farm Security Administration to help displaced Dust Bowl refugees (Okies). In this photo she is visiting a New Deal project.

9-25   HELEN GAHAGAN DOUGLAS VISITING NEW DEAL PROGRAM

**9-26   JOSEPH DANYSH, ADMINISTRATOR OF WPA FEDERAL WORKS OF
ART PROGRAM, EXCERPT ARTICLE *SAN FRANCISCO MAGAZINE,* 1976**

Testimonials

The WPA days were a fantastic period in my life. The contribution that I made was not so much as administrator and director of the project as a brash young guy that didn't worry about his own hide too much.

I knew intuitively that something as great as this couldn't last. I knew that something that had as many arrows slung at it by the opposition—by the conservative press—that it wasn't long for this world. Actually, five, seven years was an unforeseen opulence of time—I didn't realize that it would last that long. I didn't dream it would last that long. Never got used to it. Never got to the point where I went to bed one night secure in the feeling that it would be there tomorrow morning.

. . . .

There were all the human emotions that you would find in any human group endeavor, but there was another element—an element of knowing that you were involved with something that was going to live beyond the day of your eulogies and we all felt this. We fostered it and we cherished it. We knew that this was a special time.

We were among the forefront of the people of that era who were pulling out of the tragedy of the Depression something beautiful and something lasting.

> — Joseph Danysh, art dealer and administrator of the WPA Federal Works of Art Program (FAP) in the West. From *City of San Francisco* magazine, February 4, 1976, p. 20.

9-27   VANGIE BUELL, "SEVEN CARD STUD WITH MANANGS WILD," 2004

Each week, Grandma invited Manang James, Manang Jones, Manang Brown, Manang Hawkins, Manang McQuinney and Manang Baldemero over for a serious game of high stakes poker. They were Filipino women elders, aged 40 to 60 at the time. Thus, I addressed them as "manang," out of respect and endearment. Most of the women, including my grandmother, were Filipino widows of African American soldiers who were stationed in the Philippines during the Philippine-American War. Unique in their West Oakland neighborhood, they were among the very few Filipino women living in the San Francisco Bay Area before WWII. No others shared their language and customs. For the most part, their existence was isolated and lonely. So these weekly card games at Grandma's were their prime social outlet.

Manang Rosario's hair cascaded all the way to her knees. Others had their black, waist-length hair pulled back and rolled into a bun at the back of their heads, fastened with Spanish gold combs and coil-shaped pins. Two of the younger women wore the trendy, short, permanent-waved hairdos of the day. They were the typical-size Pinays, five feet to five feet four inches, slim and delicate-looking, their skins the color of creamy ivory. The faces of the two older women were etched with well-earned lines of life. Their black eyes danced with excitement when they readied themselves for the game.

Grandma began preparing for the game early in the morning. As she cooked, the enticing aroma of sautéed onions and garlic engulfed the house. Then, soaked bean threads, shrimp and chicken would be added to the pot, and a scrumptious sotanghon noodle dish blossomed.

I was Grandma's ten year old helper then. I set up the poker table and chairs and tidied up the house. The women brought *biko* and *bibingka*, rice cakes baked in coconut milk and brown sugar. They came steaming hot out of the oven, the aroma rich and tantalizing. I could hardly wait to eat. They washed down the delectable treats with Rainier Ale and ate with great gusto to the clinking sound of coins as they antied up.

The manangs sat around a green, felt-top poker table, opened their old worn purses and extracted both crumpled and crispy fresh bills. Digging down, they pulled out cloth bags bulging with coins won in past games. They piled the money carefully and methodically up front while Grandma shuffled the cards. All the while they chattered incessantly in several dialects: Pampango, Tagalog, Ilocano, Visayan and broken English. "Hesusmariosep!," they swore colorfully, interspersing this expression with other savory expletives in various dialects throughout the game. At the end of each hand, the winner would squeal happily, "Oy, my goodness!" and scoop up the winnings.

They caught up on all the news about their families in the Philippines and their children and learned how to "cook American." Grandma complained, "I can't find lumpia wrappers," so she described how she created her own very thin eggroll pancakes and shared the recipe with the others. Canned tomato sauce was a good substitute for annato (achuete) seeds to add color to some of the special dishes. Making lemon pie was quite an accomplishment for Grandma. "Don't put too much cornstarch. And stir–no matter how tired you get," she said with pride.

When it came time to eat, I would hear all the different dialect-terms for rice–*kanon, nasi, enapoy, kanin* and *bigas*. "*Saing na*. Start cooking the rice." The manangs all had to learn Tagalog in order to communicate with one another here in America. One could understand why when there were five dialects for rice!

Manang Maria and Grandma Roberta both came from Pampanga and spoke its language with relish. Hungry for the sounds of their very own tongue, they savored and spoke each word reverently, like tones of gold. The others would rattle on in Tagalog, interrupting only to tell the two Pampanga manangs to quiet down or to translate once in a while, especially if it sounded like they were missing out on some juicy gossip. The manangs vibrated with charm, warmth and delight as they socialized and played cards. They were also tough and crafty gamblers.

During the game, they told stories about their lives, their struggle to live in America, their feelings of isolation, of being cut off from their families during World War II. They often felt unwanted in their new country and longed for the love and affection of their families so far away.

"*Mahirap dito sa Amerika*. Life is difficult in America," they said. But there was also acceptance, a resolve to persevere. "I might never go back to the Philippines."

"I will die here."

"I stay with my husband."

"I must stay here to keep flowers on his grave."

I savored their feisty good humor and love of life which ensured their survival.

After much eating, chattering and several "Oy, my goodnesses," out came packages of cigarettes and cigars. They lit up, and the room became a silent haze of malodorous smoke. The game became exciting as the betting got intense. The silence was a blessed relief from the noisy chatter. The stakes were high, $50 to $200 was the norm. Cigarettes and cigars were held secure between the manangs' lips, some to one side of the mouth, others in the center moving up and down as the manangs giggled, talked and made bets. "*Makita kita*. I'll see you and raise $20."

I watched, captivated by their smoking—backwards, with the lighted end inside their mouths. How did they do that, I thought. The ashes didn't drop in their mouths and their tongues didn't burn. As they talked and laughed, cigarettes moved around their lips to the tempo of the chatter, the money piled high in the center. Still, no burning tongues.

"Alam mo is Macario, you know Macario, he ran away with a young dalaga, lass." They laughed, pulling the cigars out of their mouths in time to drop the long ashes into ashtrays, concentrating on seven-card stud, three down and four up.

One day I heard the manangs talking about a family. "*Maraming anak si Anna*. Anna has so many children. *Ang asawa, si Joey, walang trabaho*. Her husband Joey lost his job." I learned later that the manangs helped Anna and Joey buy food and clothing and pay rent with their winnings. The manangs also sent money home to the Philippines regularly to support their families. Winning was not just for themselves, but for others, and they expected nothing in return.

Many Filipinos, like the manangs, shared their resources with the Filipino community. Their homes were open to the Filipino men (later called manongs), who traveled back and forth from California farms to Alaskan fisheries, and often barred from staying in hotels and motels and eating in many restaurants. Often, these farm workers gave Grandma crates of fresh vegetables and fruits, like asparagus and tomatoes from Stockton. She and I would divide and pack them up to share with the manangs. After the poker game, each had a bag full to take home and they would reciprocate by leaving a *balato*, a tip, for the manongs.

The manangs mothered us children. We greeted them with hugs and kisses. Sometimes they asked me and my sister, Rosita, and cousin Rosario to play the piano or violin or sing for them. They took great interest in our development and school accomplishments. When they checked our report cards, they "ooh'd" and "aah'd," praising us highly to our delight and awarded us *balato*, pin money from their "Oy, my goodness.

"Here, this is for your lunch at school. You should not go hungry."

Or, "Spend this on books." I ran as fast as I could to the nearest comic book store.

"You must learn all you can. Education is important." Grandma proudly told them, "*Masipag sila*. They are hardworking." The manangs smiled with pride and called us *magandang dalagas*, beautiful young women, and we beamed as Grandma looked on approvingly. Sometimes there would be a new dress or shoes bought with the winnings from the manangs, especially when Grandma lost heavily. It would have been impolite for us to refuse the money or gifts.

At times, to ease their guilt and perhaps to salve their Catholic conscience, they would say, "Now, Ebanghelina, we want you to be good girl—no smoking, no drinking and no gambling. Very bad habit. Don't be like us. You be good woman." Little did they know, I learned great poker strategy from them despite their preaching. (To this day it is my favorite game, and my own grandchildren Joshua, Quiana, and Brielle, and I look forward to our mountain retreats every year so we can play like the manangs of long ago. It's poker chips, good food, but no smoking backwards, of course.)

During one game of five-card draw, I marveled at a loving maneuver of hands. Manang Nening said, "I open with $5." Manang Oping raised $10. Manang Maria upped the bet another $20. After a long pause, Manang Agapita blurted out, "*Makita kita!*" and ambivalently she raised $30. Manang Oping kicked her under the table. They continued playing. Soon there was a huge mound of bills and coins in the pot. Standing behind them. I caught a glimpse of the cards. One was holding a full house, another two pairs and another a straight. Then, with craft and skill, they purposely folded one by one so that Manang Rosario was left with the "winning" hand, a pair of tens. They had known she didn't have enough money to pay the PG&E and to buy groceries for the rest of the month. Her "Oy, my goodness" was music to their ears.

As the years passed, one by one the manangs folded. There were four and then three left to place their bets. I heard the last "Oy, my goodness" of the angels as they swooped down and opened their arms to scoop up to heaven the last remaining manang—my grandmother, Roberta.

9-28   VANGIE BUELL, LEFT IN FRONT ROW, 1947

QUESTION: In many cultures, women elders share a special bond and get together on a regular basis. Is this bonding among women elders part of your own cultural tradition? Think what the bond would have been for "manangs," the offspring of African Americans and Filipinos who grew up in America. What of the connections between these women in Oakland feels familiar to you; which are completely new?

9-29   VAL-MAR MOVIE THEATRE, GEORGIA ST. VALLEJO, 1945

The movies reflected the political biases of the studios that made them. Stories of struggling workers were made by Warner Brothers (where my relatives worked and I met stars at company picnics); stories of the wealthy were made by MGM, who had made the false newsreels that defeated Upton Sinclair.

People went to the movies to be inspired and to escape. Every town had at least one movie house like Napa's Uptown Theatre, which opened in 1937 with 1,200 seats. The theatre featured a central ceiling painted with a heavenly scene of angels. Former manager Thomas Malloy describes the "well-trained team of young ladies in matching uniforms" who served as usherettes. Every Saturday a new movie would be shipped to the theatre, together with a newsreel and a cartoon. Special morning matinees were scheduled for swing-shift workers from Mare Island Naval Shipyard and Basalt Rock Company.

Malloy recalls:

> After Pearl [Harbor] was bombed it was a wild time here. The manning of Monticello Road as a lookout, the presence of Mare Island, made Napans uneasy about being a potential enemy target. It was trying times, and people were looking for an outlet, to get away from things. So they went to the movies.[xxiv]

[xxiv]Rebecca Yerger, interview with Thomas Malloy, "The Movie Man," *Napa Register*, March 23, 2001.

QUESTION: What movies have inspired you? Can people find escape and inspiration on television as they used to at the movies? Do you think movie theatres will survive?

10

"You Are Helping to Make History": World War II, 1941–1946

You came out to California, put on your pants and took your lunch pail to a man's job

—Sybil Lewis, from The Home Front: America during World War II

World War II was the last war that had no significant opposition from the American people; it was also the last war to date to be formally declared by Congress. All Californians felt connected to the war; some listened intently to President Franklin Roosevelt's radio addresses, others watched newsreels at the movies every Saturday, and still others planted "Victory Gardens." Food rationing began in 1943. Commercially packed fruits, vegetables, juices, and soups were rationed, as well as coffee, meat, cheese, shoes (three pairs per year), and pressure cookers. Women received books of ration stamps that could be traded. The few restaurants that existed had to submit their menus to the ration board to prove that they were within limits. This chapter traces the very different experiences of Californians on the home front during World War II.

10-1 AIR RAID WARNING

WHAT TO DO IN AN AIR RAID

1. In any air raid or blackout, take cover immediately.
    a. If you are away from home, get off the street. You are 10 times safer in a building than standing or walking on the street. If you are in a car, pull to the side of the road immediately. DO NOT double park. Keep clear of fire plugs. Get out of the car, bus or streetcar and take shelter.
    b. If you are home, take immediate blackout precautions. Extinguish all lights. Have your fire protection equipment ready. Go to your blackout room (it should be the safest room in your home.) Stay away from windows. Bomb explosions shatter glass for considerable distances.
2. Don't use the telephone. Remember, those persons who have been trained to protect you—the air raid wardens, fire wardens, fire watchers, auxiliary firemen, auxiliary police and many others—MUST be able to get really important messages through. Your personal calls will have to wait until after the all clear signal.

3. If you are caught in the open lie down on your stomach. You are twice as safe lying down as standing up.

4. If incendiary bombs fall, play a coarse spray of water on them. Put out the fires started by the incendiaries first then devote your attention to the bomb. The coarse spray of water burns the bomb up faster. A heavy jet, stream or bucket of water will make the bomb explode. If you have no way of treating the bomb with water, cover with dry sand. Then with a blunt-nosed shovel scoop throw bomb onto a pile of sand, dump the sand and bomb in a pail; take it outside.

5. Remember, obey your air raid warden and other members of the United States Citizens Defense Corp. They are trying to help you.

6. Above all—keep cool—stay home—put out lights—take shelter—lie down—stay away from windows. You can help.

WHAT TO DO IN A GAS ATTACK

1. Serious injury may result from exposure to liquid gas which may fall from airplanes. It is, therefore, imperative to remain indoors and keep the windows closed.

2. War gases are heavier than air. If you are inside a building remain there, and, if possible, go upstairs. Do not complicate the military effort by leaving your house unless circumstances make if absolutely necessary. If you are outside and not able to immediately go indoors, walk—do not run—get out of the gas area. Avoid puddles of liquid gas, basements, valleys and other low places.

3. If the windows of your room are broken, go to another room or get out of the building.

4. If you have been exposed to a war gas—

   a. Breathe through cloths wet with baking soda solution.
   b. If you can go inside a building, do so, but first remove your outer clothing and leave it outside.
   c. Wash your hands and then your face with laundry soap and water.
   d. Wash your eyes at once with a large amount a solution of baking soda; one teaspoonful of baking soda in a glass of water.
   e. Take a bath, using plenty of laundry soap.
   f. Wash your eyes again with baking soda solution.

5. If splashes of liquid gas have gotten on you—

   a. Using small pieces of cloth, cleansing tissue or toilet paper, blot up as much of the liquid as you can being careful not to spread it.
   b. Daub the contaminated area with cloths wet with clorox, purex, sani-clor, etc.
   c. Steps B, C, D, E and F in 4 above.

6. Do not get excited. Lie down and cover yourself a blanket help. Your air raid warden will summon medical. There is no immediate serious danger from exposure any known war gas if you follow these simple rules.

10-2   GERI DIGIORNIO, *"SO WHAT'S THE WORST THAT COULD HAPPEN?"*

upstairs blackout curtains
hung from our windows
sometimes
on moonless nights
we'd hide under our pillows
listening for planes
as sirens wailed
or peer into
the black on black
looking for some image
seeing the phantom whiteness
of the air-raid captain's hat

in the daylight
we studied aircraft
so we'd know our own
and bought war stamps at school

10-3   AKEMI KIKUMURA, EXCERPT FROM *THROUGH HARSH WINTERS: THE LIFE OF A JAPANESE IMMIGRANT WOMAN*, 1942–1944

After the Japanese bombed Pearl Harbor in 1941, President Roosevelt ordered Civilian Exclusion Order Number Five, requiring all people whose parents had emigrated from countries that were at war with America to register at the local post office. Following registration, German and Italian Americans generally were put under house arrest; however, Japanese Americans were ordered out of their homes and into "relocation centers." The Cortez community, which we met in Chapter 9, was relocated to Amache Relocation Camp in Colorado. Remember Elaine Yoneda from her account of the San Francisco Longshoreman's strike? Yoneda chose to be interned during World War II, rather than be separated from her Japanese American husband, Karl Yoneda.

Two-thirds of the Japanese who were relocated were American citizens, but the U.S. Supreme Court handed down decisions upholding the relocation, including the *Korematsu, Hirabayshi,* and *Endo* decisions. Not all judges agreed. In his dissent, Justice Frank Murphy wrote that the exclusion orders had gone "over the very brink of constitutional power . . . into the ugly abyss of racism."[i] In Mitsuye Endo's case, the court decided that detention was unconstitutional, but it declined to rule whether the government had exceeded its war powers in mandating the evacuation of Californians.[ii]

---

[i]See Peter Irons, *Justice Delayed: The Record of the Japanese American Internment Cases* (1989).

[ii]See Lawson Fusao Inada (ed.), *Only What We Could Carry: The Japanese American Internment Experience* (Berkeley: Heyday Books), 2000.

We stayed in Stockton Assembly Center for two or three months until the camps in Arkansas were ready. We traveled there by train with the shades drawn down. It was better that way because quite a few Japanese people were killed by Americans before we were interned.

People closely affiliated with Japan were rounded up and imprisoned earlier. There was a young Japanese man in our town who told the FBI everything. He received money for being a rat. People said after the war they would kill him. The FBI also approached me and offered to pay me money but I said, "What are you talking about! You're crazy!" But that young man told. I would never do anything like that—tell on others to pull them down. Even if your mouth is rotten, you should never be a spy. No matter how poor I was, even if I couldn't eat tomorrow, I could not be that rotten. My lips were sealed tightly but there were people who told. A person must be human. You can't say things about others that would bring them down . . . even for money.

My biggest worry had been money for food and shelter. In camp that burden was wiped out. The government fed us and gave us a monthly allowance for $10.50. Food came out from early morning. The camp was divided into blocks and each block had a big kitchen. Everyone lined up to eat in the mess hall. Do you know what they fed us at the beginning? Corned beef and cabbage every day. Then it slowly changed.

People tried to think of things to occupy their spare time. There were English classes, flower-arrangement classes, and dance classes. They asked me to teach Japanese, but I didn't because I was pregnant again. It looks bad when you're already old [age 40] and pregnant. The pregnancy was hard on me physically but I had nothing but good thoughts.

One day our block would have a talent show, the next day a different block. Papa got pulled from block to block. They called for him constantly. He was never home to fight with. What an actor he was! When they did plays, he would always perform in them. No one could sing *Yasuki Busbi* [a Japanese folk song] better than he: Everybody said that. He would sing among thousands . . . even a professional would have run away barefooted from stage fright. When I was young . . . I always remember thinking how good he was.

The winters were cold, but we had a big stove. A fire was always burning. People went to the mountains and collected wood. They carved and polished the wood, making *obutsudans* [Buddhist altars], drawers, chairs, all sorts of things. No matter which way you faced, there were mountains. You couldn't tell which direction was east or west. Many got lost and search parties went out to look for them. There were quite a few who died there.

I grew vegetables. Everyone grew them in front of their barracks. Watermelons, eggplants, sweet potatoes . . . everything grew well. The soil was rich because no one had grown things there before. That's why Papa wanted to stay and farm.

There were two factions in camp: one who said they would stay in America, and another who said they wanted to return to Japan. About half returned to Japan. I didn't want to return to Japan. America was my home. I know I made the right decision.

In camp the Yamaguchis asked for Nesan. There were many seekers after her hand in marriage. But we knew the Yamaguchis back in. Liberty. Everyone knew the Yamaguchis. There were *bigu shatsu* [big shots]. Although they were one of the wealthiest families in Liberty, we didn't gain anything from marriage: we just lost a daughter.

We couldn't have a real wedding because it was camp time. Just the immediate relatives attended. I think Hana got married to the Maedas in camp too, but I can't remember any more.

Before the War ended, we left the camp with the Yamaguchis. We promised that we would grow food toward the war effort and they let us go. Several families left at the same time. We were already there for two years. . . .

10-4   MITSUYE ENDO, JAPANESE AMERICAN INTERNEE WHO SUCCESSFULLY SUED THAT HER DETENTION WAS UNCONSTITUTIONAL

QUESTION: Before every feature film, American moviegoers watched newsreels warning against the "Japs." In this atmosphere of fear, most Californians accepted the internment of Japanese Americans as necessary. Do you think Californians would ever again accept internment of an ethnic group deemed potentially dangerous by the government?

Because so many American citizens were employed in the war effort in the 1940s, growers persuaded the American government to create a "guest worker," or bracero, program in California to supplement the supply of workers. This program lasted from 1942 to 1964.

10-5 LUIS VEGA WITH HIS WIFE JOSEFINA VEGA-CUEVAS AND FAMILY, c. 1942

Luis Vega came to Calistoga as a bracero worker. Braceros were not allowed to join unions, and their resulting status as cheap labor was often useful to employers in preventing organizing of other immigrant workers. When the bracero program ended, daughter Emma Vega became one of the first members of Cesar Chavez's United Farm Workers Union.

10-6 GARY SOTO, "A RED PALM"

You're in this dream of cotton plants.
You raise a hoe, swing, and the first weeds
Fall with a sigh. You take another step,
Chop, and the sigh comes again,

Until you yourself are breathing that way
With each step, a sigh that will follow you into town.

That's hours later. The sun is a red blister.
Coming up in your palm. Your back is strong,
Young, not yet the broken chair
In an abandoned school of dry spiders.
Dust settles on your forehead, dirt
Smiles under each fingernail.
You chop, step, and by the end of the first row,
You can buy one splendid fish for wife
And three sons. Another row, another fish,
Until you have enough and move on to milk,
Bread, meat. Ten hours and the cupboards creak.
You can rest in the back yard under a tree.
Your hands twitch on your lap,
Not unlike the fish on a pier or the bottom
Of a boat. You drink iced tea. The minutes jerk
Like flies.

It's dusk, now night,
And the lights in your home are on.
That costs money, yellow light
In the kitchen. That's thirty steps,
You say to your hands,
Now shaped into binoculars.
You could raise them to your eyes:
You were a fool in school, now look at you.
You're a giant among cotton plants.
Now you see your oldest boy, also running.
Papa, he says, it's time to come in.

You pull him into your lap
And ask, What's forty times nine?
He knows as well as you, and you smile.
The wind makes peace with the trees,
The stars strike themselves in the dark.
You get up and walk with the sigh of cotton plants.
You go to sleep with a red sun on your palm,
The sore light you see when you first stir in bed.

QUESTION: How does Gary Soto help us understand what it feels like to do farm labor?
Which line(s) stand out for you and why?

10-7   FILIPINO MEN SERVING IN A SEGREGATED REGIMENT, THE FILIPINO INFANTRY BATTALION, FORT ORD, c. 1945

In addition to the Navy, some Filipinos served in one of the Army's all Filipino regiments. Faustino Bacus of Vallejo is pictured here in the middle of this 1940 photograph at Fort Ord. A member of the U.S. Army's Filipino Infantry Battalion, Bacus was at Fort Ord for Army training. (Courtesy of Pat Bacol Mendoza.)

10-8   FILIPINO BROWNIE TROOP FORMED IN 1942 IN VALLEJO BECAUSE FILIPINO GIRLS WERE NOT ALLOWED TO PARTICIPATE WITH THE WHITE BROWNIES

Mel Orpilla describes the journey of his father and uncles from the Philippines to America in the mid-1920s:

> Their life here would be one of hard work, years as unmarried men, and finally the happiness of raising a family. . . . Many lived in boarding houses in old Vallejo during the pre–World War II years. The other men living in the boarding houses became their compadres for life. Growing up, I called them either "uncle" or ninong.[iii]

[iii]Mel Orpilla, "And Then There was One," in Helen Toribio (ed.), *Seven Card Stud with Seven Manangs Wild* (San Francisco: T'boli Publishing), 2002.

Prior to the Japanese invasion of the Philippines, one could see signs that read "Dogs and Filipinos positively not allowed" throughout the West Coast. However, after Americans fought alongside Filipinos against the Japanese, a significant shift occurred in attitudes toward Filipinos. The Chinese Exclusion Act was repealed in 1943, allowing people of Chinese ancestry to become American citizens, and in 1946 Filipino emigrants became eligible, finally, for American citizenship.

Because Mel Orpilla's father served as a steward in the Navy during World War II, "he was allowed to bring a wife to America as a non-quota immigrant, according to the War Brides Act passed in 1946. He met, fell in love with, and proposed to my mother through letters."[iv] Filipino Americans, Latinos, African Americans, and Japanese Americans all enlisted and served enthusiastically in the war effort, each in segregated units. Mary Helen Ponce gives us a vivid account of her segregation experience at the Saturday movies.

A Filipino Brownie troop was formed in 1942 because Filipino girls were not allowed to participate with the "white" Brownies. Among the members are Pat and Juanita Bacol, Ester and Lilly Reyes, and Lydia Guilling. (Courtesy of Pat Bacol Mendoza.)

[iv]Mel Orpilla, *Filipinos in Vallejo* (Charleston, South Carolina: Arcadia Publishing), 2004, 33.

10-9   MARY ELLEN PONCE, "CHOCHIS AND THE MOVIES AT SANFER," 1984

I remember when as children we attended movies in the nearby town of San Fernando, where of the two movie theaters, Mexicans were welcome in one, the San Fernando Theater. The other, El Rennie Theater, catered to Anglos and was off limits to the *chicanada* of Pacoima and Sanfer. It was not until World War II and soon after that Mexican-Americans (as we were then known) were allowed to patronize local movie houses and restaurants. Many barrio men were wounded, killed and decorated while fighting for their country, the good ole USA. It was not considered patriotic to turn away non-whites in uniform so we were let inside. However, by the time we were admitted to the Rennie Theater we had already chosen to attend el San Fernando Theater, where the owner, Mort, was friendly and made us feel welcome. Mort was Jewish, and tolerant of other minorities. He was a good businessman, but more than that, he was kind to Mexican people. For the Mexican-Americans of Pacas and Sanfer, the place to go for fun on a Sunday afternoon was el Towne, on Brand Street.

The "draw" to the special Sunday matinees were the weekly serials. We took the long bus ride and then stood in line, eager to see the latest escapades of the blonde heroine of *The Perils of Pauline*, and the curvaceous girl who was Nyoka of the Jungle. Both young women were usually caught up in adventures that had us sitting on the edge of our seats, gasping from excitement. The movie would end with Pauline and Nyoka on the brink of death as they waited to be rescued by the handsome hero who later reappeared in other episodes. When the words "to be continued next week" flashed on the screen we sank back in our seats, exhausted but exhilarated. We exited the theatre, and on the way to the bus stop, we talked of nothing else but the coming episode, and of our plans to return the following Sunday.

My friends faithfully attended the movies. I went once in a while. Most of the families of Pacoima (like ours) were of the working-class, with large families and little money to spend frivolously. We rarely had spending money, other than a few pennies and *cincos* earned from returning bottles to La Tienda de Don Jesus; yet my father was forever fixing our house, putting up a new fence, and my mother made sure we had "church clothes." Perhaps what we had were different values.

I remember some of my friends lived in run-down homes yet always had spending money, and went often to the movies. Not until I was older did I realize our parents' first priorities were to feed, clothe, and provide a comfortable home for us. There was little money left over for fun. When on Sundays I saw my friends walking to the bus stop on the way to the "show," I was filled with envy but only for a minute. In time I was more grateful for our home with the white picket fence and well-tended rose bushes.

Although none of my friends dated or went steady, by the time we were twelve or so, we made arrangements to "sit" at the movies with someone we liked. One year, George Sanchez, or Chochis as his mother called him, asked me to go with him to a matinee. I wasn't too thrilled as Chochis was *un gordito*. The fact that I too was chubby was of no consequence to me. I mean we didn't have to be *gordinflones*.

It was fun to "sit" with George. He ate all during the movie. Popcorn, peanuts and candy. He would load up before the movie, during intermission, and just before the movie ended. To be with him was to partake in a continuous feed. Food was happiness for Chochis, and for me, happiness was sitting with him.

There was a certain amount of security in being with Chochis. He was content to stuff himself all during the movie so that he never had time to get fresh with me. All he ever did was put his arm around me. One arm on my shoulder, the other entwined around a big bag of buttered popcorn. While the other girls were busy fighting off *los frescos*, I munched contentedly throughout the entire movie, mesmerized by the antics of Pauline and Nyoka, secure with an array of Baby Ruths, Milk Duds and Snickers.

The movies included war news of World War II. These were in black and white, produced by Pathe News. Scenes of battles, soldiers and tanks flashed on the screen: fighting men of the USA! Although we were interested in the fighting overseas, the war seemed far away. The war news appeared to be another movie, part of the entertainment offered to youngsters on a Sunday afternoon.

One time during intermission a short propaganda movie was shown. This included a funny jingle, which the audience was urged to sing. The words evade me now, but sounded like this:

Stinky Jap, off the map

Benito's jaw, oh ho ho

The song was an allusion to the enemy, the Japanese and Mussolini. We sang several verses, all funny and clever. I stopped eating long enough to sing along. I liked to sing and didn't want to miss either the words or beat. We sang and sang. The theater rocked with shouts of laughter and jeers. Aha, ha ha.

I remember thinking it was wrong to be making fun of the Japanese. We were not exactly blonde and blue-eyed. We were brown. Light and dark brown, but nonetheless, brown. *Morenos, trigueños, prietos.* Not white enough to be accepted in the predominately white Rennie Theater but able to laugh at others who, like our ancestors, had fought a war against this country, men who were mocked and called "dirty Mexicans," not "dirty Japs."

When this "short" was not screened again I was grateful as I felt uncomfortable laughing at other minorities. My parents were not racist, and neither were we kids. I think Mort disliked the movie too, as we never saw it again. As I said, he was a nice man.

QUESTION: Have you ever witnessed racial stereotyping and not known how to respond, as Mary Ellen did at the movies? What else could she have done?

10-10 VLADIMIR SHKURKIN, "HELPING TO MAKE HISTORY," VALLEJO, c. 1940, DESIGNED TO INSPIRE PARTICIPATION IN WAR EFFORT AT MARE ISLAND

HELPING TO MAKE HISTORY. No other event in Vallejo's history had a greater impact than World War II. Mare Island played a critical role in the war effort as thousands of people labored around the clock building and repairing ships at the navy yard. Workers were urged to redouble their efforts with inspiring, patriotic banners like the one shown here, painted by artist Vladimir Shkurkin.

10-11 MARGARET ALMSTROM, WELDER AT MARE ISLAND, c. 1943

Former welder Margaret Almstrom described her wartime experiences to me one hot afternoon: "All the girls I went with wanted to be welders and I didn't. I wanted to drive a truck." She tells how one friend got her into welding by a small trick of raising her hand behind Margaret's head. Next thing she heard was, "All the welders and YOU (Margaret) come with the lady boss to be trained to weld."

Ahlstrom started at third class; first class earned $10/hour. She wore jeans at Mare Island Naval Shipyard and describes it as the only place you didn't have to wear a dress. She recalls with a smile how a male welder got angry with her and raised her helmet to expose her eyes to the flames, impairing her vision for several days. Almstrom worked at Mare Island until the war ended. She was offered a job welding lightweight material after the war, but "I couldn't keep my spark down low." At the age of eighty, she comments wistfully, "When I see a sign saying 'welder wanted,' I always wonder if I would be able to strike up a weld."[v]

Margaret Almstrom was also a welder at Mare Island in the 1940s.

---

[v]Interviewed by Lauren Coodley, June 2003.

More than a million African Americans left the South during the war, and eighty-five percent of those migrants came to California for employment opportunities.[vi] As Douglas Daniels notes, the war created the San Francisco Bay Area's first Black working-class population.[vii] African American women were employed in blue-collar jobs where they found decent pay and a sense of companionship with fellow workers, which they hoped to maintain when the war ended.

10-12 FANNY WALKER MEMOIR, *ILWU DISPATCHER*, FEBRUARY 1996

'The treatment of black people by the whites changed a lot on account of the union.'

I was born in Louisiana in 1904. My grandmother raised me; my grandfather was a sharecropper. I come up pretty hard. You worked in the fields in early morning and evening, when it was cool. I was 12 when I started. Growing up, I did housework. You didn't make but a dollar and a half a week. The first job I had was 25 cents a week washing dishes for two old maids.

I came to California in 1940, got a job at Colgate in 1942, and retired there after 28 years. At first I worked on a conveyor machine packing washing powder and soap. You'd case so many hours and make boxes so many hours.

We had really nice foremen. They had to be nice to you because you were in the ILWU! When foremen would be nasty in different departments, the union steward went to bat for you. When different foremen would be sort of high style because they wanted to make a name, they just couldn't because the ILWU cut'em down pretty close.

I was the first black woman at Colgate. Early on, the white women had little mean things they would do. You'd put your lunch on the table; they'd take your lunch off the table. They would put your food on the floor. So I just went and put mine on the table. I said, "Now, the first one put my lunch on the floor, I'm gonna fight." So then they let me alone. I told them, "I'm going to stay here. You're not going to make me quit." The next day, this girl brought me a sweater. We were friends from then on.

The treatment of black people by the whites changed a lot. It changed a lot on account of the union, because they had stewards in different departments. If anything went wrong, you'd report it to your steward.

[vi]San Francisco's Black population alone increased by 600% between 1940 and 1945—from 5,000 to 43,000.

[vii]Preface, Douglas Henry Daniels, *Pioneer Urbanites: A Social and Cultural History of Black San Francisco* (Philadelphia), 1980, xvii.

10-13 PARADE, VALLEJO. THIS FLOAT WAS SPONSORED BY THE MARE ISLAND EX-APPRENTICE ASSOCIATION, c. 1943

BOND RALLIES AND PARADES. Vallejoans were urged to support the war effort by buying war bonds. Bond rallies in Vallejo and at Mare Island often featured popular entertainers encouraging those in attendance to purchase bonds. Local movie theaters offered free admission with each bond sold.

10-14 MAXINE MEYERS, LETTERS, *RICHMOND TIMES*, OCTOBER 11, 2000

Meyers, who worked in the Richmond shipyards as a welder, saved many of the letters she sent to her husband serving overseas during the war. Excerpts from two are below.

June 15, 1944

Dearest Baby,

Last night at 8 we launched our first Victory ship. Of course, I didn't get to see it go down the ways as that time is swing-time, but I went aboard last night, or rather, this morning at about 5:30. She's a honey! You should see how pretty she is. Much nicer than the Liberties, and bigger, too. It's the USS Sarasota. This morning when work slowed down from a drag to a complete stop (at least my part of it), I left the assembly and went down to the outfitting dock to give her the once over.

Gee, I've never seen so many little rooms in all my life. Back aft on the first deck is some sort of structure that looks like one of those modern houses you see pictures of. You know the type . . . flat top with oblong porch. "Veddy" classy, but I don't know what it's for. Oh, there is just worlds of work to be done on it yet, and I don't see how they will ever get all the junk out of the engine room so that the men can get around in there, but I guess they will.

It was on the ways for 57 days, which isn't bad for the first new ship, and considering, too, that it is 40 feet longer and 10 feet wider (it looks wider than that to me) and a deck higher than the Liberties, which take an average 21 days on the ways.

At the end of the assembly where I work is a wooden fence about 7 feet high, and by sitting on this fence you can look across the bay and see the lights on the Oakland-San Francisco bridge and see the cars going into San Francisco. Last night after dinner, I climbed on the top rail of that fence and looked out over the dark bay to the gay lights beyond. Overhead was a lovely moon just wasting itself on the shipyard. The bay, as I looked across it, reminded me of the ocean that separates us . . .

May 8, 1945

My darling lover,

V-E Day! Isn't it wonderful? Of course, it would be much better if it were V-J Day but this will hasten Japan's defeat. Oh, darling, I'm so very glad that the war in Europe has ended. I cannot realize it yet as it does not seem possible, yet I know it's true. It's like that black day almost a month ago when we heard the sad news that our beloved President died. It just doesn't seem possible. We have been at war so very long that it's hard to believe Germany is at long last beaten. What a happy day it will be the day Japan suffers a likewise defeat! . . .

We were dogging down under the unit on Assembly No. 1 at 6 this morning when a flanger called to the flanger I was working with and said we could quit working and come up to hear the speech of President Truman. Just about the time I came up from under the assembly, Truman started his announcement. I ran down the road by the assembly to get nearer to the loudspeaker so as to hear better.

The yard was quiet. People stopped working and listened silently as Truman declared today to be V-E Day. After his speech they played the National Anthem and I bowed my head and cried while my thoughts were with you. After the band played the National Anthem, they read a wire from Kaiser who urged us to stay on the job, and not celebrate until Japan was whipped. Then, they played some more music.

I walked back to the assembly and the flanger I had been working for brought me a cold drink. Someone had smuggled whiskey and chasers into the yard because it was common knowledge that at 6 o'clock the news would be announced. Naturally, I did not drink any whiskey. In fact, wasn't even offered any. But I drank part of Pepsi-Cola but I don't like them. We did no more work the rest of the morning. We stood around and talked about the surrender and laughed and were glad that the war with Germany was over. What a happy, happy day it will be when the war with Japan is over. I love you, and I want to be with you. . . .

10-15 DUE TO MEAT RATIONING, THE GOVERNMENT AUTHORIZED SALE OF HORSEMEAT FOR HUMANS. MELVIN ROSSI OPENED THIS MARKET AT 717 MARIN STREET, VALLEJO, IN MARCH 1943

10-16 SYBIL LEWIS, A BLACK ROSIE THE RIVETER

When I first arrived in Los Angeles, I began to look for a job. I decided I didn't want to do maid work anymore, so I got a job as a waitress in a small black restaurant. I was making pretty good money, more money than I had in Sapulpa, but I didn't have the knack for getting good tips. Then I saw an ad in the newspaper offering to train women for defense work. I went to Lockheed Aircraft and applied. The said they'd call me, but I never got a response, so I went back and applied again. You had to be pretty persistent. Finally they accepted me. They gave me a short training program and taught me how to rivet. Then they put me to work in the plant riveting small airplane parts, mainly gasoline tanks.

The women worked in pairs. I was the riveter, and this big strong white girl from a cotton farm in Arkansas worked as the bucker. The riveter used a gun to shoot rivets through the metal and fasten it together. The bucker used a bucking bar on the other side of the metal to smooth out the rivets. Bucking was harder than shooting rivets; it required more muscle. Riveting required more skill.

I worked for a while as a riveter with this white girl, when the boss came around one day and said, "We've decided to make some changes." At this point he assigned her to do the riveting and me to do the bucking. I wanted to know why. He said, "Well, we just interchange once in a while." But I was never given the riveting job back. That was the first encounter I had with segregation in California, and it didn't sit too well with me. It brought back some of my experiences in Sapulpa—you're a Negro, so you do the hard work. I wasn't failing as a riveter—in fact, the other girl learned to rivet from me—but I felt they gave me the job of bucker because I was black.

So I applied to Douglas Aircraft in Santa Monica and was hired as a riveter there. On that job I did not encounter the same prejudice. As a matter of fact, the foreman was more congenial. But Maywood, where Lockheed was located, was a very segregated city. Going into that city, you were really going into forbidden territory. Santa Monica was not as segregated a community.

I worked in aircraft for a few years, then in '43 I saw an ad in the paper for women trainees to learn arc welding. The salary sounded good, from a dollar to a dollar-twenty-five an hour. I wanted to learn that skill and I wanted to make more money, so I answered the ad and they sent me to a short course at welding school. After I passed the trainee course, they employed me at the shipyards. That was a little different than working in aircraft, because in the shipyard you found mostly men. There I ran into another kind of discrimination: because I was a woman I was paid less than a man for doing the same job.

I was an arc welder, I'd passed both the army and navy tests, and I knew I could do the job, but I found from talking with some of the men that they made more money. You'd ask about this, but they'd say, "Well, you don't have the experience," or "The men have to lift some heavy pieces of steel and you don't have to," but I knew that I had to help lift steel, too.

They started everyone off at a dollar-twenty an hour. There were higher-paying jobs, though, like chippers and crane operators, that were for men only. Once, the foreman told me I had to go on the skids—the long docks along the hull. I said, "That sounds pretty dangerous. Will I make more than one-twenty an hour?" And he said, "No, one-twenty is the top pay you'll get." But the men got more.

It was interesting that although they didn't pay women as well as men, the men treated you differently if you wore slacks. I noticed, for example, that when you'd get on the bus or the streetcar, you stood all the way, more than the lady who would get on with a dress. I never could understand why men wouldn't give women in slacks a seat. At the shipyards the language wasn't the best. Nobody respected you enough to clean up the way they spoke. It didn't seem to bother the men that you were a woman. During the war years men began to say, "You have a man's job and you're getting paid almost the same, so we don't have to give you a seat anymore, or show you the common courtesies that men show women." All those little niceties were lost.

I enjoyed working at the shipyard: it was a unique job for a woman, and I liked the challenge. But it was a dangerous job. The safety measures were very poor. Many people were injured by falling steel. Finally I was assigned to a very hazardous area and I asked to be transferred into a safer area. I was not granted that. They said, "You have to work where they assign you at all times." I thought it was getting too dangerous, so I quit.

The war years had a tremendous impact on women. I know for myself it was the first time I had a chance to get out of the kitchen and work in industry and make a few bucks. This was something I had never dreamed would happen. In Sapulpa all that women had to look forward to was keeping house and raising families. The war years offered new possibilities. You came out to California, put on your pants and took your lunch pail to a man's job. In Oklahoma a woman's place was in the home, and man went to work and provided. This was the beginning of women's feeling that they could do something more. We were trained to do this kind of work because of the war, but there was no question that this was an interim period. We were all told that when the war was over we would not be needed anymore.

10-17 JOSEPH JAMES, WHO CAMPAIGNED FOR FAIR TREATMENT FOR AFRICAN AMERICAN WORKERS, SINGING AT THE LAUNCHING OF A SHIP AT MARINSHIP YARD, SAUSALITO, 1943

James was a leader in the efforts of black shipyard workers to win equal treatment in the Bay Area. He came to San Francisco as a singer in 1939, was hired at Marinship in 1942, and by 1943 he had become an expert welder. He performed regularly as a singer at Marinship launchings as well. James led a struggle to strengthen the Boilermakers Union "by insisting that Blacks be granted full and equal membership rights," according to historian Chuck Wollenberg.[viii]

On November 27, 1943, Joseph James and a group of almost 800 workers protested at the Marinship Yard, an event described by the local paper as "Marin's greatest labor demonstration . . . since the San Francisco General Strike in the summer of 1934."[ix] Eventually the argument went to the California Supreme Court as *James v. Marinship*. The court ruled in favor of James and his colleagues in January 1945. By then James was president of the San Francisco chapter of the National Association for the Advancement of Colored People (NAACP).

[viii]Charles Wollenberg, "*James vs. Marinship*: Trouble on the New Black Frontier, *California History*, Fall 1981, 269.

[ix]*San Rafael Daily Independent*, November 27, 1943.

10-18 ETHEL MAE GARY, OAKLAND, 1945

Ashlee Gary writes:

> This is my grandmother, Ethel Mae Gary, Magnolia Street, Oakland, 1945. . . . She and my grandfather moved to California where they bought a house and raised their six children, where she still lives and still wears that same look of honesty and wisdom. She is our family treasure and holds us together.[x]

---

[x]Ashlee Gary, Faces of America Photo Contest, Napa College, 2000.

10-19 BILLIE ROBERTS HENDRICKS AND DAUGHTER SALLIE, FEBRUARY 1945

10-20 INTERVIEW WITH BILLIE HENDRICKS, MARCH 2005

I grew up on an Iowa farm. I'm 76 now. My mother was the only one of eight children not born in a log cabin near Prairie View. My grandmother rode to Iowa in a covered wagon and my grandfather went through the Civil War as a Yank with the Eighth Iowa Cavalry. We've got family trees until it comes out of your ears. Some of my relatives wanted to join the Daughters of the American Revolution (DAR), but I never joined. It's so stuffy!

My parents were married in 1904. They weren't rich, but they owned their farm, 80 acres of corn, oats and livestock in Van Buren County, Iowa. My folks raised me to be a little lady and marry a "professional man." Well, by age 17 the farm was choking me. I would wake up and see the sun come in over the corn field and settle over the corn field. The world was my oyster, but there was nothing to do, just grow up and pick flowers in the summer. We were five miles out of any little town.

I'd read books where you get out and see the world. I wanted to leave the farm, be on my own and go to school. My father wanted me to stay home and raise chickens, but that didn't appeal to me at all. So I went to Lawrence, Kansas where my Aunt Lucy took me in and I went to college. I wanted to be a school teacher. You didn't have to have a college certificate to do that in those days. So I took a teaching job when I was 19 or 20.

For two years I taught grade school in the small Kansas towns of Bayshore and Heifer. I had to sign a paper that I'd go to church at least twice a month. Remember, this was rural America in the 1920s. I was supposed to stay in the village of Bayshore, and I couldn't smoke, get married or go out with high school boys. After I won a $5 box of candy in a local lottery, the school board charged me with gambling. So, when I was invited to my uncle's in Chicago, I went. I took a job there and stayed for 18 months.

In Chicago I met a man who was 20 years my senior. He'd been married several times, once to a silent movie star in Hollywood. He was selling and traveling from coast to coast when he wasn't drinking. He said, "If you want to go to Los Angeles, I'll get you a little house with red roses around it and you can pick oranges off the trees." I quit my job in the middle of the day, got married and came to California!

That's when the big 1929 crash came. The Great Depression shot my husband's sales business. At first I couldn't get a job. I'd go to those big all-night markets they had in Los Angeles, where vegetables were a penny a bunch, if you had the penny. I would go to Elysian Park and look under the trees where the lovers were, and pick around and maybe find a dime.

I finally got a job in a little scab restaurant. Everything in Los Angeles was scab then. Each time I called the order in, the short-order cook would give me a punch on the back side. That incensed me to death. Now, I'd curse him back, after all my years in the ILWU. Then I just went home and told my stuck-up college husband. He said, "You must have encouraged him." Imagine!

We came up to San Francisco in 1932. A lady I knew said, "There's jobs opening in this whiskey place." That was around 1933. The first job I got, and it was before we were organized into the union, was at South End Warehouse. As soon as Prohibition was repealed in late '33 the foreman opened his own place, Distillers Distributing. He asked several of us to go with him, including me, and I went. These were small businesses. It was before the big companies started, like Schenley's and Hiram Walker's.

At South End Warehouse I got 32 cents an hour for eight hours' work, if I was lucky. If you were wanted for a second shift, it was eight hours more at 32 cents an hour. All we got between shifts was coffee, no meals. There was no such thing as hours-a-week or overtime. But mostly, we'd go in and work a few hours and then they'd say, "There are no more orders. Go home." We'd work two hours, sit there and wait two more hours until the mail came, and then go home.

I worked on a line with a big machine, and it would drive you crazy. We pasted labels on whisky flasks and put the bottles in cases, 24 to a case. If you wasn't careful, if the boys didn't get it right, the glass would fly. The floors were wet. You had to wear certain shoes. You wore your own gloves. These were old warehouses. Sometimes they weren't even heated. After they were union you had clean uniforms supplied and you bought your own shoes. They supplied gloves.

Before the union, the women that worked the fastest got to stay the longest. Then the boss would come along and say, "Fire all the old bags, and keep all the pretty ones with pretty legs." Here the poor old gals were working their tails off and needed the money and was better workers. You never knew when you were going to be let out and when you weren't.

When the three-day San Francisco general strike came along in July 1934 everybody was out. The town was ours. We were just on top of the world. Nobody dared tell us we were poor. We knew we were going to win. There was nobody quitting and saying, "We can't make a living, we'll go someplace else." During the long maritime strike, before and after the general strike, I was working at South End Warehouse. When the National Guard patrolled the waterfront following the police killings on "Bloody Thursday," the longshoremen gave me a pass to go through. The women weren't organized yet, but they weren't "anti."

Actually it was our dream to be unionized. Imagine belonging to a group like the longshoremen that stuck up for your rights, saw that you had seniority, and saw that the boss couldn't harrass you or sleep with you. Harry Ludden, the foreman at South End Warehouse, used to say, "Come out to my house tonight." We didn't dare say, "No." We were tired, but when we were invited to the boss' party, we went. Once he made us all get down on our hands and knees and bark like a dog for our state of supper!

The first group of organized warehouses we heard about was the coffee houses. We went down to the hall to get in the union. But the work wasn't too steady. We would go to the hall and be dispatched out to work.

During the years right after the 1934 strike people flocked to the warehouse local. All the Italian women from North Beach rushed down to join the union. Those were the years the longshoremen worked to start other unions going. They inspired everyone. The garment workers and the flour workers were organizing. Everybody wanted to get their home base, just like the longshoremen.

My first union meeting must have been about 1936. The women would just listen back then. We did think our organizers—Gene Paton, who became a wonderful Local 6 president in 1937, Lou Goldblatt, the Heide brothers, Bob Robertson—were "it." And Lou knew how to get things rolling. He started our steward system. But we didn't have much of a voice. The men would make all the rules. There was nothing we could do but be a rubber stamp for them.

Between 1937 and 1942 the women had their own separate meetings. Our male Local 6 leaders weren't much interested in women's problems in those early days. Neither was

Harry, although we were thrilled when he came to meetings. The men thought "the girls" were only going to work until they got married or made some extra money. I was on the Women's Division Executive Board, but we didn't have much real power. We didn't meet with the men until we bellowed. Then we got amalgamated with them. We wanted to be known as workers. I never knew about this Equal Rights Amendment (ERA) business. I always thought I was a worker.

Sometimes when we were dispatched out of the union hall for jobs we were sent to a place that wasn't organized. We would talk union to the workers. Then we would vote to get the union in. We were called "Red Hots" because we organized. The bosses hated us. We had some pretty rough times. Whenever anybody struck, we were on that picket line. This little Judy Anderson always had a long sock with a Sweetheart Soap bar in it. If she was bothered by scabs, they'd get hit with a "sweetheart."

My husband and I divorced before very long. Then I married a man named Roberts. While I was working at Distillers Distributors I became pregnant. When my daughter Sallie was 18 months old, Roberts left me to marry someone else. But by then I had a good Local 6 job and was determined to keep care of my little girl.

I became interested in a group called Working Mothers with Children. As my daughter grew up, for the next seven or eight years, I went to every meeting they had. There were several Local 6 people who were interested in child care, including Tillie Olsen, the famous author, and Hazel Drummond, who wrote a column for *The Dispatcher* in the mid-1940s. We'd meet with the Board of Education and rant and rave about getting a center for working mothers' kids. All the unions sent delegates, including the longshoremen.

Right at the end of 1939 or in 1940 I went over to Schenley's Liquors. It was just starting up. The union wanted volunteers to go in and help organize the place. One of the officers asked me to go. The company was avid to get workers. We just went down and asked for a job. We succeeded in organizing Schenley's into Local 6, too. I'd been working at the MJB Coffee warehouse packing tea bags on a belt line. It was a wrench to give up your seniority in a house, but I did.

When the bosses figured out I was organizing, they called me "that red button girl" and gave me the dirtiest job there was. I was stuck off in this washroom, standing up all the time washing bales and bales of dirty rags with glue on them and then passing them along. When the other workers put the labels on the bottles they had nice clean cloths to wipe the extra glue off. In this job, though, I sometimes got to walk up and down the line and, when I wasn't caught, talk union.

I also got on every Local 6 committee I could. We had a Publicity Committee that put out a little magazine on yellow sheets. We would send these yellow sheets around to everybody so they'd know what the other shops were doing. I was on our Uniform Committee, too. Each of us got a cap and a white, starched uniform for parades. On Labor Day we were out in force on Market Street. We'd pass the reviewing stand and then get a walkaway shrimp cocktail down at the beach. We were the proudest things you ever did see!

Usually when there was a committee meeting I'd take my daughter with me. The Local 6 hall was our second home. Everybody knew Sallie at the union. From nine to four, while I was working at Schenley's, I could leave her at the St. Francis Day Home, which was close to where I lived. It only cost me 35 cents a day. Otherwise Sallie went everywhere with me. Of course, if there was a night meeting or a potentially dangerous situation, someone else would take care of her.

About 1940 there was a particularly rough strike at Euclid Candy Company. We had joined the picket line and were walking back and forth across the company's door when the cops dove in. They weren't nice cops and they were on horseback. We tried to put our arms together and keep walking. They kept pushing with their horses. A horse's hoof almost stepped on my foot. One of our boys had a pocket knife and he gave the horse a job to make it move away.

The Local 10 longshoremen showed up to reinforce the Euclid picket line. They were all in their white hats, work shirts and black jeans. That was kind of an ILWU uniform. The cops saw this one longshoreman I recognized who was always an organizer. They said, "All right, Hendricks, step back." That was the first time I ever heard the name of Hendricks. I thought, "That guy's for me." He wasn't afraid of the devil. At Easter, anybody else would bring his sweetheart an Easter lily. Not Frank Hendricks! He brought an Easter basket with a bunny in it for my baby. We were married in 1943.

When the United States got into World War II in the early 1940s and most of the men went into the service, I took what had been considered a "man's job." I got a marvelous wage and I was now called a receiving clerk. This was at Schenley's. The boss said, "Are you afraid to go downstairs to shipping and receiving, you and Alice Moore?" We weren't. Alice became a shipping clerk. We each got our own little office.

I used to get this solution that came in five gallon cans. It went over the top of the liquor to keep the government stamps intact. I took in supplies for the machine shop, too. All the boys were helpful, although there was one old man who used to say, "Why don't you girls go home and raise your family? Why do you want to do men's work?" What an old son-of-a-gun he was. We had to live, you know?

I was also quite into the blood donor scene during World War II. This was around 1944–1945. They needed blood for the wounded. I represented Schenley's, Local 6, and the San Francisco Industrial Union Council, CIO in this big contest to elect Queens of the Purple Hearts. When you gave a pint of blood you cast a vote for queen. I got 400 votes for 400 pints donated. We had it so well organized in warehouse. There were big signs that said, "Vote for Billie Roberts." I gave a lot of blood myself, too. You'd think I was a mainliner. But I had lots of blood. I was a strong person.

When Schenley's and all the other liquor houses closed down in 1951, I went to work in a top grade restaurant at the Clift Hotel and became a member of the AFL Waitresses Union. They were a very so-so outfit. You didn't have to go to union meetings. In early Local 6 days we couldn't wait for our two meetings a month. But in the Waitresses Union, if you didn't want to go, you just had to pay your month's dues.

They thought I was the craziest thing they ever saw because instead of paying for someone to picket one of the restaurants, I went and picketed after my job. They never heard of anyone getting out and walking again after she'd walked all day.

Of course, I was always in political action as a good Democrat. When Franklin Delano Roosevelt was running for president, Sylvia Maker from Local 6 and I took pamphlets around. We walked for blocks to put fliers in front windows. It didn't occur to us to charge. The Waitresses Union didn't care who was running. They didn't care if you voted or not. It was very different.

The waitresses, too, always worked for tips and were jealous of each other. There wasn't that comradeship like we had in the ILWU, where you knew that you belonged. You weren't fighting alone. All of my life, for the last 30 or 40 years, I've remembered those Local 6 kids. They were like the buddies, I guess, in a war. We were together against the enemy every day.

I love the ILWU. I'm so proud of it. I don't know what life would have been for me without the union. It was certainly a wonderful way of life. When you were a school teacher you had to get out and wrestle your own job, or go in all dressed up to see the boss, with him looking you up and down wondering what kind of a lay you were. But it was nothing seeing the boss after there was a union and we got our dispatch hail.

I never got into anything before where I thought the workers would get their just desserts. When I was in college, they used to say, "What good are unions? They're only for stupid people. Anybody with any ingenuity can get their own job." You know, stuff like that. But when I found out these workers were organizing, I thought it was beautiful.

10-21   LOCAL #6 MEMBERS, LABOR DAY PARADE, SAN FRANCISCO, 1945

Labor activism continued during World War II; First Lady Eleanor Roosevelt had insisted that defense plants be racially integrated and unionized. As active union members, women like Billie Hendricks participated in marches like the one pictured here. Notice that the issues raised by the marchers include racial discrimination, atomic power, rights for GIs (returning vets), and jobs. Congress did pass the GI bill that paid for veterans to go to college and purchase homes. A new book describes "how members of the so-called GI Bill generation promoted academic freedom, social justice, and student self-governance"—what emerges is the story of "the college student as a highly engaged engine of civic action."[xi]

Meanwhile, women lost their jobs, usually to men returning from the war.[xii] They now had to adjust to unemployment or return to low paid work, as Billie Hendricks explains in her interview.

QUESTION: Why did factory owners recruit women during the war, but not afterward? Why do you think women's magazines began to feature articles telling women how much their children needed them at home after the war? If you have a relative who was alive during World War II, ask him or her to tell you what it was like on the home front.

[xi]Eric Hoover, "Paging the Activists," review by Eugene Schwartz, (ed.), *American Students Organize: Founding the National Student Association after World War II* (American Council of Education/Praeger, 2006), *Chronicle of Higher Education*, February 17, 2006, A41.

[xii]For an interesting contrast with Vallejo, see Kimberly Hall, "Women in Wartime: The San Diego Experience 1941–1945," and Christine Killory, "Temporary Suburbs: The Lost Opportunity of San Diego's National Defense Housing Projects," both in *Journal of San Diego History* 39 (Fall 1993).

10-22 HOWARD BASKIN, SHIPFITTER AND DRAFTSMAN, WITH DAUGHTER JANE RICHMOND, 1943

Sara Courtney writes:

> My grandfather, Howard Baskin, after a hard day's work outside government housing, Richmond, 1943. Housing was provided to shipyard employees during World War II. Having volunteered for the Navy Seabees, he began work as a ship fitter.

When they realized he could draw blueprints, he was exempted from the draft and promoted.[xiii]

Mildred Collins describes her personal experience living in the government housing called Shipyard Acres:

> The prolific farm and orchards of the Napa State Hospital were adjacent to the Acres. To the south—what is now Napa's industrial park—lay a wonderful marshland filled with flocks of singing blackbirds, both solid black and red-winged. Frogs took over the chorus on cool, breezy nights, nights when the stars and moon seemed close enough to reach up and touch.[xiv]

QUESTION: What would your life be like if your parents' employers provided housing for your family? Based on where your parent(s) work, where would you be living? Discuss the advantages and disadvantages of such an arrangement.

[xiii]Sara Courtney, Faces of America photo contest, Napa College, 2000.

[xiv]Mildred Collins, "Home is Where the Heart Is," *Napa Register*, June 5, 2002.

11

Cold War at Home, 1946–1965

Despite the miseducation they might have endured—or because of it—many people are hungry for real history.

—*Michael Parenti, History as Mystery*

The 1950s have been misunderstood as a sleepy time when mothers stayed home, dads wore suits, and children were obedient. It was the decade when television entered the American living room. Studios in Los Angeles created television shows with romanticized—and often false—images of American life, but because people watched them for weeks and months and years, they became reality.

However, a story that was not shown on 1950s television was the story of Jewish concentration camp survivors who came to America. Kenneth Kahn labored eighteen years collecting the stories of survivors who settled in Petaluma after World War II. Don Normark began documenting the Mexican American community in Chavez Ravine long before it became a baseball stadium, another astonishing and almost forgotten story. Bill Sorro tells of his Filipino family life in the Fillmore District of San Francisco, while Evelyn Velson recalls her involvement in founding Women Strike for Peace in Long Beach.

These stories fill in important missing pieces, so that those of us like Richard Katrovas or Genny Lim, who grew up watching television and feeling invisible, can find histories like our own. It was in the 1950s that Cesar Chavez began registering Latino voters in San Jose, and the Rumford Act began to address the housing discrimination suffered by African Americans. As suburbs grew, freeways were built to connect them, and "smog," a word coined during the beginning of the Industrial Revolution in London, now became a serious problem in California. In the 1950s, service station attendants wore uniforms and checked your oil, and driver training was an important rite of passage in high school.

11-1 KENNETH KANN, "THE GRINE: REFUGEES FROM THE HOLOCAUST" FROM *COMRADES AND CHICKEN RANCHERS, THE STORY OF A CALIFORNIA JEWISH COMMUNITY*, 1993

JULIA SHIFFMAN SEGAL

Grine is green. Greenhorns. That's what we called the refugees who came to Petaluma after the war. They came from the bowels of the earth. From such horrors. Our community signed up with the Jewish Agricultural Society for thirty-five families. We took them in.

BERTHA LESNER [B. 1922; MINSK, SOVIET UNION]

A lot of nice people met us at the train station in Petaluma. We arrived cold and hungry. Mr. and Mrs. Rubinstein, when we came to their house, it smelled with chicken soup they made for us! Was like coming home! The Petaluma Jewish people was so good to us. Basha Singerman, she's from my home town in Minsk, she *gave* us her car, an old Nash. I'll never forget it as long as I live.

As soon as we could we rented a ranch and rolled up the sleeves. When we first came to America, in New York my husband worked on an assembly line. Here we worked for ourselves on our own ranch. Here was a good place for the children. Was hard work with the chickens, but we know how to work hard. After what we went through with Hitler, a chicken ranch is freedom.

ROSE YARMULSHEFSKY [B. 1921; ZGIERZ, POLAND]

Petaluma was good to all the newcomers. The people who were survivors from the Nazis—we were taken in like family by the whole Jewish community.

There is no people in the world like American people. I'm not just saying so—it is the truth! The first day on the ranch the neighbor—very beautiful lady—she asked if I need some food. When I went for clothes for the children, at Montgomery Wards they knocked me down the price. I went to order a telephone—by that time I speak a few words English—and the lady who talked to me said, "You are doing beautiful." That is good for strangers. The American people make welcome.

Raise chickens? After you go through so much, you know everything! If you can make ammunition in a Nazi concentration camp, why can't you work with chickens? You need to make a living in America so you make a living. When you have no other choice, courage is big.

ESTELLE EDELSTEIN [B. 1920; KRASNOVCE, CZECHOSLOVAKIA]

The first time I went to the Center, they looked at me like a *grine*—a greenhorn. I sat there very shy. But people came up to me. Right away they made me feel it is home.

Petaluma Jewish community is something special. We moved in here, Mrs. Feinstein came to see if we need something. If you miss an affair at the Center, right away Mrs. Katz calls: "What's up?" If you are sick, you can bet your life they will help you with the chickens and bring in food. It's like one bunch.

All the newcomers feel this. Still, we were always a separate bunch, the newcomers. We all went through the bad times with Hitler. We liked to enjoy in America. When there was a party at the Center, it was the newcomers who loosen up with dancing and singing. There never was a fight with the old-time community, but we were always together, the newcomers. It was not always mixing with the others. They sometimes looked at us kind of funny.

You know, they called us the *"grine."* The greenhorns. To this day, some of us do not like this name.

ELAINE BERGOWITZ HOCHMAN [B. 1950; PETALUMA]

The *grine* were weird and uptight. They had tatoos on their arms, from the concentration camps, and they hid those tatoos. They never said a word about it, but the *grine* women always wore something to cover their arms. In the Jewish community we passed clothes around from one family another, but we had to be careful with the *grine*. We never passed a short-sleeved dress or a short-sleeved shirt to these certain women. The *grine* made the whole Jewish community uptight.

ELI SALZMAN [B. 1924; BYDGOSZCZ, POLAND]

Later they got used to us, but in the beginning the Petaluma people were looking at us funny. You know, they read all kinds of stories about Jewish survivors from the concentration camps.

With me they saw a normal person. They wondered. They expected I would be different. One guy said to me, "My gosh! You have so much hair!"

I said, "Why shouldn't I have hair?"

He said, "I read reports that the hair was shaved off in the camps."

I said, "I'm no different than you. I was not in a concentration camp. I passed as a Christian for five years."

LARRY HIRSHFIELD [B. 1944; PETALUMA]

There were all kinds of rumors about the *grine*. There were stories about what happened to them in the Holocaust. There were stories about how they all got so rich.

My father said the *grine* were sponging off the Jewish community. He said Petaluma took them in, loaned them money, cosigned for their credit at the feed company, and showed them how to raise chickens. The refugees kept demanding more help, and we felt sorry for them. Then, all of a sudden, they were operating three chicken ranches and buying apartment buildings in San Francisco. While the people who had been here for thirty years were still struggling to make a living, the *grine* became rich. My father said the *grine* came to Petaluma with money. They came out of the concentration camps with gold, silver, crystal, fine tablecloths, silverware, watches—people saw it! The *grine* came here rich, and then they stepped over people to get richer.

My grandfather said that I shouldn't listen to rumors. He said the *grine* deserved all the help we could give them. He said they were courageous people who survived the Holocaust.

SAUL HOFFMAN [B. 1916; LUBLIN, POLAND]

We went through hell over there. I was not in a concentration camp. I was a partisan in the forest during the war. Ruth, my wife, she was with me all the way through. After the war, who was still a couple from before the war? But Ruth and I, we made it through hell together.

I was a veteran from the Polish cavalry. In 1942 it comes time for Jews to go to the death camps, the concentration camps. That's when I organized a partisan group. We were over eighty people living in the forest—all Jewish—women, children, men. I was the commandant. Whenever possible, we liquidated small groups of Nazi soldiers.

We lived like this for a year. Then the Polish nationalist groups and even the Polish Communist groups, they started to kill every Jew they could find. I wasn't afraid of the Nazis in the forest. But the Polacks, they can find you. You can hide from a stranger, but you can never hide from your own people. I had a few good Polaks what I could talk to. Still I didn't trust them. I could only ask them, "Do me a favor and sometimes I give you back a favor." But I ask with my rifle in my hand. Always with the rifle ready. That's the way. Yeah.

From over eighty people in my partisan group were alive maybe eight at the end. It's a long story. We went through hell. That's why I say I don't owe nobody from nothing! Nobody offered me nothing. I didn't ask for nothing.

Let me tell you, when I came to San Francisco from Europe in 1947, and my wife is going to have the second baby, the Jewish Welfare Federation called us up—they want to help us. I told them, "I take care of myself! I never took charity in my life! I'm in the best country in the world, the richest country. I'm not going there in the bread line!"

That's how I did it. I learned the tailor trade fast. I got a good job in San Francisco making ladies' garments. I went up and up. But I wanted to settle down quiet somewhere. The best place quiet was a chicken ranch in Petaluma. This was 1950.

Did the Jewish community help me start with the chickens? Let me tell you! The first people what came over to visit, I was better off than them! Even then! They owed five thousand dollars to the feed company! The first chicken was sick, they said close all the windows. The chickens almost died from no air! He didn't know what he's doing.

I didn't owe nothing to nobody here. Some newcomers, they tried to get everything they can from the Jewish people here. Not me! I never said, "You owe me help! Do everything for me!"

I never asked for nothing. For three years I worked days as a tailor in San Francisco while my wife took care the ranch and the children. The heavy work I did at night and weekends. I accumulate me enough to raise chickens on a second ranch. When the third son was born, 1953, I increased to five ranches. I said, "Now I make a living just from the chickens!"

It was a challenge. After 1953 the chicken business was tough. You had to be a hard worker—it's not just feed the chickens and go to the beach. You must know what you are doing all the time. You must understand business. You must be honest. And *pashayet*—luck—I believe in *pashayet*.

Meanwhile, we make very good friends with the other newcomers in here. Picnics, parties, music—we live it up! We like the whole Jewish community, and we are told we are an asset to the Center. They pushed me to be president, but I told them no. In Europe, with the partisans, there was a necessity. Here is so many people that want the job, let them run the Center. I be the helper.

All the newcomers liked it here. But most of them left after a few years, when the trouble comes in the chicken business. I stayed here and did good with the chickens all the way. I did good with my apartment buildings too. But most of the newcomers, they went to the city and started a grocery store, a liquor store, an ice-cream store, a restaurant, the real estate. Whatever they did, they made a successful living.

Why? When the newcomers come to this country, we got that grit—to take something and make of it. We didn't sit around and wait for gifts. We didn't have no parents to leave us fortunes. We had to start from scratch and make good ourselves.

NAOMI BERENSTEIN [B. 1923; BERLIN, GERMANY]

We was very lonesome when we came to San Francisco. We didn't speak good English and we didn't have no money and we didn't know what to do. We was completely lost because we went through the Holocaust. People don't realize what that means. You get out from the camps and you find out your family is killed and you are alone. And you come to this country and your fellow Jews don't understand. Even your relatives don't understand you. Because they *don't know* what it means to be lost.

I was working as a nurse at Mount Zion Hospital in San Francisco. My patients from Petaluma they told me, "Come to Petaluma. There are many newcomers. You will like it."

We went to Petaluma for a visit. We was greeted with open heart and open hands. They took us in like we would be family. All the old-timers who greeted us with such warmth, they found a farm for us, they loaned us money, they showed us what to do with the chickens. They gave us the love and understanding which we could not find in San Francisco.

Everybody laughed at how I worked with the chickens. Every time I had sick chickens, I made a hospital for them. I would not throw out a sick chicken. And I would not eat the chickens I raised. We worked very hard. We borrowed every penny to buy this place. And when the chicken prices went down later, we had to turn this ranch into a convalescent home to save it. But we did it, and by the way, we paid back every penny we owed.

I consider myself fortunate to live here. In Petaluma I made friends—and I *mean friends*. I gave of myself what I could to the Jewish community. And they gave me the love and understanding I did not know how to ask for. Not till years after I came here could I look in the mirror and say, "It's me. It's not somebody else."

QUESTION: Why would *immigrants* who had been in Petaluma for 20 years be so resentful of new *immigrants*? Have you noticed this phenomenon in other immigrant communities that you may be a part of? Why do you think the longtime residents were ashamed of the newcomers?

11-2   DON NORMARK, "ELINOR," CHAVEZ RAVINE

Cano Cervantes: I remember Elinor. They lived in Bishop on Davis Street. Elinor played the piano so beautiful. That was the only black family in the neighborhood. I forgot their last name. We used to love to go hear her play the piano in her house.

11-3 DON NORMARK, ELINOR'S GRANDFATHER, MR. JOHNSON

11-4   DON NORMARK, CHILDREN PLAYING

Henry Cruz: You know, a picture like this might look a little depressing to other people, but not to us. That's us right there. The reality. Look at the expression on those kids. That's the way this neighborhood was.

Reyes Guerra: It's a beautiful picture. It shows the way we used to live. Kids nowadays, they wouldn't let them play like that. People were rougher then, even the kids.

QUESTION: What can you interpret about these people's lives from the pictures Normark took then? How do their comments today complete the story? You, like Normark, could provide important clues to the past for people of the future if you document your community today.

Growing up in Los Angeles, I heard about the Dodgers every day, but nothing about the families who had been evicted to construct their baseball stadium. Don Normark has helped this community and all of us to rediscover this crucial story of Mexican American history in Los Angeles. (See http://www.pbs.org/independentlens/chavezravine.)

11-5   BILL SORRO, "A PICKLE FOR THE SUN," 2004

When I was a child around the age of seven or eight, I used to hustle the Sun Reporter news-paper up and down Fillmore Street every Saturday morning. The Sun was one of the first Black newspapers on the west coast beginning around 1936. It was also the only Black newspaper in San Francisco. At that time, Fillmore Street was the heart of the City's African American community. The year was shortly after World War II, around 1947 or '48.

I'd pick up my papers early Saturday morning at the Sun's editorial office, down the street from Onorato's Fish and Poultry store, up on the second floor of a building located at the corner of O'Farrell and Fillmore. One morning I had to step over a man passed out in the doorway of the Sun. I was so frightened and scared that I couldn't bear to look down at him; I just knew he had to be dead. When I came back down the stairs with my bundle of papers, I held my breath. Much to my surprise and relief he was gone! In those days it was highly unusual to see someone drunk and passed out in the street . . . even in the Fillmore.

With my papers under my arm I would proceed to work one side of the Fillmore from Sutter to Fulton and back up the other side. "Sun Reporter mister? Sun Reporter ma'am?" For a nickel, of which I'd get a penny, you could get the latest news about what was going on in the Black community in San Francisco. And in those years, the Fillmore was the cen-ter and heart of the community. Until I was a very young man, I always thought the Fillmore was Harlem. For me it was.

Fillmore Street was alive on Saturday mornings . . . Saturday nights too! Small shops sell-ing everything from dry goods to dry fish. Detters German delicatessen with so many differ-ent kinds of sausages, cheese and foods that we never ate in my home. What delicious smells! By the cash register was the largest jar in the world, full of dill pickles as big as your arm for only a nickel. "Hey, kid. Swap a paper for a pickle?" said the man behind the counter. Can you imagine a little kid trying to sell you a newspaper with a bundle of papers under one arm and a pickle, big as your arm under the other? "Sun, mister? Sun, ma'am?"

Wonderfully delicious aromas of fresh dark russian rye, pumpernickel and other baked goods wafted from the Ukraine bakery on McAllister and Webster streets, the center of a small Jewish community in the Fillmore. Permeating the air throughout the neighborhood was the smell of barbecue. And the very best in those days was the Kansas City Hickory Pit on Fillmore, nestled between the Long Bar Saloon (the longest bar west of the Mississippi), and the New Fillmore theater.

From the early 1940's, through the war years and into the early 1950's, large migrations of African American people settled in San Francisco, Oakland and Richmond. These migra-tions were a direct result of World War Two, especially the needs in ship building and the 'war effort,' as it was called in those days. Black people, other minorities and women were able to get jobs in the shipyards. My dad worked at AAA shipyard in Oakland during the war.

Fillmore Street was alive and bustling. People had good paying jobs and money to spend. And they did, right in their own communities. Mothers, fathers and kids shopping on Fillmore Street, buying food and other necessities for the week. You would always see or bump into people you knew. "Hey, Mama! There goes Mrs. Robles." "Hi, Sis! How are you?" The Delpinas or Campos family.

The San Francisco Filipino American community was very small in those years. In the Fillmore we all knew each other. There was always an unspoken, intimate connection that we shared as Filipinos, though not in any kind of cliquish or chauvinist way. We were Filipino and proud of it . . . and yes, we were family, too. In those days there was not the race identity of "Filipino American." As a matter of fact, in my home the use of the word "American" was to denote white people!

I'd sell all my papers, making most of my money in tips, working the bars along Fillmore. I knew every bartender working the Saturday morning shift. As long as I did not hassle their customers about buying a paper, they would let me work the bar. Always, you would meet a former newspaper kid, as the story went, and he would not only buy a paper, but give you a good tip, too! Now that's real class, ain't it?

From one joint to the next, there was always music. The beautiful sounds of Black music. Jazz, gospel, blues, boogie and swing. Up and down the block, around the corner, day and night, night and day. Music, music. Always music. Leola Kings Blue Mirror, Denny's Barrel House, The Long Bar, Chicago Barber Shop #1 & 2, Reds Shoe Shine, Uptown Bowl, Kansas City Hickory Pit, Manor Plaza Hotel. . . . "Paper, mister? Paper, ma'am?"

By the early 1950's, the Fillmore was becoming the west coast center of Black performing and visual artists, poets, writers, dancers and musicians, giving rise to what became known then as the Fillmore Renaissance.

Bobo Wado Fado Sabado. Everybody Loves Saturday Night. Indeed, the Fillmore was alive on Saturday night! The most prominent African American artists in the United States were to be seen and heard at one of the many night clubs, supper clubs, dance halls, ballrooms, jazz joints and other smaller venues. Johnson's Texas Playhouse, New Orleans Super Club, Club Alabam, The Plantation Club, Leola Kings Blue Mirror, Manor Plaza Hotel, Jimbo's Bop City, Jackson's Nook, Primalon Ball Room, Jacks of Sutter St.

The American entertainment and night club scene was totally segregated in those days. Racism, with few exceptions, had relegated Black performing artists to venues that were generally Black owned, operated and located in the community. From New York City, Chicago, Houston, Kansas City, St. Louis, New Orleans, Los Angeles, San Francisco and other little jazz and juke joints throughout this country. These clubs and joints became nationally part of what became known as the "chitlin circuit" for Black musicians and other artists.

By the time I'd finish selling my papers and paid the man at the Sun Reporter, it would be early afternoon. My belly would be full of all the good food given to me throughout the day by the baker, butcher, bartender, barbecue man and, of course, that pickle, which by now was only half eaten and wrapped in soggy newspaper and bulging through one of my pockets.

Coming home from Fillmore Street, approaching my house, I remember hordes of kids and young people always sitting, talking, playing and just cutting up as young people do. Inside our house some of my brothers and their friends would be playing *Boogie Woogie* on an old upright piano and dancing, always dancing.

When the kids were through, or if Mama got tired and ran them off, she would sometimes sit down at the piano and play herself. I would try and make myself invisible so that I would not distract her from playing. This was always such a wonderful treat, to see and hear Mama, my Mama, in a completely different context, playing the piano.

Mama was a short woman. Her legs could barely reach the piano pedals. When she played, her whole body seemed to be a part of the music, stretching her legs, standing straight up to reach the piano pedals that gave an added dimension, quality and tone to her music. I never could quite believe that this little woman sitting at the piano making this beautiful music was my Mama.

La Paloma, Spanish Eyes, Begin the Beguine, For All We Know, I'll be Seeing You. .... Music, music. Always music.

"Hey, mister! Paper? Sun Reporter, mama?"

QUESTION: Sorro gives us details about life in San Francisco's Fillmore neighborhood during World War II. Which ones stand out in your mind? Why is it important to know that different racial groups worked and played and even lived together in the past?

11-6   MARE ISLAND NAVAL SHIPYARD WORKFORCE, 1960

Defense industries, along with military bases, were the bedrock of employment in 1950s and 1960s California. Both allowed civilian employees to support their families by earning a decent wage with job security and benefits.

Employees at Mare Island Naval Shipyard worked in various "shops" laid out on the island. Mare Island built the first atomic submarine and numerous other subs, boats, and ships. In this c. 1955 photo, Pio Velasco (ninth from left top row) works in the Mare Island Sail Loft, Building 55. (Courtesy of the Vallejo Naval and Historical Museum.)

QUESTION: Why do we no longer have these kinds of jobs? See http://www .rescueamericanjobs.org for more information.

11-7   RICHARD BERMACK, EVELYN VELSON INTERVIEW, 1979

> In the author's words, Evelyn Velson and her husband Charles were active in the
> first attempts to integrate all-white neighborhoods in the Fifties. This is her
> account of being blacklisted, from an interview by Richard Bermack in 1979.

So I married Charlie Velson, and that was the beginning of an adventure. Before I married him, his father had said to me, "Do you know what you are getting into?" I said, "Of course I do," not really understanding what [he] was saying, because Charlie was hauled before every damn committee from Washington to New York. It was the McCarthy Era and from then on the FBI was to haunt us.

They went to our neighbors. The FBI implied that if they associated with us they would lose their jobs–they all worked at city or state jobs. They were scared. The FBI asked our next-door neighbor if they could put a tap on her wall. She was a good Episcopalian. She refused. She didn't tell us that until years later.

The FBI came to the house. I was home; they had already visited my employer, costing me my job. I remembered my husband's instructions, "Don't let them in." But I let them in anyway, and they got real nasty. "Where is your husband?" they asked, implying he was fooling around with other women, et cetera, et cetera, saying nasty things. Finally I started using the language my husband had instructed me to use. "You bastards, you just get the— out of here." The two of them just looked at me. They picked themselves up. "You'll be sorry for this," they said, and swaggered out.

It was a hard period. For many years my husband had been a union official, and now he returned, of necessity, as a worker. When he walked into the personnel department of the shipyards they had his name in inch-high letters on the desk to make sure no one would mistakenly hire him. Family friends would land him a job. He would work at the place a week, and the FBI would come, and he would get canned. Then he would work at another place, and again the FBI would come by and he would be fired. They would be waiting for him in the morning when he would leave the house with his lunch pail. Then he would give them a wild chase through the city by car, returning home and then starting out again, trying to elude them. This went on every single day, for I don't know how long. That year he must have had nearly 12 jobs.

You talk about economic hardships. A friend of mine would have two dollars in her purse, and I would think, miraculous, how can she do it? On Saturdays I would go to New York. I would gather milk bottles to get the carfare. The bottles were worth two cents each. And talk about isolation and social ostracism, if I went to call someone on the telephone, they would say, "Where are you calling from?" To this day there are just two people I can think of who stuck with us throughout this whole thing—who were not afraid to visit us. I have the greatest tonaness for them. Most people were just scared to death. I had absolutely no contact with my family.

They followed my three-year-old boy to nursery school, would you believe it, to get the director of the nursery to refuse the child continuing attendance. The director caved in. It was a co-operative nursery on the other side of town, where other progressive parents sent their kids, and since it was a private co-operative she was only dependent on the parents for funds and could refuse to buckle down but did not! We were constantly being harassed. It was an expenence you don't forget.

I was involved in community activities at the time. We were busy trying to break racial barriers in housing and public schools, and I must say that some devious methods were used, because they had to be used. A white person would purchase a house and sign it over to a black person, things of that sort. But it was a difficult time. I was all alone, my husband was gone a good deal of the time, and I had these young kids to raise. I just did what I could. A lot of people ran scared, and lots of us just found the fortitude to go on and face up to what was happening.

After working for the ILWU for five years, we moved to California. Charlie's work with the ILA was completed and Bridges asked him to work on the West Coast. So we ended up in San Pedro. I'll never forget it. To welcome us were big headlines in the paper, "Bridges right hand man, Communist Charles Velson, arrives. . . . " They had signs painted in the johns on the waterfront, "Charles Velson Communist, Charles Velson Communist, Charles Velson Communist." I am told those signs were still there at the time of my husband's death, five years ago. They may still be up there, I don't know.

When we first hit San Pedro, we were staggered by what we saw. I thought I was going out of my mind. People didn't seem to care about anything outside of their own lives. I saw couples, both were working, not to support one car but two cars and a boat. My husband came home one day and said, "I have never seen anything like it in my life. The guys on the waterfront, either they are reading the racing forms, or they are reading the Wall Street Journal to see how their stocks are doing. All they are interested in is buying sports cars, like MGs." I mean, this was a totally new world for both of us. We never experienced anything like it, people just involved in the materialistic way of life.

I was very disturbed by what was happening—the production of the bomb and nuclear testing, but I couldn't find anyone to work with. I was so frustrated I thought I was going mad. Then one day a little squib appeared in the women's pages of the L.A. times announcing a demonstration to be held on November 1 in Los Angeles concerning the resumption of nuclear testing. Anyone interested call this woman in Beverly Hills, the wife of Dr. so and so. I debated it. My husband would come home. He was working on the waterfront then as a marine clerk. "Did you call her?" he would ask. "No." "Well, call her." It took me a week to gather the courage, believe it or not, to call. I thought, what do I have in common with this housewife in Beverly Hills whose husband is a doctor? Finally I called her and she said, "We have leaflets announcing the demonstration. How many do you want?" I thought for a minute and said, "A dozen and a half." She went hysterical. "This is truly a housewives' movement," she laughed. "People are calling up and ordering leaflets like they order eggs."

So I got these leaflets, and got together a few other people I knew from the ILWU. We each got a few more people and we went into Los Angeles that day for the demonstration. It was astounding. Busload after busload arrived. Five thousand women came out that day. I stood there and wept. We all turned in our names, and they sent us the names of women in our area. That was the beginning of Women for Peace and Women Strike for Peace. And that was how a group of women in San Pedro and Long Beach found each other.

Shortly afterwards, we moved to Long Beach. So how do you find people? We put an ad in the local paper, "Anybody interested in working on the question of peace, get in touch with us." And this is what happened: we started to find each other. I met people who were just ordinary folk, from all walks of life, but who were just the most magnificent people with a marvelous sense of values and ethics. People who really came to the fore and were not afraid to express their opinions.

I just started talking to the people around me. I put signs on my car, "Ban the Bomb." And I thought, "Oh brother, my car is probably going to get smashed." But an interesting thing happened—my car was not smashed. Instead my neighbors started coming to me secretly to tell me how worried they were about nuclear war and then later about the war in Vietnam. They would talk about their children and grandchildren who were undergoing psychological stress and even breaking down over the fear of being drafted and having to fight in this war nobody understood. People were scared, and because they knew me and my family—they saw me every day and talked to me every day—they began to trust me.

We had a core group of five, a Quaker, an academic, a school teacher, an artist, and myself. We would go out and leaflet our neighborhood and ask people to come to meetings. Surprisingly, we got very little hostility. Instead the most amazing things happened—for example, one night in the small beach front community I lived in we turned out 125 people for a meeting in the local public school. We became very well organized. We used to canvass those neighborhoods every Sunday. We knew who were Democrats, who were Republicans, and who were independents. Then we just zeroed in on people. We knocked on thousands of doors. People got to know us and we got to know our community very well indeed.

We knew who to ask for money and how much.

People would say to me, "You must have courage to do this." They would come to me quietly and give me money and say, "Don't tell anybody I talked to you," or "Don't tell my wife or husband I gave you this." They were scared. But we were able to do the most fantastic things in that town. I don't think that town has seen the likes of us since. We were the first group that really broke through the consciousness of the American people after World War II.

11-8   EVELYN VELSON AND HUSBAND CHARLES, MID-1950s

11-9 WOMEN ON STRIKE FOR PEACE MARCH IN LOS ANGELES TO PROTEST THE RESUMPTION OF NUCLEAR WEAPONS TESTING, APRIL 27, 1962

In 1961, the United States and the Soviet Union had resumed nuclear testing. Six women in Washington, D.C., met to organize a nationwide strike that united tens of thousands of women in sixty cities across the country on November 1 of that year.

Rebecca Solnit writes:

> Using their status as middle-class moms as a shield, Women Strike for Peace activists plunged into the fray, taking risks no one else had dared . . . within a couple of years, they had helped bring into being the limited Test Ban Treaty (an achievement acknowledged by President Kennedy).[i]

---

[i]Rebecca Solnit, "Three Who Made a Revolution," *The Nation*, April 3, 2006, 32.

11-10   HANSEL MEITH, NON-SIGNERS OF LEVERING ACT, SAN FRANCISCO STATE, 1950

Mark Johnson writes:

> Hundreds of California teachers lost their jobs for refusing to sign the Levering Act oath, which required government employees to certify that they were not members of vaguely defined un-American organizations. This group was photographed by Hansel Meith in Frank Rowe's living room on Alabama Street in San Francisco. . . . The Levering Act was overturned—but not before irreparably transforming the lives of those who refused to comply because they believed it was unconstitutional.[ii]

[ii]Johnson, 69.

11-11   ROCKWELL KENT, "SAVE THIS RIGHT HAND," 1949

Harry Bridges had led the longshoremen to victory in 1934, but during the Cold War, he was often arrested and threatened with deportation. Kent, a close friend of Bridges, was one of the most famous illustrators of his era.

11-12   CÉSAR CHÁVEZ, c. 1960

Cesar Chavez was living with his family in San Jose when he met community organizer Fred Ross, who mentored him into leadership in the Community Service Organization, registering Mexican American voters and campaigning against racial and economic discrimination. By the late 1950s, Chavez had become national director, but he resigned in 1962, "leaving the security of a regular paycheck to found the National Farm Workers Association, which later became the United Farm Workers of America."[iii]

[iii]www.chavezfoundation.org/Default.aspx?pi=33.

Helen Gahagan Douglas, whom we met in Chapter 9 visiting New Deal sites, was elected to Congress in 1944, representing much of Los Angeles. When she faced Republican Richard Nixon in the general election, he smeared her as "pink right down to her underwear."[iv] The anti-Communist attack was successful; Douglas never again held public office, but she continued as a public speaker and activist until her death in 1980.

Carlos Bulosan, who wrote so powerfully about "The Thief" during the Depression, published his autobiography, *America is in the Heart*, in 1946. Bulosan was another victim of the McCarthy Era; in 1956, he died from pneumonia at the age of forty-four. Bulosan's books were out of print for decades until they were rediscovered by a new generation of Asian Americans.[v]

QUESTION: How do these stories and photos help us understand more about why some Californians were responding to the Cold War with political activism?

[iv]See www.ou.edu/special/albertctr/archives/exhibit/hgdbio.htm for more.
[v]See http://www.reflectionsofasia.com/carlosbulosan.htm for more.

11-13   RICHARD KATROVAS, "THE REPUBLIC OF BURMA SHAVE," 1985

If it were something one could actually see, I'd have seen most of it before the age of seven. It isn't; I didn't. The very word is as something made almost entirely of sugar that dissolves, leaving a faint aftertaste, in the acids of the mouth. This figure, of course, is a convention for memory, and the nexus of America and Memory—for this moment in history when Self is the supreme commodity—is childhood. In a rare fit of lucid resolve, I decided recently that I would cure myself of that peculiarly American sickness, the critical stage of which is a morose attachment to memories of childhood; however, I still watch enough television to know just how unrelenting media can be at keeping us childlike, that is, uncritically receptive. I also know that to break a fever one must ride it out.

As a child, I was as uncritically receptive as the next, and though I was born in the early fifties, smack dab in the middle of the Baby Boom and the Golden Age of Television, I did not spend as many hours as most in front of a screen. Mind you, I *loved* television, but the circumstances of my life not only made it impossible for me to watch as much as I desired, but also created an inverse relation between myself and television relative to what I now realize was, and is, the norm: I experienced it not as a means of transport from a static environment but rather as a fixed point, a touchstone.

By 1960 there would be, including my parents, seven of us, my youngest brother arriving in March of that year. We'd been on the road since before I could remember, changing cars every couple of months and staying in motels at roughly forty-eight hour intervals. I viewed America (or the vestiges of its Platonic shadow) through the window of the backseat of a car, and I also viewed it through another window when we stayed in motels. My relation to what I viewed through both windows was one of uncritical receptivity, yet whereas what passed the car window seemed distant, redundant and uncaring, the world I viewed through the TV screen was close, varied, and constantly concerned with *me*. No matter what seedy little motel in what ugly little town in what boring state we found (lost) ourselves, Captain Kangaroo and Little Miss Sunbeam would be there, waiting.

I remember leaning onto the passenger-side seat which my mother will always occupy in my memory, and asking, "What's a merica?" I was seven months from my seventh birthday. The sky was dark. Two younger brothers and a younger sister were sprawled around me, breathing through crusted nostrils, and a third younger brother lolled in the most comfortable space in the car, swelling my mother's stomach. My father was in his long-distance coma behind the wheel. The gray rabbits bounding across the road at the vague limits of our high-beams, and the furry blood-splotched pancakes of the ones which didn't make it were no less real to me than Captain Kangaroo's Bunny Rabbit—that mute, bifocaled puppet who made a lucrative career of tricking carrots from the Captain—but were certainly less engaging.

"What?" my mother whispered.

"What's a merica?" I asked again.

This may seem a naive question even for a six-year-old to ask, but I hadn't attended a single day of school yet, and wouldn't for another couple years. My mother had taught me to read a few words from comic books and to write numbers, but as prelude to my widely and irregularly spaced lessons she had never made me sit with my right hand over my heart reciting, after her, the Pledge of Allegiance. I'd probably heard of mericas in a song sung on TV late at night in a Holiday Inn just before the shows stopped and the bugs swarmed all over the inside of the screen:

> A merica, a merica,
> God shade his gray sun tree. . .

First things first. I'd find out what mericas were.

"Just a word," she mumbled, half asleep. Of course, this wasn't enough.

"But what does it *mean?*" I whispered-whined. Her eyes opened slowly. Her fingers, laced over her ninth month, began to drum lightly.

My mother was a beautiful woman. She was beautiful enough to be on television. As I stared at her shadow-softened profile, I saw that peculiar smile take shape which meant she was about to say something to me without really talking to me. It was a thin, crooked smile which meant her voice would be more breath than words.

"The Republic of Burma Shave," she breathed, letting her tired, dark beautiful head roll toward the window glass where she would keep her forehead pressed against the coolness till dawn.

I turned my cheek and rested it on my forearm which lay across the top of the seat. A rasping body curled just behind me so I couldn't sit back, but I didn't much care because the one talent all of us had developed was to achieve relative comfort in what cramped space was finally allotted when the chips, as it were, had fallen for the night. I realize now that everything I am, for better or worse, depends on that moment, which was many, many such moments: my mother pregnant and sleeping upright; my father achieving Zenlike oneness with the road; my siblings breathing as from the clogged center of the earth; the hum of rubber over asphalt vibrating up through a ton of steel, plastic, glass and flesh. My dreams were reruns.

I had only the vaguest sense of how others lived. The Nelsons, Cleavers and Ricardos lived in their own places like the people in the houses we passed in our car. Even Fred and Alice ("Mom, what's a honeymooner?") had a little place, though it looked pretty drab, a bit like motel rooms in the desert, which I hated because some of them didn't have televisions or, if they did, only got one fuzzy station.

Two days through California desert with a burlap bag strapped to the grill . . . we filled it with orange pop and the water ever after was tainted with a sugary mildew . . . another day through mountains and into snow.

Just out of the mountains ("Don't worry, there's a secret button that'll let us *float* down!") we stopped in a little town that was glazed with frost. We waited in the car while my father was "doing business." He came out of an old, brick building holding new license plates wrapped in wax paper, then took us to a motel on the outskirts of town. I knew I'd be going back with him later. I no sooner got the TV on than he made me wash up with him and change into fresh clothes. Back in the car he told me that when we got inside my name would be Mike.

I liked that bank as soon as I saw it because it had revolving doors. My father introduced me to a man in a brown suit and made me shake his hand. The man's smile reminded me of a game show. My father sat in a chair across from him and they talked like they knew each other, though I knew they didn't. My father put me on his knee, which I hated, but I knew that when my father told me I was someone else my only job was to keep my mouth shut. So I sat there balanced on his hard knee, seeing the man as my father saw him, admiring how, though he was leaning back away from his cluttered desk with his elbow propped on his chair arm and cigarette smoke swirling from his fingers around his head, he seemed to *wear* that desk. I wanted a desk like that, with a black telephone and lots of papers and pens.

At one point my father made me stand up so he could reach into his back pocket for his wallet. He plucked several cards from the good-smelling leather, and then a neatly folded rectangular piece of paper that, opened, had numbers printed on it here and there. The man smiled and nodded, then pushed something in front of my father. My father wrote on it, shook hands with the man who, at the same time with his free hand, gave something that looked like a wallet to my father. I knew as we passed through the revolving glass door that I could stop being Mike, though it didn't really matter. There wasn't much to it.

Snow fell fast that evening. My mother went into labor. Her weeping and writhing scared the younger children. I was scared, too, but I didn't cry. My father told me to watch the kids while he went out to see if there was a hospital close (there was no phone in the room, only some kind of buzzer that the office could use if a call was coming in). When he opened the door I glimpsed, in yellow-bulb light through wind-whipped swarms of snow dust, white mounds where cars had been. I told the kids to lie on the floor. I spread a blanket over them to muffle their whimpering. My mother seemed foreign and terrible. I didn't dare approach the bed. I turned on the TV. She screamed louder, making noises I'd never heard. I turned the volume as loud as it would go, draped a sheet over the cabinet, and squatted under the glowing tent. The noises my mother made were drowned out by a roaring laugh-track, but the screams weren't. I ran into the bathroom, locked the door, turned out the light, put the seat down on the toilet and pressed my cheek to the seat, mumbling *please, please . . .*

Just as the Pledge of Allegiance was not part of my backseat curriculum, neither was prayer. My pleading was raw and random. I was awakened by a pounding on the door and my father's furious voice. I opened the door. He pushed me aside, lifted the seat and pissed. The kids were still under the blanket. My mother writhed slowly and moaned gently, flushed and sweating. My father had turned down the sound on the TV. I heard a quick, sharp *honk*. My father lifted my mother, ordered me to open the door, and carried her to the cab. The cab's chains crunched them away and I watched the red taillights dissolve in the snow-swirled, late-night traffic at the out-skirts of wherever we were. I turned to the sleeping, blanketed lump left in my charge, and, as I closed the door on a cold wind, began to weep silently. I switched off the overhead light, stepped over my brothers and sister, and curled up in front of the television's gray glow. It flickered through my eye-lids and in a moment I was empty and peaceful, drifting to sleep on the violin-thickened strains of an old movie.

Artaud said somewhere that "he who does not bring back from the plunge into a fertile unconscious the sense of an atrocious nostalgia is a pig." I have often wondered how television has affected the unconscious of my generation. I don't much care about the evolution of archetypes, and my regard for questions centered on collective perceptions of ideal-types is subordinate to what I believe is a more fundamental question concerning how an individual's remembered feelings manifest in the present; I mean, when I make that plunge and return, soaked and reeling, perhaps the nostalgia I feel for people, places and things of my past is so tainted by that other conscious past, that other life, that the quality of feeling I unconsciously possess, say, for Lucille Ball is equal to that which I possess for the beautiful young woman who was my mother. It's a chilling proposition. None of us knows what his or her Rosebud will be, but Citizen Kane's pathos may be lost to a generation whose period of innocence was cloven into two worlds of consciousness both of which may bear equally upon the unconscious, for what dreadful charm is inherent in a person dying with the image of the NBC peacock frozen in that infinitesimal black space where his last synapse had sparked and faded?

The point is, from the moment I was old enough to watch television, which was before I could talk, I lived two lives, one of passive receptivity, the other alternating between active hostility towards my siblings and passive participation in relation to my parents. In neither were significant decisions made, but whereas in the former I learned quickly what to feel and when, in the latter there were only vague clues. Lucy taught me how to love her; I laughed when the TV laughed. My mother never taught me to love *her*; she was ironic and unpredictable.

Considering how different my childhood was from most, I believe that if not for television I'd probably have been just a little less antisocial than those fabled children raised by wild animals ("Mom, did Tarzan go to school?"). Television gave me *some* sense of what was "normal," and it even informed me as to what were normal problems.

My mother listened to *Queen For a Day* from the bed, pale and quiet, staring at the ceiling. My new brother was asleep in a bed we'd made from a bureau drawer. *Queen For a Day* was one of my favorite shows, though I found it puzzling. Women took turns telling how messed up their lives were, and the studio audience voted, by clapping, for the one who seemed the most messed up. I liked the part where they clapped. The winner got prizes and wept for joy. "Democracy in action!" my mother had exclaimed more than once, never explaining what democracy was; but this time she just lay there staring off. Several years later, when my father would be in prison and she'd be dying of an undiagnosed muscle disease, I'd see her like that often, though I'd be spared by dubious good luck the pain of her final pain and wretched dying.

I remember clearly that the queen for that day was a "housewife from Miami" whose husband was in an iron lung. That one gave me fits, but I didn't dare ask about iron lungs. My mother seemed in no mood for questions. I briefly tried to imagine it, but I couldn't really come up with anything. It certainly *sounded* like a winner! The audience went crazy, the needle of the little speedometer that appeared under her chin jerked to its limit, and the man with the little moustache who ran the show gave her kitchen appliances and a vacation to California and she wept for joy.

It was my job to keep the kids from messing with the baby while our father was out doing business. The kids accepted my authority because I was larger than they and quick to exhibit the inherent advantages of that fact. The burden and privilege of authority were mine, and I carried both aspects with less than regal grace. I was a brutal older brother. This new one, though, I would never brutalize. He was mine. I would raise him to the age of seven when I, thirteen, and the brother a year and a half younger than I would be taken away by our father and finally adopted by his sister and her husband in San Diego. Sixteen years from the moment I left him I'd face a twenty-three-year-old up-and-coming Cadillac salesman whose every utterance would seem obsequious and loud. He'd ask me, in his North Carolina twang, "Well, what's the bottom line on this poetry business, bub?"

But now I was a guardian angel fending off the alien hordes. My mother kept asking me to bring her glasses of water. The baby was sleeping, and she'd lift her head with much effort to cast a weary glance at the pink, swaddled product of her previous night's pain. I would never know how my father got the two of them out of the hospital so quickly, nor, of course, at the time was it within the realm of my natural considerations. I possessed fairly vivid recollections of the two previous births, and in neither case had my mother languished in professional care.

My vigil over the new citizen was interrupted only by the theme music of *The Three Stooges*, the zippy strains of which made my heart race and washed away even this solemn new sense of responsibility. I shoved the three-headed bundle from in front of the screen, and stationed myself six feet from the action, half-lotus. This was my seminar on violence, and my siblings were the nervous rabbits on which I'd perform by rote my assigned experiments. The brother a year and a half younger than I, the one who would be adopted by the same good folks who'd adopt me and therefore was the only one of my family I'd grow into adolescence and adulthood knowing, would become a career navy man and a staunch supporter of a strong defense. This, of course, was inevitable.

After the last pie had struck the last stoogey face and the credits began to roll across the screen to that adrenalin-pumping theme song—"Three Blind Mice" done double-time—I faced my second-in-command with my fist extended perpendicular to his chest, and ordered him to strike down on it. "Come on, hit it!" With side-glancing trepidation he did so, and braced for the inevitable stiff-armed three-hundred-and-sixty-degree arching hammer-fist that found its mark on the bull's eye-cowlick in the middle of his crew cut. I supplied my own stoogey sound effects and laughed hysterically. He whimpered off to a corner of the motel room, the seeds of a military temperament taking root in his four-year-old soul. The last time I saw him, his ship, a nuclear powered aircraft carrier, had docked in San Diego where I was living again, and he took me on a tour of the thing. He conducted the tour amicably and with pride, but seemed under all the spit-shine like a man itching to kill something, something big. I understand from reliable sources that he watches very little television, but spends much of his professional life stationed in front of a radar screen. He was, and no doubt still is, quite patient.

I was not very patient. After *The Three Stooges*, programming entered the wasteland of news and talk shows, and that always made me irritable. I'd turn the sound all the way down and twitch about the room for the couple of hours till prime time. Now, though, I resumed my station by the drawer, reaching in once in a while to touch the small sleeper.

The weather had calmed outside. My mother lifted herself with much effort, and took the baby from the drawer and nursed it sitting upright in bed with her eyes closed. My father came in stomping snow from his soaked black shoes. My parents' eyes met and my father smiled broadly and arched his eyebrows. This was a facial gesture I would come to hate, but now it signaled good news so it made me excited. I knew it meant we had a new car and probably a bigger one than the last. He was holding two white bags which made me very excited. I could smell the french fries and see the grease stains at the bottom of the bags. My heart began to pound. We'd not eaten since the night before. He doled out the burgers and fries, and my siblings took their rations and moved as far from me as they could. They didn't want to be close when I was in a feeding frenzy. From the moment I ripped the wrapper off my burger my mouth was filled beyond its natural capacity, and I finished just as the others were settling into their nests. My second-in-command was savvy enough to lock himself in the bathroom. The other two, my sister and former-youngest brother, three and two respectively, chewed their burgers and nibbled their fries by the bedpost together, never taking their eyes off me. I left them and their booty alone this time. From the tone of my father's voice as he spoke to my mother, we were in for a period of prosperity. There would be burgers and more burgers.

Television can be torture to a hungry child. Though I'd never seen a Television Chocolate Cake in real life—the black frosting swirled in hundreds of perfect little wavelets from top to base—I knew that a good mother was one who made them that way. The few times we'd stayed in one place long enough to occupy an apartment or kitchenette, my mother cooked very little and then almost strictly from cans. Only twice she'd baked cakes and both times the frosting was flat, thick and boring.

When we were really hungry, desperately so, and my father was out doing business, we'd wait in a motel, lethargic, watching television. Once I started crying while watching a commercial for Duncan Hines, and my brothers and sister started crying after me, and then our mother was weeping with us, and all our eyes were fixed on that frosting-swirled monument.

A few years later, while my father was in prison for his first three-years stretch and the five of us and our mother lived in relative comfort on a hundred and sixty-four dollars a month from Welfare, my friends would ask me where my father was and what he did for a living. I was told to tell them he was away at school learning a trade. That was usually enough to stop the questions. In that neighborhood, a lot of fathers were away at school learning a trade.

My father's only talents were bouncing checks and ripping off car dealers. However, his dream was to be a legitimate business man. "Legitimate" was an adjective he used often, and his dream of legitimacy soured years later into schizophrenic fantasy. The last time I saw him he was drunk, and proceeded to relate to me the shrewd manner in which he'd recently acquired offshore drilling leases in the Gulf of Mexico. Before I left his sleazy motel room, he pressed a personal check for thirty thousand dollars into my palm.

The Millionaire was coming on just as my father started packing us up. It took the *Queen For a Day* theme much farther. It was a more romantic, more civilized fiction. The plot formula was simple: a multimillionaire covertly searched out a person who was down on his luck and sent a butler to give that person a check for a million dollars. The antithesis of the Horatio Alger formula, it was, among other things, a hyperbolic metaphor for what a few years later would be called the Welfare State. On a much smaller scale, *Queen For a Day* seemed downright neighborly; its intimate game-show format within which a kind of Christian-fundamentalist witnessing took place was like a local church sending Christmas groceries to the Widow Jones. *The Millionaire*, with its pontifflike source of centralized, quiet power had an old-world grandness. In regard to his relation to money and what he thought one could and should do with it, my father's temperament and background suggested a kinship with the world of the former while his false self-image was a dream hatched in the precincts of the latter. He traversed the continent subsisting on the small though myriad payoffs a good lie told many times may garner. As liars go, he was a one-trick pony: a television character actor who could only play one kind of role, the henpecked husband or the laconic stogie-chomping gangster from Nowhere, or only the voice of commercials for toothpaste and shaving cream.

The car was large and awesome, the best we'd ever had. The *cry* in Chrysler seemed inappropriate to such a chrome-bespangled, fetching thing, though the bright vowel at the heart of the word suggested the frank and sporting glare of the thing's waxed newness. My father packed up what little we carried with us, and after several hours of the kids bouncing on the slick vinyl and all of us inhaling the heady scent of a new car's interior, night came on, clear, cold and precise with stars that seemed to follow us. The younger ones slept in a bunch on the seat under army-surplus blankets that smelled of mothballs and the loneliness of closets, and I curled up in the space at the top of the backseat covered with my father's jacket that smelled of his sweat and aftershave. The curved window was an observatory when I lay on my back, and when I turned on my side to see the faint glow of our taillights on the snowbanks at the side of the road, to see also the pearl necklace of traffic, far away, from where we had traveled, my position was one that felt like destiny. Though, of course, I had no such concept in my life, the memory of the feeling that filled me as I lay, shifting my vision between the broad field of stars that followed us and the faint lights of distant traffic, is the measure by which I now understand the word. It has little to do with where one is going, and nothing to do with where one has been. It's the supersentient moment of trust in blind movement toward anything and nothing, the dry whir of artificial heat and the steady whine of new tires through slosh.

I lay counting the stars of a moonless sky, fixing one a long time and promising myself that tomorrow night I'd find the exact same one again. As I started at my star, which was neither a faint nor a particularly bright one, an ordinary star I knew I'd lose forever after this night no matter how long or hard I stared, I visualized the letters of the first words I'd ever recognized as words: my mother would read aloud the little signs, one by one, until the last, when all of us, from my father to the two-year-old would yell in unison those words printed in bold caps. The wisdom of the land thus appeared to us on the highways of America.

And we were off again. Their stomachs full, my siblings slept as one. In the darkness of the car, I closed my eyes and dreamed a waking dream of television cakes and burgers as my American mother held a future salesman to her breast. In the Republic of Burma Shave the sins of the father can be taken to the bank, and every mother's son gets an even break.

11-14   GENNY LIM, "A JUK SING OPERA," 1988

I had this dream where I was inside a museum surrounded by ancient Chinese artifacts. The feeling of reverence and exaltation was great each time I discovered a precious object retrieved from memory or association. Silk garments with hand-embroidered dragons and phoenixes, porcelain cups, opium pipes, a hand-carved camphor chest with intricate motifs, jade and ivory carvings, vases once touched, possessed or seen in the past and long forgotten. Discovering an old rattan trunk, the type my uncle might have brought to Angel Island, I am moved to ecstasy and suddenly break into song.

The music that emerges from my mouth, however, fills me with amazement. I am singing Cantonese opera! It's as if I'm possessed by another being. My voice rises and falls in a familiar falsetto. The only time I have heard such virtuoso singing like this was as a little girl at the Great Star Theater, where the traveling operas came once a year. They, too, had to stay on Angel Island each time they came to tour. In fact, they entertained the detainees to alleviate their depression and boredom. The crowds in *Die-Fow* (San Francisco) loved them so much they would shower them with fabulous collars made of dollar bills. Now I become their idol, singing like a Hung-Sung-Nui, the famous opera star, with every soul rapt in my hand's palm. My phrasing and timing are precise, my tone clear and shrill like a flute as my voice slides through a series of varying pitches on the same syllable, turning vocal cartwheels in steep-falling rhythmic cadences.

I awaken and the opera vanishes. The illusion of transcendence and self-mastery is suddenly gone. I'm still a tongue-tied *hu-ji nuey*, an American-born Chinese girl in San Francisco.

But I can still hear the opera echoing in my ears. Its lyrical melody lingers, leading me like the zigzagging line on a highway map to a destination unknown.

As the youngest of seven children, I often felt removed from any sense of a cultural past. As a second generation American-born Chinese, I was often a living contradiction of dual values and identities. At home, my Chineseness gave way, much to mother's sadness, to American-ness; and outside, my American-ness always belied my Chinese sensibility. If the twain theoretically never met, they certainly often collided for me.

As a little girl, I bristled with shame and outrage as I heard people call my father "Chinaman." Yet his erect, proud bearing never betrayed any anger or humiliation. And I now realize the alienation that pride cost him. Because of his need for the secure kinship of fellow villagers, father never left Chinatown. He would not hear mother's constant cry to leave the ghetto for the suburbs of the city. One of the very few places where he did take us was the Sacramento Delta.

In the old days it would take Pop about four hours to wind his way through the highways to the delta. Perhaps the trip took so long because of his growing confusion over the new freeways that kept springing up overnight. Our out-of-town trips trickled to about one a year for only special clan occasions, like the Bomb Day celebration in Marysville, where a frenzy of over-zealous young men vied for the coveted prizes that signified the appeasement of the goddess, *Bok Kai*, thrown into a crowded square. Sometimes fights would erupt over the cylindrical, red-wrapped prizes, which contained a gold ring, and sometimes we would get jostled or stepped on. Once in the melee I cried in terror as I was knocked to the ground. Maybe *Bok Kai* could ward off floods, but she didn't seem effective against stampedes.

Father was part-owner of the Golden Lantern Restaurant in Sacramento. All I remember of the place were the golden lanterns strung from the ceiling, the green matchbooks with gold lanterns embossed on the cover, the steamy, bustling kitchen where we kids were not allowed, and the dark storeroom where we spent hours rolling around on a dolly and climbing up boxes stacked almost ceiling-high. I enjoyed the summer trips to Sacramento, if only as a departure from the daily existence of Chinatown. Once, we slept in an unairconditioned hotel room and I could hear my brother and sister having a water fight in the bathtub next door as I tossed and turned in bed. Once, we discovered an empty storefront and spent the morning impersonating mannequins to the amusement of passersby.

The banquets were memorable. Unlike today's banquets where people eat and run, they were all-day family affairs. Cases of Bireley's orange sodas, sparkling cider, Seagrams 7, mounds of *gwa-chi* (melon seeds), candy kisses, coconut candy, were always on hand. In the screened-off area, the men and very often the women, gambled and talked loudly, among the din of clacking *mah-jongg* tiles, dominoes and Cantonese opera blaring from the loudspeakers. One elderly woman passed water right in her chair, she was so engrossed in her game! The men liked to drink and make speeches. They toasted from table to table during the nine-course banquet, ignoring their wives' worried glances.

The Cantonese people that I knew were very different from the Chinese people I read about in newspapers or books. They did not resemble the fawning stereotypes I saw on television or films. The Cantonese I had grown up with were vibrant, adventurous, passionate, courageous, proud, and fiercely loyal family men and women. The men were given to bouts of drinking and gambling, often as their sole escape from a lifestyle of virtual exile. The women embraced their rituals and superstitions as a talisman against harm, appeasing the gods with chicken and wine on Chinese New Year's Day, consulting soothsayers and oracles from yarrow stalks and chanting to ward off evil spirits.

I am sitting in Mrs. Wong's living room in the town of Locke, which is near Sacramento, and am looking up at her wallful of memories—children, grandchildren, husband, young wife. . . . I am touched with sadness. I want to bring her oranges once a month, sit and chat with her about the size and brilliant color of her *gwa*, her infallible fishing technique, her expert knitting which she proudly holds up for my inspection. A white vest for her only son who lives in Sacramento with his family. I do not ask how often he comes because I know it is not often enough.

I become that son, sharing in his guilt. I am that generation of Chinese-American who fled the Chinatowns. The invisible breed. The shamed, who like the Jews, bury the scars of the diaspora; but unlike the Jews, we cannot escape our yellow skins behind masks of white.

She brings me an ice-cold can of 7-Up. I am not thirsty, but I graciously accept. It is safe here, better than the city. I think about my mother wandering like a frightened child in the darkness; my thoughtlessness had sent her unknowingly into the new underground metro-muni subway. The train never emerged from the tunnel and she could not read the English signs. She could not even return to her departure point because the train had switched routes at the end of the line. Mother wandered the length of the city, looking for a familiar Chinese face, any face.

It does not matter that my mother and Mrs. Wong have been in this country a majority of their lives. Their lot as Chinese women had been circumscribed, preordained here as it was in China, except that now there was no need for bound feet. Like mother, Mrs. Wong has never learned to speak English. Life in Locke and other American Chinatowns was self-sufficient, insular. You toiled in the fields, orchards, factories, sweatshops, and came home at night to your own teacup, bowl of rice, and four walls. There was a curtain that hid you from the outer world. . . .

"You hold his hand right now!" the white kindergarten teacher scolded, as the children filed out in pairs for recess. How could I explain to her what the other Chinese children had told me—that skin color was transferable. If I held the negro boy's hand, I too would turn as dark as a *see-you-guy* (soy-sauce chicken). Deep within, I sensed my attitude was perverse, yet I still spent the remainder of recess in the lavatory, scrubbing the ubiquitous mark of Cain, which the Mormon missionaries who came to Chinatown spoke about, from my palm.

I used to hide my lunches from the other kids because they laughed at my *joong* (sweet rice with a duck-egg yolk, pork and peanut filling, boiled into a glutinous lump wrapped in banana leaves), or they would wrinkle their noses in disgust at my greasy deep-fried Chinese New Year's dumplings and other such incriminating un-American concoctions. Being Chinese in America always seemed a liability to me until much later in my youth when I realized the lack of any identifying American culture.

Before father died, I tried to convey to him the importance of reclaiming our Chinese-American history. My father, like so many of his first generation cohorts, however, always felt that what history was lost was not worth retrieving. "What's the use?" he used to say with a helpless shrug. Years later, as I talked to an old man in Locke, I was to hear the same words repeated over and over. *"Mo-yoong, mo-yoong . . ."* he kept repeating bitterly. "It's no use, it's no use . . ." He tells me his family was slaughtered in the war (Sino-Japanese), and blinks back tears. "Nobody's left here," he says, gesturing around the crumbling wooden house with an age-peppered hand. "Mo-yoong-ah . . . And I'm too old."

Lim also wrote a play, *Paper Angels*, which focused on the Asian immigrants at Angel Island (for more on Angel Island, see www.angelisland.org).

QUESTION: Lim and Katrovas both grew up in the late 1950s. Whose story do you relate to? What was different about growing up then compared to today?

11-15   JOHN BECKER, "AN AIR THAT KILLS," 1956

Times were worse then
Jobs were hard to get
People were suffering more
but do you know
a man could breathe

It's as if the oxygen
were all exhausted
from the atmosphere
That's how I feel
and why I quit

Same land same sky same sea
same trees and mountains
I painted then
I guess the light went out
I saw them by

Don't make politics
out of what I say
It's just that something isn't here
that used to be
and kept us going

11-16 FAMILY PUNKIN CENTER, LOCATED ON THE EAST SIDE OF OLD HIGHWAY 40 (REPLACED BY INTERSTATE 80 IN THE 1960s) JUST SOUTH OF GEORGIA STREET, IN VALLEJO, WHERE PARENTS BROUGHT CHILDREN TO RIDE ON PONIES

600 Lincoln Hiway   PUNKIN CENTER   Vallejo, Calif.

In the 1950s, affordable cars and access to cheap gasoline created an economy in which each family was able to buy a car. Smog, made of ozone, nitrogen oxides, and carbon monoxides, is produced by emissions from cars, planes, ships, trains, industries, and any businesses and households in which polluting products are used. During the early years of World War II, Los Angeles residents began calling their doctors with symptoms that were later recognized as being caused by smog. In a 1956 survey sent out by the Los Angeles County Medical Association, ninety-five percent of physicians described a smog complex of symptoms: irritation of eyes and respiratory tract, chest pains, shortness of breath, nausea, and headache. Fifty-six percent of these doctors also reported that people were leaving Los Angeles due to smog; forty-three percent recommended their patients move away; and eighty-one percent believed that smog contributed to cancer of the lungs.[vi]

QUESTION: Have you seen "favorite places" disappear during your lifetime? Did anyone try to save them? Have any been saved? Favorite places could include trees, stores, "pumpkin centers," historic sites of any kind.

[vi]www.aqmd.gov/smog/inhealth.html#historical.

11-17 DONALD HEVERNOR, WHO TAUGHT BUSINESS AND DRIVER TRAINING IN SAN LEANDRO, RECEIVING FIRST DUAL-CONTROL INSTRUCTIONAL VEHICLE BUILT BY CHEVROLET, 1955

Kira Bulger writes:

> At left, Donald Hevernor, my grandfather, taught business, accounting, and drivers training for the San Leandro School District. This photo taken in 1955, shows him receiving their first dual control instructional vehicle built by Chevrolet. As President of the CTA [local teachers union], he worked with March Fong Eu in the development of driver education programs for the state.[vii]

This family photo is so rich in helping us understand that behind-the-wheel training for young drivers had a history. Widespread deaths from traffic accidents created a need that government officials worked to meet.

[vii]Kira Bulger, Faces of America photo contest, Napa College, 2000

11-18   TONY MAGSANAY, MANAGER OF CITY HALL SHELL STATION, VALLEJO, 1961

Tony was the manager of the City Hall Shell Station at the corner of Capitol and Marin in Vallejo. I remember the independently owned and operated service stations where knowledgeable mechanics helped customers. What happened to them? We need to know. Look at the satisfaction of doing a good job on his face. This service station was leveled and is now a parking lot for the Vallejo Naval and Historical Museum.

QUESTION: How can we learn the history of drivers training and full-service gas stations? Have they also disappeared in other states? How would we find out why we lost both of these in California?

11-19   GEORGE AND MARY ELLEN BOYET WEDDING, NAPA, 1963

George Boyet came to Napa to teach history at the community college in 1958. He met and married Mary Ellen Florea, a French teacher at Napa High School. The couple attended church at First Methodist where their minister, Andrew Juvenal, was a disciple of Gandhi. George Boyet describes Napa as a "6 pm Town, where people of color were harassed after dark."[viii]

Reverend Juvenal was saddened by the housing segregation he witnessed, so he created an Ecumenical Race Relations Committee. He requested that members of his congregation sign a pledge to buy, sell, and rent to anyone, regardless of race. George and Mary Ellen Boyet supported the minister, but others left his church in protest. In the summer of 1963, Juvenal's house was firebombed. Crosses were planted and Ku Klux Klan literature was strewn on the lawn.

[viii]For more, see James Loewen's *Sundown Towns: A Hidden Dimension of Segregation in America* (New York: Norton), 2005.

11-20   KARESE YOUNG, WASHINGTON ELEMENTARY SCHOOL, BERKELEY, 1964

Koy Lynn Hardy writes:

> Karese Young, my mother, Washington Elementary School, Berkeley 1964. This second grade photo of my mother shows one of many darling children experiencing the benefits of the civil rights movement. Karese lived across the street from the Rumford family of the famed Rumford Act that banned racial discrimination in housing in 1964.[ix]

Historian Charles Wollenberg describes the Rumford Act:

> In the 1920's, businessman D.G. Gibson had started the Appomattox Club as a way of organizing East Bay African Americans into a voting bloc. . . . In 1948 Gibson put together a coalition of CIO union activists, white liberals and African American voters to campaign for Sacramento street pharmacist William Byron Rumford, who was running for state assembly in a district that included much of Berkeley and part of Oakland. Rumford won the election, becoming the first African American from Northern California to serve in the legislature. He eventually authored two of the state's most important civil rights law—the Fair Employment Practices Act of 1959 and the Rumford Fair Housing Act of 1963.[x]

[ix]Kay Hardy, Faces of America photo contest, Napa College, 2000.

[x]Charles Wollenberg, "Berkeley: A City in History," http://berkeleypubliclibrary.org/system/Chapter8.html.

11-21 WOMAN PICKETING ELKS CLUB, SACRAMENTO, c. 1964

This photo shows how Californians protested segregation, sometimes one person at a time. We can guess that the Elks Club in her town was segregated, and that this lone woman—hat, sunglasses, and all—decided it was important enough to make her own sign and picket the club. Likewise, Lorna Smith, inspired by her experiences with the EPIC campaign in the 1930s, marched with Stokely Carmichael for civil rights.

QUESTION: If you could talk to George Boyet, Karese Young, Byron Rumford, Lorna Smith, or this unknown picketer about their civil rights work, whom would you choose and what would your questions be?

11-22   RONALD RIESTERER, MARIO SAVIO, 1964

In 1964, there was a primary battle in the Republican Party between conservative Barry Gold-water and Bill Scranton who supported desegregation of public schools. Scranton supporters came to the campus at the University of California at Berkeley to persuade students to demon-strate at the Republican convention. Hoping to squash the students' plan, Goldwater support-ers pressured university officials to ban from campus all tables displaying political flyers.

University of California student Mario Savio had just returned from registering voters in Mississippi. The fight he led on the Berkeley campus, which came to be called the Free Speech Movement, was for the right of students to engage in on-campus political advocacy. Before leading students into Sproul Hall to begin their sit-in on December 3, 1964, Savio told them:

> There is a time when the operation of the machine becomes so odious, makes you so sick at heart, that you can't take part; you can't even passively take part, and you've got to put your bodies upon the gears.[xi]

See http://bancroft.berkeley.edu/FSM/ for more on this passionate and controversial movement.

[xi]http://www.brumm.com/antiwar/mar22/45.html.

12

A Front Row Seat Watching the World Change: 1965–1980

The things we point our cameras at are tantamount to the footprints of a civilization.

—Harold Adler, The Whole World is Watching

Most Californians may not have considered themselves activists, but Leon Litwak notes this era was

> A time when significant numbers of Americans came to believe that direct, personal commitment to social justice was a moral imperative. Few have cared more deeply about this nation than some of its severest critics."[i]

Although it once seemed to historians that the anti-war movement peaked in the 1960s and ended with the withdrawal of American forces from Vietnam in 1973, recent analyses note that the other movements of the 1970s were equally transformative. These included the Chicano, Asian, American Indian, Black Power, and Women's Liberation, which included women from all of the other movements. This chapter explores that activist legacy and concludes with the election of former California Governor Ronald Reagan, a stalwart opponent of all of these movements, to the American Presidency.

12-1 GARY SOTO, "FIELD"

The wind sprays pale dirt into my mouth
The small, almost invisible scars
On my hands.

The pores in my throat and elbows
Have taken in a seed of dirt of their own.

After a day in the grape fields near Rolinda
A fine silt, washed by sweat,
Has settled into the lines
On my wrists and palms.

---

[i]Leon Litwack, "The Times they are a-Changin'," essay in *The Whole World is Watching: Peace and Social Justice Movements of the 1960s and 1970s* (Berkeley: Berkeley Art Center Association), 2001, 8.

> Already I am becoming the valley,
> A soil that sprouts nothing
> For any of us.

12-2 ALFREDO VEA, EXCERPT FROM *SILVER CLOUD CAFÉ,* "ZEFERINO'S FATHERS," 1996

During his childhood, Alfredo Vea lived with his mother in migrant camps in Stockton where her Filipino coworkers gave the boy a set of encyclopedias and taught him to read and write. Later Vea served in Vietnam, and after the war, he put himself through law school and volunteered his legal services for the United Farm Workers. Alfredo Vea is now a criminal defense attorney in San Francisco.

At the edge of the hot, shadeless fields, Zeferino the boy silently worked the furrow closest to the highway. Squash were as hard to pick as cotton, he thought. His hands were getting raw again, almost as raw as his back, which was covered now with a layer of white salt. The petroleum jelly that one of his *tios* had applied there to prevent sweat rash had been completely washed away by midmorning.

Zefe paused to look to his right. What he saw there soothed and comforted him. Señor Chavez was out there as usual, passing out handbills that protested the miserable working conditions and the slave wages. He was young and unknown and picketing all by himself, stooping now and again to carefully smell the leaves for the telltale scent of insecticides.

One day a young welfare worker came out to the fields where Zeferino was working. She looked totally out of place in her suit and heels. Someone had told her that there was a boy laboring out there who should've been in school. Zeferino remembered that she had asked where his mother was and that he had told her that he didn't know, that she never spent much time in the camps. When she asked him about his father he told her that he had no idea who he was and that he had never seen him.

"But I have lots of uncles, señora. In fact, I have over thirty of them," the boy had explained. The welfare worker didn't seem very impressed by what he had said, so she dragged the boy—kicking and screaming—out of the fields. His *tios* had protested, but they all knew that she was right. They knew that a childhood should not be spent laboring in the furrows. Though the boy hated her at the time, he understood the woman's heart was in the right place.

"I remember that she bought me some brand-new school clothes and made me take off all of my muddy gear," Zeferino said excitedly to an unconscious King and to Anatoly, who was parked in front of Radio City Music Hall. "Then she placed me into a classroom in some town that I can no longer recall. I can still see the faces of those children staring at my battered work boots. I do remember clearly that the teacher in that classroom ended the first day of class by reminding the children that in three days the school would be having their yearly Father's Day celebration. All of the children were expected to bring their fathers to school on that day."

"Pobrecito," said Raphael from above.

"I remember how miserable I felt as I walked back to the camp. I imagined myself at Father's Day, the only kid there without a father." It bothered the boy so much that he couldn't eat and even the sweet music from the Mexican Quonset couldn't cheer him up. He told one of his *tios* that he wanted to run away, that he just couldn't go back to school on Father's Day.

"Well, I must have told my *tio* the wrong day, because, on the day before Father's Day, thirty farm-workers dressed in their work clothes walked slowly, single file into the classroom. Each one had carefully combed his hair and put on his cleanest dirty workshirt. The entire classroom smelled of pomade and brilliantine and sweat.

"How could I have ever forgotten that morning?" Zeferino said, exhaling his emotions onto the rusted hood of the cab and onto the windshield. Anatoly suddenly ceased his incessant chatter as Zeferino's voice dropped to a whisper.

"There they were, forming a circle around the class, all of them shifting nervously and smiling shyly at the teacher and so proudly at me. They had their sharpened paring knives and long machetes hanging from their belts. They had taken the time to brush the mud from their knee pads and each man had carefully folded his bandanna into his shirt pocket. Each of my uncles held his straw hat respectfully in his hands.

"They were Mexicans, Pinoys, and Hindus, all missing a day's pay . . . for me." Zeferino paused while the power of the memory washed over him. Anatoly said nothing and King moaned inconsolably in the backseat. Above them all, a silent Raphael watched and listened. Zeferino's eyes glistened with emotion.

"These were strangers in America, men who had been told again and again that their own lives were a poor imitation of the lives around them. But that morning, they all braved the other world for my sake. I remember that, finally, one of them stepped forward and with a heavy accent spoke a single sentence to the class: 'We are Zeferino's father.'"

QUESTION: Vea's story shows us how important an extended friendship network has been, historically, in helping to raise children. Do you think this kind of friendship network still exists for single parents like his mother?

12-3   CÉSAR CHÁVEZ, "THE ORGANIZER'S TALE," 1966

The Organizer's Tale

It really started for me sixteen years ago in San Jose, California, when I was working on an apricot farm. We figured he was just another social worker doing a study of farm conditions, and I kept refusing to meet with him. But he was persistent. Finally, I got together some of the rough element in San Jose. We were going to have a little reception for him to teach the gringo a little bit of how we felt. There were about thirty of us in the house, young guys mostly. I was supposed to give them a signal—change my cigarette from my right hand to my left. But he started talking and the more he talked, the more wide-eyed I became and the less inclined I was to give the signal. A couple of guys who were pretty drunk at the time still wanted to give the gringo the business, but we got rid of them. This fellow was making a lot of sense, and I wanted to hear what he had to say.

His name was Fred Ross, and he was an organizer for the Community Service Organization (CSO), which was working with Mexican Americans in the cities. I became immediately really involved. Before long I was heading a voter-registration drive. All the time I was observing the things Fred did, secretly, because I wanted to learn how to organize, to see how it was done. I was impressed with his patience and understanding of people. I thought this was a tool, one of the greatest things he had.

It was pretty rough for me at first. I was changing and had to take a lot of ridicule from the kids my age, the rough characters I worked with in the fields. They would say, "Hey, big shot. Now that you're a politico, why are you working here for sixty-five cents an hour?" I might add that our neighborhood had the highest percentage of San Quentin graduates. It was a game among the pachucos in the sense that we defended ourselves from outsiders, although inside the neighborhood there was not a lot of fighting.

After six months of working every night in San Jose, Fred assigned me to take over the CSO chapter in Decoto. It was a tough spot to fill. I would suggest something, and people would say, "No, let's wait till Fred gets back" or "Fred wouldn't do it that way." This is pretty much a pattern with people, I discovered, whether I was put in Fred's position or, later, when someone else was put in my position. After the Decoto assignment I was sent to start a new chapter in Oakland. Before I left, Fred came to a place in San Jose called the Hole-in-the-Wall and we talked for half an hour over coffee. He was in a rush to leave, but I wanted to keep him talking; I was that scared of my assignment.

Those were hard times in Oakland. First of all, it was a big city and I'd get lost every time I went anywhere. Then I arranged a series of house meetings. I would get to the meeting early and drive back and forth past the house, too nervous to go in and face the people. Finally I would force myself to go inside and sit in a corner. I was quite thin then, and young, and most of the people were middle-aged. Someone would say, "Where's the organizer?" And I would pipe up, "Here I am." Then they would say in Spanish—these were very poor people and we hardly spoke anything but Spanish—"Ha! This *kid*?" Most of them said they were interested, but the hardest part was to get them to start pushing themselves, on their own initiative.

The idea was to set up a meeting and then get each attending person to call his own house meeting, inviting new people—a sort of chain-letter effect. After a house meeting I would lie awake going over the whole thing, playing the tape back, trying to see why people laughed at one point or why they were for one thing and against another. I was also learning to read and write, those late evenings. I had left school in the seventh grade after attending sixty-seven different schools, and my reading wasn't the best.

At our first organizing meeting we had 368 people; I'll never forget it because it was very important to me. You eat your heart out; the meeting is called for seven o'clock and you start to worry about four. You wait. Will they show up? Then the first one arrives. By seven there are only twenty people; you have everything in order, you have to look calm. But little by little they filter in, and at a certain point you know it will be a success.

After four months in Oakland, I was transferred. The chapter was beginning to move on its own, so Fred assigned me to organize the San Joaquin Valley. Over the months I developed what I used to call schemes or tricks—now I call them techniques—of making initial contacts. The main thing in convincing someone is to spend time with him. It doesn't matter if he can read, write, or even speak well. What is important is that he is a man and, second, that he has shown some initial interest. One good way to develop leadership is to take a man with you in your car. And it works a lot better if you're doing the driving; that way you are in charge. You drive, he sits there, and you talk. These little things were very important to me; I was caught in a big game by then, figuring out what makes people work. I found that if you work hard enough, you can usually shake people into working too, those who are concerned. You work harder and they work harder still—up to a point, and then they pass you. Then, of course, they're on their own.

I also learned to keep away from the established groups and so-called leaders, and to guard against philosophizing. Working with low-income people is very different from working with the professionals, who like to sit around talking about how to play politics. When you're trying to recruit a farmworker, you have to paint a little picture, and then you have to color the picture in. We found out that the harder a guy is to convince, the better leader or member he becomes. When you exert yourself to convince him, you have his confidence and he has good motivation. A lot of people who say OK right away wind up hanging around the office, taking up the workers' time.

During the McCarthy era in one Valley town, I was subjected to a lot of red-baiting. We had been recruiting people for citizenship classes at the high school when we got into a quarrel with the naturalization examiner. He was rejecting people on the grounds that they were just parroting what they learned in citizenship class. One day we had a meeting about it in Fresno, and I took along some of the leaders of our local chapter. Some red-baiting official gave us a hard time, and the people got scared and took his side. They did it because it seemed easy at the moment, even though they knew that sticking with me was the right thing to do. It was disgusting. When we left the building, they walked by themselves ahead of me as if I had some kind of communicable disease. I had been working with these people for three months and I was very sad to see that. It taught me a great lesson.

That night I learned that the chapter officers were holding a meeting to review my letters and printed materials to see if I really was a Communist. So I drove out there and walked right in on their meeting. I said, "I hear you've been discussing me, and I thought it would be nice if I was here to defend myself. Not that it matters that much to you or even to me, because as far as I'm concerned you are a bunch of cowards." At that they began to apologize. "Let's forget it," they said. "You're a nice guy."

But I didn't want apologies. I wanted a full discussion. I told them that they had to learn to distinguish fact from what appeared to be a fact because of fear. I kept them there till two in the morning. Some of the women cried. I don't know if they investigated me any further, but I stayed on another few months and things worked out.

This was not an isolated case. Often when we'd leave people to themselves, they would get frightened and draw back into their shells where they had been all the years. And I learned quickly that there is no real appreciation. Whatever you do, and no matter what reasons you may give to others, you do it because you want to see it done, or maybe because you want power. And there shouldn't be any appreciation, understandably. I know good organizers who were destroyed, washed out, because they expected people to appreciate what they'd done. Things don't work that way.

For more than ten years I worked for the CSO. As the organization grew, we found ourselves meeting in fancier and fancier motels and holding expensive conventions. Doctors, lawyers, and politicians began joining. They would get elected to some office in the organization and then, for all practical purposes, leave. Intent on using the CSO for their own prestige purposes, these "leaders," many of them, lacked the urgency we had to have. When I became general director, I began to press for a program to organize farmworkers into a union—an idea most of the leadership opposed. So I started a revolt within the CSO. I refused to sit at the head table at meetings, refused to wear a suit and tie, and finally I even refused to shave and cut my hair. It used to embarrass some of the professionals.

At every meeting I got up and gave my standard speech: we shouldn't meet in fancy motels, we were getting away from the people, farmworkers had to be organized. But nothing happened. In March of '62 I resigned and came to Delano to begin organizing the Valley on my own.

I drew a map of all the towns between Arvin and Stockton—eighty-six of them, including farming camps—and decided to hit them all to get a small nucleus of people working in each. For six months I traveled around, planting an idea. We had a simple questionnaire, a little card with space for name, address, and how much the worker thought he ought to be paid. My wife, Helen, mimeographed them, and we took our kids for two- or three-day jaunts to these towns, distributing the cards door to door and to camps and groceries.

Some eighty thousand cards were sent back from eight Valley counties. I got a lot of contacts that way, but I was shocked at the wages the people were asking. The growers were paying $1.00 and $1.15, and maybe 95 percent of the people thought they should be getting only $1.25. Sometimes people scribbled messages on the cards: "I hope to God we win" or "Do you think we can win?" or "I'd like to know more." So I separated the cards with the penciled notes, got in my car, and went to those people.

We didn't have any money at all in those days, none for gas and hardly any for food. So I went to people and started asking for food. It turned out to be about the best thing I could have done, although at first it's hard on your pride. Some of our best members came in that way. If people give you their food, they'll give you their hearts. Several months and many meetings later we had a working organization, and this time the leaders were the people.

None of the farmworkers had collective bargaining contracts, and I thought it would take ten years before we got that first contract. I wanted desperately to get some color into the movement, to give people something they could identify with, like a flag. I was reading some books about how various leaders discovered what colors contrasted and stood out the best. The Egyptians had found that a red field with a white circle and a black emblem in the center crashed into your eyes like nothing else. I wanted to use the Aztec eagle in the center, as on the Mexican flag. So I told my cousin Manuel, "Draw an Aztec eagle." Manuel had a little trouble with it, so we modified the eagle to make it easier for people to draw.

The first big meeting of what we decided to call the National Farm Workers Association was held in September 1962, at Fresno, with 287 people. We had our huge red flag on the wall, with paper tacked over it. When the time came, Manuel pulled a cord, ripping the paper off the flag, and all of a sudden it hit the people. Some of them wondered if it was a Communist flag, and I said it probably looked more like a neo-Nazi emblem than anything else. But they wanted an explanation, so Manuel got up and said, "When that eagle flies— that's when the farmworkers' problems are going to be solved."

One of the first things I decided was that outside money wasn't going to organize people, at least not in the beginning. I even turned down a grant from a private group— $50,000 to go directly to organize farmworkers—for just this reason. Even when there are no strings attached, you are still compromised because you feel you have to produce immediate results. This is bad, because it takes a long time to build a movement, and your organization suffers if you get too far ahead of the people it belongs to. We set the dues at $42 a year per family—really meaningful dues—but of the 212 families we got to pay, only twelve remained by June of '63. We were discouraged at that, but not enough to make us quit.

Money was always a problem. Once we were facing a $180 gas bill on a credit card I'd got a long time ago and was about to lose. And we *had* to keep that credit card.

One day my wife and I were picking cotton, pulling bolls, to make a little money to live on. Helen said to me, "Do you put all this in the bag, or just the cotton?" I thought she was kidding and told her to throw the whole boll in, so that she had nothing but a sack of bolls at the weighing.

The man said, "Whose sack is this?" I said, "Well, my wife's," and he told us we were fired.

Helen and I started laughing. We were going anyway. We took the $4 we had earned and spent it at a grocery store where they were giving away a $100 prize. Each time you shopped they'd give you one of the letters of M-O-N-E-Y or a flag; you had to have M-O-N-E-Y plus the flag to win. Helen had already collected the letters and just needed the flag. Anyway, they gave her the ticket. She screamed, "A flag? I don't believe it," ran in, and got the $100. She said, "Now we're going to eat steak." But I said, "No, we're going to pay the gas bill." I don't know if she cried, but I think she did.

It was rough in those early years. Helen was having babies and I was not there when she was at the hospital. But if you haven't got your wife behind you, you can't do many things. There's got to be peace at home. So I did, I think, a fairly good job of organizing her. When we were kids, she lived in Delano and I came to town as a migrant. Once on a date we had a bad experience about segregation at a movie theater, and I put up a fight. We were together then, and still are. I think I'm more of a pacifist than she is. Her father, Fabela, was a colonel with Pancho Villa in the Mexican Revolution. Sometimes she gets angry and tells me, "These scabs—you should deal with them sternly," and I kid her, "It must be too much of that Fabela blood in you."

The Movement really caught on in '64. By August we had a thousand members. We'd had a beautiful ninety-day drive in Corcoran, where they had the Battle of the Corcoran

Farm Camp thirty years ago, and by November we had assets of $25,000 in our credit union, which helped to stabilize the membership. I had gone without pay the whole of 1963. The next year the members voted me a $40-a-week salary, after Helen had to quit working in the fields to manage the credit union.

Our first strike was in May of '65—a small one but it prepared us for the big one. A farmworker from McFarland named Epifanio Camacho came to see me. He said he was sick and tired of how people working the roses were being treated, and was willing to "go the limit."

I assigned Manuel and Gilbert Padilla to hold meetings at Camacho's house. The people wanted union recognition, but the real issue, as in most cases when you begin, was wages. They were promised $9.00 a thousand, but they were actually getting $6.50 and $7.00 for grafting roses. Most of them signed cards giving us the right to bargain for them. We chose the biggest company, with about eighty-five employees, not counting the irrigators and supervisors, and we held a series of meetings to prepare the strike and call the vote. There would be no picket line; everyone pledged on their honor not to break the strike.

Early on the first morning of the strike, we sent out ten cars to check the people's homes. We found lights in five or six homes and knocked on the doors. The men were getting up, and we'd say, "Where are you going?" They would dodge. "Oh, uh . . . I was just getting up, you know." We'd say, "Well, you're not going to work, are you?" And they'd say no. Dolores Huerta, who was driving the green panel truck, saw a light in one house where four rose workers lived. They told her they were going to work, even after she reminded them of their pledge. So she moved the truck so it blocked their driveway, turned off the key, put it in her purse, and sat there alone.

That morning the company foreman refused to talk to us. None of the grafters had shown up for work. At 10:30 we started to go to the company office, but it occurred to us that maybe a woman would have a better chance. So Dolores knocked on the office door, saying, "I'm Dolores Huerta from the National Farm Workers Association."

"Get out!" the man said. "You Communist. Get out!" I guess they were expecting us, because as Dolores stood arguing with him the cops came and told her to leave. She left.

For two days the fields were idle. On Wednesday they recruited a group of Filipinos from out of town who knew nothing of the strike, maybe thirty-five of them. They drove through escorted by three sheriff's patrol cars—one in front, one in the middle, and one at the rear with a dog. We didn't have a picket line, but we parked across the street and just watched them go through, not saying a word. All but seven stopped working after half an hour, and the rest had quit by midafternoon.

The company made an offer the evening of the fourth day, a package deal that amounted to a 120-percent wage increase, but no contract. We wanted to hold out for a contract and more benefits, but a majority of the rose workers wanted to accept the offer and go back. We are a democratic union, so we had to support what they wanted to do. They had a meeting and voted to settle. Then we had a problem with a few militants who wanted to hold out. We had to convince them to go back to work, as a united front, because otherwise they could be canned. So we worked—Tony Orendain and I, Dolores and Gilbert, Jim Drake and all the organizers—knocking on doors till two in the morning, telling people, "You have to go back or you'll lose your job."

And they did. They worked.

Our second strike, and our last before the big one at Delano, was in the grapes at Martin's Ranch. The people were getting a raw deal there, being pushed around pretty badly. Gilbert went out to the field, climbed on top of a car, and took a strike vote. They voted unanimously to go out. Right away they started bringing in strikebreakers, so we launched a tough attack on the labor contractors, distributed leaflets portraying them as really low characters. We attacked one so badly that he just gave up the job, and he took twenty-seven of his men out with him. All he asked was that we distribute another leaflet reinstating him in the community. And we did. What was unusual was that the grower would still talk to us. The grower kept saying, "I can't pay. I just haven't got the money." I guess he must have found the money somewhere, because we were asking $1.40 and we got it.

We had just finished the Martin strike when the Agricultural Workers Organizing Committee (AFL-CIO) started a strike against the grape growers, DiGiorgio, Schenley liquors, and small growers, asking $1.40 an hour and 25 cents a box. There was a lot of pressure from our members for us to join the strike, but we had some misgivings. We didn't feel ready for a big strike like this one, one that was sure to last a long time. Having no money—just $87 in the strike fund—meant we'd have to depend on God knows who.

Eight days after the strike started—it takes time to get twelve hundred people together from all over the Valley—we held a meeting in Delano and voted to go out. I asked the membership to release us from the pledge not to accept outside money, because we'd need it now, a lot of it. The help came. It started because of the close, and I would say even beautiful, relationship that we've had with the Migrant Ministry for some years. They were the first to come to our rescue, financially and in every other way, and they spread the word to other benefactors.

We had planned, before, to start a labor school in November. It never happened, but we have the best labor school we could ever have, in the strike. The strike is only a temporary condition, however. We have over three thousand members spread out over a wide area, and we have to service them when they have problems. We get letters from New Mexico, Colorado, Texas, California, from farmworkers saying, "We're getting together and we need an organizer."

It kills you when you haven't got the personnel and resources. You feel badly about not sending an organizer because you look back and remember all the difficulty you had in getting two or three people together, and here *they're* together. Of course, we're training organizers, many of them younger than I was when I started in CSO. They can work twenty hours a day, sleep four, and be ready to hit it again; when you get to be thirty-nine it's a different story.

The people who took part in the strike and the march have something more than their material interest going for them. If it were only material, they wouldn't have stayed on the strike long enough to win. It is difficult to explain. But it flows out in the ordinary things they say. For instance, some of the younger guys are saying, "Where do you think's going to be the next strike?"

I say, "Well, we have to win in Delano."

They say, "We'll win, but where do we go next?"

I say, "Maybe most of us will be working in the fields."

They say, "No, I don't want to go and work in the fields. I want to organize. There are a lot of people that need our help."

So I say, "You're going to be pretty poor then, because when you strike you don't have much money." They say they don't care much about that.

And others are saying, "I have friends who are working in Texas. If we could only help them."

It is bigger, certainly, than just a strike. And if this spirit grows within the farm labor movement, one day we can use the force that we have to help correct a lot of things that are wrong in this society. But that is for the future. Before you can run, you have to learn to walk.

There are vivid memories from my childhood—what we had to go through because of low wages and the conditions, basically because there was no union. I suppose if I wanted to be fair, I could say that I'm trying to settle a personal score. I could dramatize it by saying that I want to bring social justice to farmworkers. But the truth is that I went through a lot of hell, and a lot of people did. If we can even the score a little for the workers, then we are doing something. Besides, I don't know any other work I like to do better than this. I really don't, you know.

12-4   END OF CÉSAR CHÁVEZ FAST WITH ROBERT KENNEDY, DELANO, 1968

12-5 JOSE GARCIA'S IDENTIFICATION CARD, AGE 25, 1955

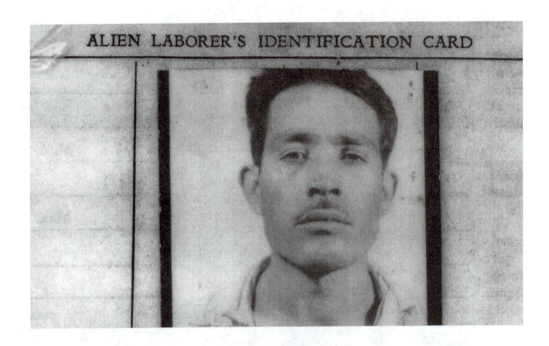

ALIEN LABORER'S IDENTIFICATION CARD

Rosa Tijero writes:

Jose Garcia, my father, alien labor ID card, taken 12/7/55, prior to coming to California to work in the fields of Salinas, where he toiled for 25 years, providing for his family in Mexico. In 1969, he marched with César Chávez. He retired from the fields in 1985 and lives with his daughter (me) in Napa.[ii]

[ii]Rosa Tijero, Faces of America photo contest, Napa College, 2000.

12-6   GRAPE STRIKERS, *UCLA DAILY BRUIN*, MAY 2, 1966

Desde Delano hasta Sacramento—the grapestrikers' march

Rene Nunez

Sacramento, California—Easter Sunday, 1966— A blustery day with scattered showers and a threatening black sky; for motorists trying to cross Sacramento's main street, West Capitol Drive, it also must have been a frustrating day as 8,000 "pilgrims," four abreast, marching to the cadence of "Huelga, huelga, huelga" (strike), dominated the city. I had joined the march two days earlier at Freeport, a fishing haven a few miles outside of the city, and for those two days I became part of what must have been a fantastic site for many unaware people. Led by a banner depicting Our Lady of Guadalupe (patron sait of the Mexican people), the flags of the United States and Mexico, interspersed with signs designating supporting organizations and hundreds of bright red flags embossed with the black eagle emblem of the National Farm Workers Association (NFWA), we marched to West Sacramento on Saturday and into Sacramento on Easter Sunday. As we entered the city and the capitol building came into view, the spirit of the "pilgrims" grew and shouts of "Viva la causa" (Long live the cause), "Viva la revolucion" (Long live the revolution), and "Viva la Virgen de Guadalupe;" (Long live our Lady of Guadalupe) with answering roars of "Viva" from the throng reverberated from the buildings.

HISTORICAL AND UNIQUE

Some of the "pilgrims" had joined the march but a few days earlier, some had been part of the march off and on, some had been on the road for twenty-five days travelling 300 miles all the way from Delano, California, the spot of an historical and unique event in the history of farm labor, the GRAPE STRIKE. Some had just walked up as the rally, at the foot of the capitol steps began—but all of these people caught the spirit and feeling of the "huelgistas" and "peregrinos", who, with their religious theme, had come to ask the governor to hear them in their struggle to achieve a decent level of dignity and living condition.

Three basic feelings were felt from these people: (1) bitterness toward an absent Governor Brown, who "traditionally spends these holidays with his family" but couldn't recognize that so do many other Americans namely 8,000 of them. A bitterness that was best expressed by the statement "apparently he (Brown) is either indifferent or hostile to the needs of the poor of Calif;" (2) the joy of knowing victory after such a long battle (on April 7, Schenley Industry Corporation recognized NFWA as sole bargaining agent for its vineyard workers and signed an agreement to begin negotiations for a contract within 30 days); and (3) the hope inspired by the Plan of Delano, a declaration by the farmworkers that change is coming, which in essence says: "Our sweat and our blood have fallen on this land (San Joaquin Valley) to make other men rich." and continues with six propositions:

1. "We seek our basic, God given rights as human beings . . . We are ready to give up everything, even our lives, in our fight for social justice."
2. "The farm worker has been abandoned to his own fate—without representation, without power—subject to the mercy and the caprice of the rancher. We are tired of words, of betrayels of indifference. To the politicians we say that the years are gone when the farm worker said nothing and did nothing to help himself."
3. "God shall not abandon us."
4. "Our men, women and children have suffered not only the basic brutality of stoop labor, and the most obvious injustice of the system; they have also suffered the desperation of knowing that that system caters to the greed of callous men and not to our needs. They have imposed hunger upon us and now we hunger for justice. ENOUGH!"
5. "The strength of the poor is also in union. We know that the poverty of the Mexican or Filipino worker in California is the same as that of the farm workers across the country . . . of all the races that comprise the oppressed minorities of the U.S. . . . We must use the only strength that we have, the force of numbers. UNITED WE SHALL STAND."
6. "We shall strike. We shall pursue the REVOLUTION we have proposed. Our revolution shall not be armed but we want the existing social order to dissolve, we want a new social order. We are poor, we are humble, and our only choice is to STRIKE in those ranches where we are not treated with the respect we deserve as working men, where our rights as free and sovereign men are not recognized."

NO LONGER IMPOTENT

To me the amazing thing about this occasion and its uniqueness was that amid the fiesta-like atmosphere of the rally; amid the guitars, the singing and the hatwaving; amid the "vivas" and the "gritos", many of us realized that, as one of the speakers put it: We (the Mexican-American people) have been taken advantage of because of our impotency—we are no longer impotent; we have been cheated because of our weaknesses—we are no longer weak; we are men." This feeling of emergence in the area of farm labor has been strengthened by Schenley's recognition of NFWA; a second breakthrough came on April 12, when Christian Brothers of California, winemakers, recognized and began bargaining with the Cesar Chavez of the NFWA—they also stated that a campaign has been started to form an employer association of other grape growers to bargain with the unions.

What has been hailed, in some quarters, as a third breakthrough, the DiGiorgio Corporation's agreement to elections on the question of unions, I believe has to be looked at from another point of view. DiGiorgio has declared that it wants to have an election of its present employees to see if they desire a union and it also wants a clause of compulsory arbitration of labor disputes. NFWA and the Agricultural Workers Organizing Committee (AWOC), an affiliate of AFL-CIO, the other striking union, have both denounced this offer, saying that the elections would call for only "scabs" (strike-breakers), to vote and that the arbitration clause is a "no-strike pledge," thus the major interest of this offer is to continue a system of worker control now held by the growers; the two unions refused to attend conciliatory meetings set up under Gov. Brown's orders and held in Fresno by the State Counciliation Service.

CLOSED DOOR MEETINGS

Another aspect of this offer of DiGiorgio's can be seen in the reaction of the Council of California Growers, which on the one hand has called Schenley's unconditional recognition of NFWA "not representative of California's agriculture" (Schenley is the second largest employer in the strike area) and "a sellout", and on the other hand has approved the DiGiorgio move. Nevertheless, representatives of NFWA and AWOC have been having closed door meetings with the growers in an effort to come to some sort of agreement.

In the meantime, the boycott which was instrumental in the signing of Schenley, has now been switched to DiGiorgio subsidiaries which include, Treesweet and S&W, with full national support of the Teamsters union. The UCLA Committee to Aid Farmworkers (SCAF), which since September of 1965, has been actively supporting the strike, the boycott and the co-op operations of the NFWA, is ready to go into Los Angeles to picket selected markets which carry Treesweet and S&W products within the next few days if DiGiorgio does not come to terms.

An interesting and somewhat revolutionary side issue has developed from the strike. Leroy Chatfield, formally Brother Golbert of the Catholic order of Christian Bros, began giving life to an idea a few months ago: A Co-op for farmworkers, a discount store in the farmlands, a non-profit organization to which farm workers could belong to. It would include a garage and an auto parts store, a building to house these, a pharmacy and a credit union. Chatfield started in the Berkeley-San Francisco area where he was able to raise $10,000 with which he bought a plot of land in Delano, laid a foundation and sunk a water-well. Now he is in Los Angeles trying to raise another $10,000 to erect a building and to make his idea reality. The UCLA Farmworkers Committee last Wednesday inagurated a program in which honorary membership to NFWA can be procured for $2, the money thus collected going to the co-op.

FORGOTTEN AREA

The co-op idea, if successful, may revolutionize an area of America that has been forgotten except by the people who are forced to endure the conditions of that area. This may be one of the answers for a people who, unlike industrial workers, are not covered by federal laws such as minimum wage, unemployment insurance and the National Labor Relations Act, which sets up procedures for holding union representation elections.

The co-op, the strike, the boycott—weapons of the poor, church, union and student support; and an historic pilgrimage to Sacremento that rivaled the civil rights march on Washington, are forces that are beginning to lift a giant whose voice one day will be heard throughout this nation—a giant who is starting to undo the bonds that have held him fast—a giant who is no longer impotent and weak— "From this movement shall spring leaders who shall understand us, lead us, be faithful to us . . . WE SHALL BE HEARD!

12-7   BOB FITCH, DOROTHY DAY, FOUNDER OF CATHOLIC WORKER MOVEMENT, WITH UFW PICKETERS IN ORANGE GROVES, LAMONT, 1973

QUESTION: The United Farm Workers introduced a new model of labor organizing within a multiracial and spiritual movement. After reading Chavez, Tijero, and Vea, looking at the photographs, and thinking back to Dorothy Day's Depression era interview with Tom Mooney, would you have wished to be part of this movement? For the story of a similar movement, see http://www.aflcio.org/aboutus/unionsummer.

By 1965, California was the leading state in receiving federal defense dollars, and during the Vietnam War, the Oakland Army Base was the largest military port complex in the world. While thousands of soldiers came through California on their way to "Nam," Californians passionately debated about the war. As political scientist Jeff Lustig has noted:

> In Panorama City in 1967, Navy veteran JD Copping burned himself to death in protest
> . . . a week later a Buddhist woman in San Diego did the same . . . Florence Beaumont,
> the leader of the San Gabriel Valley Council Against the War, followed. . . . By 1970,

George Winne had also committed suicide at University of California in San Diego. . . .
California thus accounted for four of the seven known tragic self-immolations in protest
against the war.[iii]

12-8 RONALD RIESTERER, STUDENTS HOLDING SIGNS AT CHARTER DAY, UNIVERSITY OF CALIFORNIA AT BERKELEY, 1966

We are fortunate to have the accounts of civil rights activists like Carson and Davis. But millions of young people in the 1960s who joined them remain largely unknown. We see their
faces in Riesterer's powerful photo of a protest in 1966 on Charter Day at University of
California Berkeley where U.S. Ambassador to the United Nations Arthur Goldberg was
speaking in defense of President Lyndon Johnson's Vietnam policies.

[iii]Jeff Lustig, "The War at Home: California's Struggle to Stop the Vietnam War," in *What's Going On: California and the Vietnam Era*, edited by Eymann and Wollenberg (Berkeley: University of California), 2004, 71.

12-9   ABRAHAM IGNACIO, JR., "THE TURNING POINT"

Like other communities of color during the 1960's and 1970's, the Filipino American community became involved with the struggles for civil rights and later to end U.S. intervention in Vietnam. The second-generation college age Filipino Americans on the west coast spearheaded the community's entry into broader political struggles of the time. Many of us joined the anti-war marches and student strikes for ethnic studies on college campuses. We began to question the second class status of Filipinos in American society. Many of us joined community struggles around issues like low-cost housing, equal job opportunity, immigrant rights and affirmative action. Out of these struggles arose a Filipino Identity movement among Filipino teenagers and young adults.

I reached a turning point in my life in the mid-1970's with the reading of a book— *America is in the Heart* by Carlos Bulosan. It was my first year in college at the University of California at San Diego. I was so captivated by the book I read it in one sitting. I could not put it down. The story it told of our people's experiences during the 1920's and 1930's brought out many different emotions and thoughts within me. At times anger seethed within me, then deep sadness took over. It was a book that was read by hundreds of my generation and revealed to us a history which was untold in our school books. It started me on a path to political activism in the Filipino community.

12-10   NACIO JAN BROWN, HIGH SCHOOL STUDENTS,
SAN FRANCISCO, 1969

12-11 ANGELA DAVIS, EXCERPT FROM *WITH MY MIND ON FREEDOM: AN AUTOBIOGRAPHY*

In October 1966 the Black Panther Party was organized in Oakland. Panther leaders spoke publicly against the war and pointed out that African Americans were serving in front-line combat at a disproportionately high rate. Historian Clayborne Carson remembers handing out anti-war leaflets at the Los Angeles train station, where he was repeatedly arrested. His efforts to gain conscientious objector status failed, and eventually, he and his wife left the U.S. in order to avoid being sent to Vietnam.

They returned to Los Angeles in 1969 where Carson began attending Professor Gary Nash's new class at the University of California Los Angeles on race relations in the United States. He remembers: "As one of a small number of black college graduates on campus, I was soon recruited to be an informal teaching assistant, leading a section of Nash's course devoted to black political thought."[iv] Carson, who is now director of the Stanford University Martin Luther Junior papers, concludes:

> Having lived through a uniquely volatile period of the state's history, I felt fortunate to have witnessed the transformation. Although racial boundaries still remain, I have come to see California as a place where there is much to be learned by crossing them.[v]

When I arrived in Southern California a few weeks later, one of the first things I did was look up the address Stokely had given me. There was no such number. After desperately knocking on door after door, it was clear that no one in the neighborhood had ever heard of Tommy J. Because I was straining toward a permanent involvement, not being able to find this brother depressed me enormously. Reluctantly, I left for San Diego without any contacts in or concrete information about the movement in Southern California.

In San Diego, the only people I knew were graduate students in the philosophy department, primarily students who were there because of Marcuse. Ricky Sherover and Bill Leiss, for example, had been graduate students at Brandeis during my senior year and had accompanied Marcuse to UCSD. Nevertheless, I did manage to get the telephone numbers of two Black community leaders: the director of a youth organization in San Diego, and a man who I later discovered was a member of the Communist Party.

I telephoned the first brother.

"Hello, this is Angela Davis. I've just arrived in San Diego to study philosophy at the university. I've been abroad for the last two years, and I want to try to contribute whatever I can to the Black movement here. Someone gave me your name and number . . ."

[iv]Clayborne Carson, 111. Carson now directs the Martin Luther King Papers Project at Stanford University.
[v]Carson, 111.

At the end of my little speech there was only silence. I did not realize then how I must have sounded—like an effervescent adolescent, or like an agent trying to worm her way to the inside. The silence continued for a while, then he finally promised to call me soon and tell me about a meeting I could attend. I didn't detect very much enthusiasm in his voice and I didn't really expect to hear from him after I hung up. I was right.

The days clumped by, the chances of a speedy acceptance into the San Diego community becoming more and more remote. Sometimes I would get into my car and, out of sheer frustration, drive into San Diego and head toward Logan Heights, where the largest concentration of Black people lived, and drive around aimlessly, daydreaming, trying to devise some way of escaping this terrible isolation.

There was little more to do than wait for classes at the university to begin. And so I studied, socialized with the philosophy students and professors, and waited, waited. At last the dormitories came alive with students returning to campus. As the resident student body grew, so did my disappointment. Not everyone had arrived, but I was hard at work searching every corner and crevice for sisters and brothers. Each day brought on a more profound dejection, for there were still no Black people on campus.

I was like an explorer who returns to his homeland after many years, with precious bounty and no one to give it to. I believed my energy, my commitment, my convictions were the treasure I had accumulated, and I looked high and low for a way to spend it. I roamed the campus, examined the bulletin boards, read the newspapers, talked to everyone who might know: Where are my people? It was as if I would be churned up and destroyed inside by these irrepressible desires to become a part of a liberation movement if I did not soon discover an outlet for them. Therefore, I turned to the radical students' organization on campus, and participated in the planning of an action against the war in Vietnam.

In 1967 masses of people had not yet arrived at the conclusion that the war ought to come to an immediate halt. Consequently many of our efforts to talk to the people in the streets of San Diego were immediately and abruptly rebuffed. Many refused to even take our literature. But since this was my first demonstration in the United States, for a number of years, I was enthusiastic and excited. The hostile attitudes of the people in the streets gave me all the more reason to talk harder, longer and more persuasively.

As zealous as I felt, as clearly as I understood the political necessity for this demonstration, I still experienced a sense of alienation among these students. Emotionally I was a stranger—in a way that I had never been a stranger among white people before. It was not the feeling of my childhood in the South. It was not the alienation I experienced in New York upon realizing that many of the whites around me were going out of their way to make me feel that they were not racist. It was a new strangeness that I felt. But one I would have to deal with later.

Meanwhile, the contingent of police overseeing our demonstration grew larger. A police car was stationed on every corner now. Uniformed and plain-clothes agents were all around. San Diego was not used to such demonstrations. That its defenses would be extreme could have been predicted beforehand.

When the atmosphere seemed to be reaching a boiling point, the decision was made to return to the campus and pick up reinforcements. Since my '58 Buick was one of the largest cars we had, I accepted the assignment of making the fifteen-mile trip back to La Jolla. But by the time we reached the university, a call had come in telling us that arrests had already been made.

The next step was to retrieve the prisoners. We mustered up enough for the bond. Three of us, a man, another woman and I, went down to the jail, posted the money and awaited the release of our companions. The charges that had been lodged against them were still an enigma to us. We inquired about the precise circumstances surrounding the arrest. Previously we had been told that the charge was "obstructing pedestrian traffic."

Since no one in the front office could satisfy us, we were directed to the chambers of the patrol captain, We entered into a dark room musty with the odor of San Diego justice. Again, we posed the question. Why the arrests? Again the answer was mechanically spouted out to us: "obstructing pedestrian traffic on the side-walk." We were persistent. What does that mean? We ourselves were passing out literature as well; we knew we did not prevent anyone from passing.

"Well," said the patrol captain, "as long as you are standing on the sidewalk, you may be considered to be obstructing pedestrian traffic."

"Then how many times have you arrested Jehovah's Witnesses distributing their religious literature?"

Silence.

"Sir, could you be a little more explicit and a little clearer in your explanation of the reasons for the arrests of our friends?"

The captain began to say something, but became so completely tongue-tied he was not able to get the words out. Finally, out of sheer frustration and evidently disturbed by our logic, he blurted out—"It is not the police's job to understand the law; that is the job of the district attorney. If you want to understand the meaning of this law, go to the D.A.!"

Although we realized that we were in the chambers of our enemy, this remark was so stupid and so funny that all three of us roared with laughter.

"Get out of this place! Get out!" the captain, now out of control, screamed.

We were trying to regain our composure when we noticed him dialing a number on his telephone. In less than a minute, his office was full of policemen who came for a single purpose: to throw us into jail.

Our male companion was carted off; Anna and I were handcuffed and pushed into the back seat of a patrol car parked in the steaming hot courtyard of the city jail complex. The windows were closed, and we saw that police cars have no door handles on the inside. The police officer slammed the doors and walked away. Fifteen minutes passed, then twenty. The heat had become absolutely intolerable. Sweat was pouring down our faces and our clothes were drenched. We banged on the windows and screamed. No one came.

Just as our fear began to approach panic, the officer walked toward the car, got in and started up the motor.

"What do you girls do for a living?" he asked.

"We don't have jobs," we answered.

"If you don't have a job, then we can pin vagrancy on you."

"We have money in our purses; that proves we aren't vagrants."

"That's even better," he said. "If you have money, but no job, we can charge you with robbery—or better than that, armed robbery."

On the way to the jail, we looked at San Diego through the windows of the police car. The screeching of the siren attracted stares from the crowds of people in the downtown area. What were they thinking? Were we prostitutes, drug users, robbers, or had we gotten caught in a confidence game? I doubt if the idea crossed any of their minds that we might be revolutionaries.

In the woman's section of the county jail, we were directed to a room and instructed to remove all of our clothes in the presence of a matron. Anna and I protested this degradation long and hard before we were forced to acquiesce. The next stage was a hot shower in a room where a heavy iron door was locked behind us. After being left for an hour in the shower room, we were placed in separate silvery-colored, padded cells, where we had to suffer through another waiting period. Thinking I could use some of this time constructively, I scratched political slogans on the walls with a burnt match for the benefit of the sisters who would occupy this cell next.

Many hours passed before the mug shots and fingerprints were finally taken, our booking sheet written up. We made the telephone calls due us and, dressed in prisoner's uniforms, were taken to the jail population upstairs.

They put us in a large tank separated from the outside corridor by a double gate of electrically operated bars. The first gate slid open at the push of a button. Anna and I stepped inside between the two gates. It slid closed. Only when it was securely locked did the second gate leading into the tank open.

The tank itself was as depressingly sterile as jail tanks are meant to be. It was divided into two sections—one with the bunks for sleeping and the other for eating and game-playing. We explained to each sister who inquired what we had done to be arrested. Our explanation singled us out, in 1967, as curiosities. Many of the sisters, in jail on such charges as possession of drugs and prostitution, tried to comfort us. They felt that the charges against us were silly and would be dropped.

They were right. At long last we were released.

In the meantime other demonstrators had informed the news media that three people in San Diego had been arrested when they tried to inquire about the nature of a law. A rock station based in Los Angeles was running a spot every hour: "Have you heard about the people down south who got arrested because they wanted to know about the law?"

The university agreed to lodge an official protest, and within two days, the district attorney of San Diego dropped the charges and made a formal apology.

A few days later, during a meeting of the group that had organized the demonstration, I was excited to see a young Black couple sitting on the other side of the room. They were the first Black students I had seen on the campus—and their presence at the meeting meant they were interested in the movement. After the meeting, we introduced ourselves, and within a short time Liz and Ed and I decided to try to organize a Black Student Union.

QUESTION: Do the students in Riesterer's photo look like your image of anti-war demonstrators? What new impressions did you gain from Nacio Jan Brown's photograph and Abraham Ignacio, Jr.'s, essay?

Ronald Reagan began his career as an actor and as president of the Screen Actor's Guild. By the late 1940s, he had evolved, says historian Jules Tygiel, into "a militant anti-communist, operating as an informant for the FBI, assisting in the enforcement of the Hollywood blacklist."[vi] In the 1950s, Reagan became the national spokesperson for General Electric, who then fired him in the 1960s for what Tygiel calls "his often shrill conservatism."[vii]

In 1964, the California Real Estate Association labeled the anti-discrimination Rumford Fair Housing Act as "forced housing." The Association placed an initiative on the ballot, Proposition 14, seeking to overturn the Rumford Act. Reagan was an ardent supporter of Proposition 14, arguing, "if an individual wants to discriminate against Negroes or others in selling or renting his home, he has a right to do so."[viii]

California voters passed Proposition 14. Encouraged by this victory, Republican leaders concluded that Reagan could overcome the 3–2 majority of registered Democrats in the state and nominated him to run for governor. During the 1966 campaign, Reagan began to denounce the anti-war movement, particularly "the mess at Berkeley."[ix] Despite possessing, in the description of one of his advisers, "zero" knowledge about California, Reagan won the California gubernatorial election. Tygiel argues that this election broadened the message of conservatism "from an ideology of the privileged elites to one with a populist base," and that it "may be the most significant legacy of California during the Vietnam War Era."[x]

12-12 ESTER GULICK, CATHERINE KERR, AND SYLVIA MCLAUGHLIN, *SAVING THE BAY*

Another legacy of this era was a victory in the fight to save San Francisco Bay. *California Going, Going*, published in 1962, was one of the earliest indictments of environmental decay.[xi] The booklet warned that because of environmental changes and massive population growth, California was "running out of space, causing congestion and straining other finite resources such as air, water, forests and wilderness."[xii]

Thousands of acres of tidal flats and marshes in the San Francisco Bay were being covered by landfill every year for commercial development. Had the practice continued, the bay would have been reduced to a few polluted channels by 2000. When Governor Reagan opposed plans developed by the three East Bay women in this document, they responded by

---

[vi]Jules Tygiel, "Reagan and the Triumph of Conservatism," in *What's Going On: California and the Vietnam Era*, edited by Eymann and Wollenberg (Berkeley: University of California), 2004, 48.

[vii]Jules Tygiel, 48.

[viii]Lisa McGirr, *Suburban Warriors: The Origins of the New American Right* (Princeton, New Jersey: Princeton University Press), 2001.

[ix]See Matthew Dallek, *The Right Moment: Ronald Reagan's First Victory and the Decisive Turning Point in American Politics* (New York: Free Press), 2000.

[x]Tygiel, 52.

[xi]Samuel Wood and Alfred Heller, *California Going Going* (San Francisco: California Tomorrow), 1962.

[xii]Rice, Bullough, and Orsi, *Elusive Eden*, 600.

presenting him with 200,000 signatures on petitions, which they stretched around the Capitol. According to the history posted at http://www.safesfbay.org:

> This first modern grassroots environmental movement in the Bay Area won a revolution-
> ary change—tens of thousands of Save the Bay members forced the State of California
> to acknowledge that the Bay belonged to the public. Save The Bay won a legislative
> moratorium against placing fill in the Bay in 1965, the McAteer-Petris Act. The Bay
> Conservation and Development Commission (BCDC) was established by the State to
> plan protection of the Bay, regulate shoreline development, and ensure public access,
> which at the time was almost non-existent. BCDC became a permanent agency in 1969,
> and continues today, the first coastal zone management agency and the model for most
> others in the world.

Kay Kerr, Sylvia McLaughlin and I are very grateful for the kind words expressed in our introduction. We have had other names bestowed upon us, such as enemies of progress, impractical idealists, do-gooders, posy pickers, eco-freaks, enviromaniacs, little old ladies in tennis shoes and almond cookie revolutionaries.

We were very much concerned about what was happening to our Bay, but it was a hap-penstance that we came together. Kay and Sylvia were talking at a tea and they discussed the Army Corps of Engineers' map that had been printed in the *Oakland Tribune* in Decem-ber, 1959. It showed that the Bay could end up being nothing but a deep water ship chan-nel by the year 2020 because of the enormous amount of fill being planned. The Corps had made a study for the United States Department of Commerce and it had just been released. Shortly before Christmas in 1960 I took some almond cookies over to Kay's house, partic-ularly for her husband because they were his favorites. It was a beautiful day and the Bay was as blue as it could be. Of course, we talked about the Corps' map and Kay asked me if I thought I would have time to help do something about it. Little did I know what that was going to mean!

The three of us discussed how we could start. Berkeley's City Council and the busi-ness and industrial sector, supported by the *Berkeley Gazette*, were anxious to put over 2,000 acres of fill in the Bay so that Berkeley could almost double its size. There were grandiose plans of having an airport, industrial and commercial buildings, houses, apart-ments, a hotel or two, a parking lot and so on. Other cities had similar plans. We decided we would present the problems to some of the leaders of the larger conservation organiza-tions. We asked a group of them to meet at my home in January 1961. They were very interested and thought it was an excellent idea but, unfortunately, they all said they were much too busy to take on anything more. They thought it was essential to form another group. However, they said they would help all they could. As they left they wished us much luck. It was clear that if anything was going to be done we were "it," so we went to work, green as grass as we were.

Acquiring members was probably the most important first step so we composed a letter and sent it to people we knew, as well as to the Berkeley names on the lists we had received. We had a wonderful response—more than 90 percent. People could not believe that the pub-lic did not own the Bay. Most citizens did not know, just as we did not until a short time before, that approximately 70 percent of the Bay was less than 20 feet deep and very suscep-tible to being filled. As Mel Scott, who was with the University's Institute of Governmental

Studies, wrote: "To attorneys, developers, title insurance companies, manufacturers of salt and cement, innumerable government officials, members of the state legislature and many others, it is some of the most valuable real estate in California." The State much earlier had sold a great deal of the Bay for no more than a dollar an acre. These sales were stopped in 1879 when a new constitution was adopted.

In 1850, when California was admitted to the Union, the Bay was approximately 680 square miles. A little more than 100 years later this had been reduced by dikes and fills to about 430 square miles. There were at least 40 garbage dumps on the Bay shoreline. In Berkeley we have seen discarded furniture, old automobile tires and batteries, old mattresses and many other things, in addition to garden clippings and kitchen garbage. It was a common sight to see these dumps burning and smoking. Much of the refuse also spilled over into the water. There was a stench along the shoreline, particularly where raw sewage poured into the Bay. At the same time when there was this massive fill proposed for Berkeley, there was also a serious proposal to fill Berkeley's Aquatic Park and use the site for industry. This area had been part of the Bay until the freeway was built. The Aquatic Park proposal was defeated by only one vote of the City Council.

In 1962 Berkeley secured an amendment to its tideland grant. This allowed fills in the Bay to be used "for all commercial and industrial uses and purposes, and the construction, reconstruction, repair and maintenance of commercial and industrial buildings, plants and facilities, as may be specified by the City Council after public hearing." Save San Francisco Bay Association tried to prevent the passage of the amendment, but unfortunately failed. However, we got much favorable publicity and more members. At the end of 1962 our total membership was 2,500.

It became very clear that numerous cities and counties around the Bay had plans in various stages of development to fill many more square miles. In 1963 and again in 1964 Assemblyman Nicholas Petris introduced bills in the state legislature to protect the Bay with a moratorium on fill while the problem was studied. Although these bills lost, they alerted the legislature to the destructive threats to the Bay.

A bill was introduced into the legislature in early 1963 which would allow the Construction Aggregates Corporation of Chicago to dredge massive amounts of sand from the Potato Patch Shoal, the important ecological area just outside the Golden Gate. According to testimony of scientists, removal of the sand in the Potato Patch Shoal would have a detrimental effect also on the beaches to the south. Testimony was presented by crab and sports fishermen and concerned citizens. A multitude of letters in opposition were received by the legislators. Fortunately, the bill lost.

The Chicago corporation estimated the fill required for the projects that were being considered for the Bay as more than 1,330,000,000 cubic yards, which would mean many square miles of filling.

But back to the critical situation in Berkeley. We talked with many professional people about the proposed Berkeley fill. We spoke with engineers, economists, city planners, architects and others. Throughout the years, many of the University's faculty had donated their time and expertise to the Association. Mel Scott's book "The Future of San Francisco Bay," written for the Institute of Governmental Studies, was an invaluable resource and the definitive book about San Francisco Bay. We were extremely fortunate and are very grateful to all those who provided so much help. Many of our members also donated help in innumerable ways. We learned a great deal and took some of this knowledge to the City Council. They began to listen to us. Also, they were impressed at the great concern so many citizens had over the concept of substantial fill and so-called balanced development.

Experts speaking for Save-the-Bay were hard to refute. The master plan became a political issue and more and more people spoke against it. The City Council made a complete change in policy at the end of 1963. A waterfront advisory committee was set up and existing plans were replaced by an interim waterfront plan which would greatly limit fill and development. It also defined the lines of how far out the fill would extend. The composition of the City Council had changed after an election and the new members were much more conscious of what many of their constituents wanted with regard to the preservation of the Bay.

Early in 1964 Kay, who knew Senator Eugene McAteer, went to see him in San Francisco and talked about the need to protect the Bay. Senator McAteer was the most powerful legislator in the Senate and was known for his devotion to San Francisco. He realized that many of those who had fill plans also had a great deal of political clout. McAteer thought that the legislature should study the problem before any action was taken. In 1964 a bill was passed to create the San Francisco Bay Conservation Study Commission. The new commission had four months and a budget of $75,000 to study the Bay fill (from September 1964 until the end of the year). Then it was to report its findings and recommendations to the governor and the legislature. The commission had nine members and McAteer was chairman. Twelve public hearings were held and the commission heard the views of many diverse people. There were those who had plans for expansion by dredging and filling as well as those who worried about the Bay and the lack of access to its water.

The press and the public began to pay attention. Don Sherwood, the Bay Area's most popular disc jockey, knew McAteer and he also had a 6 to 9 A.M. program on KSFO. He had the largest audience around the Bay and he would tell his listeners to be sure to write to their legislators before they had that second cup of coffee or started the day's work. Sherwood was highly successful in getting people to write, as were the conservation groups, and many cartons of mail were delivered daily to the legislators.

One committee meeting that will never be forgotten was the hearing on John Knox's Bill #AB 2057. It was the same as the McAteer-Petris Bill. KQED telecast this hearing to the Bay Area. The meeting room was packed and the large room next to it where one could hear, but not see what was going on, was also filled. People stood out in the hall. The lawyer for Westbay spoke passionately against the bill. Finally, John Knox asked him if he had read it. He said no.

The final vote was the climax of years of hard work. The developers' highly-paid lobbyists had also been very active.

During the last session some legislators were still speaking against the bill. Sylvia and I were watching this dramatic event. Under Howard Way's very astute leadership the bill passed by one vote and the Bay Conservation and Development Commission became permanent. For us, and for our thousands of supporters, this was the ultimate victory.

12-13 NACIO JAN BROWN, DEMONSTRATORS BEATEN DURING STRIKE FOR ETHNIC STUDIES, SAN FRANCISCO STATE UNIVERSITY, 1969

One of the goals of the college and high school strikes of 1968 and 1969 was to develop ethnic studies classes. The outrage that students of color felt about the skyrocketing death rates of racial minorities in Vietnam translated into a passionate campaign to create classes that would document and illuminate their own experiences.

**12-14   VISITACION PABELICO FULGENCIO IN FRONT OF HER HOME
IN COLLEGE PARK ON RED WING STREET, ONE
OF THE FIRST FILIPINO FAMILIES TO LIVE IN A DESEGREGATED
NEIGHBORHOOD, VALLEJO, 1969**

Following World War II and until the 1960s, Filipinos lived in segregated
neighborhoods, often finding it hard to buy homes from people who
resisted selling to a "person of color." The Fulgencio family persevered
and was one of the first Filipino families to live in the desirable College
Park neighborhood. Visitacion Pabelico Fulgencio is shown here in front
of her home in College Park on Redwing Street, c. 1969. (Courtesy of
Rena Fulgencio.)

12-15 ALCATRAZ OCCUPATION, 1969

In November 1969, ninety American Indians, calling themselves Indians of All Tribes, claimed Alcatraz Island as Indian land. Leader Richard Oakes leans on wall as supporters bring supplies through a Coast Guard blockade of "The Rock" on November 23.

In 1969, while students campaigned for ethnic studies on college campuses, Visitacion Fulgencio was able to buy a home in a previously segregated neighborhood in Vallejo. That same year, a group of American Indians chartered a boat, circled Alcatraz, and later occupied it. Inspired by other social movements, the American Indian Movement was founded in the early 1970s. Howard Zinn writes: "As if a plant left to die refused to do so, began to flourish . . . Indians were already gathering their energy for resistance, thinking about how to change the situation."[xiii]

Native American scholar Edward Castillo remembers:

> On October 28, 1969, the San Francisco Indian Center, a focal point for Native American residents, was gutted by fire. That spark ignited a powder keg of pent-up frustration and growing impatience with the fact that reform for American Indians lagged far behind that for other ethnic groups. The combination of the robust local anti-war movement and public announcement that Alcatraz was likely to be developed into a private tourist attraction prompted yet another attempt to seize it. On November 9, a group of 14 Indian college students occupied the island for 19 hours. Like the first attempt, the justification offered for the seizure was based on terms of a treaty with the Sioux in 1868. This document promised that the federal government would return any abandoned federal outposts to the Indians."[xiv]

The next expedition to Alcatraz was led by Richard Oakes, who directed Indian Studies at San Francisco State College, and by Grace Thorpe, a Sac and Fox Indian, daughter of Jim Thorpe, Olympic triathlete. Castillo writes:

> Oakes traveled to UCLA in mid-November to seek recruits among the large American Indian student population enrolled in UCLA's newly established Native American program. About 40 Indian students and one professor (this author) volunteered for the campaign. On the evening of November 20, 1969, about 80 American Indians (mostly college students from UC Berkeley, UCLA, and San Francisco State) boarded boats in Sausalito for a midnight trip to Alcatraz Island. The next day we awoke to the sound of helicopters and expected to be arrested by federal marshals. Instead it was the press. This time the sheer number of Indians commanded a serious investigation into the causes of such a dramatic demonstration."[xv]

Richard Oakes never wrote his own story of what happened at Alcatraz, which included personal tragedy, but he told an interviewer: "It was there [at San Francisco State] that one of the older people said 'All you young people, listen: We have been looking forward to this day when there would be something for you to do . . . Alcatraz is not only here on the island, but it's part of every reservation, it's a part of every person."[xvi]

[xiii]Howard Zinn, *People's History*, 385.

[xiv]Edward Castillo, "Native American Activism," in *The Whole World's Watching: Peace and Social Justice Movements of the 1960's and 1970's* (Berkeley: Berkeley Art Center Association), 2001, 96.

[xv]Troy Johnson (ed.), *Alcatraz: Indian Land Forever* (Los Angeles: University of California), 1994. Visitors to Alcatraz in 2000 found "Red Power" scrawled on rocks.

[xvi]Richard Oakes, *California History* (Spring 1983).

12-16 ALCATRAZ PROCLAMATION

To the Great White Father and All His People—

We, the native Americans, re-claim the land known as Alcatraz Island in the name of all American Indians by right of discovery.

We wish to be fair and honorable in our dealings with the Caucasian inhabitants of this land, and hereby offer the following treaty:

We will purchase said Alcatraz Island for twenty-four dollars (24) in glass beads and red cloth, a precedent set by the white man's purchase of a similar island about 300 years ago. We know that $24 in trade goods for these 16 acres is more than was paid when Manhattan Island was sold, but we know that land values have risen over the years. Our offer of $1.24 per acre is greater than the 47 cents per acre the white men are now paying the California Indians for their land.

We will give to the inhabitants of this island a portion of the land for their own to be held in trust by the American Indian Affairs and by the bureau of Caucasian Affairs to hold in perpetuity—for as long as the sun shall rise and the rivers go down to the sea. We will further guide the inhabitants in the proper way of living. We will offer them our religion, our education, our life-ways, in order to help them achieve our level of civilization and thus raise them and all their white brothers up from their savage and unhappy state. We offer this treaty in good faith and wish to be fair and honorable in our dealings with all white men.

We feel that this so-called Alcatraz Island is more than suitable for an Indian reservation, as determined by the white man's own standards. By this we mean that this place resembles most Indian reservations in that:

1. It is isolated from modern facilities, and without adequate means of transportation.
2. It has no fresh running water.
3. It has inadequate sanitation facilities.
4. There are no oil or mine rights.
5. There is no industry and so unemployment is very great.
6. The population has always exceeded the land base.
7. The population has always been held as prisoners and kept dependent upon others.

Further, it would be fitting and symbolic that ships from all over the world, entering the Golden Gate, would first see Indian land, and thus be reminded of the true history of this nation. This tiny island would be a symbol of the great lands once ruled by free and noble Indians.

What use will we make of this land?

Since the San Francisco Indian Center burned down, there is no place for Indians to assemble and carry on tribal life here in the white man's city. Therefore, we plan to develop on this island several Indian institutions:

1. A Center for Native American Studies which will educate them to the skills and knowledge relevant to improve the lives and spirits of all Indian peoples.
2. An American Indian Spiritual Center which will practice our ancient tribal religious and sacred healing ceremonies. . . .

3. An Indian Center of Ecology which will train and support our young people in scientific research and practice to restore our lands and waters to their pure and natural state. . . .

4. A Great Indian Training School will be developed to teach our people how to make a living in the world, improve our standard of living, and to end hunger and unemployment among all our people. . . .

Some of the present buildings will be taken over to develop an AMERICAN INDIAN MUSEUM which will depict our native food & other cultural contributions we have given to the world. Another part of the museum will present some of the things the white man has given to the Indians in return for the land and life he took: disease, alcohol, poverty and cultural decimation (As symbolized by old tin cans, barbed wire, rubber tires, plastic containers, etc.). . . .

In the name of all Indians, therefore, we claim this island for our Indian nations. . . .

Eventually six hundred Native Americans were living on the island, which they held from November 20, 1969, until June 11, 1971. The federal government cut off phones, electricity, and water, and eventually sent the U.S. Coast Guard to remove them from the Island. Alcatraz historian Troy Johnson notes that this occupation is barely noted in history books, "even though it represents the longest continuous occupation of a federal facility by any minority group in the history of this nation."[xvii]

QUESTION: How does the Alcatraz occupation make sense to you—or does it—based on the earlier history of California indigenous peoples that we have examined?

12-17 TERESITA CATAAG BAUTISTA "MY MANONG DAD, WAR BRIDE MOM, AND MAVERICK ME"

Teresita Cataag Bautista describes herself as a $1\frac{1}{2}$ generation Pinay. Her memoir demonstrates the ways that Filipino American young people of all races became part of the social movements that swept through California in the late 1960s and early 1970s.

I was born in a kitchen on August 12, 1946, in Aringay, La Union, my father's hometown. After a month-long ocean journey in March 1946, my 20-year old mother, Florentina Catayoc Cataag Bautista from Ormoc, Leyte, and I docked in Seattle, Washington. Together with hundreds of World War II war brides and their babies, we arrived on the military tanker David S. Schenk. You can still see the military tanker dry-docked with the mothball fleet in the bay outside of Martinez, about 25 miles from San Francisco.

We took a train to re-unite with my father, Eutiquio Guillermo.

When I finally transferred to UC Berkeley in 1969, I was main-streamed my first year as an English major, a member of the college choir, and as a setter on the UC Varsity Volleyball Team. Up to then, I had an assortment of jobs to get me through school. I worked as a student clerk for Merritt's Foreign Student Adviser. In the evenings and weekends I sold patterns at New York Fabric's by City Hall. Before going downtown in the evenings I played with kids as a Recreation Leader in after school programs. My highest

---

[xvii]Troy Johnson, *The Occupation of Alcatraz Island.* University of Illinois, 1996.

paying job, $3.50 an hour, twice the minimum wage then, was a two-year stint as a casual mail carrier at the Temescal Post Office. I resigned when I couldn't accept carrying all the election junk mail for Nixon's presidential campaign. The UC Educational Opportunity Program (EOP), landed me a job as an art history slide binder in the Bancroft Library. I was one independent woman!

At UC, I reconnected with Filipinos in 1970. We were over 40 strong in the Pilipino American Alliance (PAA). The next year brought me another work-study job at the International Institute of the East Bay (IIEB), where as Project Aide my assignment was to organize new arrival workshops which developed into the Filipino Immigrant Services (FIS) project. By graduation in 1972, I had my BA in Humanities and Interdisciplinary Studies, but was also deeply involved as an organizer in Oakland Chinatown. I gave up a Minority Scholarship in Education, I took a job in the Asian American Studies Department as a Field Work Assistant and led the sections on community organizing.

Inspired by the struggle to save the International Hotel in San Francisco, student efforts went to building a low-cost hotel in downtown Oakland. The program, Project Manong, operated out of a three-story hotel being renovated for occupancy on 16th Street. Scores of students and youth conducted outreach to isolated and displaced seniors, who were "regulars" at the local pool halls and cafes in the Chinatown neighborhoods targeted for redevelopment and high-rise buildings. This outreach was highly successful. Youth and young adults had come to respect the Filipino elders, our Manongs, for their contributions to the agribusiness industry of California and Hawaii. The young people were growing in the consciousness of themselves as Filipinos in the U.S. This knowledge compelled them to seek change in the living conditions of these dear elders, peers of their own fathers and grandfathers.

Martial law was declared in the Philippines in 1972. For the first time I saw masses of Filipinos in the streets, where I used to walk with hundreds of thousands of anti-war protesters. Now the focus was on Marcos and his military rule. This issue was one of the most controversial and polarizing debates in the Filipino community, lasting 14 years. Those of us who dared to take a strong position again Marcos were blacklisted, redbaited and, often silenced in community events. So many of us younger Filipinos understood the need for involvement in issues shaped by US national policy affecting our community. We developed and provided leadership for resistance and protest to military oppression in the Philippines.

At the same time, the community response to issues affecting Filipinos in the US because of racism and a lack of a strong Filipino voice in mainstream society was equally, if not more, engaging and controversial. Activists of all ages created community-based organizations. These groups addressed social, political, and economic needs of workers. I will be forever proud of my participation, and those of long-time friends, in building community institutions, like Filipinos for Affirmative Action, and groups that brought these issues to the awareness of government, funding agencies, and the broader community. We challenged backward community leadership that was self-serving and more interested in photo-ops with government officials.

I landed my first, full-time job in 1973 when I became the Filipino Liaison in the Office Community Relations for Oakland Public Schools. My anti-martial stance would find me in my supervisor's office every so many months. He would say, "I'm getting those calls again." Pro-Marcos community people would call him to complain, and even asked that I be discharged from my position because I openly criticized the Manila government. That was also the year I was asked to join the Union of Democratic Filipinos (KDP).

Besides going to junior and senior high schools to extinguish flare-ups and ease interracial tensions, I was able to train teachers on reviewing textbooks for omissions and distortions in books that mentioned Filipinos and the Philippines. We, the Filipino Far West Task Force on Education, went to Sacramento many times to lobby the California Board of Education. The group prepared citations from textbooks that reflected inaccurate and insufficient information on the Philippines and Filipinos in US history. It was quite an education to see how publishers lobbied officials and invested time to testify that their texts were relevant.

The Filipino community was so dynamic that initiatives abounded. We even had a local, bilingual TV program *Asians Now* on KTVU. Every Saturday morning we would see history, culture, and current concerns of the diverse Asian communities. For the first time, we saw our stories portrayed by us on television.

12-18 CHICANO MORATORIUM, ANTI-WAR MARCH, LOS ANGELES, AUGUST 1970

As scholar Jorge Mariscal has noted:

> The darkest areas on military casualty maps from the Vietnam War era reveal a dense concentration of fatalities in California's Central, San Joaquin, and Imperial Valleys. Home to large Chicano communities, these regions of the state sacrificed an unusually high percentage of their young men to the U.S. war in Southeast Asia.[xviii]

The most significant Chicano anti-war protest was held in Laguna Park, East Los Angeles, bringing at least twenty thousand marchers. The marchers carried signs that read, "Traiga a mis carnales ahora" and "A mi me dieron una medalla y $10,000 por mi unico hijo."[xix] Although it was later acknowledged that the police attacked the marchers, which caused a panic, the next day *The New York Times* reported that only seven thousand people attended and described the gathering as a riot where "five hundred policemen and Sheriff's deputies tried to break up roaming gangs."[xx] However, at the same time, Spanish-language newspapers published editorials on "La rebellion de los Chicanos," acknowledging the incendiary role played by government agencies and infiltrators and police spies who encouraged illegal behavior in order to discredit the marchers.

Meanwhile, Chicanos, like UCLA student body president Rosalio Munoz, found support on college campuses for refusing military induction. For example, in 1970, student Manuel Gomez wrote to his draft board, "The Vietnamese people are not my enemy, but brothers involved in the same struggle for justice against a common enemy. We are all under the same sky."[xxi]

By 1972, Chicana activists Lea Ybarra and Nina Genera produced a bilingual pamphlet offering "legal ways to stay out of the military," advising young Chicanos in high schools and colleges throughout Northern California.[xxii] Ybarra, who had 18 cousins serving in Vietnam, remembers performing anti-war skits and reciting Daniel Valdez's "Corrido de Ricardo Campos":

> You are dead, Richard Campos, you are gone
> You are dead, and I bid you goodbye
> But now that you're gone, there's a doubt in my mind
> What would have happened if you never would have died?[xxiii]

[xviii]George Mariscal, "Chicano and Chicana Experiences of the War," essay in *What's Going On: California and the Vietnam Era*, edited by Eymann and Wollenberg (Berkeley: University of California), 2004. Mariscal himself, a grandson of Mexican immigrants, was drafted in 1968 and served in Vietnam.

[xix]Translated as "Bring my homeboys home now" and "They gave me a medal and $10,000 for my only son."

[xx]Mariscal cites Armando Morales, *Ando sangrando (I am Bleeding): A study of Mexican American Police Conflict* (La Puente: Perspectiva), 1972.

[xxi]Manel Gomez, "Letter to Draft Board," *La Raza* 1, 1970. As I worked on this book, another generation resumed the practice of nonviolent marches to protest the treatment of immigrants. Inspired by the HBO film *Walkout*, written and directed by many of participants in the Chicano Moratorium, hundreds of thousands of young people, including in Vallejo and Napa where my students live, had their first experience of peaceful protest in 2005; see www.atzlan.net/la_gran_marcha.htm for more.

[xxii]Nine Genera and Lea Ybarra, *La batalla esta aqui: Chicano and the War* (El Cerrito: Chicano Draft Help), 1972.

[xxiii]Ybarra, phone interview with Mariscal, 1997. The real Richard Campos, a native of Northern California, was killed in South Vietnam on December 6, 1966.

12-19 JEFFREY BLANKFORT, SERVICEMEN FROM ALL BRANCHES OF THE MILITARY PARTICIPATING IN AN ANTI-WAR MARCH IN LOS ANGELES, 1969

The Movement for a Democratic Military, founded by African American marines at Camp Pendleton in 1967, spread through the San Diego naval complex, then to Alameda and beyond. Jeffrey Lustig writes that "Marines staged a violent brig rebellion in August 1969; California was now the point of contagion for an epidemic of GI resistance and combat refusals."[xxiv] Anti-war activists opened coffeehouses near military bases, creating a safe space for GIs to meet; by 1970 there were seven in California.[xxv]

[xxiv]Jeff Lustig, 73. For information on Camp Pendleton, he cites Robert Sherrill, "Anderson by the Sea: The Pendleton Brig," *The Nation*, September 15, 1969.

[xxv]See www.vvaw.org for more on this organization, and http://grunt.space.swri.edu/calmem.htm.

12-20 JEFFREY BLANKFORT, RON KOVIC, AUTHOR OF *BORN ON THE FOURTH OF JULY*, CALIFORNIA VETERANS OFFICE, 1971

Ron Kovic is well known from Tom Cruise's portrayal of him in *Born on the Fourth of July*,[xxvi] but less well known is the extent of organizing among other veterans. The California veterans' movement had many goals, including recognition of posttraumatic stress disorder, acknowledgments of the effects of the herbicide known as Agent Orange, and a restructuring of the Veterans Administration to address their issues.

Six thousand young California men died in Vietnam. At the State Capitol, you can visit a memorial to them, which is also on the Web at www.cdva.ca.gov/memorial/cvvm.asp.

QUESTION: The Vietnam Veteran's and Chicano movements, the occupation of Alcatraz, and the struggles to create ethnic studies courses in colleges and universities are four of the least-known movements of this period. How do these photographs and narratives challenge the portrayal of this period that you may have seen in movies or television?

[xxvi]Ron Kovic, *Born on the Fourth of July* (New York: Akashic Books), 2005. Hollywood provided contrasting interpretation of the war, ranging from the pro-war *Green Berets* to the populism of *Platoon* and *Born on the Fourth of July.*

12-21 PAM BROOKS, MEMOIR, 1980

Pam Brooks's description of her experience forming a union at a country club and Cathy Cade's photograph of stewardesses contradict the media distortion that feminism was a movement of privileged women who merely wanted prestigious careers.

On June 13, 1970 I, along with nearly one thousand other young people, graduated from Napa High School. Most of us went directly from "student" to "job-seeker", some being more prepared for this transition than others. My curriculum had consisted of "college preparatory" classes and, after commencement, I found myself qualified for only one vocation—that of college student. However, I was engaged to be married and our plan was to first provide him with a college education (he had already completed his freshman year) and then I would resume my education. We needed money; I needed a job. After many inquiries, I discovered that the most lucrative employment for unskilled laborers was as a housekeeper at the prestigious Silvarado Country Club. Not long after I started working there I saw why the women in this minimum-wage job were receiving larger pay-checks than women in similar occupations.

My first day on the job, as I was being introduced to the other housekeepers, I was surprised to see that I was at least ten years younger than the others. I also could not help but notice how tired they appeared. (Although now, in retrospect, perhaps hopeless would be a more accurate description).

Challenge echoed in my head. It was pure stubborness that got me through that first grueling week, that and the fact that I was getting closer and closer to pay-day.

I eagerly tore open my first pay envelope. I couldn't believe what I saw. My fifty-six hours of back-breaking work had only grossed $92.40! I decided it must be a mistake, so I took my check to our boss to be corrected. He quickly calculated the figures: $56 \times \$1.65 = \$92.40$. He smugly handed me back my check.

"But what about the forty-hour work week?" "What about my sixteen hours of overtime?" I stammered.

"No such animal here" he replied curtly. "If you don't like it, plenty of others waitin' to take your place. However, I'm satisfied with your work, even gonna give you a raise if you decide to stay—nickel an hour. Customers are pleased too. Even gonna add some more "young skirts" to the staff" he said as he exited his office, leaving me sitting there in disbelief.

Within two months from the date Christie, Paula and Candy had been hired, we had our first of many clandestine meetings with the representative from the Housekeepers, Waitress and Bartenders Union. Bill Richardson was stunned, then outraged, upon hearing the descriptions of our working conditions. Immediately he began to advise us on how to proceed.

The first step would be for us to approach other maids who we thought could be persuaded to join us, being cautious not to tip our hand to anyone who might leak our plan to the "higher-ups" (this included Fran and Gerry) before we had gained enough support. Should this happen, the four of us would simply be fired and replaced—our plan for unionization squashed. Convincing the others of the benifits of union representation and protection was more difficult than I had anticipated. They were fearful of losing their jobs; they asked us who else would hire an aging, uneducated, unskilled woman. Slowly though, one by one, we began to sway them. But we were still not sure that if push came to shove who they would side with.

The next day Bill and the four of us were ushered upstairs to the Executive Conference Room to begin negotiations. We won some; we lost some. To me our most significant victories were 1) a forty hour work week 2) time-and-a-half pay for over-time and 3) retroactive pay for all previous over-time hours accrued. The day the retroactive pay-checks were passed out Eva openly wept. Her check amounted to several thousand dollars.

I had all but forgotten this entire experience until I enrolled in History 150 taught by Lauren Coodley. Reading about women union organizors such as Sarah Bagley, Elizabeth Gurley Flynn, Mother Jones and Clara Lemlich made me stop and wonder how many thousands of Evas they had given hope to for a better future.

Incidently, one issue we failed to win concerned the dress-code. My last day on the job I let the hem out of my uniform and wore it a frumpy four inches below my knees; the others did the same thing to their uniforms. I heard that shortly after I left the dresses had been replaced with smocks and comfortable slacks. I think that Elizabeth Smith Miller and Amelia Bloomer would have approved.

12-22 CATHY CADE, TWA STEWARDESSES ON STRIKE, SAN FRANCISCO, 1973

QUESTION: What do Cathy Cade's photo and Pam Brooks's story demonstrate about the feminism in the 1970s and working women's fight for dignity?

Inspired by her discovery of a fifty-year-old volume, *A Short History of Women,* June Stephenson (remember her account of the 1934 General Strike in Chapter 9?) developed and taught the first women's history class at Napa High School.[xxvii] When Stephenson left to write her own book, *Women's Roots,*[xxviii] women's history was removed from the curriculum and was taught only at a separate program, Hill and Valley, that teacher Sudie Pollock created for pregnant girls.[xvix] Pollock recalls:

> In the summer of 1963, my best friend got pregnant and was kicked out of school. She wasn't allowed to be around the rest of us because, she was told, she had "carnal knowledge." She didn't get her diploma. . . . I saw what happened to her and didn't want that to ever happen to another girl. . . . It was very apparent to me that we needed to increase the self-esteem of these girls. Watching my students over the years go through childbirth . . . raising children alone, dealing with difficult family situations, boys and men who sometimes walked away, made a raging feminist out of me.[xxx]

In addition to the Hill and Valley program, Pollock developed Women's History Week celebrations in the public schools. Just before her retirement, she got back in touch with the best friend, who inspired her work, and found that her friend's mother "used to send her all the clippings about my school. It really touched her that I was able to provide a much better situation for other pregnant girls." [xxxi]

[xxvii]Stephenson, letter to Lauren Coodley, June 2003.

[xxviii]See http://junestephenson.com/books/roots/htm for more.

[xxii]When Pollock retired, women's history was again eliminated from the curriculum at the high school.

[xxx]Elizabeth Sagehorn, "Over Hill and Valley," *Napa Register,* October 7, 2002.

[xxxi]Sagehorn, October 7, 2002.

12-23 SUDIE POLLOCK AND FRIENDS, NAPA, c. 1978

QUESTION: Have you known a teacher like Sudie Pollock whose activism made a difference in the lives of her students? What do you see as the risks and benefits of being this kind of teacher?

Historian Ruth Rosen writes: "Between 1965 and 1980, tens of thousands of women participated in an enormous 'archeological dig,' excavating crimes and secrets that used to be called, with a shrug, 'life.'"[xxxii] She notes the contributions of Californian women to this effort: their "digging" revealed rape as an act not of sexual desire, but of power, thus helped end the silence that surrounded incest. Some of these women went on to create clandestine shelters for victims of marital abuse; others pioneered a revolution in health practices managed by and for women. Between 1973 and 1983, classes, and then majors, in women's studies were fought for, and achieved.

[xxxii]Ruth Rosen, "The Feminist Revolution in California," in *What's Going On: California and the Vietnam Era*, edited by Eymann and Wollenberg (Berkeley: University of California), 2004.

12-24   SAWYER TANNERY, NAPA, c. 1978

Meanwhile, most Californians continued their working lives amidst the deaths in Vietnam and the anti-war protests around the state. No one imagined that blue-collar jobs like the one pictured here at Sawyer Tannery would soon begin to disappear, and with them the good pay and benefits that many took for granted.

12-25   *SUPPORT THE KENTUCKY MINERS*, SAN FRANCISCO POSTER BRIGADE, 1978

San Francisco continued to be a strong labor town. The International Longshoremen's and Warehouse Union, under the leadership of Harry Bridges (remember the efforts to deport him?) thrived. Its members are pictured here protesting against "Nixonomics," their drill team standing in the foreground. Sympathetic artists created posters like the one shown here to help labor struggles as far away as Kentucky. Californians hoped that workers in other states would gain the protections we had here.[xxxiii]

[xxxiii]Mark Johnson writes that "artists Wilfred Owens, Rachel Romero, and others revived the high-contrast woodcut style associated with Mexican *tallers* in works that promoted worker solidarity, 73.

But in 1978, Proposition 13 was on the November ballot. Even its most enthusiastic proponents may not have foreseen the changes it would bring to California. Richard Reeves, in his essay "The Tax Revolt that Wrecked California," writes:

> Inevitably, as revenues fell, spending and critical public services were cut. In California, those cuts have led to crises in education, medical care and public safety . . . There's no free lunch; you get what you pay for.[xxxiv]

See http://www.pbs.org/merrow/tv/ftw/prop13.html for arguments for and against this far-reaching measure.

QUESTION: Do you think people today realize how much their quality of life and access to services was affected by the passage of Proposition 13? Think about the long-term costs of Prop 13 in closed drug/alcohol treatment centers, schools, hospitals, and libraries. If you could choose the line items that taxes would pay for, what would you want our taxes to fund?

[xxxiv]Richard Reeves, *San Francisco Chronicle*, January 23, 1994.

13

Life is a Great and Mighty March: 1980–2000

If we tried
To sink the past beneath our feet, be sure
The future would not stand.

—Elizabeth Barret Browning, Aurora Leigh

Each town in California can be seen as a small story of the de-industrialization that swept our country, and our state, through the Eighties and Nineties. In my own town of Napa, I watched the industrial heart of the city begin to stop beating in these decades. Our town's largest employer, the State Hospital, had lost most of its patients based on Governor Reagan's policy of sending patients out to live in board and care settings, which often turned out to be on the streets. Thousands of psychiatric technicians were unemployed, and hundreds of newly homeless people wandered through our streets, a sight that was last seen during the Great Depression in the Thirties. I gradually learned that forces far outside our town were affecting many parts of across California. The adoption of what was called "free trade policies" in Washington allowed corporations to close American companies and open them around the world in wherever labor is cheapest. In California, as in much of America, these policies began to erode our industrial base.

After the end of the Cold War with the Soviet Union in the late Eighties, the Presidential Base Closure Commission decidede to shut down bases all over California; historian Richard Rice notes that these closures were "a laborious and painful process and most replacement jobs offered much lower pay levels."[i] And yet, despite the setbacks of these last twenty years of the Twentieth Century, California experienced many transcendent moments in which positive changes were wrenched through human effort. The story of these efforts led singer Holly Near to pen the lines "Life is a Great and Mighty March," and these triumphant struggles (as well as their costs) are the theme of this chapter.

---

[i]Richard Rice, et al, Elusive Eden, 3rd edition (New York: McGraw Hill), 2002, 631.

318

13-1 "RAY GUNN," POEM BY GERI DIGIORNIO

at the homeless center
ray is looking for a quarter
for the dryer
i tell him i'll give him one
if he comes to the collage class
and he does

a week later i see him in line at the kitchen
he comes running over when he sees me
says he's got to tell me something

ever since he did the collage class
every where he looks he sees collage
in the street
the newspaper
magazines
on tv
he's collaging the walls in his room
he says

Homelessness returned to California for a number of reasons. Wages stagnated, while housing prices soared. Homes that poor people had lived in for half a century were torn down and not replaced, After Prop 13, reduced local income from taxes forced major cuts in funding for counseling, drug treatment and housing assistance. As a result, a third of the homeless were Vietnam Veterans; others were formerly housed in the state's mental hospitals.

QUESTION: California between 1940 and 1980 was a place with very few homeless people. Would you be willing to see your tax dollars bringing back the conditions before Proposition 13, re-opening the state hospitals and creating low-income housing solutions?

13-2   CARITHERS DEPARTMENT STORE CLERKS

In my town, strikes in 1981 and 1982 were led primarily by female workers. Their actions were a local example of the national struggles of unionized workers, which began when President Reagan fired ten thousand air traffic controllers in 1980. One was led by clerks at Carithers, the last union department store in Napa.

The local chapter of the National Women's Political Caucus collected canned foods for the strikers and organized fundraisers, including a dance in the Labor Temple on Main Street. The clerks were inspired by watching films of historic labor struggles, films that had just been created by the new field of women's history. One 19 year old clerk brought her infant to the picket line in a stroller adorned with a sign reading "Don't be a Scab," inspired by the Shirtwaist strikers of 1915.

The clerks won the strike and credited the community for its support as they returned to work. Their union newsletter characterized the victory:

> It was like David slaying Goliath: a relative handful of determined union women pick-
> eted their employer, Carithers, part of a mammoth corporation, in order to maintain a
> decent living standard and win dignity in their place of work. They never gave up. They
> walked for four and one half months, from the beginning of spring on through the parch-
> ing heat of summer—and prevailed.[ii]

[ii]UFCW newsletter, "Around the Grapevine," September 1981.

13-3   CARITHERS STRIKERS RETURNING TO WORK

around the grapevine

Official Publication of Retail Store Employees Union, Local 373

VOL. 1 NO. 2   AUGUST-SEPTEMBER 1981

PICKETS WIN CONTRACT AT CARITHERS

END OF THE STRIKE – Their picket signs are down and spirits are up as our members at Carithers in Napa approve their new contract.

QUESTION: What is the history of strikers or other labor struggles in your town? Go to the Labor Archives Research Center, www.larc.sfsu.edu, which has archived this history.

The year after the strike, Carithers closed its doors. The clerks lost their jobs as wages and conditions for all jobs in retail sales plummeted in Napa. Unionized companies began to downsize or move abroad, and the sons and daughters of welders, riveters and shipfitters faced an uncertain future, unable to buy houses or even to rent in the town where they grew up.

Ronald Reagan, now elected as President, lowered the tax rate on the very rich. Those cuts cost $70 billion loss of government revenue, while the wealthiest 1% of the population gained a trillion dollars.[iii] The widening gulf between the lives of the wealthy and the poor in California was the result, and family businesses were hit hard by the expansion of chain stores like Wal-Mart. James Sobredo, now a professor of ethnic studies at California State University in Sacramento, has written a memoir that explores the effect of political decisions on personal lives.

[iii]See Donald Barlett and James Steele. *America: What Went Wrong?* (Kansas City, Missouri: Andrews and McMeel, 1992, for more documentation.

13-4   JAMES SOBREDO, *TWO BROTHERS, TWO FILIPINO AMERICAN PERSPECTIVES*, 2004.

As a Filipino American in the 1980's and 1990's, I shall always remember Reaganomics and the "Decade of Greed." Under the Reagan administration, I saw financial aid programs and scholarships for racial and ethnic minority groups dwindle and in some cases disappear all together. I did not approve of Reagan's policies, so through it all, I was always attending demonstrations against the Reagan-Bush policies. In the 1990s, my political activism continued: I was protesting with thousands of people in San Francisco against American military actions in the Persian Gulf War.

The majority of my undergraduate Filipino friends were not like me. They were more conservative, and after college they became successful engineers, accountants, and health professionals. My Filipino friends had a fairly smooth and successful transition to the privileged professional, middle class, and they fit the media's image of Asians as "model minorities"—that is, people who worked hard, sacrificed, and, in spite of a history of racial discrimination, persevered and succeeded. Upon examination, I too seem to fit this model minority category: my family came to America as poor immigrants from the Philippines and eventually worked their way into the middle class. My father worked as a mechanic for the Navy, my mother a middle school teacher. Their son went on to attend one of the top doctoral programs in the country and received a prestigious fellowship.

Filipino Americans like me and the rest of my college-educated Filipino friends receive all the media's attention. We are the stuff that myths, like the model minority construction, are made of.

Before coming to Berkeley I was attending an Ivy league university. My younger brother Johann was pumping gas at a gas station, which caused for me, to put it mildly, a bit of "psychic disequilibrium." Johann would be dodging the local police who had a warrant out for his arrest for having outstanding tickets for illegal drag-strip racing. He was the undefeated local drag-strip champion in the quarter-mile. Johann hung out with 15 other teenagers, his buddies (his *barkada*), who formed an informal racing group called the "Eliminators." Outsiders, the media, for example, who didn't know any better, would call the Eliminators a "gang." And it's true that individual members of the Eliminators sold drugs, got involved in fights, and some were even involved in "drive-by" shootings. The crucial term here is "individual members" for they never did any of these acts as a group. In a word, they were not really a gang for they did not defend turf; they did not extort money; they had no formal initiation rites; and they had no formal gang leader who issued orders—although my brother was a sort of informal leader of the group. Fortunately, my brother never dealt drugs, never started fights or shot anyone. The Eliminators were simply a bunch of restless young men who hung out together and didn't know what they wanted in life.

The reality of the matter is, although we both came from the same family, my brother's experience in our family differs greatly from mine. I was born in the Philippines, and when my family came to America, we were very poor. So I understood how difficult life was, and consequently worked very hard to make sure that I don't stay poor and non-privileged for the rest of my life.

My younger brother, on the other hand, never experienced hardship while he was growing up, and by the time he was a senior in high school, he had his own new car complements of my parents. Then, the following year Reagan's decade of greed began. My mother went on strike, and, like the striking airport traffic controllers, whom Reagan fired, she too was fired from her job. At the same time, my father had a stroke and had to quit his job. Hence, during the decade of greed in which the rich got richer, my family dropped out of their middle-class status.

Disillusionment quickly got the better of my brother when he realized that there would be no money for him to attend college and his period of restless searching started. I taught Asian American studies at U.C. Berkeley, and I listened to lots of Filipinos talk about their experiences and also those of their friends. Their stories were similar to my Johann's. Like many young Filipinos who have no direction and consequently no hope for the future, Johann turned to hanging out with his *barkada* who were just as directionless as he was. Unfortunately, as a result of this hanging out with friends, a lot of Filipinos get into trouble, for example, with gangs, the police, drugs, and alcohol.

My brother was one of the lucky ones. On his own volition, he left the Eliminators and now works as a supervisor for Northwest Cargo. He still hasn't figured out what exactly he wants to do with his life, but at least he's planning on returning to college and getting a degree.

Thus, while the education route worked for me because my family could afford to send me to college, in the Reaganomics of the 1980's, however, it was not an option that was available to my brother. Striking workers are fired from their jobs, and scholarship funds and programs were eliminated. My brother's experience shows the reality behind the myth of the "model minority."

QUESTION: James Sobredo, now a professor of ethnic studies at California State University in Sacramento, has written a memoir that explores the effect of political decisions on personal lives. Do you know families where one member went to college and another ended up on the streets?

---

barkada, a social group of close friends, gang.

N.b. there is no comma after "Filipinos," so this is a restrictive claus, which means I am talking about Filipinos "who have no direction". This is not to say that all Filipino youth have no direction, or that they all get into trouble.

13-5   NUCLEAR FREEZE MARCH, NAPA, 1983

After Ronald Reagan was elected President in 1980, thousands of Americans mobilized to push for an end to the arms race. Dr. Randall Carolyn Forsberg founded the Nuclear Freeze Weapons Campaign, a grassroots confederation of groups across the country. In California, the Freeze campaigned for a Congressional ballot initiative limiting nuclear testing. Many towns had small offices from which hundreds of volunteers worked to end the use of nuclear weapons. This history has gone largely unrecorded; when I tried to find the files from the Napa office, no one knew what had become of them. I finally tracked them to a box in some-one's garage, the repository of much untold history. I found a copy of the "Freeze" newsletter where I read:

> We waged a successful petition drive and delivered over 3,000 Napa County signatures to President Reagan. We collected more than $1200 to pay for a full page ad in the *Napa Register.*[iv]

The week after their ad came out, local Congressional Representative Doug Bosco signed on as a co-sponsor of a bill to cut off funds for nuclear testing. A massive peace march began in Los Angeles. Singer Holly Near remembers:

> The Great Peace Marchers decorated L.A.'s Griffith Park with their beautiful colored tents. I could feel the excitement as twelve hundred brave people said goodbye to friends and family and began to meet those with whom they would walk across this huge country. I would fly across the country many times before the marchers arrived in D.C. and would often look down and think of them in the desert, in the snow, at com-munity meetings. But tonight I would teach them the song I wrote especially for them. It was getting dark as we gathered on a hillside together. As I began to conduct the parts, a few campers got out their flashlights to focus light on my hands. And a beautiful choir of voices rose from the black night.[v]

[iv]Freeze newsletter, Volume 3, No. 4, December 1985.

[v]Holly Near, Fire in the Rain, Singer in the Storm (New York: William Morrow), 1990, 243. See also http://wochica. tripod.com/lostjournals for a fascinating meditation on this event.

13-6 "THE GREAT PEACE MARCH" SONG BY HOLLY NEAR, 1983

Ancient eyes are watching in the night
The stars come out to guide the way
The sun still shines despite the clouds
And the dawn is dusk is dawn is dusk is day

Farmers rise and dream to feed the world
The world awakes to feed the heart
Hearts beat while a thousand flags are waving
And the farmer sees a dream has played a part

Chorus:
We will have peace, we will because we must
We must because we cherish life
And believe it or not, as daring as it may seem
It is not an empty dream, to walk in a powerful path
Neither the first nor the last Great Peace March
Life is a great and mighty march
Forever, for love and for life
On the Great Peace March

Are you black like night or red like clay
Are you gold like sun or brown like earth
Grey like mist or white like moon
My love for you is the reason for my birth

Peace can start with just one heart
From a small step to leaps and bounds
A walk becomes a race for time
And a brave child calls out from the crowd
Chorus

(© 1986 Hereford Music (ASCAP)
Use/Reprint by Permission Only.)

13-7   ANTI-APARTHEID PROTEST, SAN FRANCISCO

President's Reagan's policy of support for the apartheid government in South Africa provoked a strong opposition. As a result of marches like the one pictured here, in 1986 Congress overrode President Reagan's veto and moved forward with imposing economic sanctions against the South African government. Organized citizen protests brought results: African National Congress leader Nelson Mandela was released from prison in 1990 and was elected President of South Africa in 1994.

Jerry Brown's election as Governor had made possible the passage of legislation addressing the plight of farmworkers . Brown had attended Catholic seminary. He travelled with Dorothy Day's Catholic Worker's group to visit farmworkers, and later marched with Cesar Chavez in the Coachella Valley.

Jerry Brown was elected Governor of California in 1974, along with the first African American Lieutenant governor Mervyn Dymally, the first Asian Secretary of State March Fong Eu, and the first African American Superintendent of Schools, Wilson Riles. Brown appointed more than 1500 women to positions in state government. Among them was Rose Bird, his Berkeley undergraduate classmate, whom he nominated to be Chief Justice of the State Supreme Court. One of Brown's first acts as governor was to collaborate with Bird to draft the Agricultural Labor Relations Act of 1975, which gave farm workers the right to organize and to enjoy all the rights of other union members.

In 1986, Rose Bird and two other justices were defeated in an election with important implications for California. Some historians thought their defeat was due to their support of farm workers. As Dick Meister writes:

> It was under her leadership that the state banned use of the short-handled hoe, a torturous tool that kept thousands of field workers bent almost double for most of their working day. Although using Bird's opposition to the death penalty as the campaign's main theme and enlisting prosecutors to lead it [the campaign], the wealthy growers and other business interests who bankrolled the effort were concerned mainly with the court's pro-labor stance. They ran one of the most vicious election campaigns in California history in finally convincing voters to oust Bird and two other liberal justices, Cruz Reynoso and Joseph Grodin..[vi]

[vi]http://www.labornet.org/viewpoints/meister/rosebird.htm

13-8   LUIS VALDEZ MEMOIR, "ENVISIONING CALIFORNIA," 1989

The year was 1946. I was six years old, walking along a dirt road along the middle of a tomato patch in the Santa Clara Valley, by Moffett Field. Lockheed, I believe, occupies the same acreage now, right by the Bayshore Freeway. There was no Bayshore in 1946. The highway to San Francisco was the El Camino Real. So we were out there, in the middle of nowhere, except for Moffett Field. I was walking along, and there, at my feet, I suddenly spotted a dead rattlesnake. I didn't know at the moment that the snake was dead; it just looked fierce and terrifying. So I tried to cry out to my parents who were a couple of rows down, but no voice came out. I was paralyzed with fear. At that instant, something caught my eye, and I looked up at the sky. My cry came out as I spotted this huge blimp heading for one of those giant hangars at Moffett Field. Between that moment of silence and the cry, I sensed the depth and breath of my being. I sensed fear and I sensed exhilaration. It couldn't have happened anywhere but in that tomato patch in the Santa Clara Valley in 1946. Moffett Field was a magical place, with airships floating through the sky and land-ing. Even as a farmworker, as a child, I felt privileged to be in this magic land. That's a unique California experience.

Let's flash forward more than 30 years to another experience of California which didn't even happen in this state. It was in a small apartment across the street from Columbia University in New York City. I rang the doorbell at a very humble apartment to encounter one of the great Californians of our century, Carey McWilliams. This is a man who was and remains one of my heroes, a man who has shaped my vision of the world through his book, *North from Mexico,* which I had read in 1959. And now here I was in 1977, in New York City, about to interview him about his role in the Sleepy Lagoon Defense Committee back in 1942, in defense of the Pachucos. Of course, that research led to *Zoot Suit,* the play, and *Zoot Suit,* the movie. He was quite generous and open. We spoke for hours, until his wife Iris came and stopped us, because he was just as fascinated with the subject as I was—the subject of California. But it was getting late in the day.

Flash forward a couple of years. At the time I had talked to McWilliams I had said, "I'm researching for a play that I want to write for the Mark Taper Forum in Los Angeles. We have hopes that maybe some day this can come to New York City." He just smiled. In fact, when we opened on Broadway at the Winter Garden Theater in 1979, he was there. He said, "You know, I thought you were going to make it." It was wonderful. It was wonderful that he was there, and it was wonderful to bring the "Zoot suit" riots and the Pachuco experience and the Chicano vision to New York City.

As you may know, we ran into a critical blank wall, a wall that is the East Coast. One of the first things I did when I got back to San Juan Bautista, where I live with my wife and three kids and the larger family of Teatro Campesino, was that I made a sign for myself with felt pens. I pinned it up on the wall of my office. The sign contained a single word, and that word was CALIFORNIA. The trip to New York had taught me who I was: yes I was Chicano, yes I was an ex-farmworker, yes I was this, yes I was that. But, above all, I was a Californian. I realized in New York City the uniqueness of my California origin. I decided then, in 1979, that this would become the foundation of a greater exploration of my history, of our history, of our take on reality.

I, like many of you, started here. This is where I opened my eyes. Not in Mexico, but here in California, right here in *el valle*. This place, this valley, is where I took root. *I am not an immigrant.* My parents were born in the United States. I am a native. And so I speak with a native tongue and a sense of native belonging, of having been born in this place.

But I was born in Delano, California, in 1940, and in 1940, Delano was the asshole of the universe. It was bad, let me tell you. There was a white side, and there was a brown side, and a railroad and Highway 99 sliced right down the middle. Everybody knew the town was segregated, but no one admitted it. Filipinos and the *chinos* and a few Japanese lived in Chinatown. We lived in that nether region which is also a California phenomenon— the *barrio*. Most of it was Filipino actually; but to this day my parents' idea of an evening out is to go to a Chinese restaurant, because of the Pagoda Restaurant on the west side in Delano, the first restaurant I ever knew. Next to it was the Montecarlo, and so forth. What I didn't know, but soon learned, is that there were 13 whorehouses in Delano; this is in a town of 10,000 people. Somebody was awfully active there—lots of aerobics. It so happens there were a lot of single men, a lot of Filipinos who weren't allowed to marry white women. There were a lot of ugly rumors, and racism on both sides of the fence. What I didn't know then was that the Filipinos were Hispanic, but they looked *chino* to me.

There is another image too that comes from the early days of California, Spanish California at any rate. When they were gathering those parties back in Sonora, Mexico, to come and colonize Alta California, they had to bring whomever they could find, any-one who was willing to come to this farflung wilderness on the edge of the earth. So who came? *Mestizos, mulatos, filipinos, chinos, negroes, tercerones* (one thirders), *saltatraces* (the ones who bounce back, the racial retards, the throwbacks). These are the people who settled the early Spanish California pueblos of Los Angeles, San Jose, and San Francisco. San Francisco was settled, among others, by a man called José Tiburcio Vasquez, who came and laid the foundations for the city. A generation later, his son was the Sheriff-Mayor of San Jose, and their adobe stood in the plaza right beside the site of the modern convention center on Market Street. A generation after that Tiburcio Vasquez, José's great-grandson became the last of the California bandits, and the last man to be publicly hanged in California. He died less than two blocks from the adobe of his grandfather, the late Sheriff-Mayor of San Jose.

What happened after 1848? An enormous upheaval, the Gold Rush, which we all know about, the search for El Dorado. As it turns out, that is only a manifestation of some-thing else, of a vision that this land for some reason or another has always inspired in its inhabitants.

Did you know that here, in California, before the Spaniards arrived, was the largest concentration of Native Americans in the continental United States? A quarter of a mil-lion Indians lived in the hills and valleys of this fabled land. The Spanish came, but not in great numbers. When the Americans arrived in 1848, because of the Gold Rush, there were just barely 10,000 Spanish Californians. That's not even a good sized barrio these days. Only 10,000 Hispanics (or as I like to say, "High Spanics") were spread over this vast territory.

And yet, I was not always a migrant. I was born in 1940, and we all know what hap-pened December 7, 1941. Not September 7, but December 7, 1941. There were a lot of

Japanese American farmers working the San Joaquin Valley in the 1940s. They were doing quite well tilling small pieces of land; they had done a lot to make row crops productive. They were showing American agriculture how to grow things like watermelons and cantaloupes and cucumbers, produce that had not been known and seen in this valley. They had the art, the skill, the gift. Naturally, this produced competition, and human beings being what they are, someone took advantage of the historical moment, and all Japanese farms were vacated when their farmers and families were sent to concentration camps in 1942.

Suddenly the U.S. Army was responsible for hundreds of farms across California. Who was to take charge? They turned them over to the Mexican farmworkers. One of them was my father. They asked him if he would like to run a farm. Well he went for it, and suddenly we were *rancheros!* So World War II was a very prosperous time for my family. We had a "new" car (a 1939-1940, but they did not make new cars during the war). We had food, a house—two houses. We had acreage. My dad was farming; it was wonderful. The only *patron* we had to deal with was the U.S. Army, which showed up occasionally.

But a strange and tragic thing had happened on our ranch before we got it. The Japanese farmer who had lived on it refused to go to a concentration camp. So he hanged himself in the kitchen. Growing up with my older brother, I would be afraid to go into the kitchen after certain hours. One night our parents were gone. Our cousins were there, and we started telling ghost stories. I could see the farmer hanging from the lamp. So my cousin, who was about 15 at the time, got out the holy water, and she went around blessing the house from corner to corner. "Help us." We were saved.

Then in 1945, a more terrible thing happened. The U.S. won the war. The G.I.s came back, and the Mexican farmers for one reason or another began to lose their farms. So from utter prosperity, my family fell to utter poverty. In 1946 we hit the road, and I got to pick those tomatoes next to Moffett Field, and watch the blimps go by. That is a California story.

I did not understand it then. I did not understand the energies of this state. I did not understand, for instance, that Delano has been the focal point of some of the greatest labor struggles in the history of this country and in the history of this century. I was not aware of the residue of social consciousness that existed in Delano. I did not know that for at least another 20 years, until I went back and joined Cesar Chavez and the United Farmworkers, in an effort to try to make some changes happen. *La huelga* led to the Grape Boycott, which led to the first farm labor collective bargaining agreements in U.S. history. Change did happen, but then the Teamsters and the growers got together and the pendulum swung back. All those contracts were lost.

This state will not be able to achieve its greatness until it deals with its gut, until it deals with its agriculture, until it deals with injustice on the land where we grow our food. This is not just a repetition, a warning that comes from the past. This is a warning for the future. The pesticides and other poisons that are seeping into the richest farmland in the world are going to impoverish our grandchildren. It is happening in the Imperial Valley as well. Why is it happening? Because of human intransigence, because of human insensitivity, because one ethnic group believes in the American dream and wants to deny it to another.

We are enmeshed in the future, but we are entangled in the past. The only way out is for us to get to the very core of the issue. The core of the issue has something to do with the way we view who we are, what we are, where we are, where we are going. This idea of Manifest Destiny—that somehow the only progression that has ever come to California has come from the east to the west—is only half of the vision. There's a progression from the south to the north, and, if you will go back to that little line of nomads coming down twenty thousand years ago across the Bering Strait, from the north to the south. We must cross the "T", we must square the circle, in order to understand who it is we are.

There are borders. One of the traditional conflicts in this state has been between north and south. Of course, you must know there were Spanish Californians involved in the creation of the California Constitution, which was based in part on the law that already existed here among the Spanish-speaking peoples. I rush to say these were not Spanish, these were not Chicanos per se; these were *mulatos, filipinos, chinos, indios, criollos*. From its very inception, California was a multi-cultural land. It was the destiny of this corner of the world to square the circle. Even so, before too long after the Gold Rush, the state suddenly found itself divided into northern and southern California. Bear Flaggers would accuse the southern *californios* of putting a drag on the development of California as part of the United States, because they wanted to maintain political control. For a while there was talk of secession and of splitting the state into two separate states, northern California and southern California.

I think one of the most beautiful parts of California is the unpopulated part in the middle. We see the rolling hills, benign and soft, almost poetic in their natural rhythms. This is the faithful California, the California of old. But I am sure I am not the only one driving those freeways; nor are you. Many other kinds of visionaries are driving those freeways, and they see one city from San Francisco to Los Angeles. That too is part of our future; north to south. Will it become that? It depends on what we see.

And, then, as narrow as the state is, there is an east and west, and that is the most important, fascinating part of our California. I could not define it when I was 6, but I knew the moment we packed our belongings into the pickup and headed down Highway 99 and then up to 152 over Pacheco Pass, and came down the hills to Gilroy that we were suddenly in *la costa*, the coast. *La costa* was a magical land. We used to speak of it; our parents used to tell us stories about *la costa*. They used to say, "look to the *duendes*." The *duendes* are our spirits—little leprechauns, little creative spirits—and maybe it was just a way to keep us picking. But, you know, it worked. Because they were magical, and I was picking up the *duendes* all along and did not even know it. I sensed it in the ecology of *la costa*.

Back in 1946 we did not know the word "ecology" existed. It was "nature" then. We saw it around us in the rivers, in the clumps of live oaks, in California poison oak, and in those hills. The Santa Clara Valley and San Fernando Valley were amazing because they were magical, and they were open, and they were free. Now they're full. I wouldn't keep anybody out of the state, far from it. But I sense the loss, that the newcomers never saw that openness. They never really got a chance to look for the *duendes,* even as children.

What I did not know was that I was looking at a geological phenomenon; that mythical line called the San Andreas Fault, which you encounter just west of Pacheco Pass, is the boundary between two continental plates, the North American plate and the Pacific plate. The Pacific plate rose out of the sea a million years after the North American plate. So the flora and the fauna are new.

The history of agriculture has taught us many things. Unfortunately, it has not taught us quickly enough. When Europeans came to America, they discovered a miraculous new system of agriculture. They discovered some very essential things. For instance, the humble potato that I used to pick outside Bakersfield in mid-July. (That was in a place called Fomosa. In 1950, there were headlines that the Red Chinese had invaded *Formosa*. We were picking outside *Fomosa* and I was trying to look to see if we could see any Chinese.) Anyway, the potato took root in the San Joaquin Valley, and a tremendous amount of money was made. I don't know if you know about the potato: the Irish potato, the Idaho potato, the sweet potato. The potato was developed by the Inca. One theory was that it was developed in Machu Picchu on step levels. The Inca bred potatoes that would grow in any kind of weather. The potato is medicinal, the potato is alcoholic, the potato is food; the uses of the potato alone are incredible. One of the things it did was to solve a tremendous problem in northern Europe. Being a vegetable that could grow in cold climates —because it came from the Inca—the potato solved the problem of famine, and it joined the world's food supply and became a natural treasure, along with the gold of America, some of it from California.

An ancient myth sustains my everyday progress into this maddening reality of ours. Ultimately we are all Maya; we are all part of the roots of America. The Maya believed that in that place where the conscious meets with the subconscious—in the navel of the universe—the four heavenly roads converge. The yellow road, the black road, the white road, and the red road. Squaring the circle. They had a symbolic image of God. No name, but an image. A square inside a circle. They called it *hunabku*. That's as close as they ever got to the picture of God; God as a mathematical vector.

I did not know this when I reared my head in Delano. Nobody told me I was a mathematician, I had to find that out for myself. So in my first year of college I married math and physics. I majored in math and physics. Ultimately, mathematics embraces us all, and it comes back to the question of who we are. We are an unfinished equation that continues to unravel itself. As Lou Diamond Phillips said in *Stand and Deliver* . . . "Cal-coo-loose." There is the calculus of our minds. There is the beat of the universe, as it hums like clockwork and can be described in numbers. There is the magic of the human mind as it perceives and makes sense of its own experience. Sometimes the vision precedes, outlining a road; sometimes the vision emerges from experience. But the vision is always there. And that vision always brings us back to our essential nature as spiritual beings. We are conscious energy. The word "wisdom" comes from the word "vision." It's the same word. In order for California to be wise, it must enlarge its vision to include all humanity.

I leave you with one final thought. The future belongs to those who can imagine it. Thank you.

13-9   CÉSAR CHÁVEZ "FARMWORKERS AT RISK," 1993

There is nothing we care more about than the lives and safety of our families. There is nothing we share more deeply in common with the people of North America than the safety of the food we all rely upon.

The chemical companies that manufacture the pesticides and the growers who use them want us to believe that they are the health-givers, that because of pesticides people are not dying of malaria and starvation. They have convinced the politicians and the government regulators that pesticides are the cure-all, the key to an abundance of food. So they don't ban the worst of these poisons because some farm workers give birth to children who contract cancer or to babies who are born with deformities. They don't imperil millions of dollars in profits today because, some day, some consumers might get cancer. They allow all of us who place our faith in the safety of the nation's food supply to consume grapes and other produce that contain residues from pesticides that cause cancer and birth defects. We accept decades of environmental damage these poisons have brought upon the land. The growers and the chemical companies, the politicians and the bureaucrats, all say that these are acceptable levels of exposure. Acceptable to whom? . . .

Acceptable to all the other farm workers and their children who have known tragedy from pesticides? Acceptable to 300,000 farm workers who are poisoned each year in the United States, according to a 1985 study by the World Resources Institute? Or the eight hundred to one thousand who die each year from exposure to pesticides, according to a study by the U.S. Food and Drug Administration?

There is no acceptable level of exposure to any chemical that causes cancer. We cannot tolerate any toxic substance that causes miscarriages stillbirths, and deformed infants. . . .

Compared with other jobs, farm workers are one of the least-protected groups in the nation. They are specifically excluded, either totally partially, from health and safety standards under the federal Occupational Safety and Health Act as well as the Fair Labor Standards Act. Many are excluded from state worker compensation and unemployment insurance laws. Thus we lack effective legal remedies. Growers are not even required to tell workers the specific chemicals being used or to provide protective clothing. For one of the most hazardous occupations in the nation, three and one half million farm workers live under a double standard. . . .

In 1965, our infant farm workers' union led a major strike against Delano-area grape producers. That walkout was also headed for the same fate as its predecessors, until we tried something different: We asked consumers across North America to boycott California table grapes.

In 1992, the United Farm Workers marked its 30th anniversary. It has been almost twenty-seven years since our union cause first touched the hearts and consciences of people across America and around the world by letting them know about the abuses suffered by farm workers and their families.

In 1967, the farm workers dramatically transformed the simple act of refusing to buy fresh table grapes into a powerful statement against unfairness and injustice. The grape boycott was a hallmark of the 1960s and `70s. It rallied millions of Americans to the cause of migrant farm workers. And it worked. The first real collective-bargaining relationship was established between an agricultural employer and farm workers when we signed our first union contract with a Delano-area grape grower. . . .

Although UFW contracts in 1967 provided protection from dangerous pesticides, most farm workers still remained unprotected in 1982, when corporate growers gave the gubernatorial election campaign of Republican George Deukmejian more than $1 million. . . .

Many of these same growers also spent millions of dollars to help kill Proposition 128, California's 1990 Big Green initiative supported by environmental groups and the UFW, which would have protected California's last stands of privately held redwoods and banned cancer-causing pesticides.

Growers and other opponents of Proposition 128 would be mistaken to view the election results as a rejection of the need for reforms, such as the protection of old-growth forests and restrictions on the use of pesticides that produce birth defects. . . .

All my life, I have been driven by one dream, one goal, one vision: To overthrow a farm-labor system in this nation that treats farm workers as if we are not important human beings. Farm workers are not agricultural implements of beasts of burden to be used and discarded. . . .

How could we progress as a people, even if we lived in the cities, while the farm workers—men and women of our color—were condemned to a life without pride? How could we progress as a people while the farm workers, who symbolized our history in this were denied self-respect? How could our people believe that their children could become lawyers, doctors, judges, and professional people while permitting this shame and injustice to continue? . . .

Tens of thousands of the children and grandchildren of farm workers, and the children and grandchildren of poor Latinos, are moving out of the fields and the barrios. That movement cannot be overturned. Once social change begins, it cannot be reversed. You cannot uneducate the person who has learned to read. You cannot humiliate the person who feels pride. You cannot oppress the people who are not afraid anymore.

Boycott grapes!

QUESTION: César Chávez fasted 35 days in 1988 to call attention to the high cancer rates of farmworkers. How would you investigate if the food safety issues that concerned him still exist?

Although farmworkers lost much of their collective bargaining due to the hostility of the Governors who followed Jerry Brown, immigrants continued to organize. Proposition 187, passed in 1994, restricted welfare, social benefits and education to undocumented immigrants. Millions of Latinos registered to vote against it, and it was eventually ruled unconstitutional by a U.S. District Judge. Thousands of farmworkers and their supporters gathered to travel to La Paz for the funeral of César Chávez that same year. This photograph was taken by Aurelio Hurtado, who had worked with Chávez in the Sixties.

13-10 PHOTOGRAPH FROM CESAR CHAVEZ FUNERAL, 1994.

The increasing degree of impoverishment of low-income citizens that occurred during in the Reagan-Bush years hit Black families hardest. At the end of the Eighties, at least 1/3 of African American families fell below the official poverty level. Maxine Waters began working at age 13 in segregated restaurants. After moving to Los Angeles, she worked in garment factories and at the telephone company.

Waters attended California State University at Los Angeles, where she earned a Bachelor of Arts degree. She began her career in public service as a teacher and a volunteer coordinator in the Head Start program. Elected in November 2002 to her seventh term in the House of Representatives, Congresswoman Maxine Waters represents a large part of South Central Los Angeles, the Westchester community and the diverse cities of Gardena, Hawthorne, Inglewood and Lawndale.[vii]

[vii]http://www.house.gov/waters/bio.htm

13-11 "CAUSES OF LA RIOTS" TESTIMONY BY CONG. MAXINE WATERS TO SENATE BANKING COMMITTEE, *CONGRESSIONAL RECORD*, 1992.

Many of us have watched our country—including our government—neglect the problems, indeed the people, of our inner-cities for years—even as matters reached a crisis stage.

The verdict in the Rodney King case did not cause what happened in Los Angeles. It was only the most recent injustice—piled upon many other injustices—suffered by the poor, minorities and the hopeless people living in this nation's cities. For years, they have been crying out for help. For years, their cries have not been heard.

I recently came across a statement made more than 25 years ago by Robert Kennedy, just two months before his violent death. He was talking about the violence that had erupted in cities across America. His words were wise and thoughtful:

> There is another kind of violence in America, slower but just as deadly, destructive as the shot or bomb in the night. . . . This is the violence of institutions; indifference and inaction and slow decay. This is the violence that afflicts the poor, that poisons relations between men and women because their skin is different colors. This is the slow destruction of a child by hunger, and schools without books and homes without heat in winter.

What a tragedy it is that America has still, in 1992, not learned such an important lesson.

I have represented the people of South Central Los Angeles in the U.S. Congress and the California state Assembly for close to 20 years. I have seen our community continually and systematically ravaged by banks who would not lend to us, by governments which abandoned us or punished us for our poverty, and by big businesses who exported our jobs to Third-World countries for cheap labor.

In LA, between 40 and 50 percent of all African-American men are unemployed. The poverty rate is 32.9 percent. According to the most recent census, 40,000 teenagers—that is 20 percent of the city's 16 to 19 year olds—are both out of school and unemployed. . . .

We have created in many areas of this country a breeding ground for hopelessness, anger and despair. All the traditional mechanisms for empowerment, opportunity and self-improvement have been closed.

We are in the midst of a grand economic experiment that suggests if we "get the government off people's backs," and let the economy grow, everyone, including the poor, will somehow be better off. . . . The results of this experiment have been devastating. Today, more than 12 million children live in poverty, despite a decade of "economic growth," the precise mechanism we were told would reduce poverty. Today, one in five children in America lives in poverty. . . .

While the budget cuts of the eighties were literally forcing millions of Americans into poverty, there were other social and economic trends destroying inner-city communities at the same time.

I'm sure everyone in this room has read the results of the Federal Reserve Board's study on mortgage discrimination that demonstrates African Americans . . . are twice as likely as whites of the same income to be denied mortgages. . . .

In law enforcement, the problems are longstanding and well documented as well.

Is it any wonder our children have no hope? The systems are failing us. I could go on and on. . . . We simply cannot afford the continued terror and benign neglect that has characterized the federal government's response to the cities since the late 1970s.

13-12 "THE TEN MILLION FLAMES OF LOS ANGELES: A NEW YEAR'S POEM, 1994" BY AMY UYEMATSU

I've always been afraid of death by fire,
I am eight or nine when I see the remnants of a cross
burning on the Jacobs' front lawn,
seventeen when Watts explodes in '65,
forty-four when Watts blazes again in 1992.
For days the sky scatters soot and ash which cling to my skin,
the smell of burning metal everywhere. And I recall
James Baldwin's warning about the fire next time.

> *Fires keep burning in my city of the angels,*
> *from South Central to Hollywood,*
> *burn, baby, burn.*

In '93 LA's Santana winds incinerate Laguna and Malibu.
Once the firestorm begins, wind and heat regenerate
on their own, unleashing a fury so unforgiving
it must be a warning from the gods.

> *Fires keep burning in my city of the angels,*
> *how many does it take,*
> *burn, LA burn.*

Everybody says we're all going to hell.
No home safe
from any tagger, gangster, carjacker, neighbor.
LA gets meaner by the minute
as we turn our backs
on another generation of young men,
become too used to this condition
of children killing children.
I wonder who to fear more.

> *Fires keep burning in my city of angels,*
> *but I hear someone whisper,*
> *"Mi angelita, come closer."*

Though I ready myself for the next conflagration,
I feel myself giving in to something I can't name.
I smile more at strangers, leave big tips to waitresses,
laugh when I'm stuck on the freeway, content
just listening to B.B. King's "Why I Sing the Blues."

> *"Mi angelita, mi angelita."*

I'm starting to believe in a flame
which tries to breathe in each of us.

I see young Chicanos fasting one more day
in a hunger strike for education,
read about gang members preaching peace in the 'hood
hear Reginald Denny forgiving the men
who nearly beat him to death.
I look at people I know, as if for the first time,
sure that some are angels. I like the unlikeliness
of this unhandsome crew—the men losing their hair,
needing a shave, those with dark shining
eyes, and the grey-haired women, rage
and grace in each sturdy step.
What is this fire I feel, this fire which breathes freely
inside without burning them alive?

> *Fires keep burning in my city of angels,*
> *but someone calls to me,*
> *"Angelita, do not run from the flame."*

QUESTION: How do Waters' testimony and Uyematsu's poem combine to help explain what has been called the "Los Angeles uprising"?

13-13 EXCERPT, JANET STICKMON, *CRUSHING SOFT RUBIES*, 2005

Janet Stickmon was born to an African American father and a Filipino mother; both her parents died by the time she was a teenager growing up in Lancaster, near Bakersfield. In this excerpt from her memoir, Janet describes what it was like to be at college and to connect with a multiracial group of students.

Tangled in the stress of trying to graduate and getting used to my new friends, was still my experience at UCLA. As I became more aware of myself as a Black and Filipino woman, I also discovered all the things I didn't know about both cultures. I didn't know how to speak *Cebuano* or *Tagalog*. I knew what *Tinikling* was, but not *Singkil* or *Vinta*. I learned that Ferdinand Magellan had "discovered" the Philippines, but I didn't know that Opung Lapulapu killed him. I had heard about Jose Rizal but not Andre Bonifacio. I knew Ferdinand and Imelda Marcos were corrupt, but I didn't know exactly how corrupt they were. In short, I knew very little about the basics in Filipino and Filipino-American history.

The few Filipinos that I knew as a child were those who were children of Mom's closest friends; some of them were also Black and Filipino. Being accepted by them never seemed to be an issue. I didn't have many Filipino classmates in elementary, junior high, or high school, but I was still proud to tell everyone I was half Filipino, mostly because people seemed to find me more intriguing. The few second generation Filipinos I met in college, with the exception of those I met at UCLA, were disconnected from their roots, like me. The most we could do was share the memories of *lumpia* and *adobo*, imitate and laugh about the familiar, endearing sound of our elders' Filipino accents, and long for the day we'd return to our parents' homeland.

And as far as my Black side, I had the same problem. I barely knew anything about African and African-American history. I knew about slavery, Booker T. Washington, and Martin Luther King, Jr. That was it. I didn't know much about Africa prior to slavery, W.E.B. Du Bois, or Malcolm X. Didn't recognize names like Fannie Lou Hamer, James Baldwin, Audre Lorde, Lorraine Hansberry, Bayard Rustin, Mary McLeod Bethune, Gil Scott-Heron, or Mae Jemison. When I heard "African Diaspora" or the "Reconstruction Era," I didn't know what was meant. I didn't know what Kwanzaa was or why many African-Americans in college felt a connection to Egyptian mythology or a connection to countries in western Africa.

I was never completely comfortable with some of my Black sisters and brothers because I was insecure about my own Blackness; I was never sure if I was "Black enough." Often in the presence of other Black people, I felt I had to compete with them. This competitiveness took its origin in being the sole Black person in most of my social and academic circles. I learned to gain great satisfaction from being, by default, the "expert," a position expected of me by non-Blacks in my company. Many of these folks that I hung out with were the same people who tried using Black slang, acting animated around me, deeming me the "nice" Black person they could talk to, and addressing me as "sista" because they thought that was how they could effectively relate to me since I was a Black woman. And I just dismissed it all.

My need to compete could be traced to my choice to separate myself from other Blacks as early as the second grade. In elementary school, I noticed some of my Black classmates who didn't do their homework or got in trouble and made the decision not to associate with them so I wouldn't be labeled as "bad." I subconsciously put on the shroud of the "good Negro" which later evolved into an official uniform that helped me to assume the leverage to judge all of my sisters and brothers according to how they spoke, whether or not they smiled, how they dressed, and whether or not they were formally educated. I never knew that I was using the same standards of judgment and condemnation that some whites, Asians, and Latinos used to judge us.

The more I became aware of what I didn't know and the connection I didn't have with my people(s), the more difficult it was to learn what I was missing. What was holding me back? Embarrassment clung to every admission I made to not knowing my cultural histories. If other Filipinos discovered I didn't know who Lapulapu was, I knew I'd be judged. I'd embarrass myself if I began spending time at the Black Student Union, and people discovered I didn't know who Angela Davis, Marcus Garvey, or Maulana Karenga were. To save myself the public embarrassment, I avoided these circles and never placed myself in situations where I was a "learner" of my own cultures. I feared being vulnerable to criticism.

Because of this fear, I gravitated toward Chicanos. Having friends like Shayra, Rosario, Gerardo, and Samantha influenced my language, my mannerisms, and my interests. I didn't necessarily seek them out because they were Mexican. They were just among the few people of color in the physical science and engineering department that I had met. They had not assimilated into mainstream white culture, but they weren't exactly militant revolutionaries either.

Being with them was comforting. My mother was an immigrant to this country like many of their parents. We understood what it meant to be the descendents of those in search of the "American Dream," and thus knew what it meant to be among the first in our families to graduate from college. With them, I was never held accountable for what I didn't know about my Black and Filipino backgrounds. Since I was not Mexican, there was never any pressure to be an expert in their Mexican heritage. I was free to learn without being stigmatized. And I enjoyed that luxury. However, something needed to change.

Thermodynamics always frustrated me. I flipped through the pages of the book as if reading a foreign language. Devon sat across from me studying diligently. He was wearing a black knit cap with the initials "N.S.B.E." on it.

"Devon, what's N.S.B.E.?" I asked.

"N.S.B.E. is the National Society of Black Engineers. It's a student-run organization divided into regions, each holding annual conferences. They have an annual national conventions, too."

"What do you do at the conferences?"

"Oh, there so much fun. They have a lot of workshops on corporate environments and resume writing, things like that. There's a career fair where large corporations come to offer summer internships and information about their company. And a college fair . . . different colleges come to distribute information about their university. Oh, and roll call . . . I can't explain it . . .you have to see it. You should join and come to one of the conferences. I think you'd like it."

Thousands of Black people filled the convention center from wall to wall—skin tones from dark black to olive, eyes of deep brown to hazel, hair from relaxed to afros and dreads. As we walked passed each other, there was no fear, no hesitation . . . we were connected and it was only natural that we caught eyes and said, "Hello, my brotha. Hello, my sista," exchanging smiles and nods of acknowledgement . . . the way Da'y greeted other Black men when I was little. During roll call at the opening plenary session, the officers called out the names of each school, and instead of answering "Here" or "Present", the members of each chapter stood and sang chants (sometimes to the tune of Black sitcoms like the *Jeffersons* or *Good Times*) while the rest of students sat doubled over in their seats, laughing, throwing their heads back, cheering on the group, eager to see what the rest of the chapters would do for roll call. After the session, stepping through the massive double doors of the ballroom, I found the career fair: corporations like 3M, Merck, and Anderson Consulting passed out souvenirs and pamphlets with information about their company and internship programs. Up the hall was the college fair where hundreds of universities like Cornell, Purdue, Prairie View A & M, University of Illinois at Urbana-Champaign, Georgia Tech, and Howard had representatives speaking to students individually about graduate school programs. I watched all the students walking past. Handsome brothas looked at me, while I snuck glances at them. The young men were dressed in dark three-piece suits and ties; the women wore smooth dress suits and heels; leather planners and briefcases replaced the 3-ring binders and backpacks used at school. Undergraduate and graduate students alike looked professional, carrying themselves with dignity: serious, but not aloof; confident, but not cocky.

I was in an atmosphere where all of us, as Black people, were college-educated and no one was made to feel ashamed; amongst each other, being smart was celebrated, not ridiculed. By admiring the beauty of my people across the room, I was admiring my own beauty. I had no reason to look at my nappy hair with contempt or disgust and no longer thought of my Blackness as the reason why boys weren't attracted to me. I was beautiful; and I was beautiful because I came from beautiful people.

I traveled from room to room, listening to speakers from the corporate world and academia who were eager to share their knowledge and experience. I absorbed the information, recklessly taking notes as they spoke about maintaining one's African-American identity in corporate America, making wise investments, studying U.S. history from an African-American perspective. They "talked back" to comments made about African-Americans often heard in corporations and universities like, "Yes, but are they qualified?" or "Well, we just didn't have `any' apply for the job." With each workshop I attended, I understood why it was important to nurture and rebuild cultures that have been hated, questioned, ostracized, fetishized, and excluded from society. As I continued listening, I felt like I had arrived home without even knowing how far I had wandered away; many of these ideas crossed my mind, but I could never articulate them; hearing these presentations brought me so much relief and comfort that I wondered what sort of oblivion I had grown used to living in.

13-14 JANET STICKMON

QUESTION: Have you ever had an experience like this one, where you feel that your eyes were opened for the first time?

Another Californian who had a moment of awakening was Judi Bari, who became a carpenter in Mendocino County. While on the job, she became curious about the redwood boards she was handling. She learned they came from trees that were over one thousand years old. This awakening inspired her to work with others in her county to eventually save several thousand acres of old growth forest in the Cahto Wilderness Area.

Bari joined an effort to support mill workers who had been exposed to toxic PCB's in a 1989 Georgia-Pacific sawmill accident in Fort Bragg. She helped organize the injured workers into the Industrial Workers of the World. Judi Bari wrote an article for the IWW newspaper in 1989 about the need to protect and organize timber workers.[viii] In 1996, she told journalist Eric Brazil that these workers no longer believed that environmentalism was the main threats to their jobs: "What we've been saying is true: it's corporations versus the rural community. We just want sustainable logging."[ix] When diagnosed in 1997 with breast cancer, Bari continued working as long as she could on behalf of timber workers and the redwoods. She died later that year.

13-15 EXCERPT FROM OBITUARY FOR JUDI BARI BY HOLLY NEAR, 1997

The IWW, active in California during the Twenties, and rejuvenated by Judi Bari on behalf of timber workers, has never been completely forgotten. During the Fifties, San Pedro longshoreman Art Almeida, whose grandfather had been one of the 1923 strikers at Liberty Hill, met an elderly IWW member. That meeting triggered in Almeida "an insatiable appetite to know more."[x] Art Almeida worked for twenty years to establish a State Historic Landmark at Liberty Hill. On May 21, 1998, his dream came true: a stonemason created a monument of rock and shells, now installed in front of the Los Angeles Harbor workers community center, one of a handful of labor history sites in California.[xi]

[xiii]http://www.iww.org/union/iu120/local-1/labor/TLGarner1.shtml, August 15, 1990.

[ix]Eric Brazil, *San Francisco Examiner*, December 15, 1996.

[x]Lauren Coodley, oral history of Art Almeida, "Liberty Hill becomes a State Historic Landmark," ILWU *Dispatcher*, March 1998.

[xi]Liberty Hill is Landmark No. 1021.

13-16 DEDICATION CEREMONY, LIBERTY HILL MEMORIAL, 1998. ALMEIDA AND GRANDSON SEATED BY PODIUM.

13-17 SUPREME COURT JUSTICE ROSE BIRD

Jerry Brown was elected Governor of California in 1974, along with the first African American Lieutenant governor Mervyn Dymally, the first Asian Secretary of State March Fong Eu, and the first African American Superintendent of Schools, Wilson Riles. Brown appointed more than 1500 women to positions in state government. Among them was Rose Bird, his Berkeley undergraduate classmate, whom he nominated to be Chief Justice of the State Supreme Court. One of Brown's first acts as governor was to collaborate with Bird to draft the Agricultural Labor Relations Act of 1975, which gave farm workers the right to organize and to enjoy all the rights of other union members.

In 1986, Rose Bird and two other justices were defeated in an election. Some historians thought the loss was due to their support of farm workers.

13-18 CALIFORNIA SUPREME COURT JUSTICES, ROSE BIRD MEMORIAL COMMENTS, 1999

Justice Reynoso

May it please the court, Mr. Chief Justice and Associate Justices. Thank you for the opportunity to share with you remembrances of an extraordinary woman and Chief Justice of California, Rose Elizabeth Bird.

Her sojourn on this planet was not a long one. Her accomplishments in the service of her fellow Californians were many and lasting. Foremost, it seems to me, was her example to us all that one could implement one's most noble ideals and live a satisfying and fulfilling life.

I met Chief Justice Bird after she was named to the bench. I was then serving as an associate justice of the Court of Appeal in Sacramento. Aside from meeting her informally, I was soon asked to join the Supreme Court on assignment. She personally took time to extend the invitation, to explain the Supreme Court internal practices, to make me feel welcome, and to later thank me for service to this court. A few years thereafter, I joined the court. I was honored that Chief Justice Rose Bird administered my oath of office.

The press reported, at that time, that there were tensions among the justices. So, since I knew and respected each justice I was determined, I told myself, to bring peace to the court. However, when I arrived, I looked in vain for the reported friction. Rather, I found vigorous but respectful agreement and disagreement among the justices.

She had come to her position as Chief Justice at an age young of years, but full of accomplishments. She graduated from Boalt Hall in 1965, at a time when women represented no more than three percent of the bar, and whose presence on the bench was rare. She was 41 years of age when she was named Chief Justice by Governor Edmund G. (Jerry) Brown, Jr.

The Chief Justice had been raised poor, first in Arizona and later in New York, where her mother supported her and her two brothers by working at a factory job. Before attending law school, she worked as a legal secretary. She knew life as those without power live it. The perspective of those who do not have power guided her sense of justice.

When she graduated from Boalt Hall, after clerking for the Nevada Supreme Court, her first attorney position was that of a public defender of Santa Clara County. She had already begun her role as a trailblazer. She had been the first woman law clerk at the Nevada Supreme Court, and she was the first woman to work as a public defender in San Jose.

She, like the other seven or eight attorneys, worked long hours. The inside joke, according to Judge Takei, who then worked with the Chief Justice, was that the defense attorneys spent more time in jail than their clients. The Chief Justice quickly advanced from trial attorney to senior trial deputy, to chief of the unit working on appeals and writs.

Judge Takei remembers an incident which typified the dedication that the Chief Justice had to her clients. She had defended a woman charged with prostitution. The woman was poor and had recently arrived in the city from a rural Indian reservation. The accused was acquitted, but she had no place to go. The Chief took her to her home and subsequently paid for her return trip to her native reservation.

By the early-and mid-1970's, the Chief Justice was teaching at Stanford as a clinical professor. Her students voted her the most popular professor. As a clinical professor, she had what one former student called "the miraculous power to give strength." She was close to her students, many later worked with her in her executive and judicial roles.

Governor Jerry Brown, then newly elected, named Chief Justice Bird as Secretary of Agricultural Services, the first woman again "ascendicated" ever to hold a cabinet position in the state government. In that position, she stretched her energies even more. In short order, she incorporated lay persons into professional commissions, banned the short-handled hoe, and regulated toxic waste.

I learned only recently that her cancer which eventually took her life appeared while she was in state service. Her time, she may have felt, was limited and there was much she wanted to accomplish.

Democracy, we all know, is a most difficult form of government. I serve as vice-chair of the United States Commission on Civil Rights. Too often when we have hearings on police-community tensions, the public officials, mayors, district attorneys, police chiefs and sheriffs testify that all is well in the community. Citizen surveys confirm strong support for the police, yet dozens of church and community leaders, as well as countless individuals, will follow with their own testimony questioning actions they consider seriously hurtful to the citizenry. It is hard to give voice to a political minority when officials are beholden to an electoral majority. At the same time, the people may speak, but political realities impede implementing that public will. Thus, poll after poll indicate that Californians are willing to pay more for a head of lettuce or a pound of carrots to enhance the lives of farmworkers. Yet that public opinion, supportive of farmworkers, had not realized its potential until then Secretary Rose Bird structured the Agricultural Labor Relations Act. She understood democracy, it seems to me, and made it work.

My own observation is that as Chief Justice, she had three passions. Her first passion was the law. She would agree with Daniel Webster that "The law, it has honored us, may we honor it." Chief Justice Rose Bird honored the law, even when she disagreed with it.

Her second passion related to the first, an abiding faith that the law should protect all, the weak and the strong. Those who were weak in political or economic power could look to the black robes for protection, be they consumers, renters, farmworkers or those politically unloved.

The third passion was her conviction that justice would be best served if those black robes were on the shoulders of judges representing both genders and all ethnic and racial groups who make California home.

Those who worked most closely with the Chief speak of her as headstrong and stubborn, yet gentle in compassion. They agree that she was an inspiring judge.

During her tenure, the body politic of California changed. For decades, there had been an unstated agreement among the political parties that the judiciary would not be the subject of partisan political attack.

I recall my own 1976 appointment to the Court of Appeal Chief Justice Donald Wright called to congratulate me. He advised me that I need not appear at the constitutionally required hearing and assured me that I would be confirmed in light of my background. A few weeks thereafter he called with the expected good news, that I had been confirmed. That was it.

Just over five years thereafter when I was named to this court, the change was dramatic, the hearing was contentious, many witnesses appeared and the vote was divided. Partisan politics were in full bloom.

During Chief Justice Rose Bird's tenure, she was subjected to several recall petition campaigns and to two confirmation votes. She understood that court decisions which angered powerful groups or protected nonmajoritarian rights would jeopardize her position. She remained true to her oath of office, she enforced the Constitution and applied it equally to all.

As a member of the American Bar Association's committee to select recipients of the annual Thurgood Marshall Award, I have reviewed hundreds of attorney and judicial profiles. Many judges, federal and state, have shown great courage; but no judge, in my view, has been more courageous than Chief Justice Rose Bird, who performed her judicial tasks in the face of physical and political threats. She suffered a vote of nonconfirmation and retired from the bench in 1987.

There is life after the bench. Perhaps out of the public's glare the true character of Chief Justice Rose Bird can be better understood. She lived a private life. She volunteered in a food kitchen which served those in need. She assisted the East Palo Alto Law Clinic which represents the poor. She cared for her elderly mother and loved her dog, Nellie.

Father Eugene Boyle, who served Palo Alto's St. Anne's Chapel, refers to Chief Justice Bird as a person of deeply religious principles, those of truth, justice and compassion. The description, it seems to me, is apt. I am proud to have been a friend and colleague of Chief Justice Rose Elizabeth Bird. History will note her trailblazing career and the good she did for us all.

MR. SCOTT SUGARMAN: I Knew Chief Justice Bird for Nearly 30 Years.

We met in the early 1970's, when I was her student at Stanford Law School. She taught an advanced course in criminal procedure, a very demanding clinical seminar. She was widely regarded as one of the best teachers on the faculty because of her remarkable devotion to her students, her insight and intelligence, and her commitment to teaching law students to be real lawyers.

She was extraordinarily hardworking. She worked days, nights, weekends, holidays; it did not matter. There was work to be done and she was going to do it all. And she demanded no less of her staff. Let me tell you about my first day.

In 1978, when she had been Chief Justice only a year, the biggest political issue of the day came to the Supreme Court—the constitutionality of Proposition 13. Proposition 13 radically altered the payment of property taxes in California, and thus changed the way California was governed then, and to this day. The initiative had passed with the support of a substantial majority of the voters.

Predictably, within days of its passage, challenges to Prop. 13 from cities, counties and others throughout the state poured into the court. The way in which Chief Justice Bird dealt with that case illustrates much about her character.

Once the briefs were in, the Chiefs instructions to her law clerks were simple. Read all the petitions and evaluate the best arguments that could be made about the constitutionality of Proposition 13. No prejudgment, no stacking the deck.

Once the Supreme Court voted to hear those petitions, the case was on the fast track. The Chief's clerks soon met with her to discuss the issues raised in that case, and how relevant prior judicial opinions related to the issues presented. She did not want law clerks who were compliant, who would only mirror what she wanted to hear. She asked for, and got, our independent views.

After she personally reviewed the briefs and applicable precedents, she told us that, on reflection, she was deeply troubled by the fact that homeowners sitting side by side, with homes of the same value, would be required to pay very different amounts in taxes to the state for the same public services. Chief Justice Bird concluded that making those homeowners pay different taxes violated the equal protection clause of the United States Constitution. She held strong views about the importance of equal treatment in our society and, in her view, Proposition 13 treated identically situated individuals differently.

Her opinion in *Amador Valley v. State Board of Equalization* (1978) 22 Cal.3d 208 was an open book of her thoughts and expressed her views on what a judge must do. She believed in the people and their right to govern their own lives. In the very first sentence of her opinion, she wrote that judges must accord great deference to the expressed will of the people. A judge must construe an initiative "so that the will of the people is given full weight and authority." However, she explained that if this or any initiative or legislative act was in conflict with the United States Constitution, judges were duty bound to uphold the mandate of the Constitution. As she wrote, judges . . . must be devoted to the preservation of the great constitutional principles which history has bequeathed to us."

In her opinion, she was quick to admit that her conclusion that Proposition 13 was unconstitutional had not come easily. She acknowledged that the issue was close and that the emotions on the question ran high. However, particularly in such an environment, she wrote, "a judge must follow the law and do what it requires."

Each of the six other judges on the Supreme Court—including a man she admired and respected greatly, Justice Matthew Tobriner—concluded that the initiative was constitutional. It is little short of astounding that she was willing to stand alone in opposition to Proposition 13 just two months before her first confirmation election in 1978. It would have been easy to join the court's six-member majority and stay silent. Her vote could not alter the court's decision to uphold the constitutionality of Proposition 13. However, she believed that to abandon her true understanding of the mandate of the Constitution would betray her core responsibility as a judge. While she understood that her expressed opinion might cost her the election and her office as Chief Justice of California she would not bend to adopt a course she believed was contrary to her duty.

She knew that powerful political forces would be arrayed against her. She knew she could not defend herself other than in her written opinion. Yet she truly had the courage of her convictions, and a fundamental belief in the independence of the judiciary. It is her courage and her integrity that shine through.

She was, and is, an unequaled model of integrity and fidelity to the mandates of the Constitution and the Bill of Rights. As her decision in *Amador Valley* illustrates, she was a judicial example of character, strength and courage.

Predictably, Chief Justice Bird's opinion in the Proposition 13 case garnered much attention in the press. I think it is fair to say that no judge in California has ever endured as much day-to-day critical commentary, speculation and coverage as Chief Justice Bird. Yet, for all of that commentary, it is little short of shocking that so little has been said about the scholarship of the body of her opinions.

Whether she was writing about a poor woman's access to government funding for an abortion as in *Committee to Defend Reproductive Rights v. Meyers* (1982) 29 Cal.3d 252, or the right of the family of a rich and famous man to control the commercial exploitation of his likeness and life's work as in *Lugosi v. Universal Pictures* (1979) 25 Cal.3d 813, or the ban on the admission of statements taken from suspects in violation of their right to remain silent as in *People v. Rucker* (1980) 26 Cal.3d 368, her opinions reflect exhaustive research, principled decisionmaking and compelling analytical thought.

While I and some of my colleagues concluded our clerkships with the Chief Justice some 20 years ago, the clarity of her opinions and her commitment to individual rights and judicial independence remain powerful guides to our understanding of new cases and new controversies.

Maybe because she was the first woman to serve as a law clerk in the Nevada Supreme Court, or because she was the first woman to serve as a deputy public defender in Santa Clara County, or because she was the first woman to serve as a cabinet officer in the State of California, or because she was the first woman to serve on the California Supreme Court, Chief Justice Bird was keenly sensitive to the struggles of the outsider and the dispossessed, of the power exercised by the "haves" on the "have nots," of the power used by government agents and officers on those who are powerless.

She was a passionate advocate for justice and fair and equal treatment. While she was well aware of the role of the Supreme Court as a court which set precedent, she firmly believed that the court must hear cases to do justice, especially for those whose access to the legislative or executive branches was limited or denied. While she believed every person was entitled to justice and equal treatment under the law, she spoke with a rare passion for those who were powerless or penniless, neglected or notorious.

Chief Justice Bird expressed her vision more eloquently than I can recreate, in the last speech she gave as Chief Justice in January of 1987, at the Annual Law School Deans' Luncheon. There, she said:

"Our humanity informs us and instructs us in what it is to live lives of decency and dignity. As lawyers and judges, we bring unique perspective to our humanity that, if used wisely and well, can enhance the quality of justice in our society.

"That is not a task for tomorrow. It is something we must live every day. And if we live it fully — with all of our intelligence, compassion and courage — then we will have truly fulfilled the promise of justice our titles imply.

"If we judges and lawyers are not to be popular, let it be because we are standing on the forefront of protecting people's rights during a time of transition. Let it be because we have the courage to represent unsympathetic individuals and make difficult rulings in order to give life and breath to our constitutional guarantees.

"Let it be because we have the integrity to do justice, even though such actions may be met with criticism and disapproval. Let it be because we see our role from the perspective of its noble traditions, not from the pressured viewpoint of the moment.

"Let it be because we stand up for a just society and stand firm for the rule of law."

From the same place inside her from which came her passionate commitment to justice came her enormous caring and compassion for the men and women around her. Not a birthday, anniversary, or holiday came which she did not remember with a personal card or gift. During the winter holidays, her chambers would be filled with laughter and good food, much of which the Chief Justice personally prepared. For each staff member, she obtained an individual memento or gift, tailored to his or her traits. She never bought 20 identical pens or pet rocks, but spent the time and effort to find some gift that would fit the recipient. And, at Thanksgiving or the New Year, she would send flowers to our homes.

We, who were fortunate enough to serve as her law clerks, and to work with her, thus learned lessons not just by her instruction, but by the life she lived and the decisions she made each day.

Her beacon is now gone. However, her spirit, her integrity, her brilliance, her vision is preserved in our hearts and minds, and is evident in the hundreds of judicial opinions which she authored and in which she participated during her nearly ten years as Chief Justice of the Supreme Court. *(Derived from Supreme Court minutes and 22 Cal.4th.)*

QUESTION: It is difficult to find Rose Bird's story in histories of California. What factors might have caused historians to leave her out?

Recently, Yosemite Park Ranger Shelton Johnson found a photograph of five U.S. Army troopers on horseback. This unit of Buffalo Soldiers from the San Francisco Presidio were sent to Yosemite, after returning from the Philippines, to patrol the national parks in the late 19th century against Indians. (The name "Buffalo Soldier" had been given to these Black soldiers by the Plains Indians as a badge of honor, because they were as fierce as the buffalo that they hunted and revered). The photo inspired Johnson to create performances in which he portrays Sgt. Elizy Boman, a veteran of the U.S. war against the Filipino insurrection. Johnson says his work is in honor of his father, who enlisted in the Army to get out of the South: "I had to think why do we remember what we do? Who has the power over what is written down?"[xii]

Johnson's question is one of the guiding themes of this book. In the early 1990's, Susheel Bibb began to study Mary Ellen Pleasant, resulting in a theatrical performances in which she herself portrays Mary Ellen Pleasant. In 1994, actor Ian Ruskin began to develop a one-man show as Harry Bridges, an effort which, writes Chronicle reporter Carl Hall, "has moved to tears even some battle-scarred veterans of the great 1934 General Strike, which started on the waterfront and grew into the largest general strike in American history."[xiii]

13-19 "WHAT HAPPENS WHEN A MANANG DIES," BY JEANNETTE LAZAM, 2004.

> *Dedicated to all the Pinays that came before me, all the Pinays that stand with me, and all those who come after me and my generation of strong-willed sistahs!*

We all know what happens when a manong passes on. He gets talked about at home, at the barbershop, the corner store, at the neighborhood restaurant, at the local newsstand.

But what happens when a Manang dies?

We all know that his friends will reminisce about the good old days, will miss him when they come to Chinatown to play pai gaw or at the horse races; sing sad and old songs of long ago; tip their hats in reverence and slowly move through life as though they will be the next in line to go.

But what happens when a Manang dies?

We all know that a manong is an icon, the true Filipino trailblazer - pioneer of sorts. As such, there is no more dancing or humming, laughing or joking, tickling and scratching, no more of anything.

But what happens when a Manang dies?

We all know that the end has come to the smell of stale cigars, heavy-starched white long-sleeved shirts, cuff links and tie clips, gray overcoats and shined shoes, pomade and greasy combs in the bathroom, and folded boxer shorts and Italian cut undershirts.

[xii]Interviewed by Carl Nolte, "Buffalo Soldiers Story," *San Francisco Chronicle*, February 1, 2003, A15.

[xiii] Carl Hall, "Actor Brings Labor's Harry Bridges to Life," *San Francisco Chronicle*, July 9, 2002.

But what happens when a Manang dies?

We all know that our men folk want to cry but they don't. And we all know that we will never smell that Old Spice aftershave lotion, or hear the clink of the gold plated key chain as it swings in motion to unlock the front door. We all know that a period of life, a slice of time will now be looked upon in photo albums and Sony camcorder videos of Lolo kissing the grandchildren and tickling them until they lose their breath.

But what happens when a Manang dies?

We all know that the tiyo's and tiya's will burn-up the telephone lines making arrangements for the last dinner, the last farewell to this Filipino old timer who braved the discrimination and prejudice of whites and others as he searched for employment and housing in the United States.

But what happens when a Manang dies?

We all know that come time to clean out his closer and dresser drawers, his wife, children and quite possibly grandchildren, will find things they never knew about him: girly magazines, nude women playing cards, unused condoms, Las Vegas and Reno one dollar coins, pictures of Jesus Christ and the Virgin Mary, bank books dated 1937 and earlier, an extra set of false teeth, his union cards, money clip, wrinkled and torn photos of him and his barkada in their army uniforms, cook and waiter outfits, and a 1941 snapshot of them standing on the footbridge in Central Park, dressed to the nines.

But what happens when a Manang dies?

Please tell me, what happens when a manang dies? We simply know because it rains softly and ever so gently, and then, we tuck her memory away deep in our heart and soul - for the loss is too great to deal with at the moment, and for an eternity

Recently, Yosemite Park Ranger Shelton Johnson found a photograph of five U.S. Army troopers on horseback. This unit of Buffalo Soldiers from the San Francisco Presidio were sent to Yosemite, after returning from the Philippines, to patrol the national parks in the late 19th century against Indians. (The name "Buffalo Soldier" had been given to these Black soldiers by the Plains Indians as a badge of honor, because they were as fierce as the buffalo that they hunted and revered). The photo inspired Johnson to create performances in which he portrays Sgt. Elizy Boman, a veteran of the U.S. war against the Filipino insurrection. Johnson says his work is in honor of his father, who enlisted in the Army to get out of the South: "I had to think why do we remember what we do? Who has the power over what is written down?"[xiv]

Lolo, grandfather, adaptation of Spanish abuelo

tiyo, tiya, uncle, aunt, adaptation of Spanish tio, tia

[xiv]Carl Nolte, "Buffalo Soldiers Story," *San Francisco Chronicle*, February 1, 2003, A 15.

Johnson's question is one of the guiding themes of this book. In the early 1990's, Susheel Bibb began to study Mary Ellen Pleasant, resulting in a theatrical performances in which she herself portrays Mary Ellen Pleasant. In 1994, actor Ian Ruskin began to develop a one-man show as Harry Bridges, an effort which, writes Chronicle reporter Carl Hall, "has moved to tears even some battle-scarred veterans of the great 1934 General Strike, which started on the waterfront and grew into the largest general strike in American history."[xv]

13-20 SUSHEEL BIBB AS MARY ELLEN PLEASANT

[xv]Carl Hall, "Actor Brings Labor's Harry Bridges to Life," *San Francisco Chronicle*, July 9, 2002.

13-21 IAN RUSKIN AS HARRY BRIDGES

The past is a thread that weaves us powerfully into the present moment. As Shelton observed, "Most of history is like an iceberg. It's hidden. Most of history is an act of revelation."[xvi] What happens in your life, and the lives of everyone around you, compose "a great and mighty march," and deserve to become part of history. This book has suggested some ways to become active within the historical moment, and some ways to record the stories of those whom you think should be added to the historical record. I look forward to your contributions in this effort.

[xvi]Nolte, A 15.